Kirtley Library
Columbia College
8th and Rogers
Columbia, MO. 65201

New Uses for Old Buildings

New Uses for Old Buildings

Sherban Cantacuzino

Whitney Library of Design
An Imprint of Watson-Guptill Publications, New York

First published in the United States 1975
by Watson-Guptill Publications,
a division of Billboard Publications, Inc.,
One Astor Plaza, New York, New York
10036

Copyright © 1975 by
The Architectural Press Ltd.
First published 1975 in Great Britain by
The Architectural Press, Ltd.,
9 Queen Anne's Gate, London SW1H 9BY

All rights reserved. No part of this
publication may be reproduced or used
in any form or by any means—
graphic, electronic, or mechanical,
including photocopying, recording,
taping, or information storage and
retrieval systems—without written
permission of the publisher.

Manufactured in Great Britain

**Library of Congress Cataloging in Publication
Data**
Cantacuzino, Sherban.
　New uses for old buildings.
　Includes bibliographical references.
　1. Buildings—Repair and reconstruction. 2. Architecture—Conservation
and restoration. I. Title.
TH3401.C35 1975　690　74-14580
ISBN 0-8230-7390-4

Contents

Acknowledgments   vii
General Introduction   viii

Churches and chapels
Introduction   1
Augustiner Kirche, Munich   *Museum and shops*   5
St. John's, Smith Square, London   *Cultural centre and concert hall*   9
St. George's, Charlotte Square, Edinburgh   *Archives*   13
Holy Trinity, Southwark, London (project)   *Orchestra rehearsal hall*   16
All Saints, Oxford (project)   *Library*   19
Trinity Almshouses Chapel, Mile End Road, London   *Social Hall*   21
Nonconformist Meeting Hall, Hove, Sussex   *Showroom and offices*   23

Monastic and other religious establishments
Introduction   26
La Commanderie des Templiers, Coulommiers, France   *Youth centre and museum*   28
Monastery, Macerata, Italy   *University faculties*   32
Monastery, Urbino (project)   *University faculty*   37
Convent, Urbino   *University faculty*   40
Convent, Montreal   *Offices, shops and restaurant*   45
Quaker Friars, Bristol   *Exhibition centre*   48
Holy Jesus Hospital, Newcastle-upon-Tyne   *Museum*   51

Fortifications, gates and barracks
Introduction   56
Southsea Castle, Portsmouth   *Museum*   59
Clarence Barracks, Portsmouth   *Museum*   63
Old Barracks, Lincoln   *Museum*   66
Magazine Gateway, Leicester   *Museum*   70
Martello Tower, Dunlaoghaire, Eire   *James Joyce museum*   74
Orto dell'Abbondanza, Urbino (project)   *University mensa*   77

Town houses, country houses, outhouses and other ancillaries
Introduction   80
Sveti Stefan, Montenegro, Yugoslavia   *Tourist island village*   83
Prospect House, Princeton, New Jersey   *University social centre*   85
Mount Clare, Roehampton, London   *Social centre and classrooms*   88
Private House, Krefeld, German Federal Republic   *Art gallery*   90
Carriage House, Lockport, New York   *Theatre*   92
Commercial Buildings, Boston, Massachusetts   *Private house*   95
Gothic Temple, Stowe, Buckinghamshire   *Holiday house*   99
Dovecot, Tixover Grange, Rutland   *School tuckshop*   102
Dovecot, Bicester, Oxfordshire   *Meeting hall*   104

Schools
Introduction   106
Board School, Wellingborough, Northamptonshire   *Youth club*   108
Village School, Haynes, Bedfordshire   *Private house*   110
St. Paul's Hall, Hunton Bridge, Hertfordshire   *Private house and office*   112
Village Schoolroom, Rampton, Cambridgeshire   *Private house*   115

Corn exchanges
Introduction   118
Corn exchange, Sudbury, Suffolk   *Library*   120
Corn exchange, Cambridge (project)   *Concert hall*   122
Corn exchange, Bishop's Stortford, Hertfordshire (project)   *Offices*   125

Barns and granaries
Introduction   127
Farm Buildings, Great Barrington, Massachusetts   *School art centre*   129
Barns, Hamar, Norway   *Archaeological museum*   132
Barn, East Hendred, Berkshire   *Private house*   135
Granary, Blakeney, Norfolk   *Flats*   139
Barns, Knebworth House, Hertfordshire   *Restaurants*   142

Mills
Introduction   146
Abbey Mill, Bradford-on-Avon, Wiltshire   *Offices*   149
Grain Mill, Ellingham, Suffolk   *Private house*   151
Wolfen Mill, Chipping, Lancashire   *Private house*   156
Arlington Mill, Bibury, Gloucestershire   *Museum*   159
Tide Mill, Woodbridge, Suffolk   *Museum*   162
Moorside Mills, Bradford, Yorkshire   *Museum*   165

Maltings and breweries
Introduction   168
Old Brewery, Freshford, Somerset   *Office*   170
Maltings, Snape, Suffolk   *Concert hall and arts centre*   174
Maltings, Ely, Cambridgeshire   *Multi-purpose hall*   178
Taylor's Maltings, Bishop's Stortford, Hertfordshire (project)   *Arts centre*   180
Maltings, Beccles, Suffolk   *Flats*   183
Maltings, Farnham, Surrey (project)   *Arts centre*   187

Warehouses and other industrial buildings
Introduction   189
Salines Royales de Chaux, Arc-et-Senans, France   *Conference centre*   192
Ghirardelli Square, San Francisco, California   *Mixed public use*   198
Cannery, San Francisco, California   *Mixed public use*   202
Canal Square, Washington, D.C.   *Mixed public use*   205
Warehouses, Skipton, Yorkshire   *Shop, restaurant*   209
Copper and Arsenic Mine, Calstock, Cornwall   *Holiday house*   213
Ice Houses, San Francisco, California   *Wholesale showrooms*   218
Warehouse, San Francisco, California   *Offices*   221
Warehouse, San Francisco, California   *Offices*   225
Commercial Buildings, San Antonio, Texas   *Restaurant*   229
Car Showroom and Garage, Washington, D.C.   *Cinemas, restaurant and car park*   234
Printing Works, Hanover, German Federal Republic   *School of architecture*   237
'I' Warehouse, St. Katharine Docks, London   *Yacht club and flats*   240
Warehouse, Oliver's Wharf, Wapping, London   *Flats*   244
Seed Warehouse, Norwich   *Showrooms and shop*   249
Old City Hall, Boston, Massachusetts   *Offices*   252
Railway Station, Brunswick, German Federal Republic   *Bank*   255
The Round House, Camden, London   *Theatre*   259

Three pumping stations
Abbey pumping station, Leicester   *Museum*   261
Ryhope pumping station, Sunderland, County Durham   *Museum*   262
Markfield Road pumping station and sewage works, Haringey, London   *Children's playground*   264

Acknowledgments

This book is about old buildings and their conversion to new uses. It is about all the building owners and architects who together conceived the plans which have prolonged the useful life of structures threatened with redundancy and demolition. It could never have been produced without their help, without the information and material which many of them provided so unstintingly.

Some of the material was first published in a special number of *The Architectural Review* in May 1972, which I edited, and which was also entitled 'New Uses for Old Buildings'. In addition a few examples have appeared in other numbers of the *Review*, but the greater part of the book—some fifty out of the seventy-three examples—is new. Much of it is concerned with buildings that were the product of the Industrial Revolution, with an industrial vernacular now commonly referred to as 'the functional tradition', a phrase first coined in the pages of *The Architectural Review* and subsequently embodied in a book of the same name: *The Functional Tradition in Early Industrial Buildings* by Sir James Richards with photographs by Eric de Maré (Architectural Press, 1958 and 1968).

This new book is a logical consequence of that earlier book which first made people aware of the value of industrial buildings such as warehouses, mills and maltings, and underlined the urgent need to find new uses in order to avert irreparable loss through demolition. Several examples in the earlier book reappear in this one, already converted or in the process of conversion to new uses. My debt to Sir James Richards and Eric de Maré is very great indeed.

I would like to thank all the photographers who made special journeys at my request, especially Bill Toomey, Peter Baistow and Dan Cruickshank, and above all my editorial assistant, Susan Brandt, who worked tirelessly at editing and organising the enormous amount of material that a book of this nature involves.

London, February 1974   *Sherban Cantacuzino*

General Introduction

Because their structure tends to outlive their function, buildings have continuously been adapted to new uses—a fact which has enabled generation after generation to derive a sense of continuity and stability from their physical surroundings. When buildings were abandoned, pilfered for materials or condemned for political reasons, the process of destruction was often slow and incomplete compared to the effect of the modern bulldozer. Paradoxically while it is possible today to demolish and rebuild whole areas faster than ever before, it may take ten years to design and erect a large hospital, by which time the ideas on hospital planning that prevailed at the time of the design will have become outdated. The dissatisfaction expressed by the users of so many new buildings has directed attention back to some fundamental ecological and sociological problems and has forced governments to make more money available for conservation. Yet it is unfortunately true that the process of wholesale and indiscriminate destruction will go on as long as there are local authorities who continue to see redevelopment as a matter of prestige, or find in the developer's proposals an irresistible opportunity to increase their revenue from rates.

Not surprisingly, the growing interest shown in old buildings of every kind—an interest which remains healthy as long as it is used in the service of true conservation—has developed parallel to a quickening tempo in building. In Britain the Civic Amenities Act of 1967 was as important for concerning itself with areas rather than individual buildings as for the possibilities which it created. Active conservation implies far more than merely declaring conservation areas as the act requires. In collaboration with local amenity societies, local authorities must continue the logical process of conservation: examine and classify the building stock in each area, earmark the danger points, anticipate redundancy, prepare strict criteria for sympathetic redevelopment, alternatively propose new uses or other means of preservation, and document buildings by measuring and photographing them, if necessary with the help of local art colleges or architectural schools. In collaboration with the county planning authority local authorities must determine their conservationist policies in the wider context of a county structure plan. Only in this way can the knowledge needed to evolve a proper theory of conservation be acquired: and a proper balance between conservation and development be achieved.

This book is about one specific aspect of conservation—the need to find new uses when old buildings are threatened with redundancy. In the absence of economic pressure from rising land values, new uses in the past tended to 'happen' quite casually. The Victorian Gothic cotton exchange at Preston, for example, is now a cinema, while the corn exchange at Banbury conceals a public house behind its grandiose neo-classical facade. Neither building makes the best of its new use, but each owes its survival to it and each is a landmark in its respective town.

Since the last war the pace of change has accelerated to such an extent that redundancy, followed by demolition, has become a common pattern in urban centres. The wrong application of planning controls has often led to the departure of industrial and commercial activities in central areas to suburban or rural zones allocated exclusively to such uses. Buildings which housed these activities like warehouses and maltings, often situated on increasingly valuable land, have been demolished to make way for more profitable development such as shopping centres and offices. Local authorities have built new housing estates like mushrooms around the edge of towns without rehabilitating existing central urban housing. Many churches and other community buildings in the centre have consequently lost their role. If our towns are to remain living organisms, planning must now concentrate on combatting rising land values and encouraging a richer mix of uses in central areas. This means, amongst other things, finding suitable new uses for buildings that formerly provided this richer mix.

The examples illustrated in this book were selected for three main reasons: for their visual importance in the urban or rural context, for the social or cultural importance of their new use and for the quality of their design, having regard to the character of the original building. The seventy-three examples are taken from all over the world, with forty-six examples from Britain, thirteen from the United States, four each from Germany and Italy, two from France and one each from Canada, Ireland, Norway and Yugoslavia. Even if the British bias needs no justification in a British book, it can to some extent be explained by the great wealth of late eighteenth- and nineteenth-century industrial buildings which exists in Great Britain. About one-third of this book is thus devoted to conversions of buildings belonging to that *functional tradition* within which 'new and more sophisticated standards are achieved gradually and unselfconsciously as one anonymous mind after another applies itself to the improvement or modification of an established pattern'.* Finding new uses for these buildings is important not only because of the intrinsic value of the buildings themselves, but because the very act of converting them may teach today's architects something about this established pattern. The conversion of a Georgian textile mill or a Victorian warehouse, moreover, offers considerably more freedom than the conversion of a building of outstanding architectural or historic interest,

---

The Functional Tradition in Early Industrial Buildings by J. M. Richards. Architectural Press, 1958 and 1968.

which demands scholarly restoration and inhibits the choice of a new use.

It will be apparent from the examples illustrated that not enough good established architects are prepared to devote their talents to conversion work. How many architects, for instance, of Giancarlo De Carlo's standing in the world would be prepared to rehabilitate painstakingly, year after year, one city block after another? To show that such work can be creative and not just hack is one purpose of this book. Indeed, the very constraints of conversion can make positive contributions in the physical interpretation of the brief. It is unlikely, for instance, that Sverre Fehn would have solved the problem of the circulation in his archaeological museum at Hamar in the way he did, had he not had the precise form of a medieval barn to work on. Michelangelo's solution for the church of Santa Maria degli Angeli in the central hall of Diocletian's baths in Rome resulted from the conflicting claims of two existing axes; the most common form of church plan—a nave and two aisles— might have turned out otherwise if the early Christians had not made use of Roman basilicas; and monastic planning might have taken a different course if the first Benedictines had not settled in the courtyards of a *villa rustica*.

The ten chapters into which the book is divided represent ten different building types before conversion. This places the emphasis on the original character of the building and the onus on the architect to preserve some of that character in his conversion. That is why each example begins with the headings 'Site', 'History' and 'Character', which contrive to tell the reader as much as possible about the building before conversion. The introduction to each chapter tries to identify the essence of the building type and to suggest suitable new uses.

Approximate costs related to dates are provided in the majority of cases, and it does not take long to see that in the recent past it has been more often than not substantially cheaper—sometimes ridiculously so—to convert than to build new. The economic argument for rehabilitation or conversion is indeed a powerful one, for most of the examples illustrated are not just concerned with maintaining the fabric of an old building, but introduce completely new standards and services. On another level, Dr. P. A. Stone* has pointed out that 'urban quality depends more on the standard of maintenance and improvement of the existing stock than on the standards to which new stock is built', because the annual addition to the stock is proportionately very small. The division of national resources between new buildings and maintenance ought, he argues, to be nearer 50:50 than the 75:25 that it was at the time of writing. Unfortunately, the mounting rate of inflation and the growing scarcity of the craftsman builder in recent years have narrowed the margin between the cost of conversion and that of new work. Most of the examples illustrated pre-date this trend, but some of the more recent

---

*'The cost of quality' Official Architecture and Planning, November 1971.

projects suggest that new uses for old buildings may be economically justified in the future only if the unquantifiable value of age and character is added to the sum. The latest evidence shows nevertheless that more and more conversions are being undertaken. One of the problems of compiling this book has been the continuous flow of material and the temptation of adding new examples up to the very last minute.

The size of projects, too, seems to be increasing as the momentum of conservation gathers pace. The Faneuil Hall market district in Boston, a waterfront development built between 1825 and 1829 which is being comprehensively converted into outdoor cafés, restaurants and shops, will eventually form part of a larger recreational area with parks, marinas, a nautical museum and an aquarium. At Louvain, the university have preferred to rehabilitate the Grand Béguinage for student residences rather than build a modern campus; and there are plans at last to save the Albert Dock at Liverpool by making use of the buildings for the Polytechnic. If one adds to this list a fourth and much older example of comprehensive conservation, the conversion of castles and monasteries in Spain into the *paradores* chain of tourist hotels, the proportion of publicly funded to privately funded work is three to one, the only example of a project supported by private developers being the Faneuil Hall market district. This proportion suggests a reversal of the trend exemplified in this book: in only one-third of the examples illustrated here is the client a public authority spending public money.

This new trend coincides happily with the Council of Europe's European Architectural Heritage Year, 1975, which, like Britain's Civic Amenities Act, is specifically concerned with the *conservation* of whole areas rather than with the *preservation* of individual monuments. At Edinburgh in January 1974, at the first of a series of seminars some of the conclusions demanded a greater share of public money for conservation and emphasised the need for more information on all economic aspects. 'There is insufficient information to be able to compare the constructional costs and social effects of restoration with those of new building.' Regarding new uses, the seminar concluded that 'the safeguarding of historic buildings often depends on the finding of a viable new use. More imagination should be employed in finding such uses.' The purpose of this book, whose publication is intended to coincide with European Architectural Heritage Year, is a practical one—to illustrate work which has been completed or is still in project form and to show where possible how much it cost, where the money came from and what some of the technical problems were. It is intended for all those people —individuals and organisations—with redundant buildings on their hands.

Churches and chapels

A church remains a monument whatever the spiritual or material loss from disuse. No apology is therefore made here for treating churches primarily as buildings of aesthetic and environmental value for which new uses must be found if they are to survive redundancy. This is not to ignore other solutions, like part conversion or joint use with churches of other denominations. Much redundancy in country churches would probably be avoided if the financial onus of keeping a church in good repair was taken on by the local community. It is arguable, for instance, that just as the elevational unity and the common ground in the centre of a Georgian square are the concern of the inhabitants of that square, so the preservation of a landmark like a village church should become the concern of the people of that village. Such views, however, are more properly the affair of the Church and of the communities involved: of general concern is the danger of demolition for apparently irrefutable economic reasons—the sale, for example, of a valuable urban site to a development company. Especially vulnerable are Victorian churches, which are less inviolable than classical or medieval churches, while at the same time often more monumental with their great towers and spires. The sale and demolition of a church in a central area which has lost its parishioners and the use of the proceeds in the construction of a new church serving the suburban area to which those parishioners have moved—the loss of a large old church whose upkeep has become increasingly costly and the gain of a new church of modest size requiring minimal maintenance—will always remain a temptation to Church authorities.

Redundancy rather than demolition is the threat to classical and medieval churches, especially where they occur in great concentrations as in the City of London or historic cities like Norwich and York. Out of a total of thirty-seven, nine City churches were recommended for redundancy* in the 1971 report of the Commission on the Churches in the City of London. The commission did not

---

*This was a recommendation only. To establish redundancy is a long process which the Church of England set up with its Pastoral Measure of 1968. Under this measure a church can be declared redundant, the ownership passing from the incumbent temporarily to the diocese. A special committee of the diocese is then given a minimum of twelve months to find a new use for the church. If it is successful the church can be leased or sold subject to suitable safeguards.

suggest specific new uses for each church, but listed what they regarded as appropriate functions, which included concert hall, library, social club, picture gallery or museum and, most interestingly, a hall for one of the City livery companies. The City of London has long been a commercial centre with only a vestigial resident community. Its empty churches perform a ceremonial and symbolic function. The problems which Norwich exhibits, if less familiar, are typical of urban areas all over Britain. Norwich churches are empty because, like the City of London churches, their supporting parishes have disappeared. So, ironically, Norwich, with a population of 170 000 and growing at a rate of 2700 every year, is experiencing a rapid decline in central area living and a move to the suburbs or beyond to the villages. Within the medieval walls there are still thirty-two churches, of which five have been turned over to other uses and nine closed. The Church's 1971 Norwich City Commission Report recommended the retention for permanent use of only six parish churches, stating unequivocally that 'if every one of the redundant medieval buildings is to be retained, some new means of financing their upkeep must be found'. In this the report was expressing a view widely held inside and outside the Church that if only the Church would drop its special exemption,* the state would provide for churches just as it already provides for other buildings of architectural merit.

There are at present in Britain three main possibilities for redundant churches. First, there is the solution adopted at Norwich (largely as a result of the report and the consequent fear of widescale demolition) where an enlightened city council has agreed to take over the freehold of all redundant churches and to assume responsibility for their preservation. Second, a redundant church can have recourse to the Redundant Churches Fund** provided it remains consecrated and is not put to any use which is incompatible with occasional worship. And third, a redundant church can be converted to a new use which is a commercially viable proposition provided this is done under the terms and procedure laid down by the Pastoral Measure.*** At Norwich, to prevent all the financial onus from falling on the local authority, two bodies—the Friends of Norwich Churches and the Norwich Churches Trust—have been formed to help raise funds where necessary. A number of local architects were invited to submit suggestions for new uses, and their proposals were exhibited in the late autumn of 1970 in one of the redundant-to-be churches, St. Michael at Plea. They included a refectory, a military museum, a doss house, a university residence and a community hall for

---

*In 1913 the Church of England obtained exemption from the Ancient Monuments Act—an exemption which secured independence for church buildings from state interference and which was written into subsequent planning laws. Today, although the Historic Buildings Council receives the yearly sum of £2½ million from the Treasury for the repair of historic buildings and buildings in conservation areas, churches in use are specially excluded by practice if not by law.

** Financed by the Church, the state and by voluntary contributions, the fund has affirmed that it will take on any redundant church of architectural or historic interest rather than see it put to an unsuitable use.

***See footnote on p. 1.

the neighbouring estates. These uses should be compared with five other Norwich churches which were already converted—into a church hall, an ecclesiastical museum, a scout headquarters, a leather store and a furniture repository.

In trying to find suitable new uses for churches, two basic requirements must be fulfilled. The new use must accord in some degree both with the spirit and with the form of a church. Thus a refectory or a livery company hall, provided the kitchens and stores can be accommodated without impinging on the main spaces, would accommodate the ritual of a body of people dining together and might well be considered a suitable use. The college hall at Oxford or Cambridge is after all not so very different from the college chapel. In spirit, too, theatrical or musical performances, lectures or debates might be thought more appropriate than museum display, despite the latter use involving the minimum change.* A library, too, is an attractive function for a church—without ritual but quiet and contemplative. In the last resort, and if the space is kept intact, it is better for a church to be used by people than by things, better as a drill hall or a scout headquarters than a furniture repository. But it is infinitely better for a church to become a furniture repository than to undergo the structural alterations which would be needed to convert it into a students' residence or private house and which would alter, radically and irreversibly, the spirit, form and character of the interior space and so of everything that spells 'church'.

This chapter is illustrated by seven examples, one of which—Holy Trinity, Southwark—is a project for a concert rehearsal hall which was approved by the special committee of the diocese in preference to an unsuitable application for converting the church into flats. Unfortunately the use of the hall will be restricted to rehearsals, the statutory requirements of escape and lavatories, to mention only the most important, being far more rigorous if the public is admitted to performances. It would have been preferable if the church could also have been used for concerts, for since church interiors have in a real sense always been public property, any new use should where possible be a public one. It is the combination of public use and careful restoration which has made St. John's, Smith Square the success it is. People regularly converge there from all around to take their place for lunchtime or evening concerts in the way that rarely happens now for church services. In retrospect it seems quite extraordinary that this church remained a ruin for nearly twenty years after the end of the last war; that it was necessary for a group of private individuals to set up a charitable trust and get a Local Act passed by Parliament in order to buy, rebuild and restore what in any other European country would have been acknowledged officially as an historic monument of unique value. In Munich the Church of the Augustinian Friars was restored

---

*One of the best examples is the Romanesque church of St. Cecilia at Cologne, now the Schnütgen Museum of church art. Another is St. Peter Hungate at Norwich, also an ecclesiastical museum.

and converted into a museum of hunting by the Bavarian State. The monumental staircase and the subdivision of the tall nave into two floors, which date from 1913, break all the rules. A church of Gothic proportions has been transformed into a 'palace' of Baroque character. But it is all done with such conviction, especially the vaulted upper hall which gives the impression that it could never have been anything else, that one comes away persuaded that the gain must be considerably greater than the loss.

The Augustinian church in Munich is the only example of Gothic origin illustrated in this chapter, and there is no doubt that the structural division of this type of church into a narrow nave and two aisles is a restricting factor when it comes to finding a new use. Both Holy Trinity and St. John's are classical churches with wide naves which can accommodate a full orchestra. St. George's at Edinburgh, though not so wide, is also a classical church. Its prime importance, however, lies in its monumental exterior which dominates the main axis of Craig's New Town. For this reason the church had at all costs to be saved, and to have spurned an offer of a viable use, even if that use meant gutting the interior and inserting a multi-storey structure for storing public records, would have shown a singular lack of judgement. An unsuitable use is made a little more palatable in this instance by the inclusion of a double-height area around the entrance where the public can visit exhibitions or consult public records.

Classical churches tend to be raised on podia over crypts, and this is another reason why they are easier to convert than Gothic churches. Both at St. John's and at Holy Trinity the crypt absorbs the ancillary accommodation which might otherwise have encroached on the church proper. In the project for All Saints at Oxford the crypt becomes an indispensable extension to the main library above, as well as providing space for essential utilities. The two chapels with which this chapter ends have similar characteristics: a single large space raised well above street level over a spacious lower floor. But they have been put to totally different uses. Trinity Chapel is more of a restoration in the sense that the space of the actual chapel has been preserved, but for social rather than religious use. The nonconformist hall at Hove has been converted into offices and an extra floor inserted. Only the break in this upper floor, which makes of it two galleries open to the main floor below, reminds one of the former space and adds to the memory of the converted building; and it is perhaps this sense of 'memory' which every architect who converts a building to a new use should leave behind him. To understand the essence of a building and to preserve enough of that essence to be meaningful should be his constant aim.

AUGUSTINER KIRCHE, MUNICH

Architect: Erwin Schleich

Client: Deutsches Jagdmuseum and Bavarian State

Site: The length of the church faces south on to Neuhauser Strasse, stretching from the junction with Ett Strasse at its west end to the junction with Augustiner Strasse at its east or choir end. To the north lies the huge complex of the police headquarters. On the other corner of Ett Strasse and standing at right angles with its gabled entrance facing Neuhauser Strasse is the Church of St. Michael. Augustiner Strasse leads to Frauen Platz and the Frauenkirche, with its twin towers rising high above the roof tops of surrounding buildings. These three churches, frequently seen together, provide one of the most striking architectural relationships in the whole of Munich. They lie in the heart of the old medieval city, which has been largely pedestrianised.

History: The first church and conventual buildings date from 1290. The church was enlarged in 1458, converted to the Baroque style in 1621 and secularised in 1803 when it became a customs depot. In 1913 the conventual buildings to the north of the church were demolished to make room for Theodor Fischer's police headquarters. Fischer also made important alterations to the church, which were mostly retained in the recent conversion. These consisted of turning the ground floor of the choir into an open arcade and forming a new entrance under it; of making shops out of the chapels in the south aisle which faces Neuhauser Strasse; of inserting two new steel floor structures and dividing the height of the nave into three unequal storeys— the bottom for shops, the middle for a police gymnasium and the top for a concert hall-cum-exhibition gallery; and of providing a monumental double staircase leading from the new entrance at the choir end up to the concert hall.

The idea of creating a national museum of hunting and shooting, first considered in 1911, finally became a reality in 1933 when an important collection came on the market. In 1938 the museum was opened in a wing at Nymphenburg, but the war caused its contents to be removed for safety. Post-war reorganisation of Nymphenburg made it imperative to find new premises for the Jagdmuseum, but it was not until 1958 that the Bavarian State made the Augustiner Kirche available and not until 1962 that conversion and restoration work was begun with financial help from the City of Munich.

Character: The lower lean-to sides and the high clerestorey crowned by a steeply pitched pantiled roof express the simple interior of nave and two aisles. The east end is buttressed and apsidal (polygonal) in plan. The walls are stucco worked into ornate flat panels in the lower storeys and brick above, but with

1, the south façade of the church facing the Neuhauser Strasse which forms part of the new pedestrian area of central Munich. The twin towers behind belong to the Franenkirche

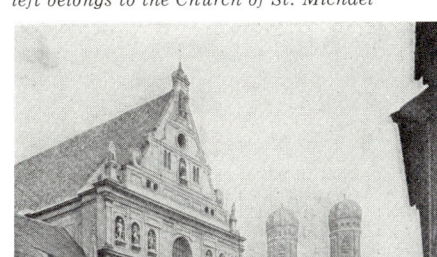

2, the same view circa 1912 before Theodor Fischer's alterations. The gabled façade to the left belongs to the Church of St. Michael

3, the apsidal east end of the church. The open arcade at ground level created by Fischer has been blocked up in the recent alterations to form and entrance hall.

stucco surrounds to the windows. The gable parapet of the west end follows a restrained Baroque curve and the aisle walls, with their strong pattern of deeply recessed round windows, terminate in a balustraded parapet with alternating obelisks and urns added in 1913. Before the alterations of 1913 the aisle wall facing Neuhauser Strasse had four semicircular-headed doors to which were added another eight similar openings to provide a continuous row of shop windows.

Internally, until 1913 the main central space of the nave retained its Gothic character in its tall proportions and in its regular rhythm of bays with quadripartite vaulting. The Baroque decoration consisted of pilasters, cornices and ceiling stucco work which were applied over a Gothic shell.

Work done: The building suffered severe war damage and had to undergo the usual repairs. All Fischer's structural alterations were retained. His monumental staircase now serves as the main way up to the museum, but regrettably the open arcade at street level has been blocked up to form the public entrance hall. The volume of the old gymnasium has been added to the museum and a new floor inserted to provide additional exhibition space. The west entrance, which had given access to the gymnasium, has been converted into a shop fronting on to Ett Strasse. The two lower floors of the museum have been fitted out with deep showcases depicting wildlife and hunting scenes. By contrast, the lofty upper floor, its vaulting and Baroque decoration painted white, displays weapons and other objects used in hunting and shooting as well as an impressive array of stags' heads and, as the *pièce de résistance* at the top of the staircase, the skeleton of a giant species of stag that became extinct around 10 000 B.C.

Accommodation: Ground floor—public entrance and ticket office to museum, staff entrance and lift, shops, stores, lavatories
First floor—museum, museum administration, upper part of shops
Second floor—museum, museum administration, upper level of shops
Third floor—museum, conservation workshops, museum administration

Date of completion: 1966

Cost: Since the essential part of the conversion dates from 1913, the cost of the recent repairs and alterations would be misleading.

4, a painting of the church and monastery in 1600 before being converted to the Baroque style

5, Fischer's upper floor plan of 1913 showing the church with its new monumental staircase and the conventual buildings replaced by the police headquarters

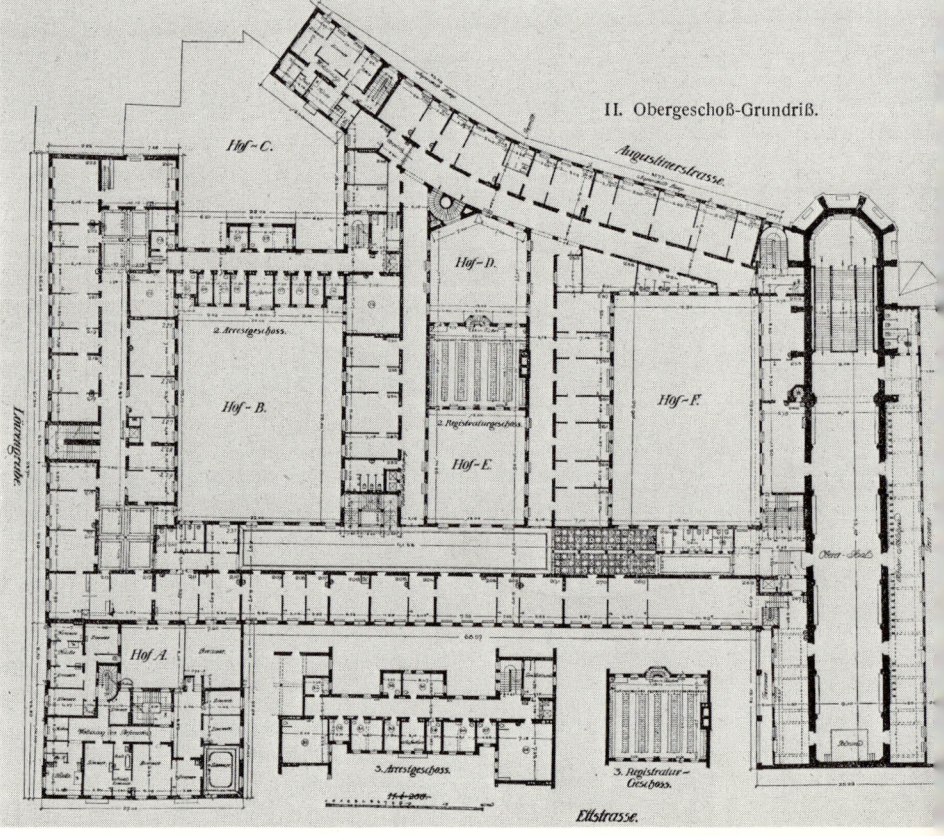

key
1, public entrance and ticket office
2, staff entrance
3, shops
4, store
5, back entrance to shops
6, police headquarters
7, museum
8, museum administration
9, conservation workshops

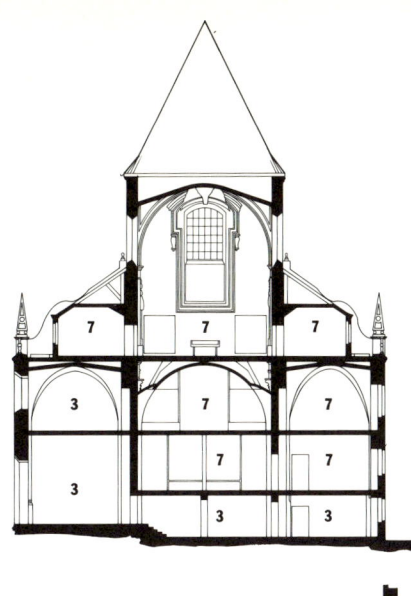

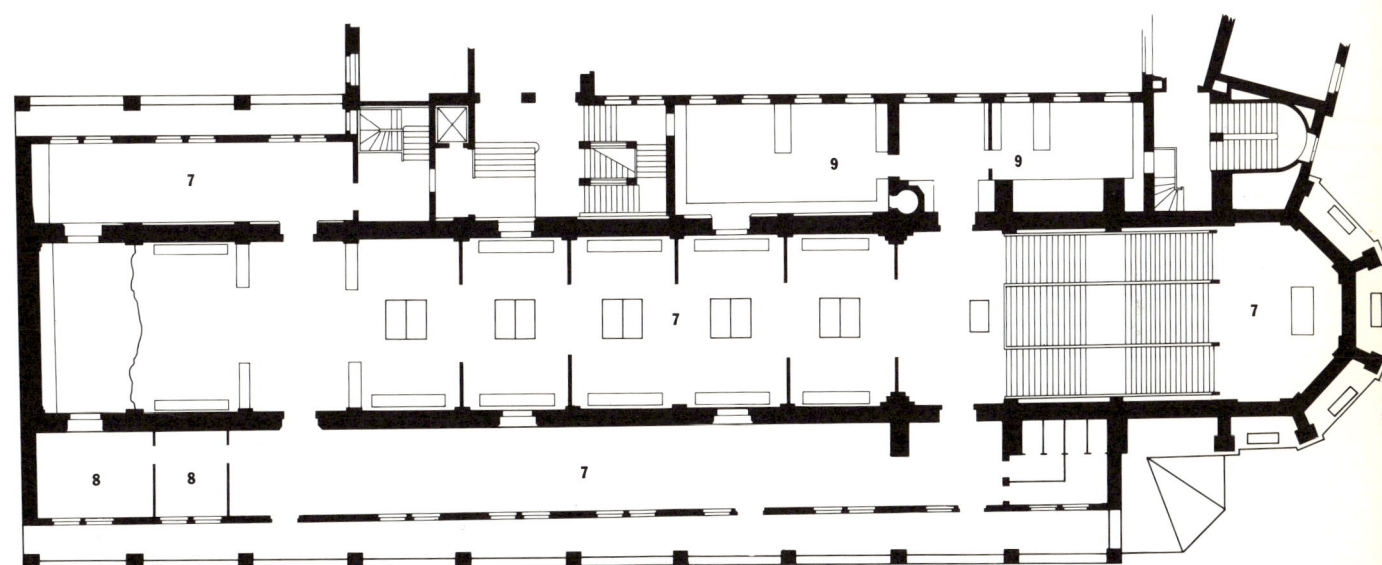

Third floor plan—scale 1 in 400

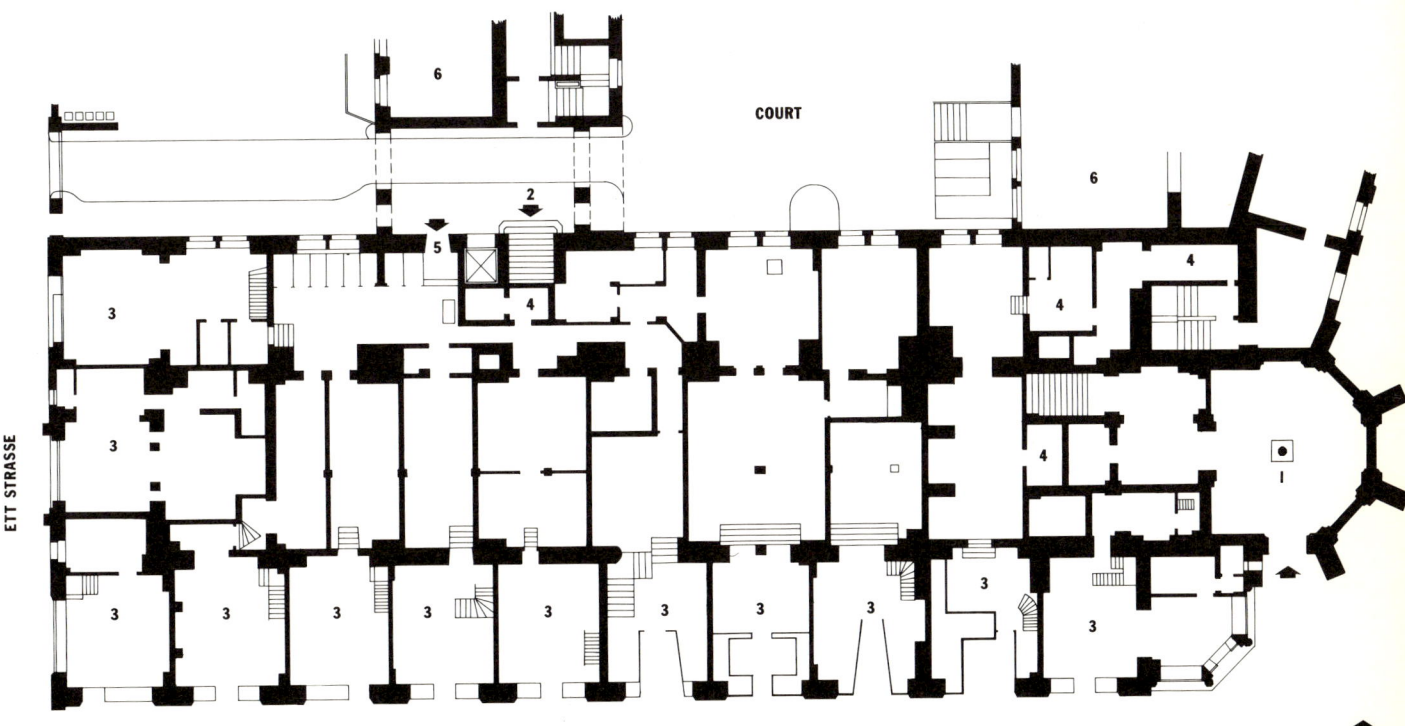

Ground floor plan—scale 1 in 400

6, the tall Gothic proportions of the nave can still be seen in this view which was taken as Fischer was inserting a new steel floor structure to create an upper hall for concerts and exhibitions

7, Fischer's monumental staircase after the recent restoration. Between the double flight can be glimpsed the intermediate floor which, like the ground floor, has been fitted out with deep showcases for the display of wild life and hunting scenes

8, the lofty upper floor, open from end to end, looking towards the apsidal east end

9, the pièce de resistance—*the skeleton of a giant species of stag that became extinct around 10000 BC—at the top of the monumental staircase*

10, the apsidal east end seen from the top of the staircase

ST. JOHN'S, SMITH SQUARE, LONDON

Architect: Marshall Sisson

Client: Friends of St. John's

Site: The church is situated in the centre of Smith Square, of which it is the focal point. Smith Square, a stone's throw from Parliament Square in Westminster, is joined by Dean Stanley Street to Millbank, which runs alongside the Thames. The houses of the square, like the houses of Trinity Church Square, were built at the same time as the church.

History: Designed by Thomas Archer, the church was one of the ten churches completed by 1730 under the Act of 1711 which ordered the building of fifty new churches. Work began in 1713 and the church was consecrated in 1728. The interior was destroyed by fire in 1742 and the first restoration by James Horne (1744–45) substituted a flat single-span ceiling for the previous vaulted one. In 1824 William Inwood and his son Henry William altered the interior to accord with the then fashionable Greek Revival style, and in May 1941 the church was gutted by incendiary bombs.

After an abortive scheme to rebuild the church as an archive for the Church Commissioners and the Diocese of London, the second restoration, which reinstates Archer's original interior in all essentials, was undertaken to provide a building for religious and cultural activities. The church remains a consecrated building but is freed by a Local Act passed by Parliament from the legal effects of consecration.

Character: St. John's is a rare example of English Baroque. Built of stone and on a monumental scale, it overwhelms the square it stands in. The north and south facades have giant colonnaded porticos surmounted by cornices and broken pediments. At each corner rises a tower of elaborate form and silhouette. Inside, the oblong church nave, 96ft. long by 62ft. wide by 48ft. high to the apex of the central groin vault, has curved corners and projecting east and west ends, both treated the same way with a broad arch decorated with rich plasterwork resting on giant Corinthian columns. Although the altar was originally in the east end, the stage was moved to the opposite end just outside the sanctuary when it was found that the performers preferred to play in front of the west window. Whereas the church is tall and brightly lit by large round-headed windows, the crypt is low and dark. The central space is divided by thick piers into square vaulted bays. The finish throughout is the exposed brick structure which was hardly affected at all by the weather during the many years that the church stood roofless.

1, the monumental scale of the Church seen against the modest Georgian houses of Lord North Street

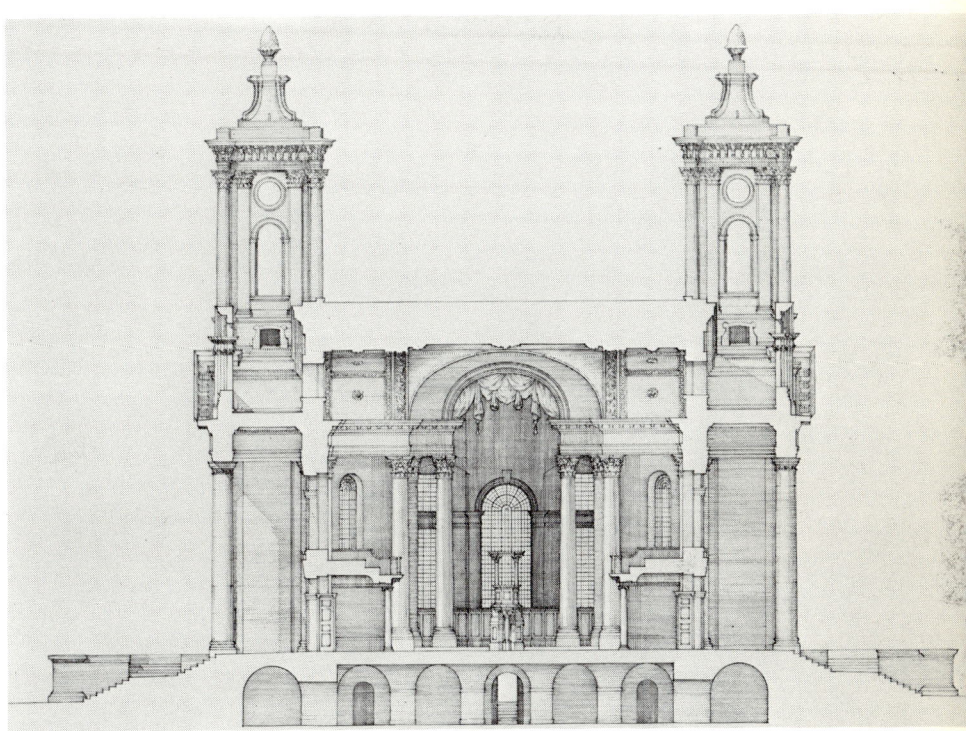

2, cross-section: drawing by Marshall Sisson

3, the size and scale of the church overwhelm the square, even today when many of the three-storey Georgian houses have been replaced by eight-storey office blocks

4, detail of the east façade

5, a contemporary engraving of Thomas Archer's church

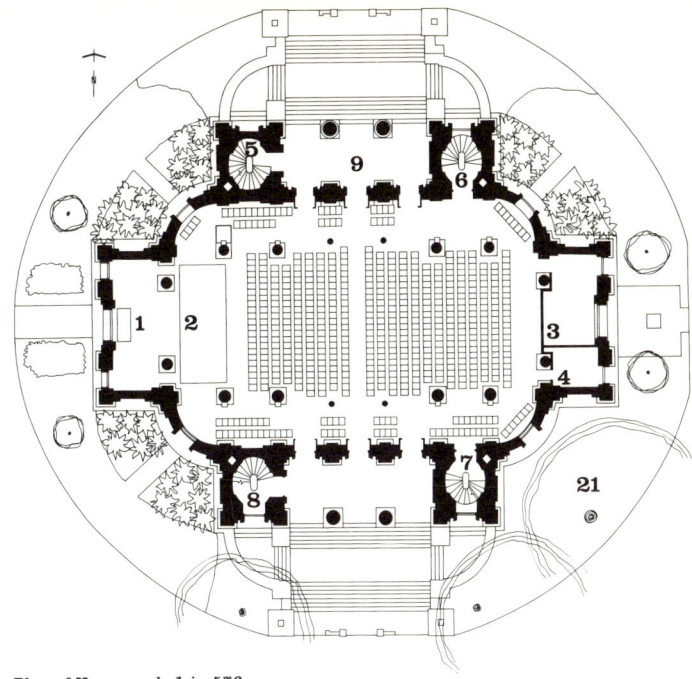

Plan of Nave—scale 1 in 576

Work done: Except for providing an office and a control room under the organ gallery, the work within the main body of the church was more or less a straight restoration job which has provided a notable addition to London's concert halls. The galleries cannot be used by the public until they are strengthened and two additional escape staircases, omitted for economy, are built. The low vaults now have excellent extract ventilation, and both church and crypt have full gas-fired central heating. Acoustic felt was fitted to all ceilings. Plate glass and later double-glazing were fitted to all windows to minimise disturbance to local residents and to exclude external noise. The garden was designed by Lanning Roper, and one of the quadrants has been made into a car park for eight or nine cars.

Accommodation: Main body of church—concert hall, control room, office
Crypt—bar and restaurant (accommodating up to 300 people standing, 100 sitting), cloakroom, caretaker's flat, store, changing rooms and lavatories for performers, kitchenette

Date of completion: October 1969

Cost: Building, £350 000 (including buying site and professional fees)
Stone cleaning, £4550
Stone repairs, £6525
Furniture and equipment, £8500
Garden, £3000
Finance was obtained from the War Damage Commission, the Historic Buildings Council, the West German Government, the Pilgrim Trust, the Leche Trust, the Transport and General Workers' Union, the Sir Robert and Lady Sainsbury Trust, industry with offices in the vicinity (with particularly generous contributions from the British-American Tobacco Company, ICI and International Nickel), residents in the locality, private and corporate donations, proceeds from concerts, recordings and other events, and the subscriptions of members of the Friends. A bank loan of £63 000 plus interest remains to be repaid.

key
1, altar
2, stage
3, control room
4, office
5, escape from crypt and gallery
6, internal access to crypt
7, internal access to roof
8, escape from gallery
9, caretaker's flat
10, store
11, bar
12, restaurant
13, cloakroom
14, boiler room
15, men's dressing room
16, women's dressing
17, women's lavatories
18, men's lavatories
19, kitchenette
20, performers' area
21, car park

6, the public part of the crypt which can be used as a restaurant and bar with the concert hall, or hired out separately

Plan of Crypt—scale 1 in 576

7, looking west towards the stage and altar. A rehearsal of chamber music is in progress

8, the same view at night with the red curtains drawn

10, looking east towards the office and control room which has been built in under the organ gallery

9, the giant Corinthian columns supporting the gallery which cannot be used by the public until further work of strengthening has been carried out

ST. GEORGE'S, CHARLOTTE SQUARE, EDINBURGH

1, the monumental east façade from Charlotte Square

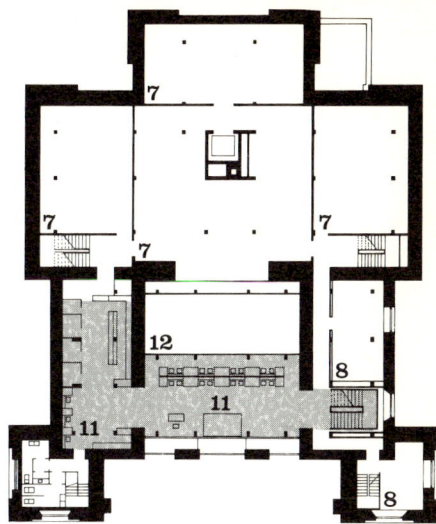

First floor plan

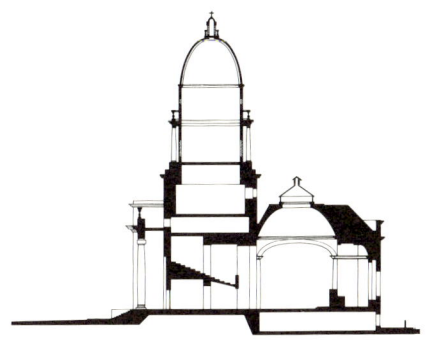

Section

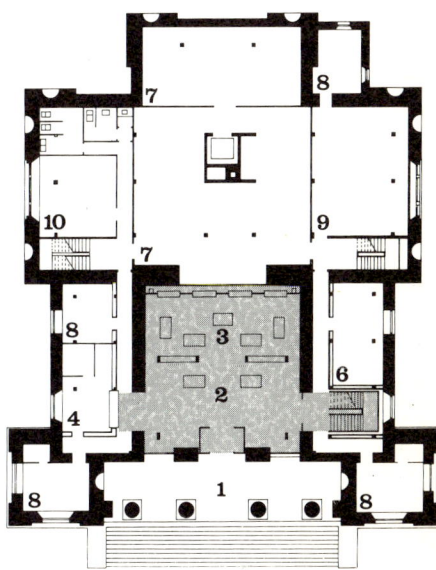

Ground floor plan

Architect: Directorate of Scottish Services, Department of the Environment

Client: Department of the Environment

Site: On the west side of Charlotte Square in Edinburgh's eighteenth-century New Town, the church holds a dominant position at the west end of George Street (the main axis of James Craig's first New Town), with the Dundas Monument providing the balance at the opposite end. It backs on to Randolph Place, which is at a lower level than Charlotte Square.

History: The church, completed in 1814, was built to a design by Robert Reid, after a more modest one by Robert Adam (who designed the adjacent houses) was rejected. In 1962 the building ceased to be used as a church and steps were taken to find a new use. Already in 1959 lack of space at Old Register House had reached a critical point, and in 1963 the Keith Committee advised that congestion should be relieved by an auxiliary repository on the outskirts of Edinburgh, a recommendation which ran counter to the views of the Scottish Records Advisory Council that separation was not practicable. By suggesting the use of St. George's, the then Ministry of Public Buildings and Works (later part of the Department of the Environment, by-passed the problem of buying an expensive site in a central area. For the city bought the building from the Church (removing thereby any risk of demolition) and offered it to the ministry at a peppercorn rent. Though separation thus became unavoidable, it was separation of only three-quarters of a mile.

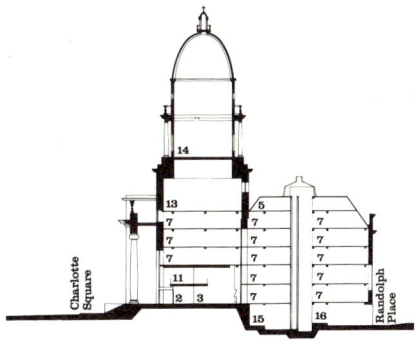

Section—scale 1 in. = 96 ft.

key
1, entrance
2, temporary exhibition
3, permanent exhibition
4, security
5, tanks
6, staff
7, storage
8, office
9, microfilm storage
10, messroom
11, search room and readers
12, void
13, future storage
14, proposed conference room
15, boiler house
16, loading bay

Character: The lower part of the church consists of massive cubic forms which build up to a tall drum and green copper dome crowned by a lantern with a gold cupola. Size and scale tend to overpower the houses in the square but are apt in the context of the New Town layout. Giant columns stand in front of a recessed portico, flanked by square blocks and surmounted by a cornice and balustrade. A low entrance under the gallery, which contrasted sharply with the tall proportions of the portico, led to a domed space lit by a lantern. The main drum and dome on Charlotte Square have been preserved for use as a possible future conference room. The interior of the church was always plain, most of the money having gone into the ambitious façade and superstructure.

Work done: The exterior (except for a glazed entrance) has been faithfully preserved. The interior of the church had initially to be gutted because of extensive dry rot. It was not practicable, considering the use to which the church was to be put, to restore the interior, which anyway was undistinguished compared to the exterior. The brief posed two distinct problems: the provision for such public functions as exhibitions and research, and the storage and preservation of documents. The first is accommodated on two floors immediately behind the new fully glazed entrance, and the second on five floors mainly within the space of the former nave. The masonry shell was retained and a free-standing steel frame on independent foundations built up within.

The whole of the storage area is in fire-resisting construction and has a smoke detection system. Temperature and humidity control provide the conditions necessary for the preservation of documents and microfilm. Mobile shelving (50 000 linear feet) has been used throughout the storage area to achieve the maximum use of space. It is calculated that the building will provide room for city records for the next fifty years.

Accommodation: Basement—boiler room and loading bay from Randolph Place
Ground floor—space for temporary and permanent exhibitions, storage space, offices, staff room, mess room
First floor—search room and reading space, storage space, offices
Second, third and fourth floors—storage space
Fifth floor—future storage space, tanks
Inside dome—proposed conference room

Date of completion: 1970

Cost: Repairs, £70 000
Conversion, including furniture, furnishings and equipment, £350 000

Rate: £7·21 per sq. ft. (£77·61 per m²). Based on the conversion.

2, the new public entrance. Full glazing is acceptable in recessed situations as here. The double height reflects the open character of the interior

3, inside the church during the demolition which preceded conversion

4, the two-storey high ground floor entrance provides exhibition space and incorporates a mezzanine floor for research work, 5

HOLY TRINITY, SOUTHWARK, LONDON (project)

Architect: Arup Associates

Client: Trustees of the Henry Wood Memorial Trust

Site: In south-east London, well situated in relation to the two important musical centres, the Festival Hall and the Barbican, the church is in the centre of an early nineteenth-century square, of which it is an integral part. Trinity Church Square and the adjoining Merrick Square were declared a conservation area in 1968.

History: The church, designed by Francis Bedford and built in 1824, was the first part of Trinity Church Square to be completed. It has not been used as a church since 1960, and was the first church in the south to be declared redundant under the Pastoral Measure of 1968. Several proposals were put before the Redundant Churches Committee, including flats with a swimming pool as well as a petrol station. Finally in 1971 the plan for using it as a rehearsal hall for the London Symphony Orchestra and the Royal Philharmonic Orchestra was accepted. On October 1, 1973, fire caused extensive damage, destroying the roof, but it was decided to continue with the conversion.

Character: The Greek Revival Holy Trinity has two distinctive external features: an entrance portico in the form of an Ionic temple front and a tall steeple carried apparently by the portico but in fact supported on the walls of the vestibule. When it comes to the interior, the structural division into nave and aisles of Gothic churches, whether medieval or Victorian, is a restricting factor in accommodating a full orchestra, and in their search for a rehearsal hall, Arup Associates rejected at least one Victorian church for this reason. Inside, Holy Trinity is 103ft. long by 60ft. wide by 35ft. high. It also has the advantage of a single-span roof structure and a 60ft. by 40ft. clear space at the choir end (where the galleries were at one time cut back), which will be ideal for rehearsing the largest orchestras when the floor has been levelled.

1, the north portico and main entrance to the church before the recent fire

Site plan

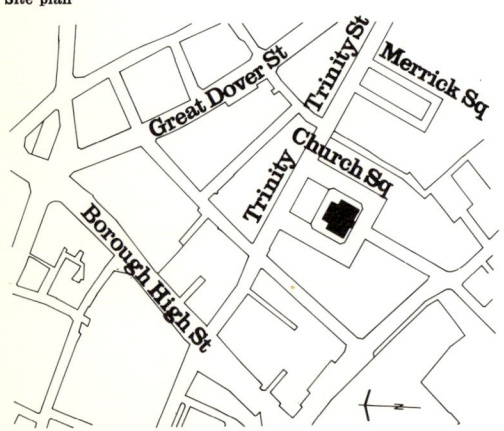

Window detail

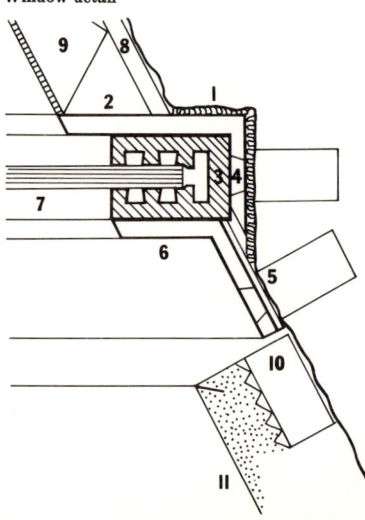

key
Detail of window
1, chase with foam seal
2, aluminium angle plugged to brickwork
3, neoprene gasket glued to angle
4, neoprene seal plug
5, neoprene seal strip
6, aluminium locking angle
7, float glass in one sheet
8, fibreboard
9, patent acoustic lining
10, softwood fillet
11, lime plaster

Work proposed: Before the fire, tests were made of the structure, and repairs were begun almost immediately after the fire. It is proposed to restore the church without making any changes in its structure except to replace the timber roof trusses with steel ones which will provide more space for installing and maintaining mechanical and electrical services. The original lead roof had already been replaced with copper, which will be used again for the new roof. The floor of the choir will be brought down to the same level as the floor of the nave and will provide a 60ft. by 61ft. space for the orchestra. The end gallery, which was destroyed by the fire, has been redesigned and returned through one bay to provide accommodation for the chorus. The architects are looking for a good organ of the period to go in the centre of the end gallery, the original organ position. Windows will be double-glazed for sound insulation, and new services installed providing heating, mechanical ventilation and full orchestral lighting. The crypt will be converted into libraries for both orchestras, a cafeteria and other facilities.

Accommodation: Crypt—music libraries for both orchestras, large cafeteria, kitchen, storerooms for orchestral and recording equipment, lavatories and cloakrooms
Nave—rehearsal hall for full orchestra, gallery to accommodate a choir of 200, recording rooms under the gallery

Date of completion: Expected to be 1975

Cost: Expected to be £450 000. A new rehearsal hall with similar facilities could cost 50 per cent more than this figure.

2, 3, the interior in the neglected state it had reached when the decision was made in 1972 to convert the church into a rehearsal and recording hall. The gallery will be restored and the floor of the sanctuary made level with the rest of the church

4, drawing showing the converted interior with an orchestral rehearsal in progress

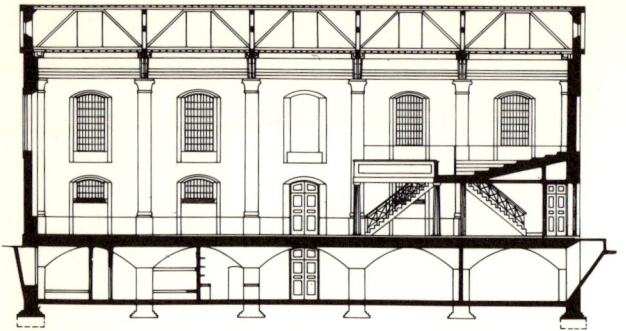

Section AA

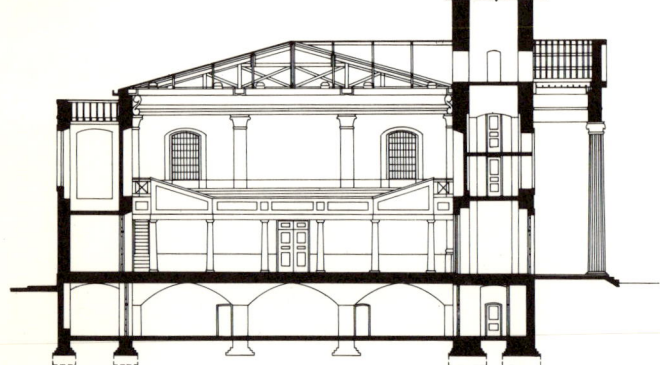

Section BB

key
Plans and sections
1, lobby
2, conductor's room
3, cafeteria
4, kitchen
5, music library
6, plant room
7, lift to crypt
8, caretaker
9, rehearsal hall
10, recording room
11, loading platform
12, manager
13, secretary
14, boiler
15, side galleries cut back and rebuilt
16, gallery front extended
17, position of original organ
18, upper part of rehearsal hall

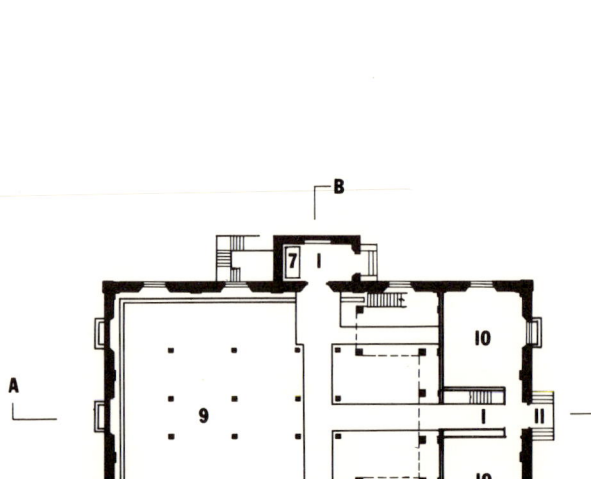

First floor plan

Ground floor plan

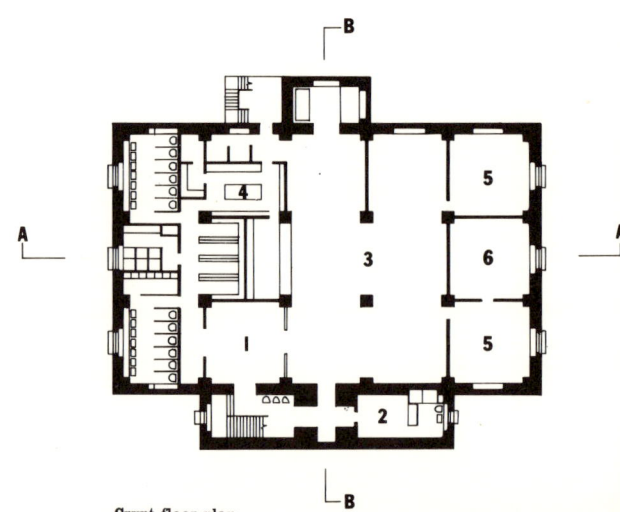

Crypt floor plan

ALL SAINTS, OXFORD (project)

1, the steeple of Dean Aldrich's All Saints—one of the many monumental 'incidents' in Oxford's High Street

Architect: Robert Potter of The Brandt, Potter, Hare Partnership

Client: Lincoln College

Site: The church stands in the High Street on the corner of Turl Street and forms one of the monumental incidents in that famous street. Its tower and spire provide one of the two major punctuations in the otherwise low facades from Magdalen Tower to Carfax Tower; seen down the narrow Turl they dramatically close the view which starts at the open end by Trinity gates. The small churchyard makes informal gaps for small trees to break through the stone frontages of these central streets.

History: The present building was erected in 1699 by public subscription, immediately after the collapse of the medieval church on the same site, to the designs of the brilliant amateur Henry Aldrich, Dean of Christ Church, an early and devout Palladian who left behind several notable works in Oxford and a book on architecture. The tower is not entirely his and may owe something to the collaboration of Hawksmoor. The church, which had been the collegiate church of the adjacent Lincoln College since the latter's foundation in 1427, was declared redundant by the diocese in 1972 and assigned to the college for use as a library.

Character: Aldrich's church is an oblong box of three by five 15ft. bays, divided by Corinthian pilasters internally and externally, and surmounted by an attic, giving a total interior height of 45ft. There is a large crypt extend-

2, a contemporary engraving of the interior showing the pews which were removed in the 1880's

3, the same view as drawn by P. E. Garbe to show the church converted into a library, with the future screen and the floor raised to the level of the top of the lost pews

ing under the whole building. The massive belfry tower abuts on to the west wall, and the west bay also has columned and pedimented doorways facing the High Street and Turl Street. Internally this west bay was fitted in the nineteenth century with a gallery cutting across the heads of the doorways. Outside, the giant order stands on a pedestal zone with blank segmental arches in each bay; inside, this zone was masked by the high oak box-pews on whose backs the main pilasters rested without any base mouldings—giving a very odd effect after the removal of the pews in the 1880's.

Work proposed: The essence of the conversion scheme is to provide a floor at the level of the tops of these lost pews, so that the main order again rests on a firm ground, some 5½ft. higher than the old floor. This changes the interior proportion, though visually it will perhaps be nearer to the original effect than it has been since the pews were taken out. The result conforms to what Aldrich's book prescribed for a 'Corinthian Oecus'—a hall of three by five bays whose pilasters may stand either on pedestals or on the floor, and which exploits the proportion of three by five in its elevations as well.

The general intention is to preserve the character and detail of the old building, employing as few new forms as possible. Fortunately there exists a wealth of contemporary woodwork from the church itself and from the demolished altar-piece of Magdalen College, now in Lincoln's possession, which can be used quite authentically. Included in the scheme of adaptation is the senior library of the college, a room now sited in a building of 1906, (but accurately conserving the proportions of the room which had housed the library since 1665, together with its furnishings and panelling, all of which will be moved to its new position with the minimum of adjustment. The rest of the college library consists of a rare-books room and a general working library of modern books used daily by undergraduates, both as a place of reference and as a congenial work-space free from noise and interruption. All these spaces will be accommodated on the lower floor of the church, lit by windows made in the blank segmental arches mentioned above.

Entrance will be by the west bay, cleared of its gallery but left with the present floor level. A central flight of steps will lead to the lower library room and senior library, etc; a double flight each side of this will lead up to the new floor level of the remaining four bays, which will constitute the main reading room. This will have eighteenth-century type bookpresses jutting out from each of the great pilasters on either side, forming 12ft. square working bays between them. In these will be desks with further shelves, formed out of existing woodwork. The best of the carved panels will form a balustrade dividing the raised floor from the lower level entrance bay. (A screen of columns across the full width may perhaps be added here at a later stage.)

The carved stone altar-piece will remain at the east end (raised to the new level); and the several good monuments will be massed on the blank west walls, the ledger stones being incorporated in the pavement of the entrance bay. The windows, now filled with indifferent Victorian grisaille and figures, will be reglazed to the old module (known from a surviving fragment) in plain glass, and double-glazed for sound insulation from the busy High Street.

All interior stonework will be cleaned, and the elaborate heraldic plaster ceiling restored. The exterior stonework, long neglected and sometimes clumsily repaired, is being completely renovated, partly through a grant from the Historic Buildings Council; the detailed carvings are being executed by Michael Black Groser and the Chichester Cathedral Works Organisation. The cost of the rest of the work is being met by the college and its old members, as well as a number of individual benefactors. The excavation of the interior was carried out by the Oxford Archaeological Society under T. Hassel, who recorded all traces found of the medieval church and earlier structures on the site.

Accommodation: Lower floor—plant room, lavatories, rare-books room, modern books reading room, senior library
Main floor—main reading room

Date of completion: Expected to be 1975

Cost: £280 000, including all restoration work
Rate: Not significant because most money was spent on external work and furnishings.

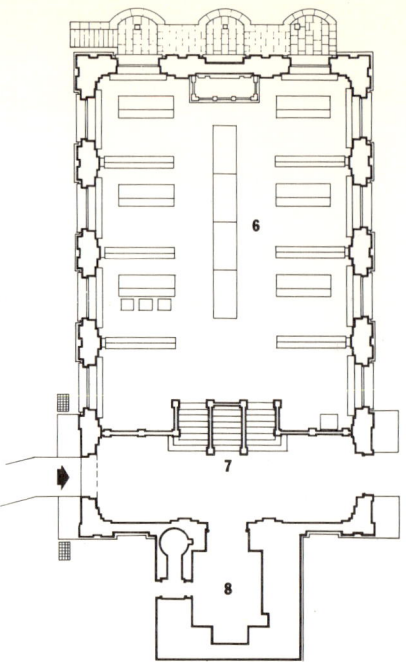

Ground floor plan

key
1, old library
2, lower reading room
3, muniment room
4, plant room
5, air extract and intake
6, upper reading room
7, entrance foyer
8, tower room

Crypt floor plan

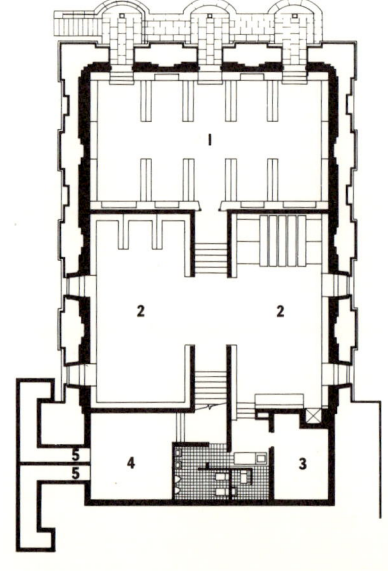

Section

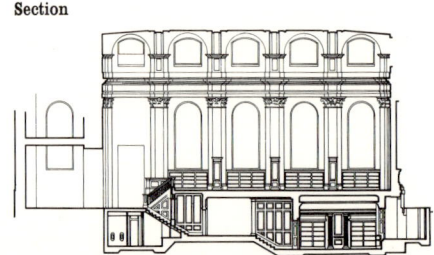

TRINITY ALMSHOUSES CHAPEL, MILE END ROAD, LONDON

Architect: London County Council (now Greater London Council) Architect's Department

Client: London County Council

History: 'THIS ALMES-HOUSE (wherein 28 decayd Masters and Comanders of Ships, or ye Widows of such are maintain'd) was built by ye CORP. of TRINITY-HOUSE AN°. 1695. The Ground was given by Capt. HENRY MUDD of Radcliff, an Elder Brother whose Widow did also contribute.' (Inscription on a memorial plaque) From the records of the Corporation of Trinity House it appears that the Mile End almshouses and chapel were built by William Ogbourne, Master of the Carpenters Company in 1724 and 1726, who was knighted in 1727.

The almshouses and chapel were in the continuous use of the corporation until the beginning of the last war, interrupted only by an event which almost caused their destruction. In the 1890's the corporation petitioned the Charity Commissioners for their demolition and for the sale of the site. There was a public outcry and, as part of the ensuing campaign for preservation, the Committee for the Survey of the Memorials of Greater London issued its first volume, *The Trinity Hospital in Mile End* by C. R. Ashbee. The corporation petition was unsuccessful; the work of the survey committee prospered and eventually developed into the present Survey of London volumes.

In 1941 the almshouses were severely damaged by enemy action and remained derelict until, in 1954, they were acquired from the corporation by the London County Council, which restored first the houses and later the chapel (1961). The houses have been modernised as two-room dwellings and let at low rents. The chapel is in use for various social purposes.

Character: At some time (possibly in the late eighteenth century) the front of the chapel was stuccoed, presumably to bring it up to date. This made it somewhat out of harmony with the red brick almshouses, and it has now been restored to its original brick and stone appearance. The chapel originally consisted of one large room, the chapel proper, approached from the forecourt up a grand flight of stone steps, with a room below it at ground floor level. Probably in the early nineteenth century, it was extended on two floors at the back.

Work done: The restoration included the new and the old parts so as to provide accommodation for three public rooms, a kitchen and lavatories. A new internal staircase was provided for general circulation and effective means of escape. This was constructed of York stone with a plain iron balustrade. The interiors are simply finished in plaster except for the chapel, which was gutted

1, the chapel flanked by almshouses and closed to the street by railings and gates. The restoration of the chapel included refacing the walls with brick slips and reconstructing the wooden bell turret from old photographs and drawings

2, the former chapel converted into a public room. The 18th century panelling came from Bradmore House. The light fittings are reproduction Dutch brass chandeliers

3, the chapel before restoration. It was gutted in 1941 by enemy action

during the war but is now lined with fine eighteenth-century panelling. When Bradmore House became a tram shed in 1908, the panelling was removed and put into store where it lay for fifty years until the discerning eye of Walter Ison spotted that it would fit into Trinity Chapel, which it did to within inches. The light fittings are simple modern ones, except in the chapel, where reproduction eighteenth-century Dutch-type brass chandeliers have been fitted. Heating is by electric convectors installed in the window embrasures except in the chapel, where a heater is fitted into the dome of a small draught lobby behind the main door designed in keeping with the panelling. The glazing is leaded lights throughout with slightly tinted, irregular glass. The new first floor has been constructed in concrete and the floor finishes are thermoplastic tiles except in the chapel, which has wide oak boards of irregular widths fixed on battens. The roof has had to be constructed new, since the building was gutted, but it has been built to the original design with fine timber trusses. It was possible to reconstruct the design of the wooden bell-turret from the measured drawings made for the survey volume and from old photographs. The roof is covered with lead and Westmorland slates. The brickwork of the front elevation was restored by hacking away the old stucco and the surface of the bricks it was adhering to and replacing with brick slips 1 in. thick. All paint was chipped away from the stonework and the stone-carved coat of arms and decoration were restored, repainted and gilded.

Accommodation: Ground floor—one public room, kitchen and lavatories
Main floor—two public rooms

Date of completion: 1961

Cost: £22 400

Rate: £9·90 per sq. ft.

Longitudinal section

key

1, general purpose
2, kitchen
3, entrance hall
4, glazed draught lobby
5, lecture room
6, craft room

Upper floor plan

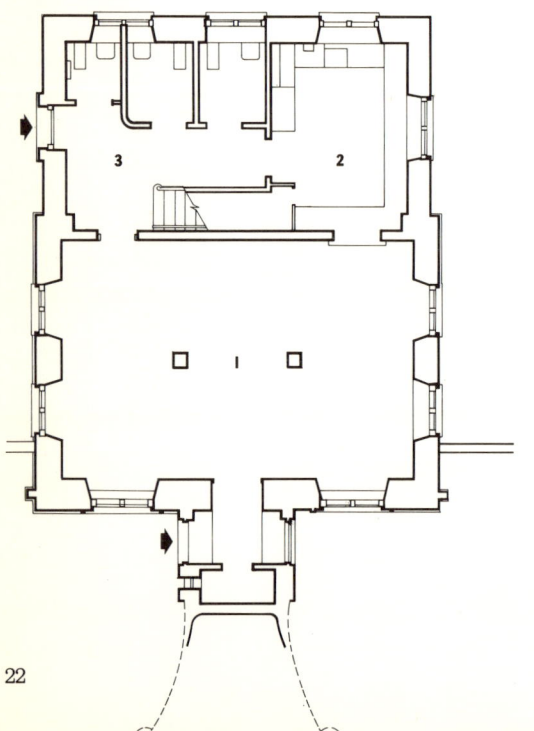

Lower floor plan

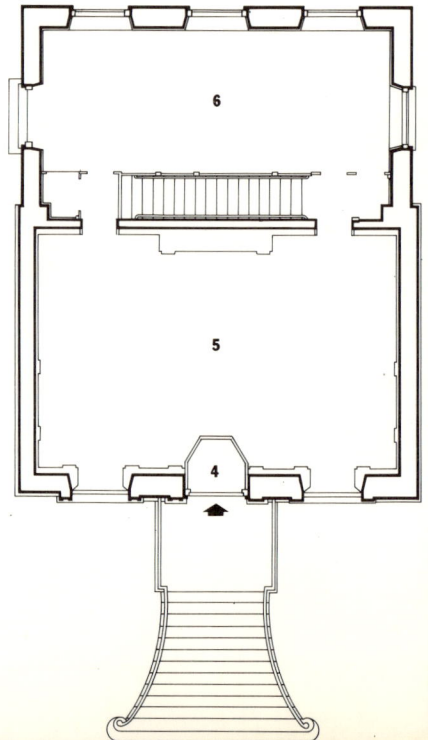

NONCONFORMIST MEETING HALL, HOVE, SUSSEX

Architect: Edward Cullinan with Michael Chassay

Client: British Olivetti Ltd.

Site: Hove is a seaside town. The meeting hall occupies a corner site in Goldstone Road, which is lined with trees and made up of three-storey Victorian houses, some with shops on the ground floor. The street runs through the town from the station to the shopping centre.

History: The building was built in 1878 as a nonconformist meeting hall and was used as such until shortly before Olivetti purchased it.

Character: A three-storey white stucco building, rusticated up to first floor level and divided by pilasters into bays. These are equal on the side elevation but unequal on the front, where the much wider central bay of three windows is crowned by a pediment with an *oeil-de-boeuf*. The two bays which flank this centre piece each contained an entrance (now a window) approached by a flight of steps (now demolished). The first floor has tall round-headed windows on the front and side.

Work done: The additions at the back and surrounding walls were demolished and the timber framed windows were replaced with large sheets of glass in slim steel frames to reveal the building's classical simplicity. The stuccoed brick shell and main timber floor were retained. A new top floor of in-situ reinforced concrete was inserted, supported on concrete columns penetrating to basement level on to new footings. A central front stair of steel and slate was added to provide access to the entrance floor corridor, which runs between the two lines of columns, is open to the floor above and leads to the new rear stair. This rear staircase is constructed of reinforced concrete and steel with neoprene gaskets and glass walls. On the main floor the offices are divided by steel and glass partitions. Heating is from a gas-fired boiler leading to fin tube convectors in perimeter ducts.

Accommodation: Basement—workshop, workshop administration, store, plant rooms, loading to basement store from rear service yard
Main floor—reception, manager's and salesmen's offices, coffee room
Top floor—showroom, two salesrooms and two salesmen's offices

Date of completion: 1971

Cost: £33 000, including carpeting

Rate: £5·04 per sq. ft.

1, the meeting hall in Goldstone Road, Hove, before conversion with its two side entrances and characteristic timber sashes

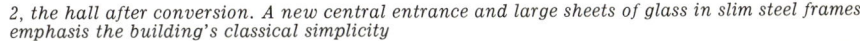

2, the hall after conversion. A new central entrance and large sheets of glass in slim steel frames emphasis the building's classical simplicity

3, the new staircase structure at the back

4, the new slate steps to the front entrance are supported on a steel structure. The splayed side reflects the fact that most people coming to the building approach it from the left

5, the entrance floor corridor is flanked on both sides by offices, between two lines of columns, and leads to the new staircase at the back. The corridor is open to the upper floor, 6, 7, which has been inserted into the double-height space of the old hall.

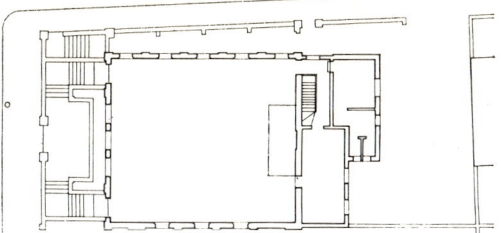

take an abandoned non-conformist meeting hall

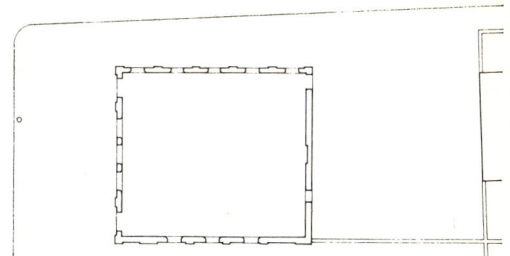

strip it down...

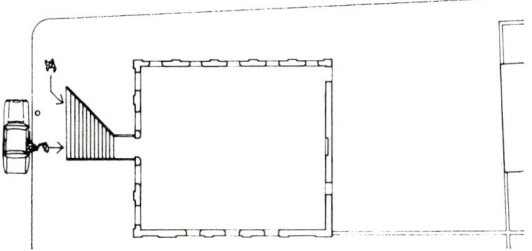

make a new entrance staircase

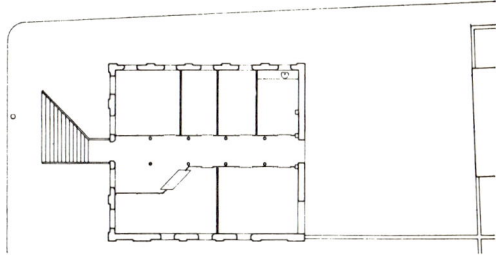

make a path through the middle with offices either side

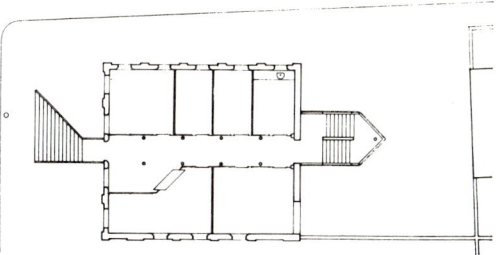

add a new back staircase connecting to...

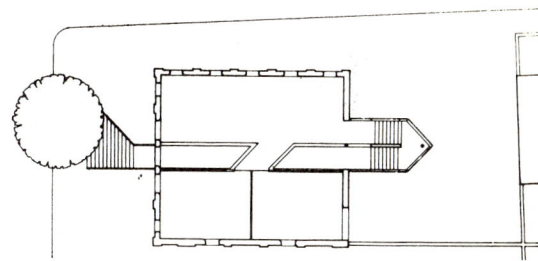

...a new floor above for a showroom and offices...

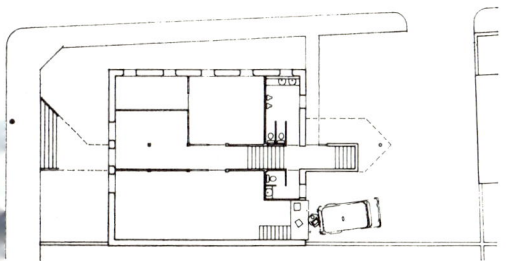

and to a workshop floor below;

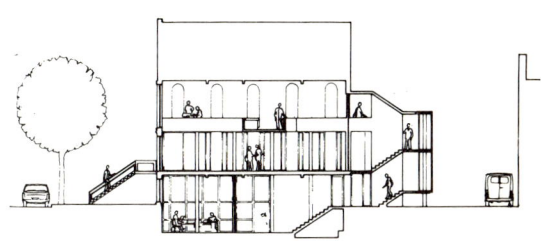

section

Monastic and other religious establishments

The conversions which follow could hardly be more different than the examples illustrated in Chapter I. Monastic buildings are, of course, related closely to chapels or churches and in one instance shown, the Commanderie des Templiers at Coulommiers in France, the chapel forms an integral part. Nevertheless the concept of a church as a large, single volume, often free-standing, as a monument which leads in the hierarchy of building types, remains fundamental to any change of use, and one must always look askance at proposals which turn a church into a cellular building.

Monastic buildings, on the other hand, can be described as a continuous web of cellular structure often arranged around courtyards. Paradoxically the monumentality of the church is fragile compared to this tough and anonymous web which seems able to absorb volumes of almost any size and to accommodate a large variety of activities. Monastic buildings could be turned to housing, students' residences, hotels, shops, offices and even some forms of light industry (a legitimate extension, surely, of traditional monastic activities). Unfortunately this last use is associated nowadays with dereliction, and two of the examples illustrated, the Commanderie and the convent stables in Montreal, suffered severe neglect respectively as a farm and a brewery, ironically the two most traditional monastic activities.

The examples in this chapter *do* include some buildings with large spans. The Commanderie has a magnificent barn, which will one day make a dining hall and a place for parties, while Quaker Friars at Bristol, with its two medieval halls, is an example of a building which had already passed through a change of use before its recent conversion into an exhibition centre. After the dissolution of the monasteries the monks' refectory and dormitory were taken over by city guilds for their meeting halls—an example of a new use which accords well enough with both the spirit and form of the space. The latest use is also apt, even if the irony of holding official planning exhibitions in the middle of some of the most insensitive post-war development in the country has not escaped notice. Of course, exhibition display can be adapted to almost any kind of building, as is shown by the museums and exhibition galleries which pervade most of the chapters in this book. But Bristol would not be able to exhibit large models of the city in a building consisting of a series of small rooms, like the Holy Jesus Hospital at Newcastle, also converted to exhibition use and also unhappily isolated by major road developments.

The most interesting examples illustrated are the three Italian monasteries, because of their role of providing continuity and consistency in urban 'grain' rather than for their intrinsic architectural quality. They illustrate well the point that a web of cellular structure can absorb volumes of almost any size. At Macerata and Urbino, large libraries have been accommodated by raising the level of the courtyards, while lecture halls and common rooms have been fitted into the existing fabric of the surrounding buildings. The outward appearance—the public face—has remained relatively unaltered, while all the major changes have taken place in the private world of the courtyard. It is a valid solution with wide implications, for one is here considering the rehabilitation of a whole city block. At Urbino, for instance, where the old city does not possess a single good hotel, such a conversion might well be aimed at a combination of the tourist and the conference business. In London, where houses tend to be narrow and tall, unproductive and unsightly backland could provide valuable commercial space with walled gardens or private outdoor space raised one or two storeys above ground level.

Much of the success of the Italian examples is due to their being large entities. Size and form play an important part: size because a large mass of building provides the client and the architect with greater flexibility; form because the courtyard plan is both compact and inward-looking. These qualities are also of great importance to the rural Commanderie. Though isolated by fields, it is already overshadowed by tall blocks of council flats and is now menaced by a hospital literally on its doorstep. The inevitable collision between the form of the Commanderie and the twentieth-century giantism of the hospital will furnish the most poignant testimony of all our failures.

LA COMMANDERIE DES TEMPLIERS, COULOMMIERS, FRANCE

Architect: Hervé Baptiste

Client: Association of the Commanderie des Templiers

Site: A compact group of monastic buildings, including a chapel, a *corps de logis* and a large barn, perched on the edge of the plateau above Coulommiers in the Brie Champenoise some 50km. east of Paris. The site is near an ancient crossing of the Roman road from Soissons to Sens and the Gallic road between Saint-Augustin and Doue. Municipal blocks of flats, water towers and two vast silos now dominate the landscape. A hospital is threatened within 100 ft. of the old buildings.

History: The Knights Templar established themselves at Coulommiers on the site of a castle (previously a Roman camp) in 1128, ten years after the foundation of the order. The chapel and exceptionally large narthex, which went up in the latter years of the thirteenth century, are the only buildings which survive from this period. In 1307 the Knights were forcibly disbanded and the Hospitallers of St. John took over the buildings. In the second half of the fifteenth century the Commanderie underwent major restoration after damage suffered in the wars against the Burgundians. The *corps de logis* was modernised, the pointed arches over the windows being replaced by square-headed openings with hoodmoulds and the fine octagonal staircase tower added. It was the start of a long prosperous period, the Commanderie having amassed from its earliest days more than 1000 hectares of land. At the Revolution, the property was sold as the 'Ferme de l'Hôpital', a name by which it was known until 1966, when compulsory purchase by the municipality for housing brought it to the attention of a group of local conservationists who formed the association which saved the buildings from demolition at the hands of a municipality which had bulldozed its Romanesque parish church the same year.

Character: A long rectangular courtyard surrounded mainly by low outhouses and barns with pitched roofs, but dominated by the much taller buildings in the south-east corner consisting of the *corps de logis* and chapel. The chapel is characteristic of Early Gothic structures with its four bays divided by buttresses and punctuated by single, tall lancet windows. The *corps de logis* is distinguished by its projecting octagonal tower built, unlike any of the other parts, in horizontal bands of alternating stone and brick. Another vertical feature of the complex is the round tower built into the narthex structure which once served as dovecot. Walls are generally random rubble roughly rendered, and roofs are tiled, those of the chapel and *corps de logis* having very steep pitches.

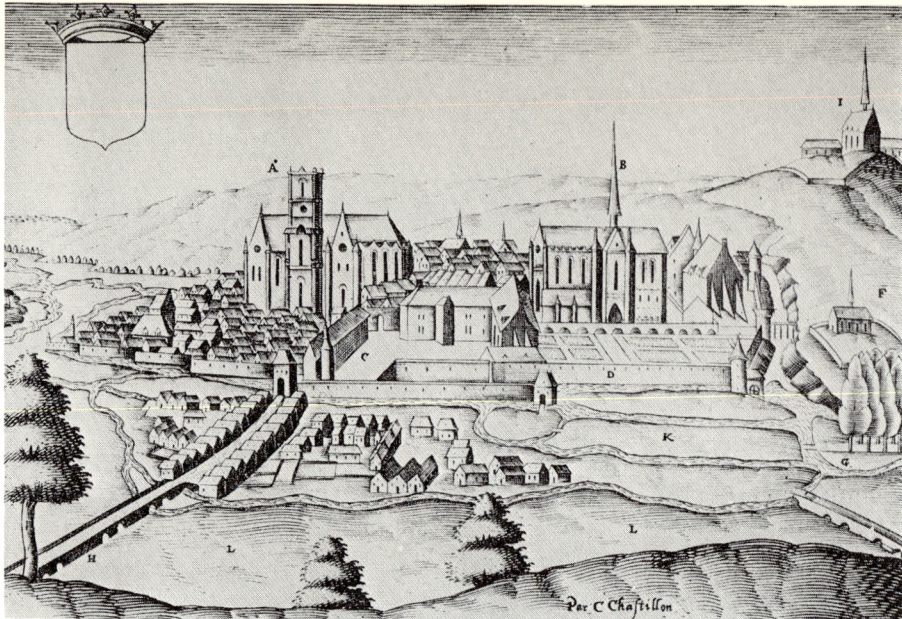

1, 16th century engraving by Chastillon of Conlommiers. Of the monuments the only one to survive is the Commanderie on the hill (top right-hand corner). The Romanesque church of St. Denis (left) was bulldozed in 1966

2, the Commanderie today (right) stands engulfed by municipal housing and overshadowed by two gigantic silos

When the association took charge of the Commanderie in 1966 it found the buildings severely mutilated. Window and door openings had been blocked up and new ones made. Upper floors had been inserted into the chapel and the narthex had been turned into part stables, part two-storey cheese dairy. The courtyard was piled high with earth and manure; the timber roof structures of the barns had been lifted to provide headroom for modern machinery. Nevertheless the quadripartite ribbed vaulting of the chapel had survived in perfect condition and the great barn of the west range had retained all its grandeur.

Work done: The intention was to restore the buildings to their former splendour and to use them as a museum (unique in France) of machinery, materials and products of the paper industry from its beginnings to the present day, and including exhibits from all over the world. A youth centre was also planned. As there was no money available, the association set up a small museum in the *corps de logis* with the help of scouts. Its success encouraged them to make an appeal through television and newspapers in January 1968, which provided a voluntary labour force of young enthusiasts during the following summer. The courtyard was cleaned out and the chapel relieved of its intruding structures. Enough money to buy tools was raised from museum entrance fees and from the sale of a specially commissioned limited edition of an engraving depicting the Commanderie. In February 1969 the Caisse Nationale de Monuments Historiques awarded the association first prize in its annual competition for restoration carried out by young voluntary labour (25 000 francs), a success which was repeated with the award of second prize (20 000 francs) the following year. Every summer holiday (except 1973), some Easter holidays and some weekends, groups of 30 to 40 school children and students, almost totally inexperienced in building, have been restoring the Commanderie bit by bit under the direction of Jean Schelstraete, founder of the association, and Hervé Baptiste, the architect. In addition to restoring the interior of the chapel, the main work has so far consisted of rebuilding six of the nine quadripartite groin vaults and two of the four columns in the narthex; re-roofing the chapel, narthex, dovecot, *corps de logis* and one of the barns; and restoring the facade of the *corps de logis*, which included renewing four large mullioned windows. Next in line is the conversion of the north range of outhouses into a youth hostel (so far volunteers have slept in the *corps de logis*) and the lowering of the ground level of the *corps de logis* by 1m. both for archaeological reasons and for headroom needed for the final installation of the museum. Having offered no support to the scheme previously, the town municipality is to organise the creation of the youth hostel and is planning to devote the enormous sum of one million francs to it.

Accommodation: Chapel—space for temporary exhibitions
Narthex ground floor—entrance to exhibitions
upper floor—permanent exhibition of specially commissioned engravings of the Commanderie and changing exhibitions explaining building operations
Corps de logis—museum of the paper industry (project)
North range—youth hostel (project)
West range—refectory, hall, kitchens (project)

Date of completion: Chapel, 1969
Roofing, 1969 and 1970
Narthex, 1970
Corps de logis (facade), 1972

Cost: 1·5 million francs for all expenses, including tools, up to the end of 1974

3, the Commanderie from the west. The steep gable on the right belongs to the 13th-century Chapel and the octagonal staircase tower in the background to the 15th-century corps de logis

4, 19th century lithograph of the Commanderie when it was used as farm buildings and called 'Ferme de l'Hôpital'. The corps de logis *is on the left and the chapel and 15th century cylindrical dovecote tower are on the right*

5, an early working party at leisure. The scaffolding behind was erected for the restoration of the roof

6, the façade of the corps de logis *under restoration in 1972. The stone surrounds of the four large square-headed windows as well as the tracery of the pointed window on the left, were renewed. The intention is to convert the* corps de logis *into a museum of the paper industry*

7, the first stage was to clean out and restore the chapel so that it could be used for exhibitions, 8, to raise money for the next stage of work. The earth floor will eventually be paved

9, 10, the upper parts—the quadripartite rib vaulting and the carving of the corbels—were found to be in almost perfect condition

11, 12, the unusually large narthex, or antichapel, had lost six of its nine quadripartite groin vaults and two of the four columns which had supported these. 11 shows the section through the narthex before restoration and the timbre centring used in the construction of the vaults. 12 shows the vaults as restored by the working party in the summer of 1970

13, the great barn by the entrance which, it is hoped, will be restored and converted into a refectory

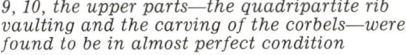
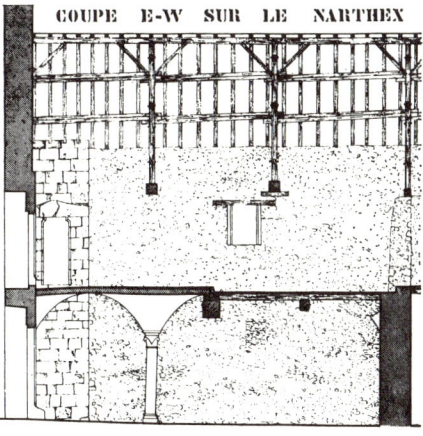
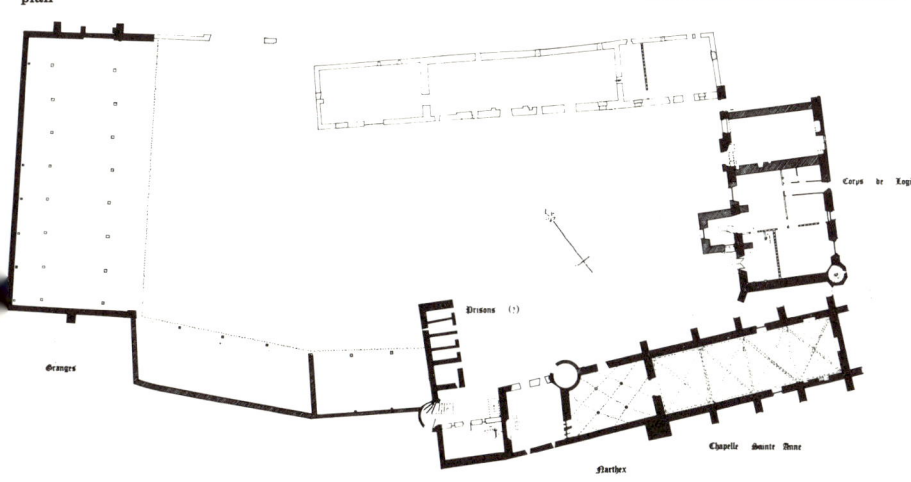

MONASTERY, MACERATA, ITALY

Monastery, Macerata,

Architect: Luciano and Giorgio Giovannini

Client: University of Macerata

Site: In the centre of Macerata, a cathedral town fourteen miles inland from the Adriatic coast and some thirty miles south of Ancona. With the church of S. Paolo, which faces the main square of the town, the Piazza della Liberta, the site takes up a whole city block. It is bounded by Via Don Minzoni to the north, Vicolo delle Scuole to the east, Via Santa Maria della Porta to the south and Piaggia dell'Universita to the west. From the piazza to the south-east corner the site falls steeply.

History: Built together with the church of S. Paolo early in the seventeenth century as a monastery for the Barnabite Fathers. The buildings had already been subjected to many alterations when in the early years of this century they ceased to house the monastery and were allocated by the municipality to a number of users, including the university (north and part of east wing), a school for surveyors (south and part of west wing) and the municipality itself for recreation, social assistance and storage. In May 1963 the municipality granted the university free use of the entire block. The university's development plan designated the buildings for the Faculty of Law (already in possession of one part), the new Institute of Medical Law and the new Faculty of Letters.

Character: The character of the external face is of prime importance because of its relationship to the town: three-, four- and five-storey walls built out of the thin 'cotto' brick typical of the town as a whole and broken by door and window openings at not very regular intervals. Along the Via Don Minzoni the facade is given greater importance by the use of window surrounds (of stone on the ground floor and brick on the upper floors), a stone band at first floor level, a pedimented doorway and a proper cornice below the eaves of the Roman-tiled roof.

The character of the courtyard was ruined in the 1930's when most of the windows (the exceptions were on the south and west elevations of the inner courtyard) were renewed in steel in a style typical of that period, and some of the courtyard walls were rendered. Except in the part occupied by the university, a series of inexpert internal alterations virtually destroyed the character of the old interior, and only a few original features, such as the vaulted passage which proceeds from the entrance on the Via Don Minzoni down the middle of the east wing, remained.

Work done: Alterations and rehabilitation work included the demolition of stairs and walls; the opening of new windows and the bricking-up of existing ones; the removal of rendering and the

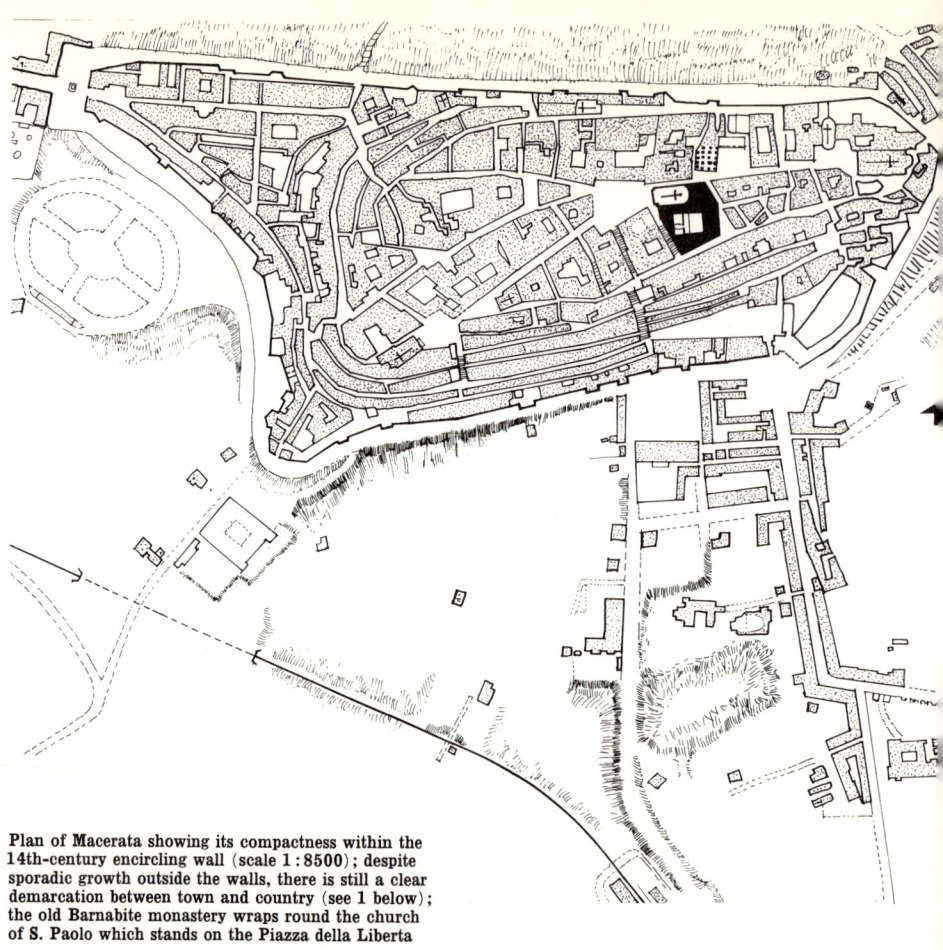

Plan of Macerata showing its compactness within the 14th-century encircling wall (scale 1:8500); despite sporadic growth outside the walls, there is still a clear demarcation between town and country (see 1 below); the old Barnabite monastery wraps round the church of S. Paolo which stands on the Piazza della Liberta

1, in the foreground the church of S. Paolo with the Barnabite monastery before conversion. The trees in the courtyard were lost when the level was raised to accommodate the new library

key to plan and
section
1, entrance
2, vaulted passage
3, rector's office
4, waiting
5, council faculty of law
6, council faculty of letters
7, students' hall
8, main lecture hall
9, lecture room
10, roof garden over new building
11, glazed link and entrance to library
12, new staircase
13, institute of medical law
14, ramp to library gallery
15, lower roof garden as extension of reading room
16, new library
17, faculty of letters
18, administration
19, faculty of law

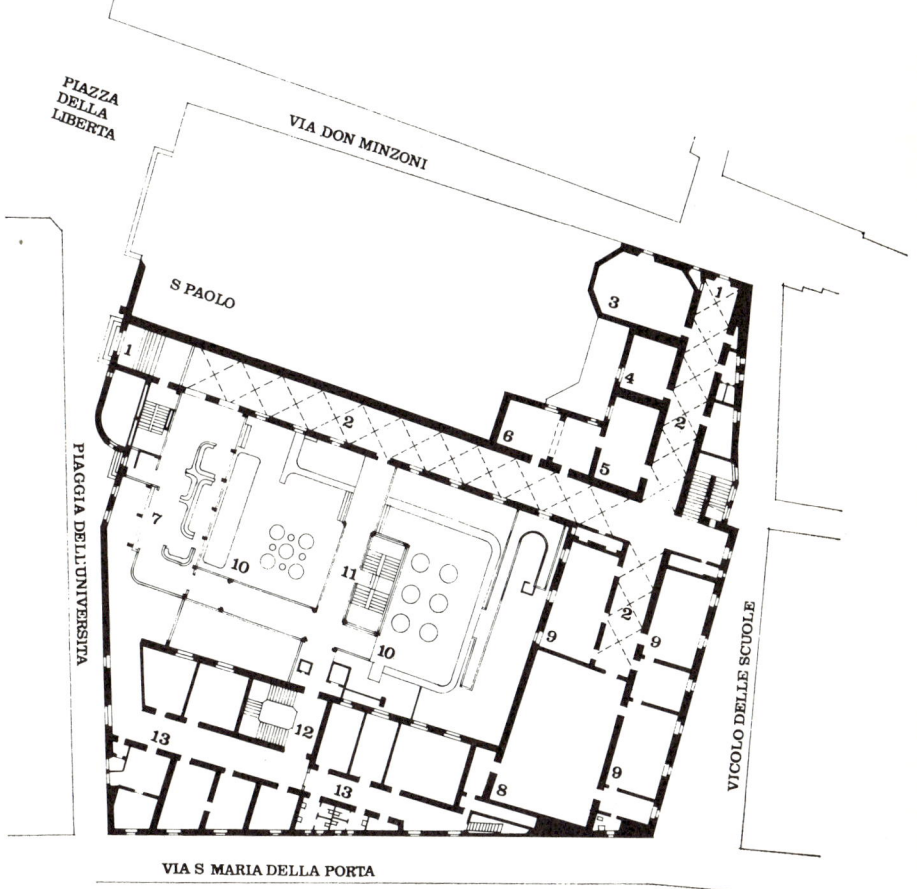

cleaning up of the brickwork on Via Santa Maria della Porta and Piaggia dell'Universita; and the lining of all window openings (except on Via Don Minzoni) with projecting steel frames painted dark brown on the outside, travertine marble on the inside and white-painted wood sashes for the windows themselves. Floor finishes are in terrazzo tiles, marble and wood. The main work consisted in the construction of a new library in the courtyard, stepped in section so as to allow light to penetrate the lower storeys of the surrounding wings, and with a roof garden across which a steel-framed glazed link provides access to the library from every part of the old building. In addition to the double staircase serving the library, a new staircase was built in the middle of the south wing, while two of the existing staircases (in the

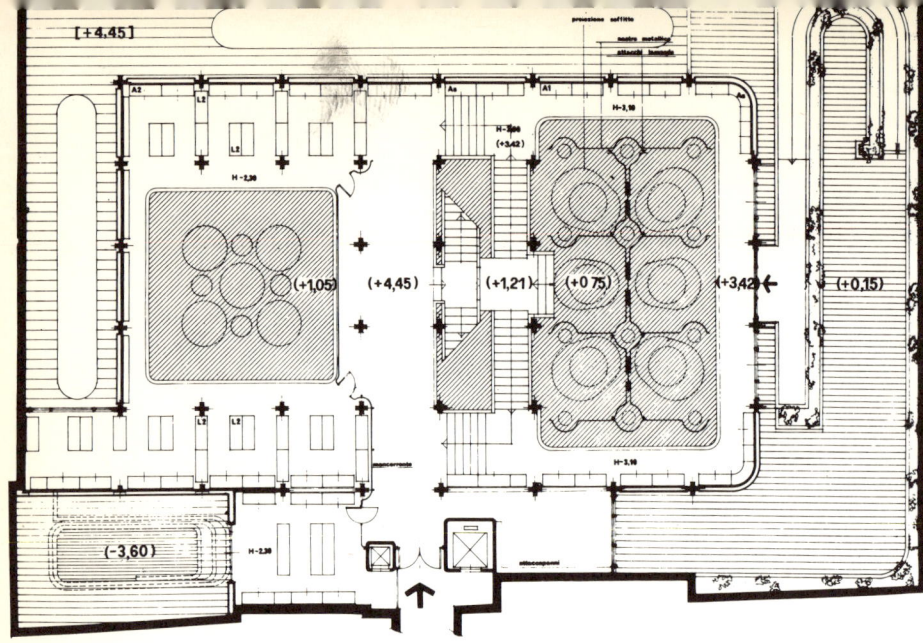

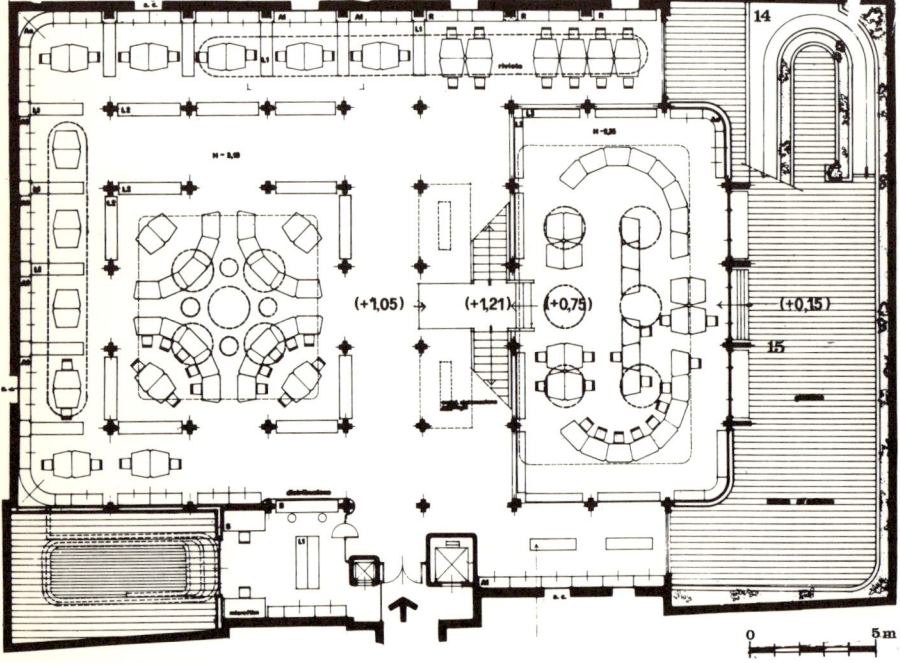

Above: plan of new library at gallery level; below: plan at reading room level (scale: 1:300)

2, the façade on Via Don Minzoni, which has not been altered. The pedimented doorway is one of two main entrances and the one which leads directly to the Institute of Medical Law

3, 4, the restored façade on the Via S. Maria della Porta. The external appearance of the monastic buildings was of no distinction. Its importance lay in the scale and relationship to the narrow streets and in the texture of the thin 'cotto' brickwork which has been restored. Though the old haphazard arrangement of windows has been maintained, all the openings have been framed with projecting steel sections painted dark brown

west and east wings) were retained and restored. The main entrance from the Piazza della Liberta was raised and made to connect by means of a new vaulted passage to the old passage which leads to the entrance on Via Don Minzoni and, via the glazed link, to the library and south wing. The construction of the library is of in-situ reinforced concrete, with column foundations unattached to the old building. Floors are of hollow clay blocks between beams. The roof is finished in copper and the rooflights are perspex. The window and door frames are in anodised aluminium. Three book conveyors connect with the different faculties and two lifts, attached to the south wing on the courtyard side, serve all the floors.

Accommodation: Library block in courtyard—double-height reading room with galleries, access from glazed link on roof above, lecture rooms below
East wing—administration, Faculty of Letters, Institute of Medical Law, entrance from Via Don Minzoni and from Via delle Scuole on level below
North wing—old gallery, church of S. Paolo
West wing—new gallery, Faculty of Law, main entrance from Piazza della Liberta
South wing—Faculty of Law, Faculty of letters, eleven lecture rooms, including the *Aula Magna* on the main floor, available to both faculties

Date of completion: 1972

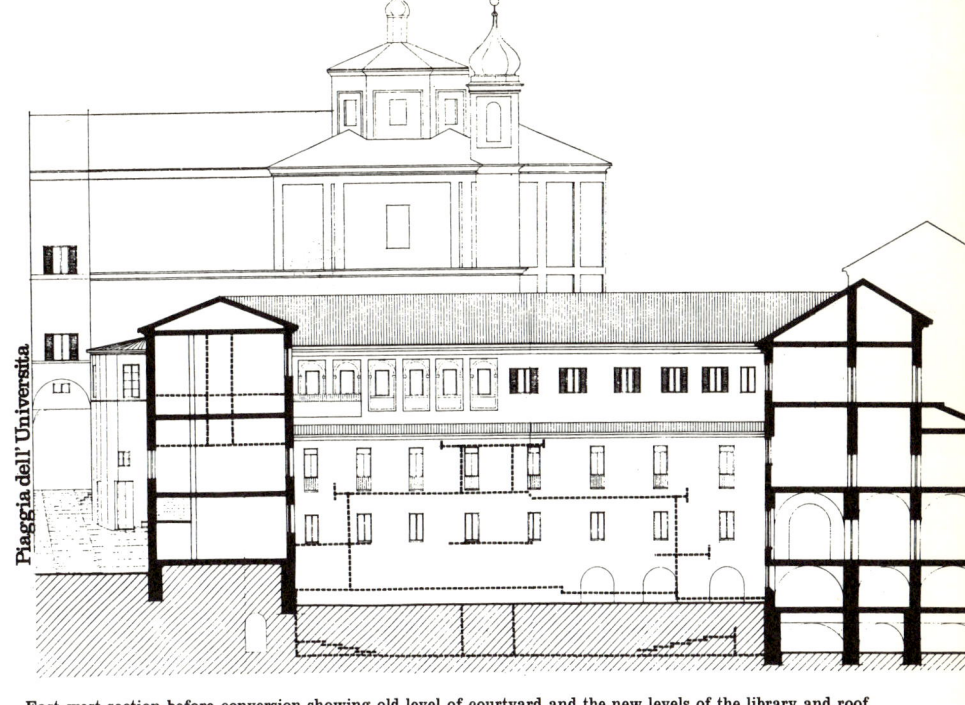

East-west section before conversion showing old level of courtyard and the new levels of the library and roof gardens dotted (scale 1:500)

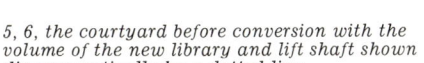

5, 6, the courtyard before conversion with the volume of the new library and lift shaft shown diagrammatically by a dotted line

7, 8, the courtyard by night and by day looking west. The only original courtyard façade preserved is the one on the right. The level of the court has been raised to accommodate a new library which is reached via a glazed link and double staircase seen in the foreground

9, the glazed link seen from the students' hall

10, 11, the symbolic and physical centre is the new library with its grand double-height reading rooms and galleries. Rooflights, ventilators and lighting ducts have been related to form an integrated ceiling pattern

12, part of the library with a lower ceiling where the roof steps down to allow light into the lower storeys of the surrounding old building

13, the foot of the double staircase serving the library and the reinforced concrete pillars supporting the gallery above

MONASTERY, URBINO (project)

Architect: Giancarlo De Carlo

Client: University of Urbino

Site: A roughly rectangular but tapering site at the southern end of the town near the walls. Bounded by Via Saffi to the west, Via S. Girolamo to the north and Via S. Maria to the south and east, the site slopes sharply down to the south and the existing buildings on Via Saffi step down with the slope. The buildings on the site are roughly L-shaped, with a walled garden making up the rectangle. On the corner of Via Saffi and Via S. Girolamo stand two private houses, and on the opposite side of Via S. Girolamo a redundant church bearing the same name as the street forms part of the project.

History: Used latterly as an orphanage, the monastery was founded in the medieval period but rebuilt in the second half of the fifteenth century and much altered subsequently.

Character: The brick walls facing outwards on to the streets are generally massive—three- and four-storeys high—with small rectangular openings for doors and windows, and the remains of arches which must once have surmounted wide openings. The roofs are covered with Roman tiles and provide deep overhangs at the eaves, except at the north end of Via Saffi, where an attractive pediment and three symmetrically placed windows with stone surrounds introduce a semblance of order. The best preserved parts are at the west end of the site and the worst preserved around the garden, which has provided space for piecemeal additions over the years. Of the interiors, only the church offers a space of distinct character worthy of preservation.

Work proposed: The programme is to use the existing site for the new Teaching Faculty of the university. The intention is to preserve, by restoring or rebuilding, the character of the outer structural face, to preserve and convert some of the structure at the west end of the site, but to demolish and rebuild

1, the monastic buildings seen from the Via Saffi. At the top of the hill, on the corner with the Via S. Girolamo stands a more formal, pedimented building which will be converted into a ceremonial hall (upper part) and a cinema (lower part)

2, model of the façade on to the Via Saffi The changes in the fenestration will be minimal

3, outbuildings in the courtyard. Only the street wall will be preserved. The lean-to structure will be replaced by the semicircular bank of lecture rooms, 4

key
1, new work
2, mainly preservation work
3, S. Girolamo, a redundant church to be converted into a ceremonial hall

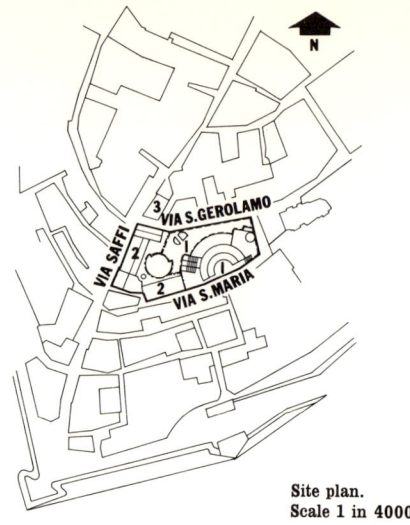

Site plan.
Scale 1 in 4000

around and over the garden, creating a series of stepped roof terraces for use as outdoor space by the students. The church, which had been used as a gymnasium by the orphanage, is to be restored inside and out, and used as a ceremonial hall, with the vestry as a dons' common room.

The plan for the project divides into two parts, the western part around a circular light well and the eastern part in the form of a great semicircle, divided segmentally into lecture rooms and lit indirectly from a skylight which takes the form of part of an inverted cone. The western part preserves the pitched and tiled roof on the perimeter, but steps upwards around the light well to a flat roof which is just below the level of the highest existing roofs. Except for a cinema and a hall on the corner of Via Saffi and Via San Girolamo, most of the spaces in the restored perimeter structure are small rooms; part of the light well is also surrounded by small teaching rooms. The eastern part accommodates on the two lowest levels six raked lecture rooms which can open up into one large hall with a gallery, seating altogether 940 people.

Accommodation: Basement—two raked lecture rooms, each seating 300; lavatories
Lower ground floor—four raked lecture rooms, two seating 100 each and two 70 each; one lecture room seating 100; lavatories, four small lecture rooms, thirteen teaching rooms, cinema (192 seats), foyer and five ancillary rooms
Ground floor—three large lecture rooms, roof garden, lavatories, four small lecture rooms, 11 teaching rooms, projector room, main entrance from Via Saffi with porter's room and offices
First floor—two large lecture rooms, roof garden, students' common room with students' entrance from Via S. Girolamo, lavatories, seven small lecture rooms or laboratories, fifteen teaching rooms, hall with anteroom, entrance from Via S. Girolamo and ticket booth to cinema below
Second floor—students' gallery with bar and related roof garden, lavatories, six small lecture rooms or laboratories, ten teaching rooms
Church—ceremonial hall

Date of completion: Expected to be summer 1975

Cost: Estimated at 800 million lire

Rate: Estimated at 25 000 lire per m³

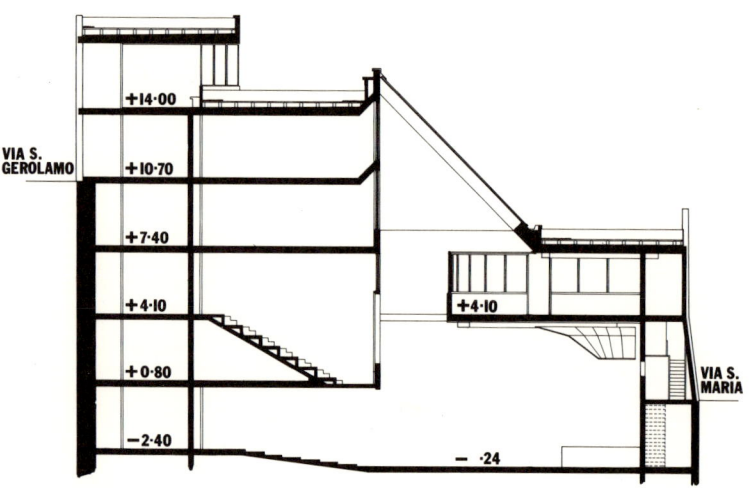

Section AA. Scale 1in. = 350ft.

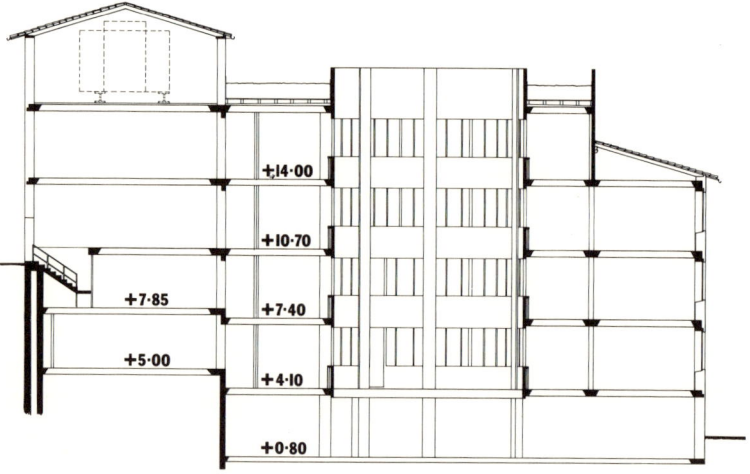

Section BB. Scale 1in. = 350ft.

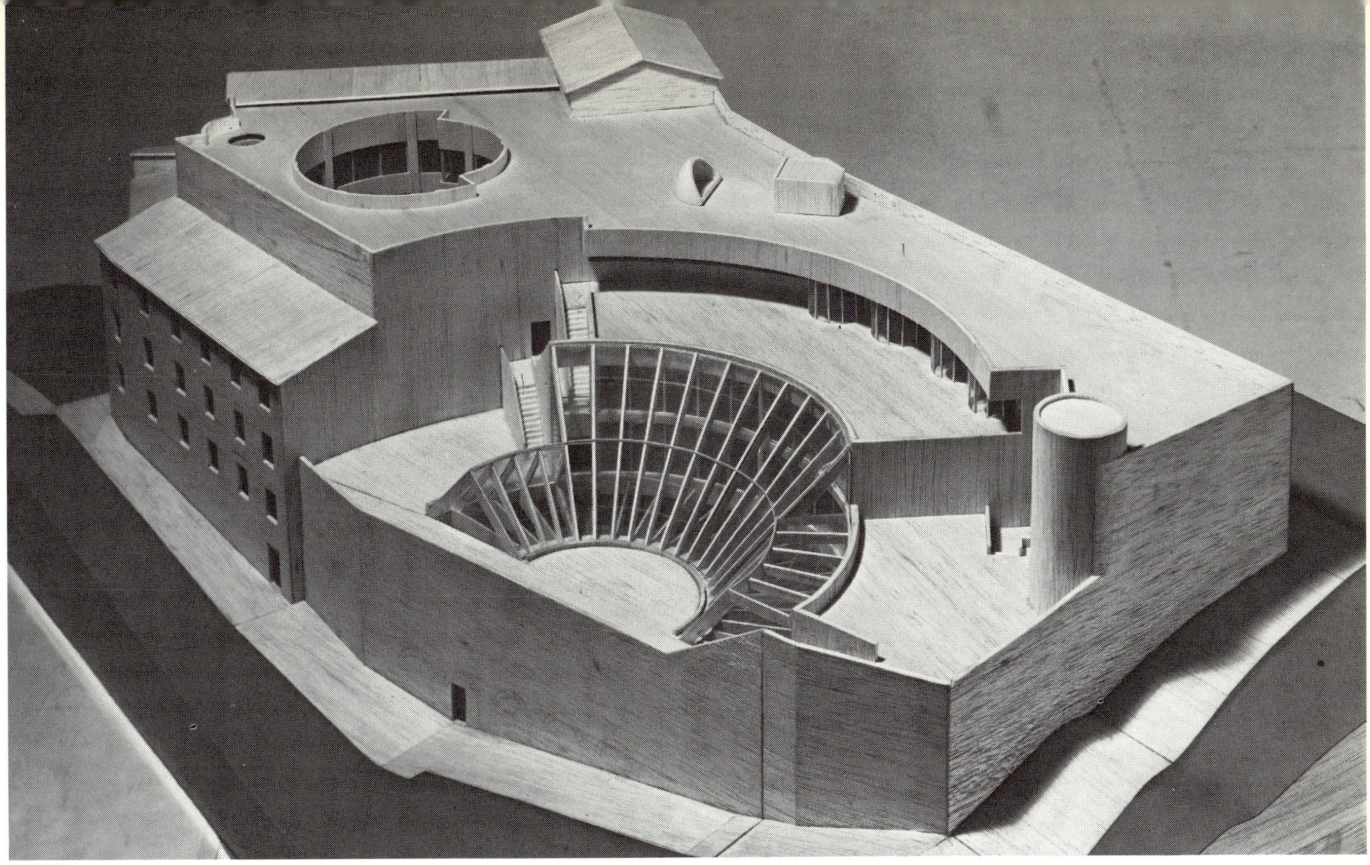

5, view of the model with Via S. Maria in the foreground

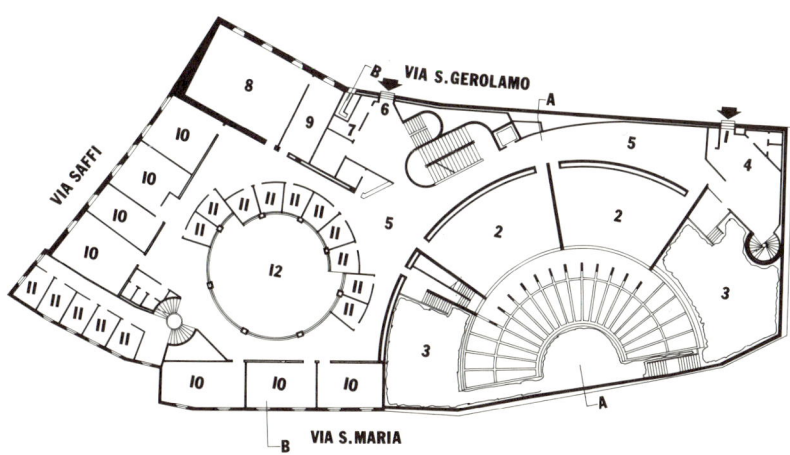

First floor plan. Scale 1 in 800

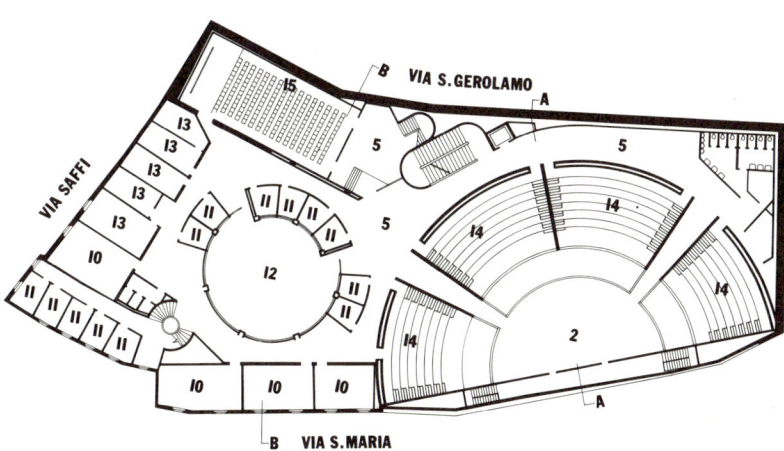

Lower ground floor plan. Scale 1 in 800

1, students' entrance
2, large lecture room seating 100
3, roof garden
4, students' common room
5, foyer
6, entrance to cinema
7, ticket booth for cinema on lower floor
8, hall
9, ante-room
10, small lecture room
11, teaching room
12, court
13, ancillary room
14, lecture room with raked seating
15, cinema

CONVENT, URBINO

Architect: Giancarlo De Carlo

Client: University of Urbino

Site: One side of the old convent abuts the walls of the church of Sant'Agostino and the other three sides face on to streets. The buildings surround a courtyard with an adjoining triangular open space which has been excavated together with the courtyard to provide space for a library. The buildings stand on a slope, so that they appear to be one storey high from the top road (Via Sant'Agostino) and three storeys high from the bottom road.

History: The late fifteenth-century buildings were once a convent attached to the church of Sant'Agostino, but more latterly they were used as an army barracks.

Character: The buildings are of brick with sloping pantiled roofs. The door and window openings round the courtyard are decorated with blind arcading at ground floor level springing from wide flat pilasters. Much of the interior was wrecked by misuse, but there are still pleasant plaster barrel and quadripartite groin vaulted ceilings.

Work done: The brief required the architect to retain as much as possible of the original structure so as to cut the cost of conversion to a minimum and to keep the old character of the buildings. The main entrance is from the side road at middle floor level, which is also courtyard level. Because of the remote placing of the secondary staircase and even more because of the lack of internal communication between lecture rooms, the courtyard can again take on the role of social catalyst. The two staircases provide easy access to the upper and lower floor levels, and a secondary entrance has been provided on the upper floor from the top road.

The lower floor is almost entirely given over to the library whose reading room, lit by day through plastic domes from a roof garden above, returns the compliment, as it were, by lighting the way into the building at night. The other main space on the lower floor is a ceremonial hall with an adjacent dons'

1, the side elevation before conversion and, 2, after conversion. It now forms the main entrance which is reached across a roof garden underneath which extends the new library

3, on the side of the lower road the building stands three storeys high. The façade has been altered as little as possible

4, the roof garden at night, with the plastic domes of the library below lighting the way into the building

key
1, university
2, law faculty
3, Palazzo Ducale
4, various university buildings
5, teaching faculty
6, future canteen and dining rooms
7, future science faculty
8, for future university use

Site plan

5, 6, two vaulted corridors on the upper floor (5 serves the dons' rooms, 6 the departments)

7, the corridor serving the ceremonial hall on the lower floor. The new concrete floor structure is left blatantly exposed on the underside

common room. The middle floor contains the entrance hall, administration and lecture rooms of various sizes, the larger vaulted rooms being on the side of the lower road. The smaller rooms, for dons and for the various departments, occupy the top floor; a long, narrow space backing on to the top road is put to good use as a students' common room.

The main facade to the lower road has been altered as little as possible, and any new windows match the old. The entrance facade, on the other hand, seen as it is across the new roof garden, has been wholly remodelled. Three narrow splayed openings, which light the secretary's office, contrast with the long horizontal entrance door. Otherwise, there is only the rich texture of plain, uninterrupted brickwork. The courtyard has had new doors and windows inserted into existing or enlarged openings. There are no shutters as on the main facade, and the effect is somewhat austere. The plasterwork inside has been carefully restored but the new concrete floor structure over the lower floor is in no way disguised. Throughout, the plain plaster and brick surfaces provide an admirable background for the modern furniture with which the building is equipped.

Accommodation: Lower floor—library, dons' common room and ceremonial hall
Middle floor—roof garden, courtyard, administration rooms and lecture rooms
Upper floor—dons' rooms, departmental offices, students' common room and lavatories

Date of completion: 1970

Cost: 200 million lire

Rate: 20 000 lire per m³

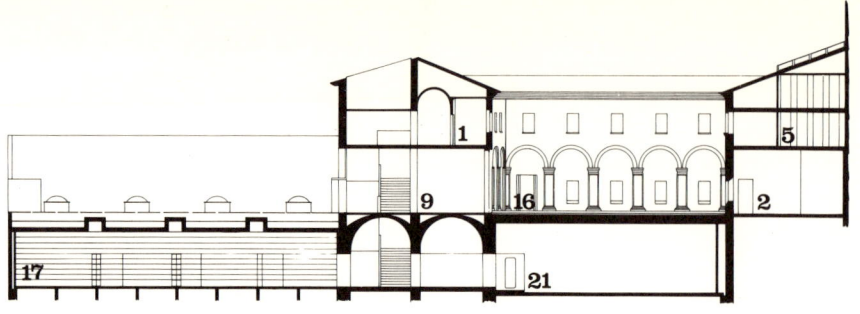

Longitudinal section
key
1, dons
2, lecture room
3, departments
4, dons' lavatory
5, male lavatories (female lavatories on half floor above)
6, porter
7, entrance
8, students' common room
9, entrance
10, secretary
11, porter
12, administration
13, cloakroom
14, garden
15, roof lights
16, courtyard
17, reading room
18, card index
19, book distribution
20, librarian
21, stack room
22, dons' common room
23, ceremonial hall
24, simultaneous translation
25, central heating installation
26, store
27, microfilms
28, dark room

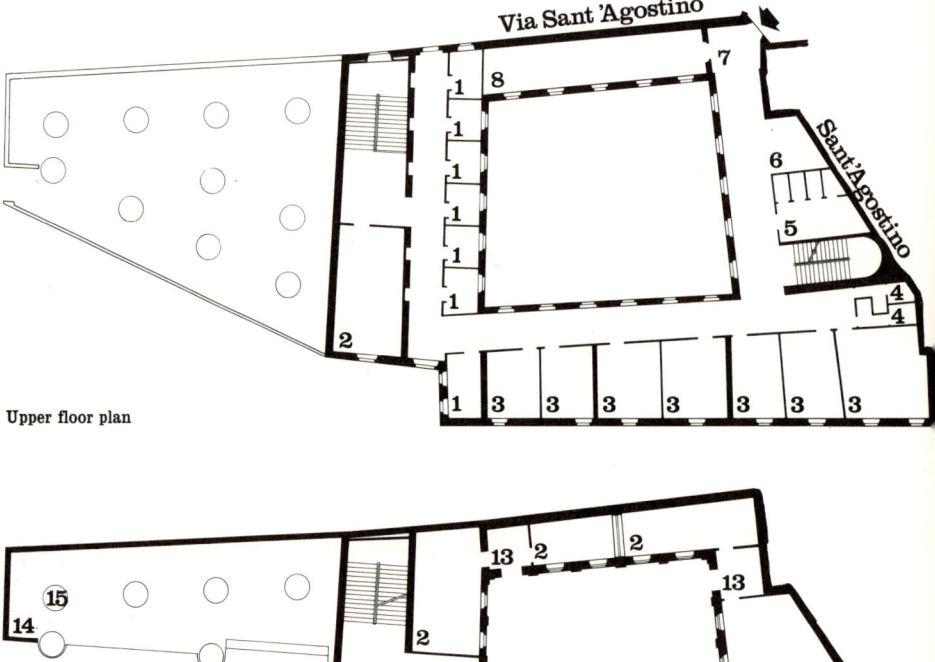

Upper floor plan

Middle floor plan

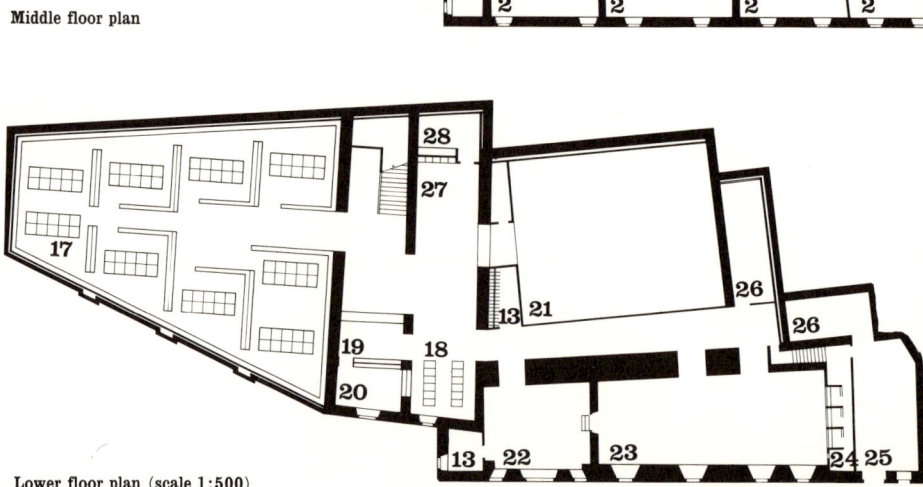

Lower floor plan (scale 1:500)

8, the courtyard has stark fenestration unrelieved by shutters. The door on the right serves the secondary staircase and the one on the left the lecture room

9, the area between the stack room and the reading room (right) on the lower floor

43

10, the dons' common room on the lower floor

11, the reading room on the lower floor, lit from above by plastic domes

12, 13, the ceremonial hall on the lower floor

CONVENT, MONTREAL

Architect: Henry W. Forster, Adepco Ltd.

Client: Youville Stables Project

Site: A building of irregular U-shape with auxiliary structures, forming part of a larger long-term project which occupies most of a city block in the lower part of the town by the St. Lawrence River. The block stretches from Commissioners Street to Common Street, which runs alongside the riverside warehouses.

History: Erected in 1747 as part of the Convent of the Grey Nuns, the buildings were used at different times as a hospital, as a school, as a brewery, as stables and, towards the end of the nineteenth century, as warehouses. Latterly they were used for light industry, by which time the space between the buildings had become filled with all kinds of excrescent structures. During the planning and building activities which preceded Expo 67, a group of fine old buildings lying between Montreal's shopping centre and harbour, though in a run-down area, was seen to have a viable commercial future. With the encouragement of the city authorities, who prepared a plan for the whole district, a private company was formed to restore and convert the remains of the convent in three phases.

Character: A two-storey building of random rubble walls with windows set in dressed stone surrounds. There is an attic storey with dormers and a pitched roof which was once covered in slates (now copper). The street facade is symmetrical, with the arched entrance in the centre, flanked by two pedimented gables with *oeil-de-boeufs*. The interiors have exposed random rubble walls and a heavy timber floor structure supported on a central line of timber columns.

Work done: The intention in phase I was to clear all excrescent structures in the courtyard and to convert the U-shaped building for commercial and office use. The only 'fixed' functions to be provided were a restaurant and kitchen, plant rooms, lavatories, two internal fireproof staircases and two external escape staircases. Otherwise the three floors were to be left open and available for commercial use on the ground floor and for office and commercial use on the upper floors.

The entire building was gutted and rebuilt with the old timber floor and roof structure. The fireproof enclosure to the staircases is either stone or 4in. concrete block. New timber windows and doors were provided and finishes were generally kept natural—stone for the walls, timber boarding for the floors and the exposed floor structure or gyproc for the ceilings.

1, aerial view showing site in relation to St. Lawrence River

2, the stables before conversion and 3, after conversion to commercial and office use

4, the new entrance gate in Commissioners Street. The three-storey warehouses in the background have since been converted into a 100-bedroom hotel

Phase II (now completed, but not included here) comprises the conversion of the three-storey block along Common Street into a luxury hotel with 100 rooms. Phase III will provide the conversion of the block between phases I and II into flats and offices.

Accommodation: Basement—restaurant, bar, kitchen, lavatories, stores, boiler room, electrical room, recording studios
Ground floor—restaurant, main entrance, unallocated commercial area
First and second floors—offices

Date of completion: Phase I, 1970
Phase II, 1973

Cost: Phase I, approximately $2 million, including purchase of property
Phase II, $4 million

Rate: Phase I, $24 per sq. ft.

5, the same view from an upstairs office

6, a shop on the ground floor. The old heavy timbers were re-used, and the stone walls as well as the timber structure left exposed

key
1, entrance to restaurant
2, cloakroom
3, restaurant
4, void over restaurant on lower floor
5, servery
6, commercial area
7, fire-escape stair
8, office area

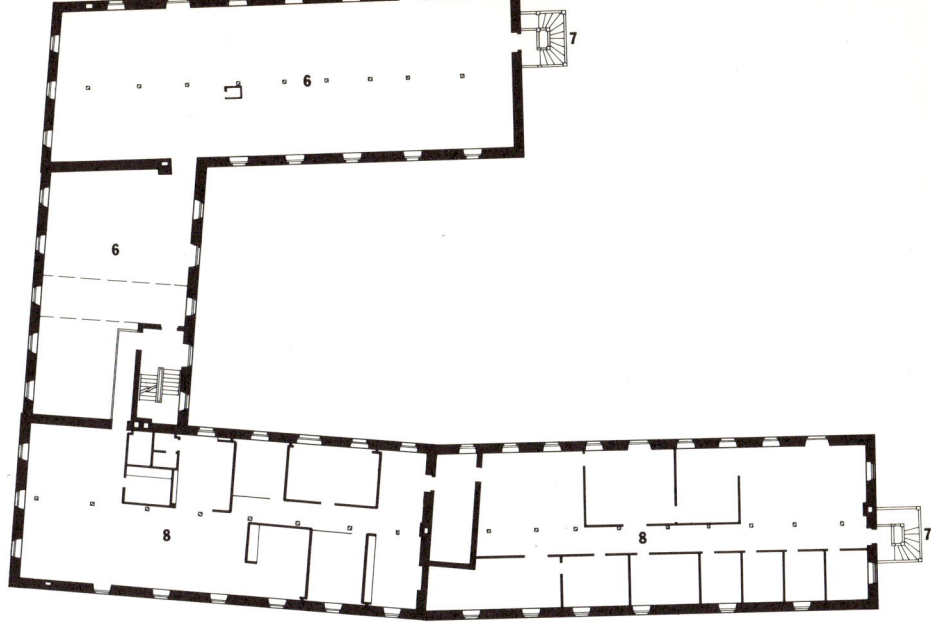

First floor plan. Scale 1 in 500

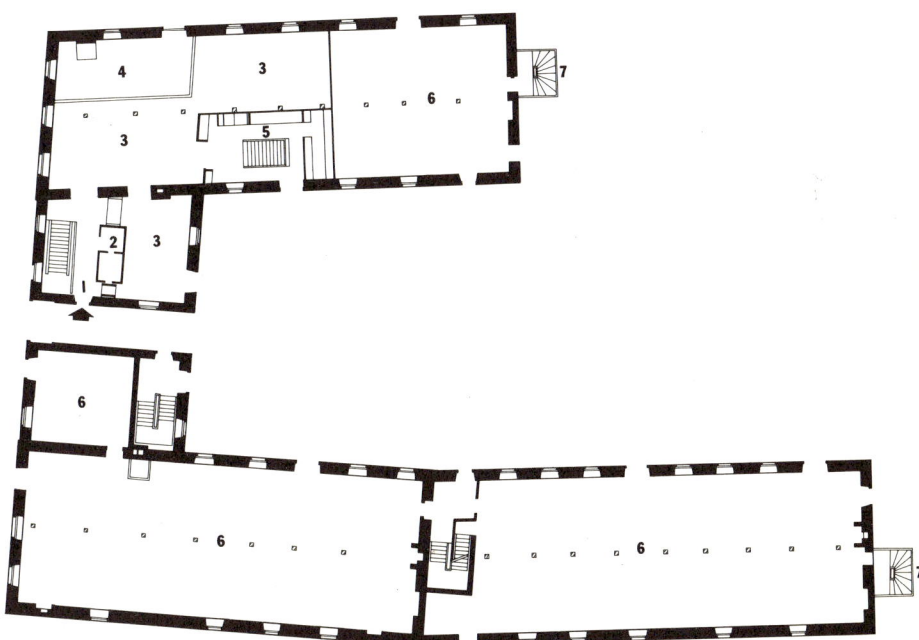

Ground floor plan. Scale 1 in 500

7, an office where the stone walls have also been left unplastered. The exceptionally wide floor boards are in sympathy with the robust character of the old building

QUAKER FRIARS, BRISTOL

Architect: Albert H. Clarke, City Architect
Exhibition design, City Engineer and Planning Department, Bristol

Client: City and County of Bristol

Site: A group of old buildings surrounded by the post-war Broadmead shopping development. The new shops form a quadrangle and face on to Broadmead, Penn Street, Broad Weir and Merchant Street. The area around Quaker Friars has consequently become a car park and a service access to the backs of shops.

History: Begun as a friary by the Dominicans in 1227 and completed by 1268, it was dissolved by Henry VIII in 1538 and subsequently bought by a local merchant. Even before the dissolution the city's Guild of Bakers had been using the old infirmary as a meeting hall, and in about 1570 the dormitory was acquired by the Cutlers, while the former refectory, long since destroyed, was used for a time by the Tanners. In 1669 the Society of Friends (Quakers) bought the friars' old cemetery and built a Meeting House (in which William Penn was married in 1696) in the ruins alongside the two guild halls—a Meeting House which was rebuilt in 1747 and still stands, converted in 1960 by the city architect into a waiting hall and offices for the registrar of births and deaths. In 1845 the Quakers bought the Bakers' and Cutlers' halls for use as schoolrooms and carried out extensive repairs which included the rebuilding of the south wall of the Cutlers' Hall and the removal of the thirteenth-century window from the east wall of the Bakers' Hall to a similar position in the Cutlers' Hall. In 1869 the Quakers built the New Hall which links the two older blocks. The whole group of buildings was bought by the local authority in 1956 and is scheduled as an Ancient Monument.

Character: The irregular U-shaped group of buildings are all built of random stonework. The Cutlers' Hall has buttresses and plate tracery windows (replicas of the original design of the cloister) on the south side, and a row of simple lancet windows on the upper floor of the north side. The south side of the Bakers' Hall has three plate tracery windows on the upper floor and a large square chimney. The pantiled roofs are high pitched and mastered by parapeted gable ends. The Victorian New Hall, built up against the back of the old Meeting House with a mono-pitch roof, has large three-light windows divided by stone mullions and transomes on the upper floor and Y-tracery windows on the ground floor. It has a flat double-pitch ceiling which is timber-boarded. The interiors of the two medieval halls have magnificent timber roof structures of the braced collar type with arched braces to the main trusses and arched wind braces longitudinally between trusses. The roof of the Cutlers' Hall was extensively overhauled before the last war, when horizontal tie beams were introduced.

1, the Bakers' Hall from the south with the Cutlers' Hall behind. The area around these medieval buildings is used as a car park and for service access to the back of the shops which enclose the so-called precinct

2, the Cutlers' Hall whose upper floor provides the main exhibition space

3, the Cutlers' Hall from the north with a discreet new entrance on the left but an unfortunate row of roof lights

Work done: The work carried out to the three halls is intended to provide space for Bristol's permanent planning exhibition, which includes lecture room facilities, the display of a large central-area model, a special historical section and a changing display of some twenty development models. The work was a continuation of the large-scale restoration work undertaken by the local authority under the direction of the city architect, Albert H. Clarke, immediately after purchasing the buildings. This included the formation of two new entrances and staircases. In the Cutlers' Hall the existing winding stair in the window recess on the west wall was demolished and a new porch, incorporating an existing seventeenth-century door, was built out at the north-east corner. It now provides the main entrance to all exhibition areas. The new entrance to the Bakers' Hall is from the west and east in the form of gates which give access to a kind of cloister which in turn leads, via a door, to the hall, lavatories and staircase. Both entrances were given stone floor paving, plastered ceilings and new wide staircases.

Other work, besides the conversion of the eighteenth-century Meeting House, included the demolition of a mortuary and a cottage on the south and west sides respectively of the Bakers' Hall; the provision of a boiler and fuel store for the whole complex on the ground floor of the Bakers' Hall and the lining of the flue in the adjacent chimney; the removal of the old leaded panes and the substitution of single sheets of plate glass for the windows; and the trimming of the roof rafters on the north slope of the Cutlers' Hall for roof lights. The ground floors of the Cutlers' Hall and New Hall were converted into a suite of rooms with their own entrance for civil marriage ceremonies.

In the Cutlers' Hall and Bakers' Hall the softwood floorboards were renewed and exhibition panels and stands were provided for all three halls. The screens in the Cutlers' Hall are set at right angles to the long walls, reflecting the original division of the room when it was a dormitory with cubicles for the friars.

4, a typical two-light plate tracery window on the upper floor of the Cutlers' Hall. Leaded lights have been replaced by large sheets of glass

5, the upper floor of the Cutlers' Hall reveals a magnificent timber roof structure. It provides the main space for the city's permanent planning exhibition

Accommodation: Bakers' Hall ground floor—entrance to Bakers' Hall with hall and lavatories, fuel store, boiler room, kitchen (part of adjacent house)
first floor—lecture room and exhibition space
New Hall ground floor—entrance to suite of rooms for civil marriages with hall and lavatories, muniment room (accessible from general office in former Meeting House)
first floor—exhibition space
Cutlers' Hall ground floor—lobby, staff room, registrar's office, anteroom, marriage room, retiring room, porch and entrance to hall on first floor
first floor—exhibition space

Date of completion: April 1963, first permanent planning exhibition opened in New Hall; Bakers' Hall used as lecture hall
1966, exhibition extended into Bakers' Hall
February 1968, Cutlers' Hall added to permanent exhibition space

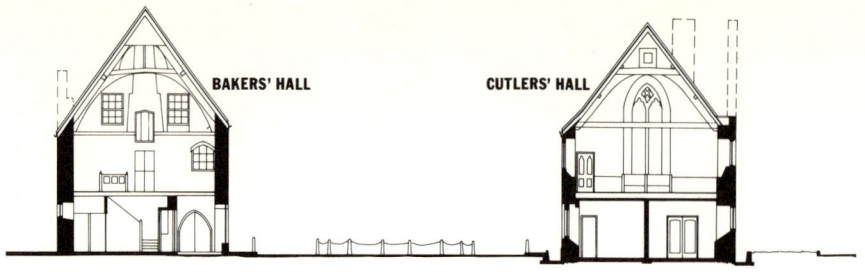

Section. Scale 1/32in. = 1ft.

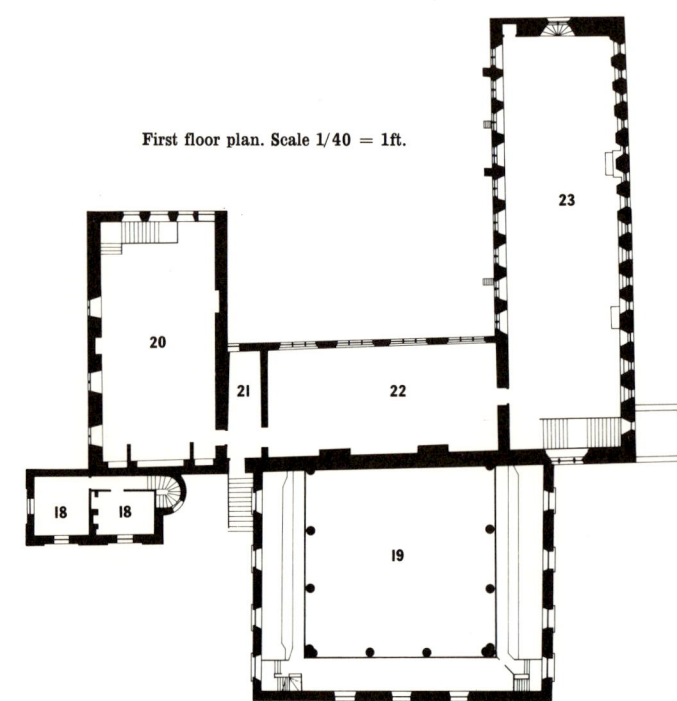

First floor plan. Scale 1/40 = 1ft.

key
1, new porch and entrance to first floor of Cutlers' Hall
2, entrance to first floor of Bakers' Hall
3, entrance to ground floor of New Hall
4, staff room
5, ante-room
6, superintending registrar
7, marriage room
8, retiring room
9, muniment room
10, general office
11, waiting room (former Meeting Hall)
12, fuel
13, boiler
14, kitchen
15, hall
16, parlour
17, walled court
18, bedroom
19, upper part of waiting room
20, Bakers' Hall—lecture room
21, store
22, New Hall—exhibition space
23, Cutlers' Hall—exhibition space

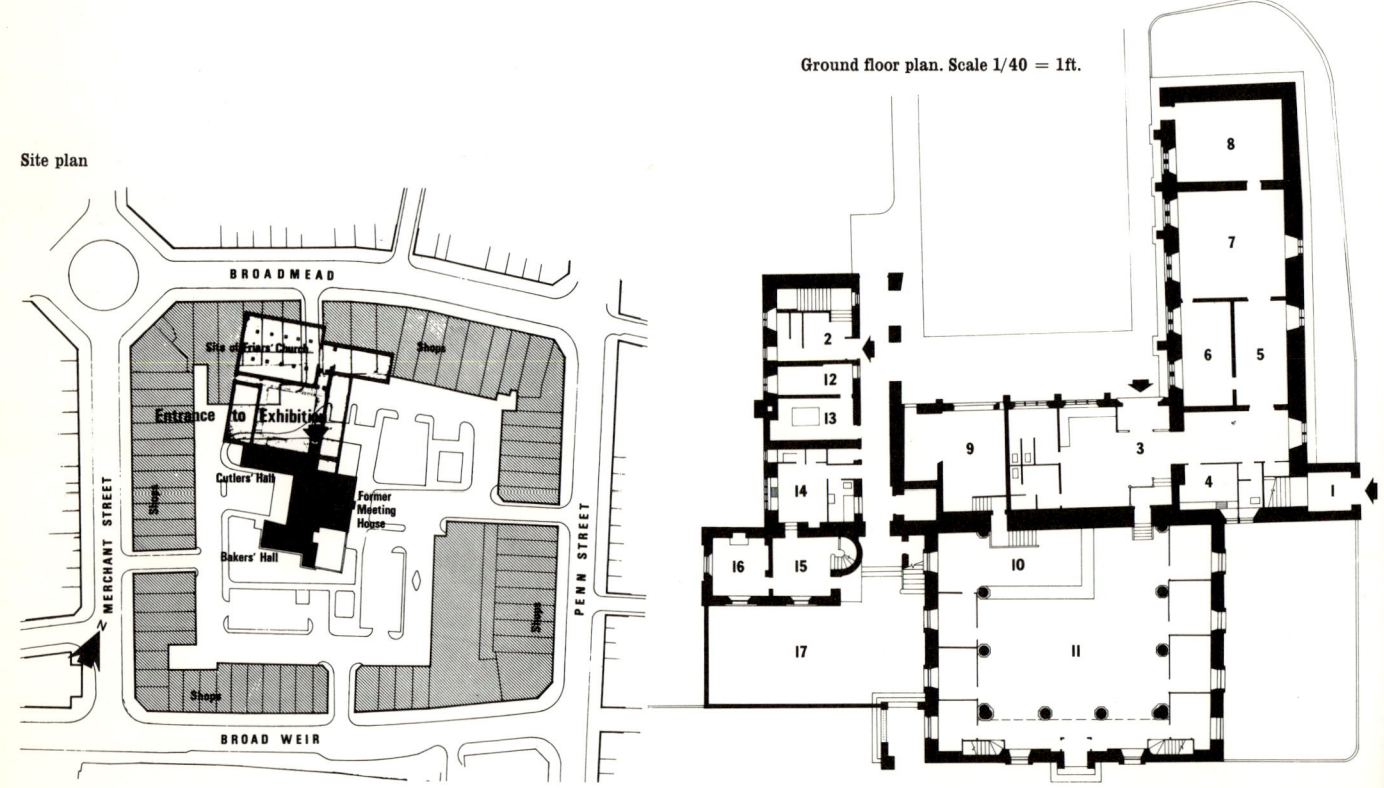

Site plan

Ground floor plan. Scale 1/40 = 1ft.

HOLY JESUS HOSPITAL, NEWCASTLE-UPON-TYNE

Architect: George Kenyon, City Architect

Client: City and County of Newcastle-upon-Tyne

Site: Holy Jesus Hospital fronts on to City Road and is immediately to the east of the Pilgrim Street roundabout which forms the northern approach to the Tyne Bridge. The buildings in the immediate vicinity are of recent construction and provide mostly office and car-parking accommodation.

History: The Holy Jesus Hospital in the Manors was founded and endowed by the Corporation of Newcastle in 1681 as a home for 'aged and impoverished freemen, their widows and daughters'. It was in continuous occupation as an almshouse until 1937, by which time it had become unfit for use so that the remaining inhabitants were transferred to the new Mary Magdalene Hospital. For over thirty years the Holy Jesus Hospital stood unoccupied while in the immediate vicinity the reconstruction of the city centre accelerated the process of decay. The trustees of the Magdalene Charity, the owners of the building, were unable to devote funds to its restoration.

There was considerable pressure to demolish the derelict hospital, but the city felt it had a responsibility to preserve the building if possible and was supported by the Royal Fine Art Commission and the Historic Buildings Council of England. In 1968 it bought the building from the Magdalene Charity. The local authority was already aware of the need for museum facilities in Newcastle and decided to use the hospital to fill this need, since its design would be easily adaptable. In March 1968 the city council instructed the city architect to prepare a detailed scheme for the restoration and conversion work; tenders were received in February 1969 and work began in June on the conversion of the hospital into the Joicey Museum.

Character: This rare example of seventeenth-century domestic architecture with its colonnade of rusticated arches is likely to become the only remaining Jacobean brick building in the city. It measures 187ft. long by 20ft. wide and contains fourteen rooms on each floor connected by a full length internal corridor on the two upper floors and by an open arcade of thirty arches on brick columns at ground floor level.

Work done: Leaks in the roof had caused extensive damage to ceilings, walls and floors at second floor level. Things were made worse by the collapse of masonry from the Austin Friars Tower through the roof at the east end and the absence of any gutters or rainwater pipes. In view of the large number of damaged and missing pantiles, the wet rot and furniture beetle in the roof timbers

1, the hospital before restoration and, 2, after restoration. First the railway and, latterly, road building have done irreparable damage to the setting of this Jacobean building

and the severely damaged ceilings, it was decided to remove the roof and restore it with new materials to its original appearance. Not one of the seventeenth-century chimney stacks remained intact above ridge level, so they were all reduced to below tile level and reconstructed with new bricks in accordance with the earliest existing illustration of the hospital that could be found. In order to keep costs within reasonable bounds it was essential for the new roof trusses to be of a standard size and it was also aesthetically desirable that a straight ridge be formed. Since the upper courses of the north and south external walls were neither straight, parallel nor level, ten courses of brickwork were taken down from the top of each wall and rebuilt to a new level. Grey-painted rectangular section aluminium gutters and rainwater pipes were added in accordance with an early illustration and conform in size to the existing wrought-iron brackets and chases through the brick string courses.

Work on the external walls commenced with the demolition of a number of nineteenth-century coalhouses built against the north wall of the hospital. The north and south external walls built of shallow stone foundations were found to be carrying the whole weight of the roof and upper floors with no support above first floor level from the numerous internal cross walls. To remove the weight from the external walls, steel columns and beams were introduced to transfer loads from the floors to the cross walls and to new foundations at ground level. Some of the brick piers of the arcade had developed vertical fractures due to excessive loading while others showed signs of settlement, probably due to the effect of traffic vibrations and inadequate foundations. About two-thirds of them were taken down and rebuilt. Repairs to external brickwork were made with Old English handmade facings manufactured to simulate Elizabethan brickwork, which were left over from a restoration job in London. On completion of the repair work all the external brickwork was cleaned down and repointed.

Except on the nineteenth-century west gable, every window frame together with its internal and external timber lintels and internal sill was replaced and lead flashings were incorporated over the external projecting brick sills. Internally, floors, plastered walls and ceilings were repaired and redecorated. The work of adaptation to a museum consisted mainly of the installation of new electrical and heating systems, a burglar alarm system, automatic hose reels and fire alarms, two internal escape staircases and lavatories.

Work has also been completed on the restoration and conversion of the medieval Austin Friars Tower, which abuts the north-east corner of the hospital and is visible in some of the photographs. It houses a display of armour and weapons as an annex to the Joicey Museum.

3, the façade to City Road before restoration and, 4, after restoration

5, city centre redevelopment towers menacingly over the old hospital

6, the brick colonnade of 30 arches on the side of the built-up City Road

Accommodation: Ground floor—entrance lobby, lavatories, stores, annex, loading bay
First floor—historical museum illustrating the history and development of the city from the Roman occupation to the present day
Second floor—furniture museum illustrating the history and development of domestic furniture and interior decoration

Date of completion: September 1970

Cost: £57 519, including all building services and finishes but excluding landscaping and consultants' fees. The cost of restoration was met by a grant from the Historic Buildings Council and the rate fund, together with contributions from two charitable trusts. The cost of conversion was met entirely by the Joicey Trust.

Rate: £4·39 per sq. ft. (£47·41 per m^2)

7, in contrast to the road side, the area behind the building has been paved and planted to provide a quiet and safe spot for museum visitors. 8, the far end is effectively closed by the Austin Friars tower which has also been converted and houses a display of armour and weapons

9, 10, the interior is a straightforward adaptation for display purposes of an existing series of small rooms served by a corridor

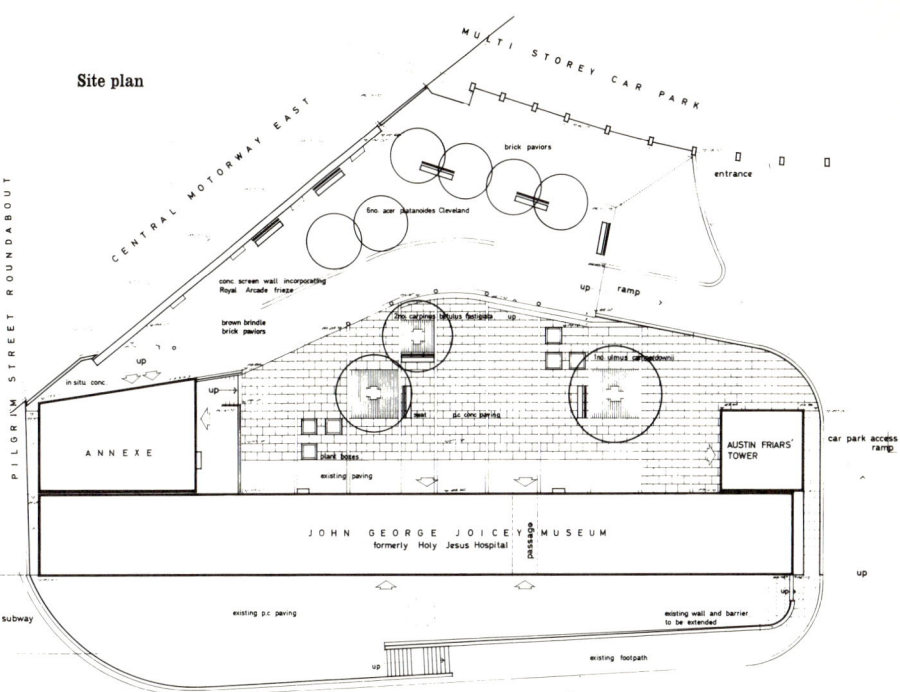

Site plan

Ground floor plan

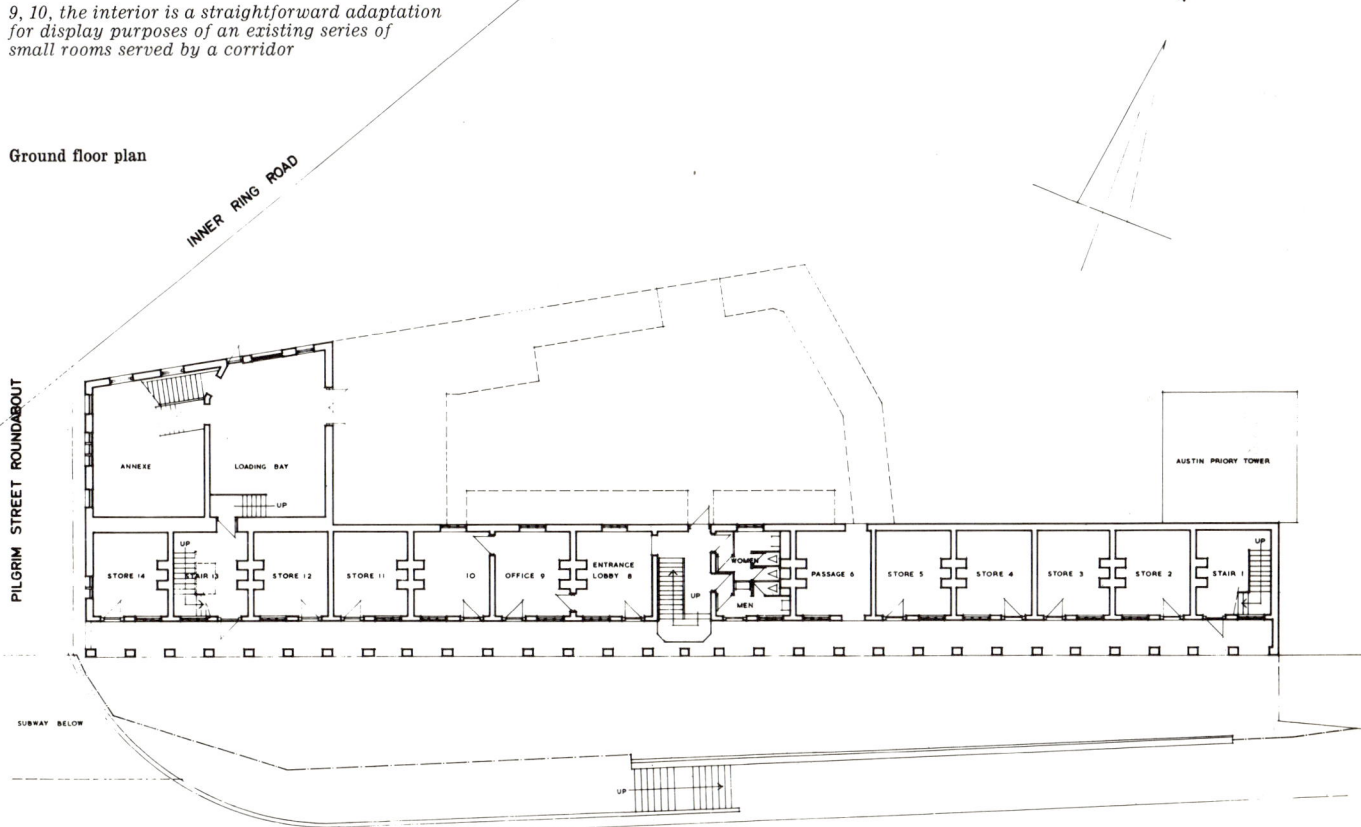

First floor plan

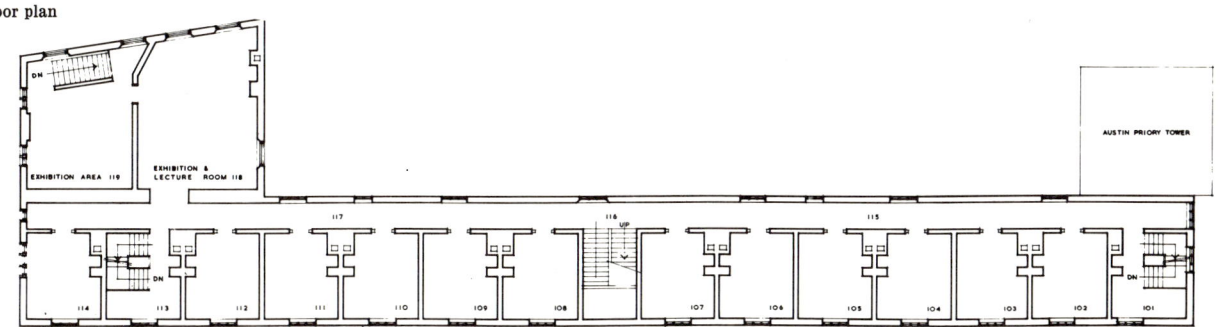

55

Fortifications, gates and barracks

If the last chapter was mainly about the importance of buildings as urban 'grain', this chapter is mainly about buildings in the round—a Henry VIII castle, a Martello tower, a late Victorian barrack block in the style of a French chateau and a medieval gateway which once formed part of a walled precinct but is now isolated on a roundabout. The exceptions are the Old Barracks at Lincoln, a castellated facade with a vast parade ground enclosed by buildings, and the old roofed garden which forms an integral part of the fortifications at the foot of the Palazzo Ducale in Urbino.

To take the last example first. Francesco di Giorgio's military engineering work incorporated what was originally a long stable block stretching between two bastions, one of which was replaced in 1830 by the Teatro Sanzio. All that is left today is a double line of walls containing a vaulted space built into the rising ground at the lower level of the Piazzale Mercatale. The roof over the upper level has long since gone, and it is at this level that the major visual change is proposed. A new mono-pitch roof of Roman tiles will enclose a space high enough to incorporate galleries over the main dining area. Reverence for the past, even when that past is represented by as functional a feature as a brick arch, has resulted in the formation of small internal gardens behind each arch, so that the modern glazing is invisible from outside. Roof lights over these gardens will brighten the interiors, but the gardens themselves will recall an earlier use which the name, Orto dell'Abbondanza, embodies. This hyper-sensitive Italian approach, which always seeks to keep the new and the old apart, should be compared with the no-nonsense approach at Quaker Friars in Bristol where the Gothic tracery is filled with single sheets of glass; and one awaits with interest De Carlo's roof lights to be able to compare them once again with Bristol, where the sweep of the pantiled surface is crudely broken by large glazed openings.

The Orto dell'Abbondanza will be a refectory for the use of students *and* the general public. Easily the most ambitious conversion in this chapter, it is the only example that is not a museum. There is a simple reason, of course, for the frequency of change to museum use: provided there is something to exhibit, most buildings can become museums with the minimum of change; and most places have rooms which can be used almost at once, so that conversion can proceed step by step with relatively small sums of money being required at any one moment. The Old Barracks at Lincoln is a good example, where the diminutive sum of £5500 was enough to buy the buildings, comply with the basic requirements of the fire officer by providing an additional staircase, devise a simple display system and open the two-storey barrack block to the public. Clarence Barracks at Portsmouth repeats the same story but on a grander scale—three distinct stages separately financed. In their form and layout, neither the Old Barracks nor Clarence Barracks suggests *museum* above all other uses. But the keep at Southsea Castle and the Magazine Gateway at Leicester do. A castle is itself a museum and so, in a less obvious way, is a medieval gateway. Both are places which people visit because they are historic, and it follows that to add some exhibits will make the visit more worthwhile and attract more people. Neither building has much space (four rooms in each), so the choice of subject and type of exhibit was limited. Both buildings chose military history, Southsea Castle the military history of Portsmouth and the Magazine Gateway the history of the Royal Leicestershire Regiment. Both subjects could be fitted into a compact area and limited to relatively small exhibits like paintings, panels, flags, firearms and showcases with minutiae like medals and belt plates.

At present the museum at Southsea Castle is limited to the keep, though there are plenty of unallocated rooms in the ranges built against the inside face of the *enceinte* into which the museum can spread. There is enough space in this outer part to provide the offices, workshops and stores that a museum invariably needs, and since all the Portsmouth museums that belong to the city come under a central organisation, these facilities will no doubt serve other museums too. At Leicester, where the organisation of museums is also centralised, the lack of space in the Magazine Gateway means that administration and conservation work have to be carried out elsewhere. All this goes to show that the flexibility obtained by adopting a centralised policy gives a local authority far more scope when deciding which buildings are suitable for museum use.

The many changes that both Southsea Castle and Magazine Gateway have undergone in their history are discouraging to the purist who would like buildings restored to their original state. But to have reinstated Southsea Castle as a Henry VIII fort would have meant not only great expense but the loss of structural changes which illustrate important aspects of later military history.

There are examples on the south coast of England of Martello towers converted into weekend houses. The need for light and air inevitably transforms this small fortification into something more like an observatory. Openings are made in the blank walls and a glass cylinder is usually placed on top to provide a living room with a view. The very essence—the gun platform—is sacrificed. Unfortunately neither the small size nor the usually remote situation of Martello towers is conducive to museum conversion, and the example in this chapter must be regarded as exceptional. It so happened that James Joyce stayed in it and set the opening scene of *Ulysses* there and that Michael Scott later bought it as part of the Joyce memorabilia he was collecting. It is the tower itself, therefore, that becomes the principal display, and any material alteration to it would have been nonsensical.

SOUTHSEA CASTLE, PORTSMOUTH

Architect: W. D. Worden, City Architect
Group architect, W. Robson
Project architect, P. Jubb

Client: Libraries and Museums Committee of Portsmouth City Council

Site: The castle is situated one mile east of the old town of Portsmouth on the southernmost apex of Portsea Island. The castle stands isolated from the built-up area of Southsea by about a quarter mile of open common ground, including Castle Field which separates it from the nearest access road, Clarence Esplanade.

History: The castle was built in 1544 by Henry VIII as part of his Solent defences against the threat of a Franco-Spanish invasion. Pevsner and Lloyd (*Hampshire and the Isle of Wight*, The Buildings of England, Penguin, 1967) describe the original plan as unusual: 'a square keep within an *enceinte* which was shaped like a diamond (or a large square at forty-five degrees with the keep) with big rectangular gun platforms at its east and west flanks'. The principal modifications to this plan were carried out by Sir Bernard de Gomme in 1683, who provided a glacis and covered way; by Major-General Sir John Fisher in 1814, who extended the northern section of the *enceinte* to accommodate a garrison of two hundred men and who rebuilt the interior of the keep in brick (as it survives today); again in 1850, when seven gun emplacements were constructed in brick in the form in which they exist today; and in the early 1860's, when the recommendations of a Royal Commission set up by Lord Palmerston were put into effect by constructing extensive new ramparts along the sea front (now landscaped, they provide walks for visitors) and enclosing the new enlarged complex within a high brick wall.

The castle remained in military occupation until 1960 when the local authority acquired it and decided to restore the building to the form in which it last functioned as a complete fortress (before the 1850 modifications) and to convert some of the interiors into a museum illustrating the military history of Portsmouth.

Character: What at first appears like a picturesque silhouette of chimney stacks, gangways, viewing platform, flagpole, lighthouse (1828) turns out to be a symmetrical fort, complete with dry moat, *enceinte*, a barbican walk with gun emplacements, and a bailey with a keep in the centre. While the exterior of the *enceinte* presents a stone face (dressed Purbeck dating from the 1814 modifications), the buildings against the inside face of the *enceinte* (also dating mostly from 1814) are all in brick. Similarly the keep presents an exterior face of Isle of Wight stone, much of it the original stonework with blocked Tudor gunports clearly visible, while the interior is lined in the

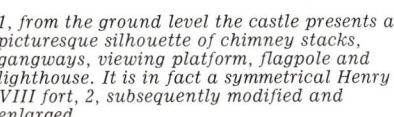

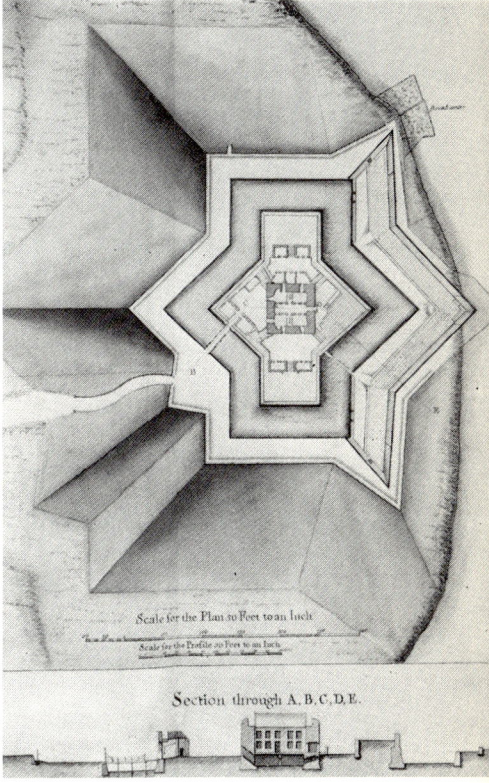

1, from the ground level the castle presents a picturesque silhouette of chimney stacks, gangways, viewing platform, flagpole and lighthouse. It is in fact a symmetrical Henry VIII fort, 2, subsequently modified and enlarged

3, plan and section, 1749 by J. P. Desmaretz from an original in the British Museum. It shows the glacis and covered way added by de Gomme in 1683

4, a view of the castle in 1666 by de Gomme before the construction of the glacis. From a drawing in the National Maritime Museum, Greenwich

brickwork of 1814 which on the first floor takes the form of two tunnel vaulted rooms connected at each end by elliptical vaults set at right angles. The brickwork was strong enough to support an open gun platform on the roof, which is reached by a cast-iron spiral stair built into the thickness of the wall dividing the two rooms. The ground floor of the keep, also two rooms, has flat ceilings with exposed main beams of timber. On both floors the great thickness of the walls is made apparent in the deep splayed reveals of the segment-headed windows.

Work done: The intention was to convert the keep into exhibition galleries and the rooms facing on to the bailey into ancillary accommodation needed by a museum, such as offices, laboratories and workshops.

Work carried out to the rooms facing on to the bailey included the glazing of loopholes and the removal of chimney breasts and brick facing to expose the stonework of the *enceinte* (east galleries); the reconstruction of the roof (west galleries); and generally the making good (or raising) and sealing of existing concrete floors (finished with wood block in the laboratory of the north range), the insulation and painting of walls and vaults, the repair or renewal of doors and windows, the formation of some new openings and the demolition of certain walls and doors.

Work carried out to the keep included the removal of partitions and of the old staircase, the construction of a new hardwood staircase, the demolition of the chimney breast and old prison cells (basement), the shoring up of floors to take out and renew defective timber, the removal of all ceiling linings and beam casings and the treatment of all timbers against infestation, and the laying of hardboard and linoleum on the ground and first floors.

The east bailey was excavated to reduce the existing level and paved with granite setts.

Accommodation: Keep basement—storage
ground and first floors—two exhibition galleries per floor
Bailey
east galleries—five unallocated rooms, smithy, lavatories (male)
west galleries—six unallocated rooms, lavatories (female)
south range—four stores, passage to caponier
north range—attendant's room, conservation laboratory, lecture room, offices for curator and museum assistants, entrance gateway with ticket office and cashier, clerical office

Date of completion: May 1967

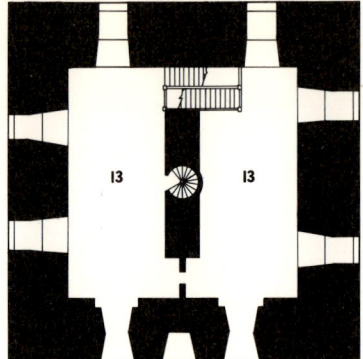

First floor plan of keep. Scale 1/32in. = 1ft.

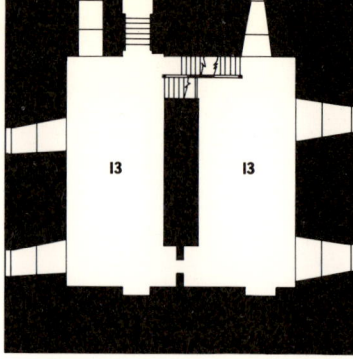

Ground floor plan of keep. Scale 1/32in. = 1ft.

key
1, storage in Keep
2, entrance gateway
3, ticket office and cashier
4, clerical office
5, attendant
6, conservation laboratory
7, lecture room
8, offices for curator and museum assistants
9, unallocated rooms
10, smithy
11, store
12, passage to caponier
13, exhibition galleries

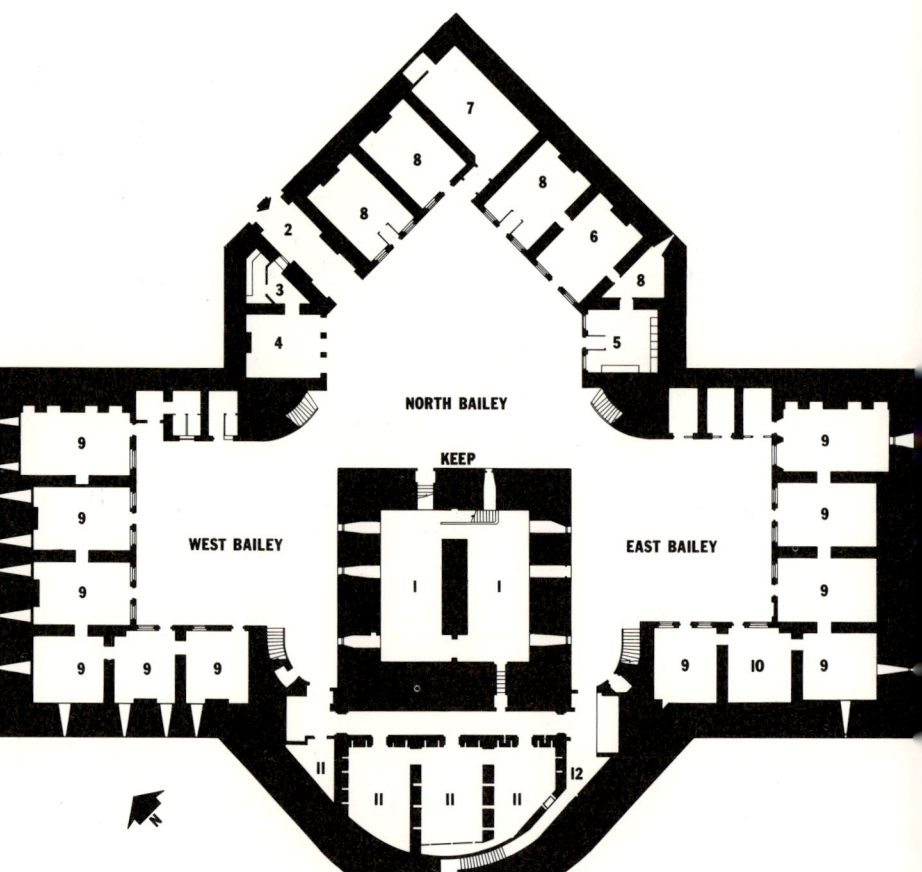

Basement plan (Bailey level). Scale 1/48in. = 1ft.

5, the bridge over the moat leading to the main gate

6, the keep which has been converted into museum galleries

7, the upper floor of the keep which consists of two tunnel-vaulted rooms. The inner brick lining dates from 1814 and was added to support an open gun platform on the roof

8, view through a window on the upper floor of the keep on to the barbican walk and gun emplacement

9, 10, one of the two museum galleries on the lower floor of the keep

CLARENCE BARRACKS, PORTSMOUTH

Architect: W. D. Worden, City Architect

Client: Libraries and Museums Committee of Portsmouth City Council

Site: The barracks front on to Alexandra Road, which runs midway between the present city centre and the seafront at Southsea. It is adjacent to the developing Polytechnic and near Old Portsmouth, the military and naval town of the eighteenth century. Next to the city museum is a single-storey Victorian military building which was used as the Regimental Institute. This has been converted into the City Records Office. To the west of the building a small cookhouse has been retained and will be restored and converted into an information centre and lecture room.

History: Barrack block E/F, for 268 men and 8 NCO's, was part of a large military complex built between 1895 and 1900. The block was at the head of a large parade ground and was constructed in 1897. As this was Queen Victoria's Golden Jubilee Year, it bears the royal coat of arms on both the front and rear pediments. The barracks were described as 'the most palatial and finest barracks in every respect in any part of the Kingdom'. They were built to the pavilion system, which gave better circulation of air and more light than the block system. They also incorporated the latest sanitary improvements.

The site of the barracks was purchased by Portsmouth City Council for residential redevelopment, with private housing as well as housing for the Royal Navy. They decided, however, to retain the best of the Victorian barrack blocks for conversion to a museum to replace one lost during the Second World War.

Character: The building, listed as of architectural or historic interest, is beautifully constructed in red brick with Portland stone lintels. It is a four-storey building about 100 metres long, modelled on the French *château* style. Roofs are covered with red tiles and the roof turrets have wrought iron finials.

Internally the building comprises five units—terminal east and west blocks, a central tower block and linking lateral blocks. Access to the top floor of the tower block is by a fine stone vice set in its own tower.

Floors generally are of 1in. hardwood boards, 4½in. wide, set in pitch on a diagonal boarded softwood sub-floor on 12in. by 3in. pine joists. The roof is made up of a series of timber king post roof trusses and rafters, covered with plain red clay peg tiles. Windows are vertical sliding sashes and the wall finishes are generally painted brickwork.

Work done: The work has been carried out in two stages, and a third will eventually complete the restoration. Stage 1 involved the conversion of the

1, the south facade of Clarence Barracks, described at the time it was built in 1897 as 'the most palatial and finest barracks in every respect in any part of the Kingdom'. To accord with its French château style, the area in front of this facade is being laid out as a parterre garden

2, 3, the central feature of the south facade consists of two closely set cylinderical towers flanking a quaint mixture of features one of which, the large bay window, lights one of the principal exhibition galleries on the first floor, 4

whole of the first floor and the east end of the ground floor. Cloakrooms at the top floor of the tower were converted to administration offices. The fire officer's requirements included fire separation doors, smoke activated where there are penetrations of the 27in. thick brick walls from the central block to the terminal blocks at each end. Escape doors were inserted on the top floor, giving access to the east and west roof voids. The stone staircases at each end of the building and in the central tower required additional infill balustrades as spacing was too wide for modern public use. (Fortunately the character of the cast-iron balustrading has not been destroyed by this requirement.) There is a completely new and extensive electrical installation which includes full fire and security protection. Electrical night storage heaters provide heating. Ceiling track lighting allows flexibility in display lighting of exhibits. A tall hollow skirting hides most electrical cables in the galleries.

Stage 2 has principally involved work to second floor galleries on similar lines to the work at first floor level in stage 1, together with extensive roof repairs. In addition, two large ground floor areas have been converted to fully air-conditioned art galleries with continuous concealed strip lighting above the hessian-covered wall screens. Stage 3, which has been postponed indefinitely, will include work to the main front entrance and the ground and second floors.

Externally, the fine original railings along the Alexandra Road boundary have been retained and the new boundary wall with brick piers and cast-iron railings includes a stone roundel and pediment taken from adjacent barrack blocks when they were demolished. To the south of the museum a French-style *parterre* garden is being laid out in keeping with the character of the building. This includes a stone balustrade complete with urns from Crichel Down House, Wiltshire, now rebuilt as a central feature of the gardens.

Accommodation: Ground floor—art galleries
First floor—galleries, bar
Second floor—museum galleries, lavatories, curators' offices, administration offices, staff rooms
Third floor—stores, technical workshops, attendants' rooms

Date of completion: 1974

Cost: Stage 1, £45 000
Stage 2, £24 000 (including a grant of £5000 from the Arts Council towards the cost of the ground floor galleries)

5, another exhibition gallery on the first floor and part of the first stage conversion

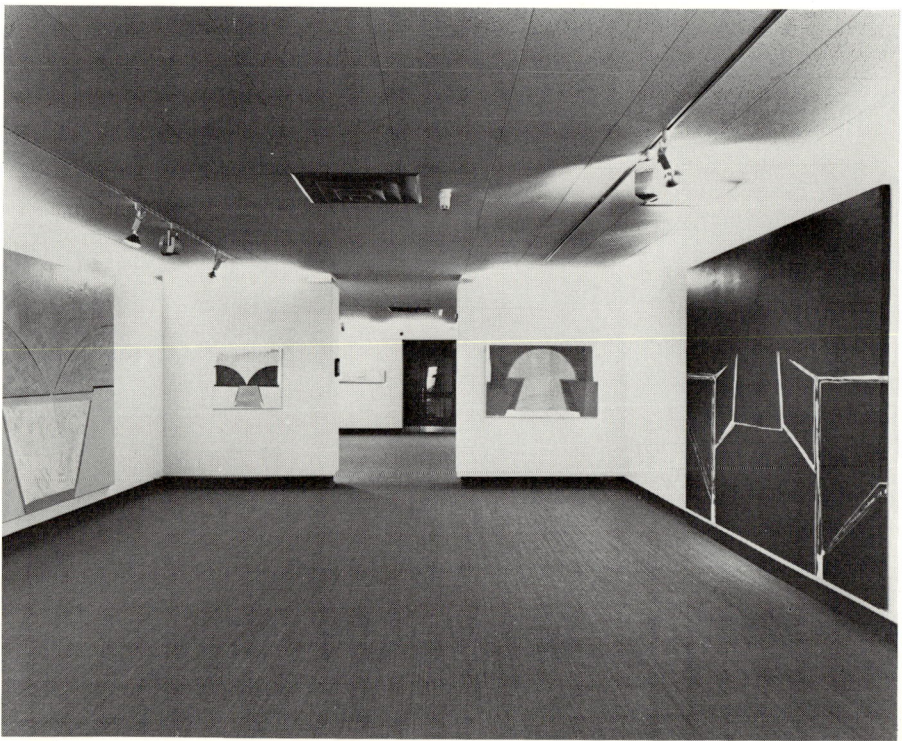

6, one of the ground floor areas which have been converted to fully air-conditioned art galleries and which formed part of the second stage conversion

key
1, temporary entrance
2, completed exhibitions room
3, gallery
4, future entrance
5, future gallery
6, contractor's temporary office
7, bar
8, offices

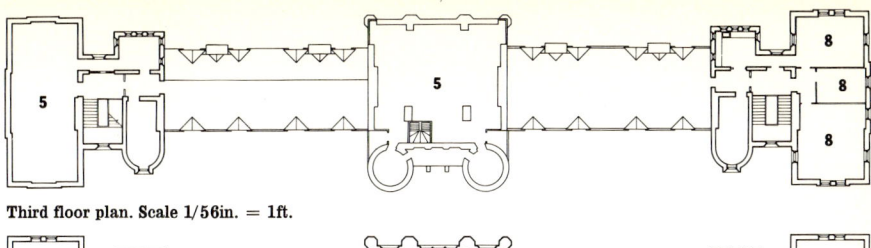

Third floor plan. Scale 1/56in. = 1ft.

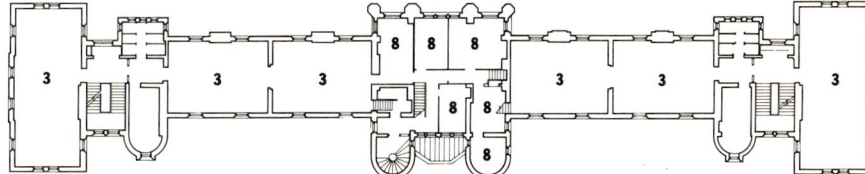

Second floor plan

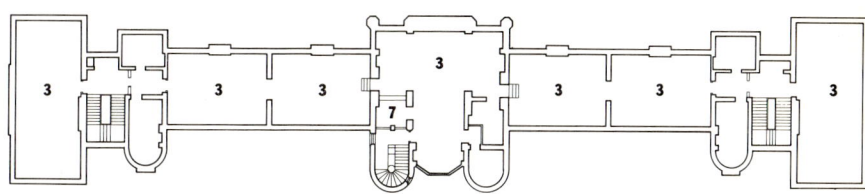

First floor plan

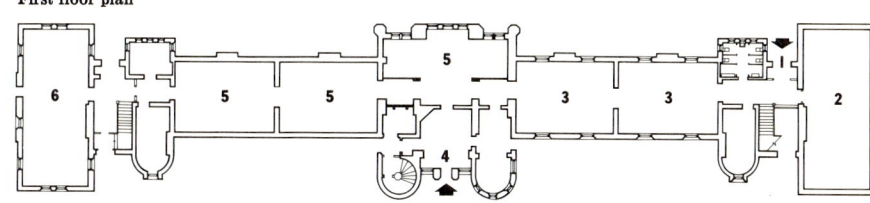

Ground floor plan

key
1, Clarence Barracks (City Museum and Art Gallery)
2, City Records Office
3, car park
4, new SEB sub-station
5, new boundary wall
6, new housing on site of old barracks

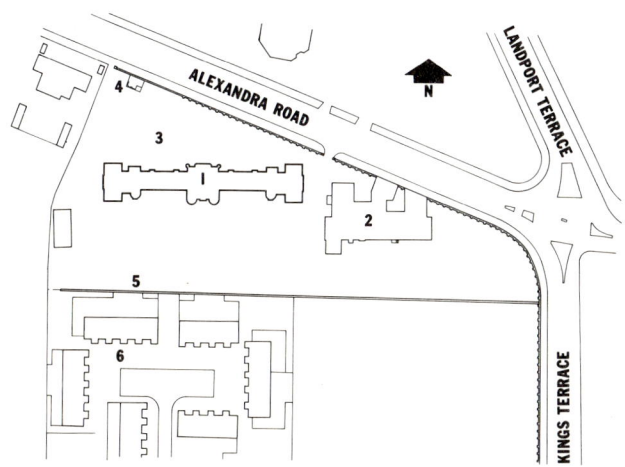

Location site plan. Scale 1 in. = 270 ft.

Longitudinal section. Scale 1/40in. = 1ft.

OLD BARRACKS, LINCOLN

Architect: Clarke Hall, Scorer and Bright

Client: Lincolnshire Association
Museum of Lincolnshire Life

Site: A deep rectangular site between Burton Road and Mill Road, a quarter mile from the cathedral and two hundred yards from the castle walls. The buildings, which are grouped around a vast courtyard, comprise the main gatehouse facing on to Burton Road, a former rifle range and drill hall and a row of cottages facing on to Mill Road behind the drill hall.

History: The gatehouse was built in 1857 for the Royal Militia (part-time soldiers). All the buildings were taken over in 1965 by the Lincolnshire Association after a long period of disuse, neglect and dilapidation.

Character: A windowless two-storey brick building (with special features in stone) of forbidding appearance faces on to Burton Road. The gateway, which stands slightly forward, has a rusticated stone plinth, a wide two-centred arch, machicolations and a castellated parapet which extends the whole length of the block. There is a large stone panel, carved in relief with the militia emblem, and recessed into a stone surround over the gate. The side wings are low, single-storey buildings with slate roofs, and the drill hall at the far end is similar, though taller, and has large multi-paned windows set in brick recesses. The ground floor of the gatehouse contains ceilings of small vaults in honeycomb bricks spanning between iron beams and supported on cast-iron columns—an early form of fireproof construction which has been preserved in the conversion.

Work done: The main part of the work has been to the gatehouse, which has been turned into museum galleries. An existing staircase to the right of the gate was rebuilt and a new staircase inserted in the left-hand half of the block to comply with fire regulations. This meant destroying some of the old prison cells, though one cell with its original door and spyhole has been preserved as an exhibit. The first floor rooms were open to the roof structure, which consists of crude metal tie beams. To provide better insulation a flat ceiling of polystyrene boards has been inserted. For reasons of economy the original asphalt floor has been retained. A simple display system of steel frames with perspex panels held at the top with a web of dyed washing line was devised for one of the first floor galleries, while the other was entirely fitted out by the curator on a do-it-yourself basis.

The museum aims to illustrate all aspects of life in Lincolnshire from Elizabeth I to Elizabeth II and lays particular emphasis on tools and machinery manufactured in the county. Rapid expansion of the collections since the opening of the museum

1, the frontage to Burton Road consists of a gatehouse (converted into museum galleries) flanked by fancifully castellated pavilions. One of the lower side wings, which enclose a vast courtyard, can be seen on the left

2, the conversion has been careful to preserve the windowless character of the street facade

has necessitated the roofing over of the western end of the courtyard to form a new gallery of 8000 sq. ft. which will house the growing industrial and transport collections.

Accommodation: Gatehouse
ground floor—reception, prison cell, store, workshop, temporary exhibitions gallery
first floor—agricultural exhibition gallery, crafts gallery, domestic and commercial gallery
Left-hand wing—offices, stores, workshops for museum, exhibition of horse-drawn transport (in former rifle range)
Right-hand wing—committee room, stores and offices for the association
Old drill hall—exhibition of hand-propelled transport

Date of completion: 1971 for gatehouse, but work continues in the other parts

Cost: £5500, which included purchase of buildings, conversion of gatehouse with display and lighting and minor alterations to the transport galleries. The money was provided by a local charity trust, the Carnegie U.K. Trust and revenue from the association, which is supported by the Arts Council.

3, over the gateway the large stone panel, carved in relief with the militia emblem, recalls the original use of the building

4, on the courtyard side the gatehouse has many windows and provides a complete contrast to its street facade

5, looking through the gateway from the courtyard towards Burton Road. The entrance to the museum is the door on the right

8, the new staircase in the gatehouse which was required to comply with fire regulations

9, the first-floor gallery in the gatehouse for which the architect and curator devised a simple display system of steel frames with perspex panels held at the top by a web of dyed washing line

10, the former rifle range which now exhibits mainly horse-drawn vehicles

6, 7, the ground floor of the gatehouse has honeycomb brick vaults spanning between iron beams and supported on iron columns

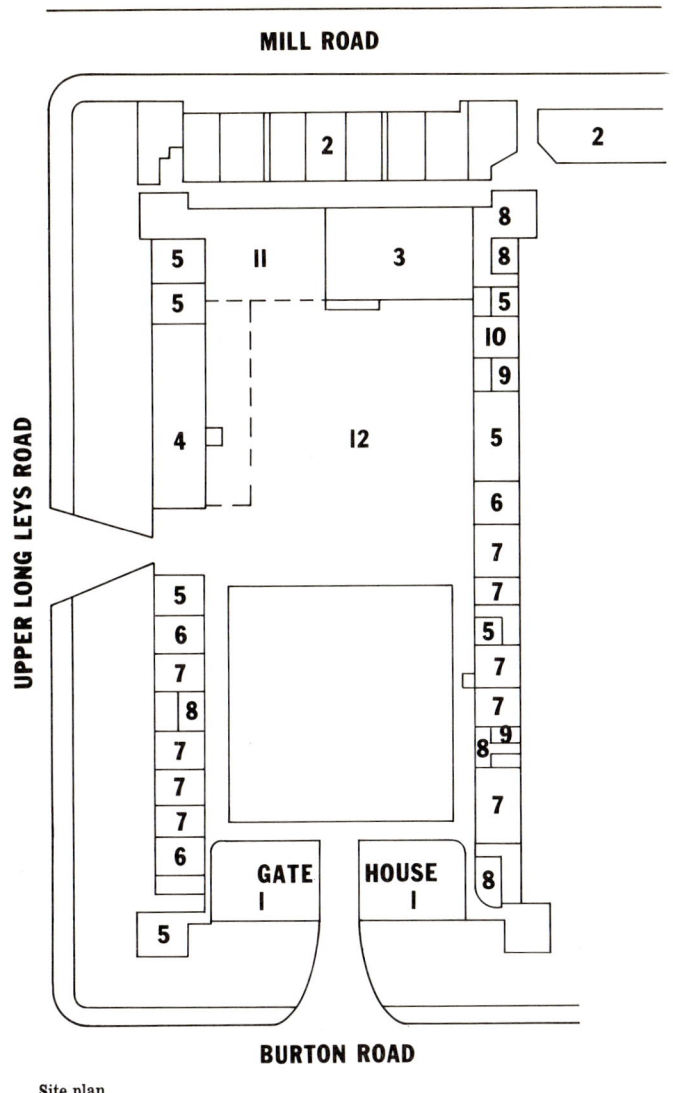

key
1, museum (formerly Gatehouse)
2, cottages
3, gallery of hand-propelled transport (formerly drill hall)
4, gallery of horse-drawn transport (formerly rifle range)
5, store
6, workshop
7, office
8, lavatories
9, kitchen
10, picture loan scheme
11, covered area for open-air exhibitions
12, car park

Site plan

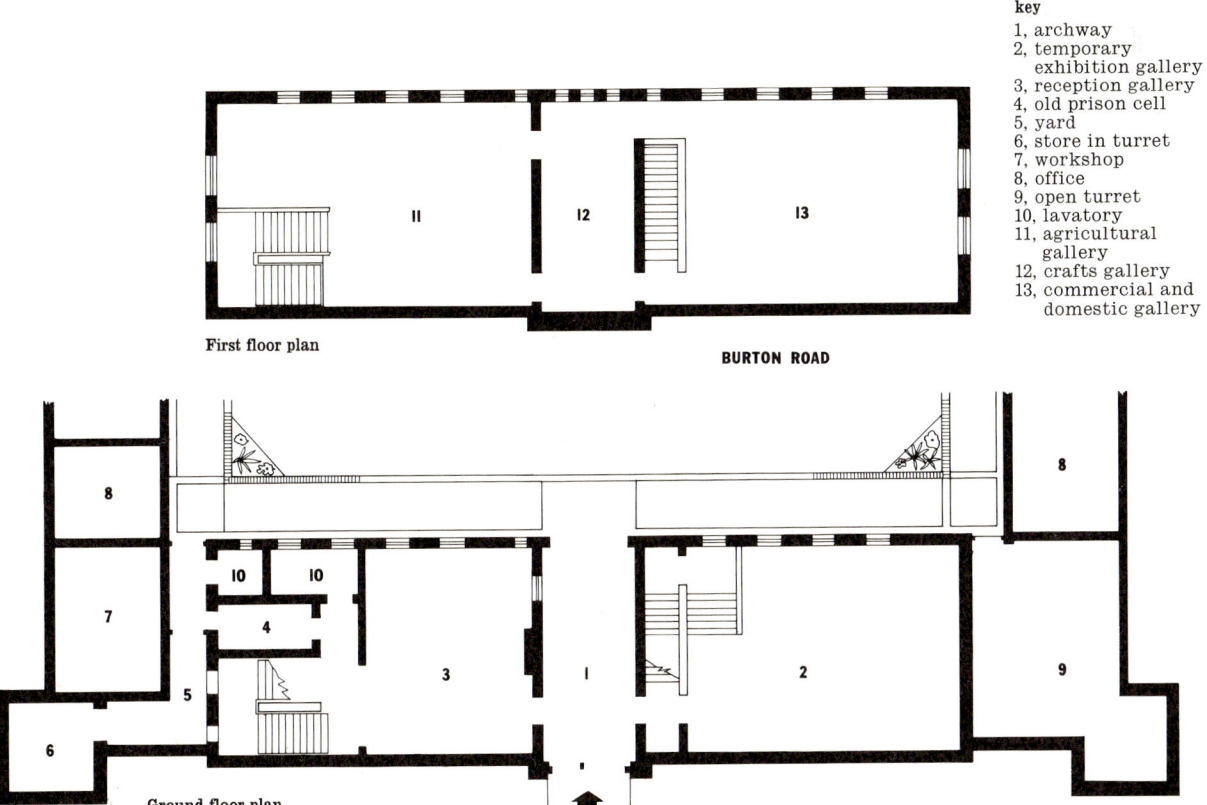

key
1, archway
2, temporary exhibition gallery
3, reception gallery
4, old prison cell
5, yard
6, store in turret
7, workshop
8, office
9, open turret
10, lavatory
11, agricultural gallery
12, crafts gallery
13, commercial and domestic gallery

First floor plan

BURTON ROAD

Ground floor plan

MAGAZINE GATEWAY, LEICESTER

Architect: Leicester City Architect's Office
Interior display, John Pound, Supplies Division Museum Group, Department of the Environment

Client: City of Leicester, Museums, Libraries and Publicity Committees

Site: A congested island site surrounded by roads south of the town centre. Leicester Polytechnic and the River Soar lie to the west.

History: The magazine probably formed part of the ambitious 'New Works' which Henry Earl of Lancaster began just outside Leicester in 1330. These consisted of almshouses and a collegiate church; a gateway and walls were provided because the area was outside the town walls. There is evidence from the fenestration that the gateway was considerably restored in the fifteenth century. The college ceased as an institution in 1548 under Edward VI's Chantries Act and some time after that the gateway became the property of the county. By 1642 it had become the county magazine and a centre of contention during the Civil War. Afterwards it remained connected with military use and a complete barrack block developed around it in the nineteenth century. It was used by wheeled traffic until 1905 when a new road was driven by its side. The construction of the Newarke underpass in 1967–68 involved the demolition of the barracks, leaving the magazine free-standing. This provided the opportunity of restoring the building and converting it into a museum for the Royal Leicestershire Regiment.

Character: A squat three-storey building of stone, with a four-centred arch to one side and a turret containing the vice off centre on the west wall. Mullioned and traceried windows with square hoodmoulds are distributed irregularly over the facades, and the parapeted top breaks into corbelled bartizans at the corners. On the west wall the roof line of the old barracks can still be seen and at the other end of the same wall there is a blocked opening at first floor level which once gave on to the rampart walk of the Newarke wall. The gateway itself has a fine quadripartite ribbed vault with tiercerons and ridge ribs. The ceilings of the ground and first floor rooms are supported on a massive centre post with three braces, and the joists rest on stone corbels in the walls, which are plastered except for the stone surround to the entrance door and two windows and a stone aumbry (wall niche) on the first floor. The high rooms of the second floor were divided by an additional third floor before restoration. These upper rooms have stone walls and exposed roof trusses, one of which is the original king post truss. The room above the gate has a relieving arch over a large fireplace which contained a Tudor overmantel

1, lithograph of the gateway in about 1826

2, the gateway today isolated on a traffic island

3, the floor inside the arch has been laid out with granite setts and precast concrete edging pieces to reflect the pattern of the rib vaulting above now collapsed. Both the first and second floors have garderobes in the thickness of the west wall connected by shafts which provided the standard form of sanitation in medieval times.

Work done: The preliminary work of demolition included the removal of partitions and a timber staircase between the ground and first floor, and of the whole of the third floor structure, leaving the second floor rooms in their original lofty state. The clearing out of foreign internal elements revealed worm infestation, dry rot and structural weaknesses usual in a building of this age. All the remedial work was carried out on a negotiated day-work basis by specialist contractors. Old slate slabs (grave headstones laid face down) quarried locally have been laid in the ground floor room. The upper floors have new hardwood strip to replace the old rush and lime cement floor. The floor of the gateway itself has been laid out with granite setts and precast concrete edging pieces to reflect the pattern of the rib vaulting above. Wall plaster has been removed throughout and renewed only on the ground and first floor. On the second floor the stonework has been cleaned and pointed. A short flight of steps in oak has been provided to connect the ground floor with the bottom of the vice. The exhibits are displayed in wall showcases, in desk-type cases in window recesses, in existing wall niches behind a simple sheet of glass, or they are fixed direct to the walls. The backs of wall showcases are removable in case a natural stone background to the display is wanted.

Accommodation: Ground floor—entrance from gateway, exhibition room, entrance counter, lavatory
First floor—exhibition room, garderobe
Second floor—two exhibition rooms, garderobes

Date of completion: 1969

Cost: £16 250 (£2000 has since been spent yearly to restore the exterior stonework.)

Rate: £10·80 per sq. ft.

4, the ground floor exhibition room. The floor has been restored with old slate slabs and a short flight of oak steps provided to connect the ground floor with the vice

5, 6, the first floor exhibition room. Walls on the ground and first floors have been replastered. Exhibits are displayed in wall showcases, desk-type cases in window recesses or fixed direct to the walls

7, where wall niches existed, these have been covered with a sheet of glass fixed direct into the stonework without a frame

8, 9, 10, 11, the second floor contains two high rooms, both of which have stone walls and exposed roof trusses.

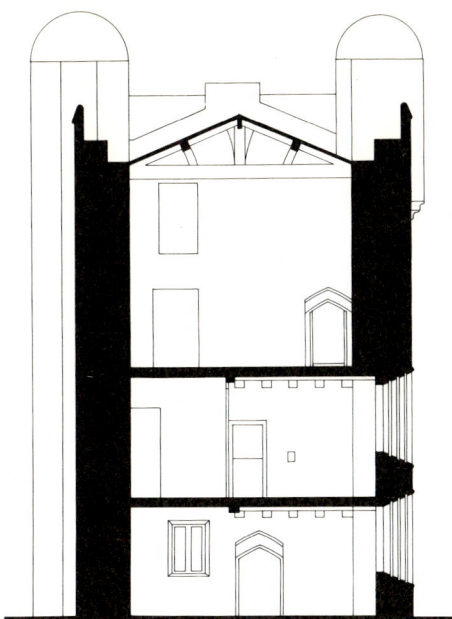
Section

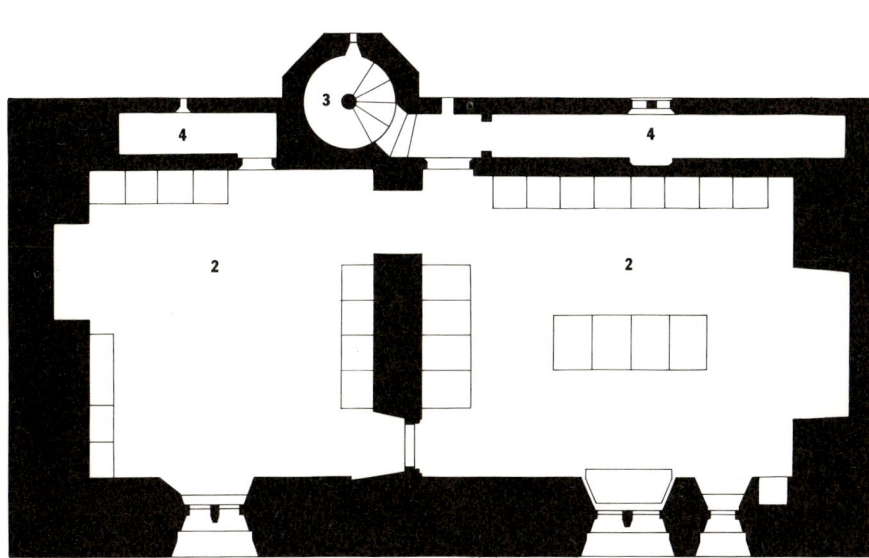
Second floor plan. Scale 1/12in. = 1ft.

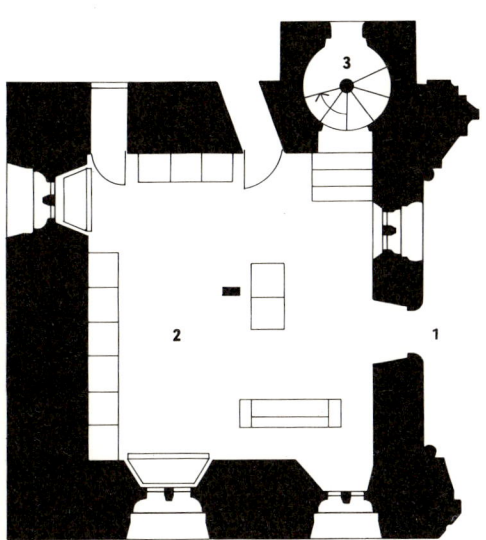
Ground floor plan

key
1, gateway
2, exhibition room
3, turret with vice
4, garderobe

MARTELLO TOWER, DUNLAOGHAIRE, EIRE

Architect: Michael Scott and Partners

Client: James Joyce Tower Committee, convened by Michael Scott, the owner

Site: A rocky promontory called Sandycove Point at Dunlaoghaire, south of Dublin. The uneven site on which the Martello tower stands is surrounded by a stone wall. One end of the wall butts into the tower and the other stops abruptly on the edge of a precipitous drop down to the sea.

History: It was built, like other Martello towers on the English and Irish coasts, in anticipation of Napoleon's invasion. The name derives from Cape Mortella in Corsica, where in 1794 a small round tower withstood the cannonade of the English fleet. The intention was to provide a small museum of James Joyce memorabilia in a building in which Joyce stayed for a short period and in which he set the opening scene of *Ulysses*. Soon after the tower opened as a Joyce museum, it was bought from Michael Scott by the Irish Tourist Board on the understanding that it would continue to be used for the same purpose.

Character: A squat circular tower, two storeys high, with battered walls nearly 8ft. thick faced externally with coursed, roughly dressed masonry. The walls are pierced by a few small, splayed openings like arrow loops and crowned by two projecting bands of stonework. A later external staircase in metal provides access at first floor level and a small vice within the wall thickness leads down to the ground floor and up to the roof or gun platform. To support the weight of the gun the roof structure is a thick stone vault which forms the ceiling of the first floor. A timber floor structure divides the first and ground floors.

Work done: Fifty timber beams and posts were inserted to strengthen the first floor, the stone walls simply whitewashed, two draught-proof doors fitted in the form of a single sheet of glass set in a metal frame, and the spaces equipped with the necessary showcases and lighting. The outside metal staircase was strengthened.

Accommodation: Ground floor—three small exhibition rooms
First floor—entrance and main exhibition room

Date of completion: June 16, 1962, to commemorate Bloomsday, the day in 1904 in which the action of *Ulysses* took place. (The opening ceremony was performed by Sylvia Beach, publisher of *Ulysses*.)

Cost: Approximately £1500. Finance was obtained from John Huston ($1000) and from the Dublin Joyce Society.

1, 2, the tower stands on a rocky promontory. Its character of a fortification has suffered little from a change of use: the addition of a few minuscule windows and of an external metal staircase

3, the machicoulis over the entrance and, 4, the gun platform survive intact

5, the first floor exhibition gallery, its stone vault simply whitewashed. The timber floor structure was largely renewed

6, the entrance into the first floor exhibition gallery preserves its original door

7, death-mask of Joyce effectively displayed against the whitewashed stone surface

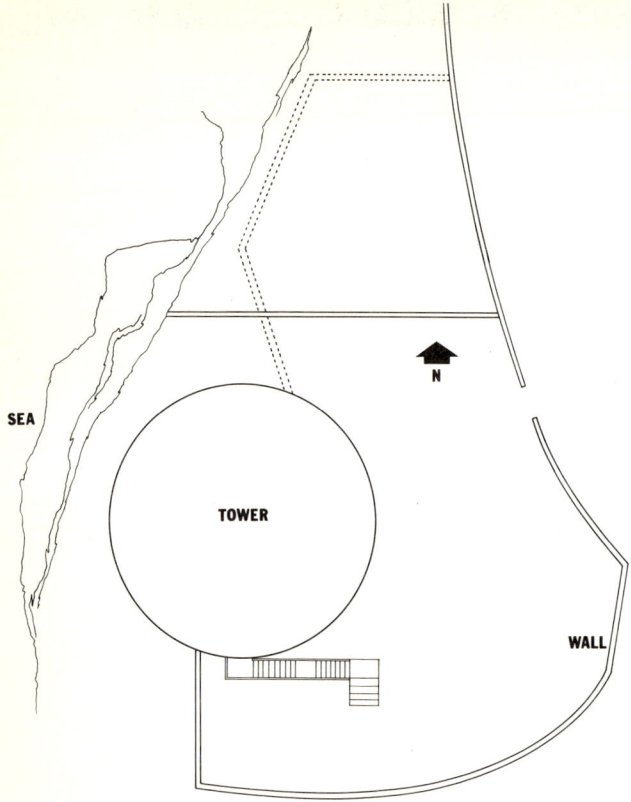

Site plan. Scale 1/24in. = 1ft.

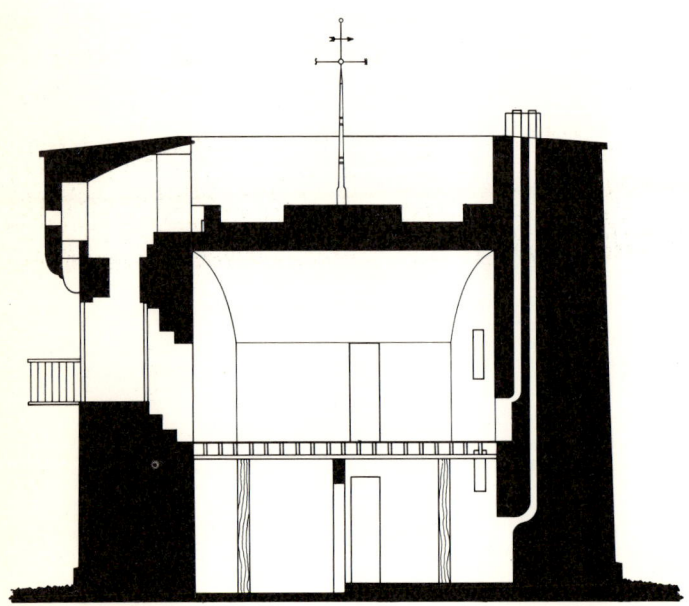

Section AA. Scale 1/12in. = 1ft.

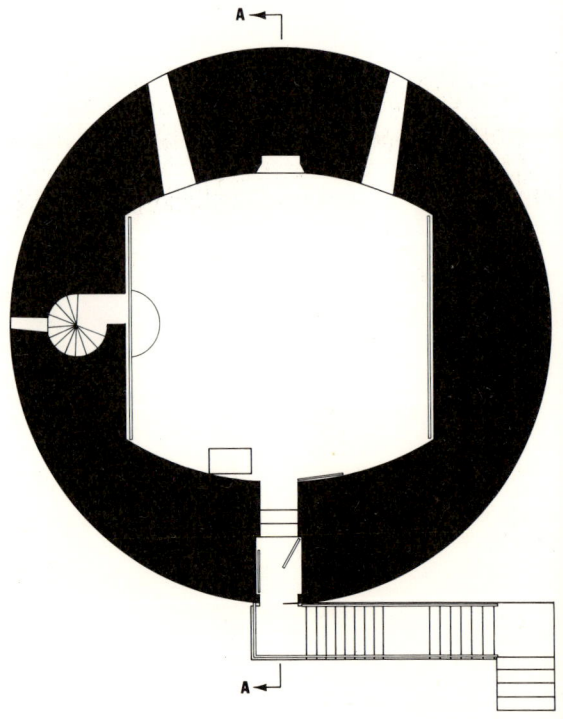

First floor. Scale 1/12in. = 1ft.

ORTO DELL'ABBONDANZA, URBINO (project)

Architect: Giancarlo De Carlo
Assistant architect, Fausto Colombo

Client: University of Urbino and the Urbino Urban Authority

Site: The Orto dell'Abbondanza is situated at the foot of the city wall of which it forms an integral part. It is a long and narrow structure on two levels, stretching between one of the bastions of the wall and the nineteenth-century Teatro Sanzio, through whose basement is the only access to the Orto. Below the main level of the Orto lies the Piazza del Mercatale and above, on the city side, runs the Via Matteotti. On the other side of the latter rises the fifteenth-century Palazzo Ducale. Nearby, on the top of the hill, is the university centre. The site is therefore in a good position for both tourists and students.

History: The Orto dell'Abbondanza was built by Francesco di Giorgio as a stable in the fifteenth century. Subsequently it became a roofed garden, but because of its inaccessibility, it was little used, the roof was allowed to collapse, and it is now in a decaying state, badly needing repair and a new use. It was chosen for the new university *mensa* because of its convenient situation and its easily adaptable form to this sort of new use.

Character: The long narrow Orto is on two levels. The lower level is divided into a series of spaces with vaulted ceilings. The upper level, which was the garden, is a long continuous space, whose front facade is pierced by open arches. The structure is of brick, and earth covers the floor of the upper level.

Work proposed: No work has yet started, but the plan is to situate the dining room of the refectory on the upper level, and to use the lower level for kitchens, staff rooms, heating plant, etc. The structure will be reinforced with concealed concrete pillars inside the walls, and the first floor will be reinforced with concrete.
The architects were obliged to retain the character of the open arches, which they have done by forming small rectangular indoor gardens inside each one, boxed in on the inside by glass. This has the double advantage of helping to break up the monotony of the long rectangular space and of diffusing the daylight let in through the windows. A roof will be constructed with skylights over each garden for additional light. The roof will be of steel, covered in old Roman tiles specially selected to blend in with the colour of the old walls.
The space on the upper floor will be high enough to allow a third level to be inserted. This is designed in the form of galleries and bridges, accessible by stairs from the main level. These galleries, made of steel for strength and lightness, can be dismantled if necessary. The interior will be laid out in as

1, the long and narrow structure of the Orto dell'Abbondanza lying between the Piazza del Mercatale (foreground) and the Via Matteotti. The Orto is terminated at one end by the 19th century Teatro Sanzio (left) and at the other by one of the bastions of the city wall. Above on the hill rises the town of Urbino with the Palazzo Ducale on the left

2, the brick wall of the Orto from the lower level of the Piazza del Mercatale which will be pierced by four entrances at ground level and by a regular series of arched openings on the upper level, 3, behind which small courtyards will be formed to admit light into the refectory

pleasant a way as possible, with seats around the internal gardens where people can wait. There will be two self-service hatches in the middle, with lifts to and from the kitchen.

The main entrance will be where offices are now, in the corner of the Sanzio theatre. A staircase and lift will lead to a common room and give access to cloakrooms and lavatories. Another entrance is planned at the opposite end of the refectory, where a staircase will go down the side of the city wall and lead into another lobby with cloakrooms and lavatories.

The refectory will hold 725 people in one sitting, 410 on the lower level and 315 on the upper level. Assuming there will be three shifts for each meal, it will thus feed 2175 people at every meal. It will be open to everybody—the public as well as students.

Accommodation: Lower level—rooms for staff, kitchens, heating plant, etc. Upper level—refectory and galleries with serving hatches, lobbies, lavatories, cloakrooms and two common rooms

Date of completion: Uncertain, but expected to take eight months once begun. No date has yet been fixed for work to begin.

Cost: 300 million lire, including 20 million for the installation of heating and 37 million for kitchen equipment. This sum does not include furnishings.

Rate: 25 000 lire per m³

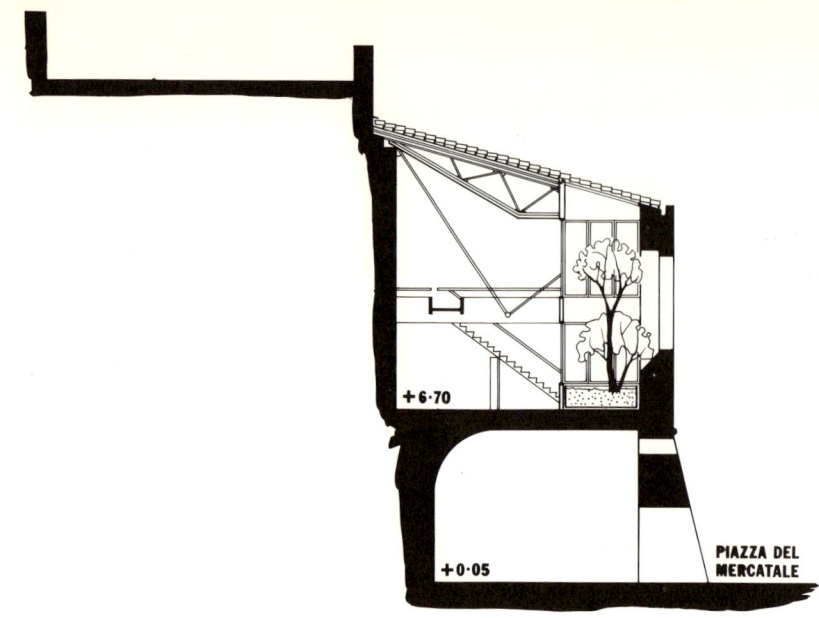

Cross section through indoor garden. Scale 1 in 300

Part longitudinal section. Scale 1 in 200

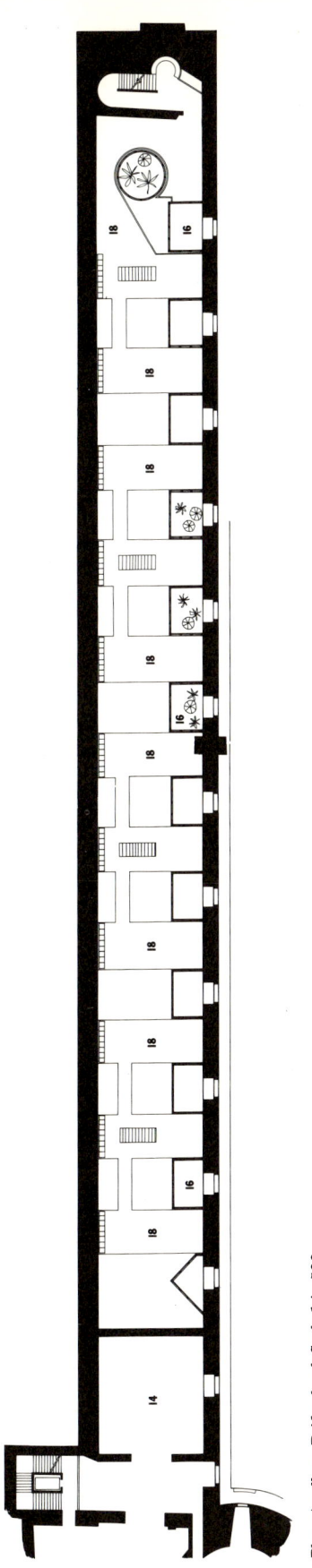

Plan at gallery. Bridge level. Scale 1 in 500

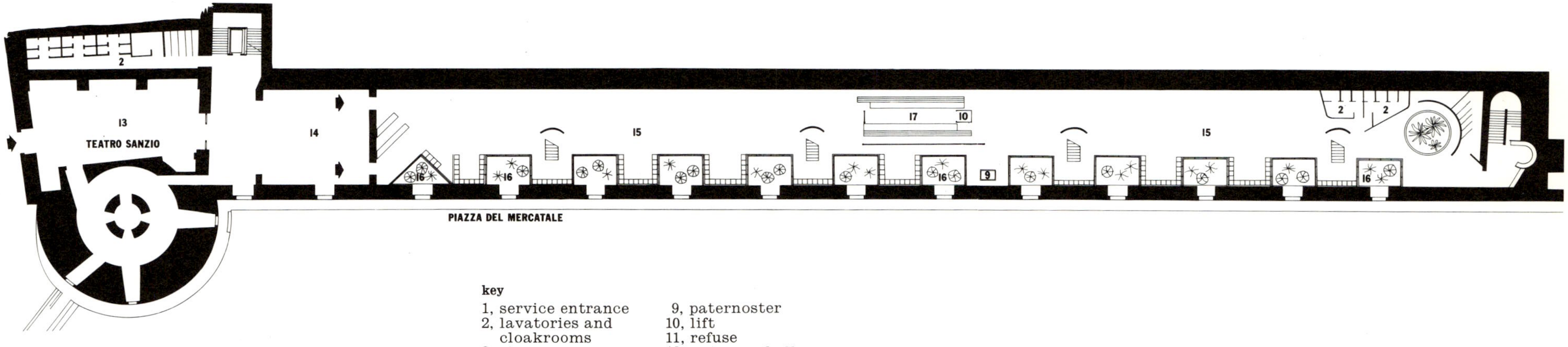

Plan at 6.70 level

Plan at 0.05 level

key
1, service entrance
2, lavatories and cloakrooms
3, store
4, electrical
5, boiler
6, preparation
7, cooking
8, wash-up
9, paternoster
10, lift
11, refuse
13, entrance hall
14, common room
15, refectory
16, indoor garden
17, self-service
18, mezzanine gallery

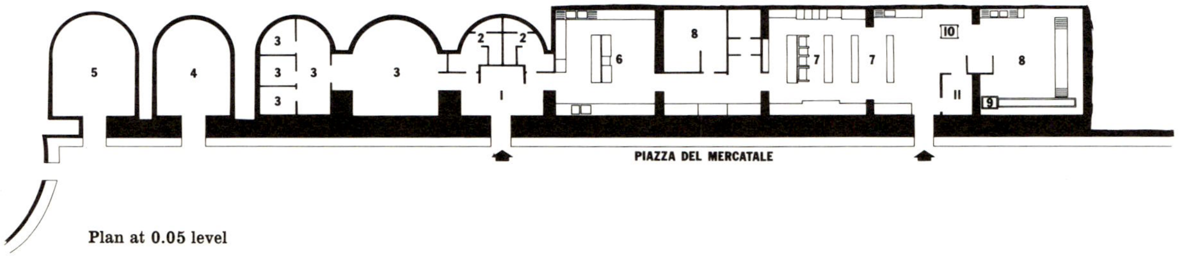

Town houses, country houses, outhouses and other ancillaries

Houses converted to flats or hotels have deliberately been excluded from this chapter. Both are common occurrences involving considerable technical problems which are rarely solved satisfactorily in the aesthetic sense. There is certainly a need for a book which explains these problems and illustrates them by good and bad examples, but to include them here would be to stray too far outside the subject of new uses arising from redundancy.

One example, however, is included because it is a special case with wide implications—the little village of Sveti Stefan which stands on a rocky spit off the Yugoslav coast. Here a deserted and derelict village has been restored to provide both the private and public accommodation normally associated with the conventional tourist hotel. A similar project is now in hand at Labro, a tiny hill town north of Rome; there is a deserted village in the hills of the Var which has been in use for many years as a centre for 'colonies de vacances'; and yet another example of an abandoned town which is gradually being restored privately for holiday use is Monemvasia in the Peloponnese. Sveti Stefan is not an example one would wish to see emulated on a wide scale, but it is better than dereliction or destruction; and it is marginally better than a faked version like Port Grimaud, whose form-language Alison and Peter Smithson (in *Without Rhetoric: An Architectural Aesthetic 1955–1972*, Latimer New Dimensions Limited, 1973) have perceptibly diagnosed as 'that of a "real life" of the past it exploits'. At least at Sveti Stefan this past is real.

An extension of the same principle, which has been proposed by Giancarlo De Carlo in his *Urbino, the History of a City and a Plan for Its Urban Evolution* (Marsilio Edition, Padua 1968), is to transform some of the space within existing city blocks into lodgings for the migrant student population, accommodation which in the summer vacation could be put to tourist uses. Whereas De Carlo's proposition is made within the context of a live city, the village of Sveti Stefan is dead at all times of the year except during the summer season.

The most modern example in the whole book is Mies van der Rohe's house for Hermann Lange at Krefeld. Five hundred years separate it from Sveti Stefan, but it is built of traditional brickwork which, unlike the more usual cement-rendered surfaces of the modern movement, has weathered well. The house itself is a classic, an exhibit in its own right. Its sequence of ground floor reception areas opening on to large terraces, were it not for the current tendency of the contemporary artist to paint ever larger canvases, would be ideally suited to exhibitions of modern art. As always in houses there is the problem of the kitchen quarters and bedrooms which are invariably planned in cellular fashion. Here the old servants' quarters are sensibly used as a caretaker's flat, and the town of Krefeld, with a centralised museum organisation like Portsmouth and Leicester (see Chapter III), is in a good position to find uses for the other rooms, which need not be directly related to the exhibition gallery but can serve the organisation as a whole.

Both the older houses in this chapter have required additions to accommodate their new use. At Roehampton, on the edge of Richmond Park, two Georgian houses became the base for a college of education. The finer of the two houses, Mount Clare, which is illustrated here, has been carefully restored and is used as common rooms (and recently as lecture rooms by day because of shortage of space). The other building, Downshire House, is used for administration and teaching. New dining rooms with residential accommodation above were provided in a separate block which has no physical link whatever with the old buildings. In contrast, at Prospect House, Princeton, a private house converted to a faculty centre, the new work literally collides with the old: a two-level contemporary dining wing has been added in front of the old building. The old house is used as kitchen, common rooms and conference rooms. Whether one rejects or accepts the collision of Princeton as a valid solution will depend on whether one is a preservationist who wants all new work to interpret the old or a modernist who believes that the architecture of the twentieth century has something unique to offer and that the contrast between old and new can be a satisfying experience. Certainly the architect, Warren Platner, performs with conviction, and one is more easily persuaded to like the extension to Prospect House—or indeed the attic to the printing works at Hanover (page 237), to give an equally convincing example from another chapter—more than the feeble integration attempted in the addition to the maltings at Ely (page 178).

The carriage houses in America are an example of different uses reflecting different social and economic situations. The pair in Boston are part of a terrace in an up-and-coming central residential area and have been converted into small houses (the client's own home and his guest house), while the one in New York is a detached building in a suburb with a strong community spirit and has been converted into a theatre. The latter is a better use for this kind of building, for it preserves the open character of the interior, while the house conversions, though interesting in themselves, have obliterated any trace of the earlier use.

To end with there are two dovecots and one eighteenth-century folly—all accessories to country seats. Neither the dovecots nor the doves were in origin ornamental. The doves provided fresh food before the development of feeding stuffs made it possible to keep livestock through the winter. There are plenty of dovecots in Britain which retain quite large populations of birds. The particular form (square, double square, circle, octagon) and diminutive size of the buildings make it desirable to maintain them as dovecots because other suitable uses are hard to find. Both the examples illustrated, a square type at Bicester and a round type in Rutland, preserve their original character and the integrity of their windowless walls. One is now a small meeting hall and the other a school tuckshop. The dovecot in Rutland still has its glover (the open lantern on the roof), but has lost its nests and is now engulfed by new buildings which butt against it. At Bicester the glover has been replaced by a perspex flèche, but the nests are still there and the dovecot remains free-standing.

The eighteenth-century folly is the Gothic temple at Stowe, which has been converted by the Landmark Trust into a weekend or holiday house. The eccentric plan does not lend itself to the more utilitarian side of living, so that the circular rooms in the towers have to serve as kitchen, bathroom and bedrooms, leaving the great central space undivided as a living room. The new use proves to be not incompatible. More important, the conversion has saved a remarkable building from further dilapidation and will ensure its maintenance in the future. The Landmark Trust was founded in 1965 by John and Christian Smith 'for preserving small buildings, structures or sites of historic interest, architectural merit, or amenity value, and where possible finding suitable uses for them; and for protecting and promoting the enjoyment of places of historic interest or natural beauty'. It has a preference for buildings which can be let furnished for short periods because this tends to avoid the more drastic work needed for permanent occupation. Besides the copper and arsenic mine in Cornwall (see page 213), the trust counts among its three dozen or so buildings at Martello tower, a railway station, a school, a chapel and two mills.

SVETI STEFAN, MONTENEGRO, YUGOSLAVIA

Architect: Branko Bon

Client: Republic of Montenegro

Site: A compact fishing village built on a rocky peninsula east of the town of Budva on the Adriatic coast. The peninsula is connected to the mainland only by a narrow sandy strip. The coast between Budva and Bar to the south has been developed with large modern hotels.

History: Sveti Stefan was built in the second half of the fifteenth century as a fortress against the Turks and became the home of famous pirates. It got its name from the little church of St. Stephen which was erected on the highest point of the peninsula. From its beginning, the fortress was associated with the Pastrovic family, who were able to maintain a considerable degree of political autonomy. The population increased, houses multiplied and Sveti Stefan prospered well into the nineteenth century. Economic decline set in around 1900, the population emigrating mainly to America. By 1955, when the project of a village hotel was put in hand, the twenty-odd inhabitants who were left were moved to other places and work began on the deserted buildings.

Character: Like a small Mediterranean hill town, the houses build up to a peak which is marked by the church. Remains of walls and bastions rise out of the sea; inside, the footpaths are steep and tortuous. Materials are stone set in lime mortar, Roman tiles and timber floor and roof structures.

Work done: In 1955 the village was in a ruined state, with the roofs and floors mostly collapsed and only the walls standing. The first task was to clean the site of waste material and undergrowth. This was followed by archaeological searches, which proved fruitless, and finally by the careful reconstruction of the buildings with traditional materials by craftsmen using traditional methods. Most of the buildings were converted into residential accommodation for tourists either in the form of rooms or flats.

Accommodation: 116 rooms with a total of 250 beds (23 single, 70 double, a few flats), restaurant, coffee bar, cocktail bars, night club, casino, hairdresser and beauty parlour, small shops, reception, parking for 80 cars

Date of completion: 1966

Cost: 80 000 new dinars per bed, excluding site and roadworks

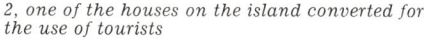

1, the island of Sveti Stefan joined to the Yugoslav mainland by a causeway and a narrow sandy strip

2, one of the houses on the island converted for the use of tourists

3, narrow, winding streets spanned by high-level bridges are typical of compact Mediterranean hill towns

Plan

4, work in progress. A small chapel (left) has been preserved

PROSPECT HOUSE, PRINCETON, NEW JERSEY

Architect: Warren Platner

Client: Princeton University

Site: The house stands on the campus of the university in a private garden surrounded by great trees. There are front and back lawns which the house commands from a terraced slope of flower gardens and hedges. Other hedges are clipped into geometric shapes and stand free on the lawn in Tuscan villa style.

History: Built as a private residence in 1849, Prospect House was bought by the university in 1878 and served as the president's house for the next ninety years. In 1968 the contribution of an anonymous donor made it possible to convert the building into a social centre, the then president having agreed to move to another house.

Character: The character of the building has been well summed up by Olga Gueft in *Interiors* (June 1970): 'It is a handsome building very grand in scale, its strong masonry masses unified under the sweeping horizontal shadows of the flaring cornices and punctuated by the emphatic verticals of the chimneys and north tower. For all the largeness of the volumes, however, the building's details and trim—the denticulating corbels, the balconies, the dark and light checkerboarding of the window and corner masonry—are refined. The building has elegance as well as a massive presence.'

Work done: The intention was to provide a social facility for dons and administrators by converting the old building and by adding a two-level dining wing in front of it. The character of the old building was to be preserved and the new dining room was to make the most of the beautiful garden.

The interior of the old building had been decorated in various styles over the years. In the conversion, emphasis has been laid on enhancing the architectural features such as the railings and cornice of the balcony circle over the entrance hall, and on furnishing each space to give it a character of its own. All rooms were painted white and the oak floors were sanded and polished and left exposed.

In the drawing room the silk curtains were cleaned and resewn. All the other windows were fitted with standard white-painted shutters. With the exception of a few old fittings, like the nineteenth-century brass chandelier in the entrance hall, all rooms were provided with modern furniture and rugs.

The extension makes use of the sloping ground and has its lower floor on the same level as the basement of the old house. The upper floor, which is at entrance level, is fully glazed on the three open sides. The reinforced concrete structure consists of a single column in each of the four corners

1, 2, the collision of an uncompromisingly modern extension with the massive but elegantly detailed forms of a mid-19th century 'Tuscan' villa. The extension provides dining rooms for the old building which has been converted into a faculty centre

supporting a coffered roof slab. Floor-to-ceiling louvred shutters slide just inside the glazing line and make it possible to control the amount of light and to provide protection at night or in bad weather. To relate the interior of the extension to the old building, oak was used for the shutters, the tables and the surround to the carpet.

Accommodation: Basement—large dining room (extension), two small dining rooms, lavatories, stores
Ground floor—large dining room (extension), kitchen, conference room, library, entrance hall, sitting rooms
First floor—several meeting and conference rooms

Date of completion: 1970

Consulting architect, Pietro Belluschi
University architect, C. Harrison Hill
Landscape architect, Michael Rapuano

3, the extension at night

4, 5, the interiors of the old buildings were painted white throughout and furnished mainly with furniture designed by the associate architect, Warren Platner

6, the new dining room on the upper level of the extension. It is fully glazed on three sides, but floor-to-ceiling sliding shutters make it possible to control the amount of light and to provide protection at night or in bad weather

Site plan

First floor plan

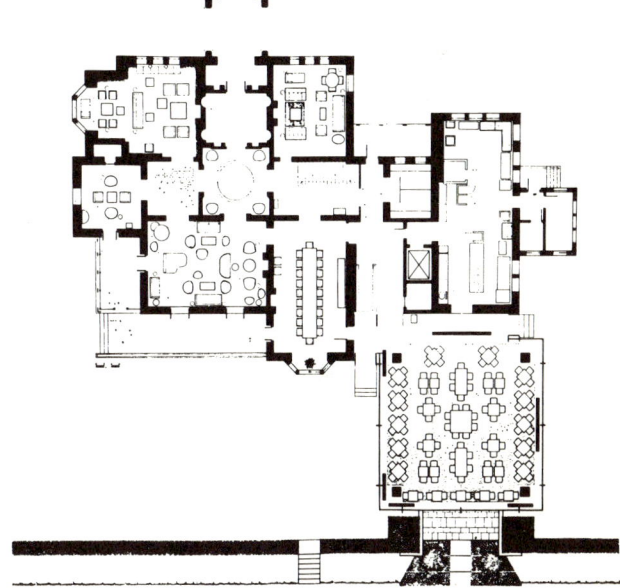

Ground floor plan

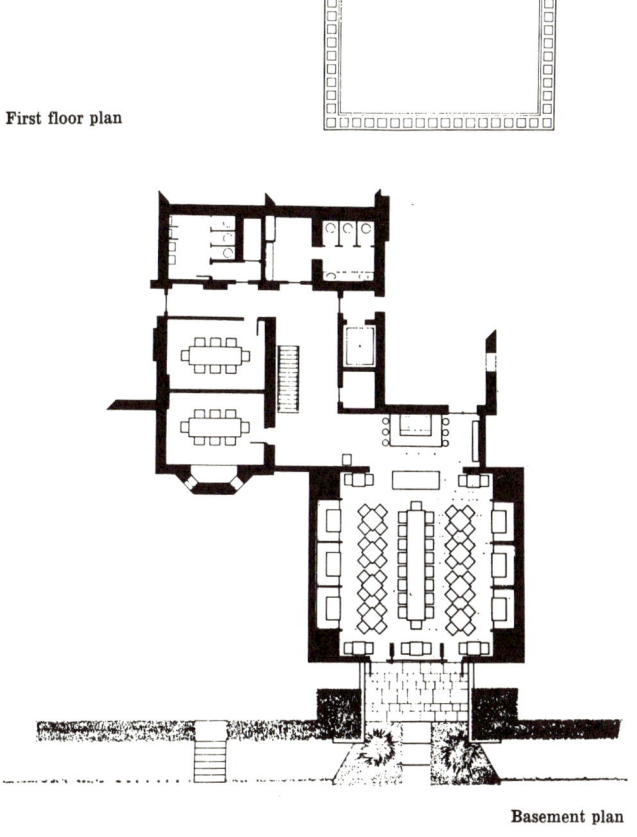

Basement plan

87

MOUNT CLARE, ROEHAMPTON, LONDON

Architect: London County Council (now Greater London Council) Architect's Department

Client: London County Council Education Department (now Inner London Education Authority)

Site: The house is set in its own grounds in Roehampton, a western suburb of London near Richmond Park. Nearby is the Roehampton housing estate, which was built by the London County Council.

History: In 1770 George Clive, the cousin of Lord Clive of India, bought thirty-five acres of land adjoining Richmond Park and Parkstead House and two years later built a house which he named Mount Clare as a compliment to his cousin, whose house at Esher was called Claremont. Henry Holland, who worked on Claremont, probably designed Mount Clare, whilst Lancelot Brown laid out the grounds. The house was sold in 1780 to Sir John Dick who commissioned Placidio Columbani, a Milanese architect, to add the Doric

1, the graceful 18th century house after the removal of 19th century extensions and its conversion into student and staff common rooms for a college of education. The view shows the house in relation to the new residential block and dining rooms (left). The single-storey buildings in the foreground (left) are part of the Roehampton housing estate

2, the garden front

portico and some of the interior decorations. The house remained in private hands until the estate was purchased by the London County Council after the Second World War. Many proposals for the use of the house were examined until eventually it was agreed that it should provide the student and staff common rooms (the neighbouring Downshire House would provide the lecture rooms) of the Garnett College of Education, which was moved to Roehampton from the Old Kent Road.

Character: The house is finished in stucco and consists of two principal floors over a rusticated semi-basement which contained the service rooms. It is approached up curved stone steps leading to a Doric portico. The two principal rooms, the entrance hall and the octagon beyond it, are very fine examples of late eighteenth-century interior decoration. The staircase and remaining rooms are simple and elegant.

Work done: The nineteenth-century extensions to Mount Clare were pulled down, and a block containing new dining rooms with residential accommodation above was erected close to it. The principal's house was built in an enclave of the former garden enclosing the eighteenth-century garden temple. Apart from the furniture, the house is now restored nearly to the appearance it presented in 1780. Gradually the original colour schemes are being re-established in the principal rooms. It makes an admirable social centre for the college and it is almost continuously in use for seminars during vacations. It is still set about with the mature trees of the eighteenth-century landscape.

The repairs and restorations were carried out in two separate contracts by different builders. The house is heated by hot water radiators fed from a calorifier connected to the district heating system of Roehampton housing estate.

Accommodation: Basement—lavatories, laundry and heating installation
Principal floors—common rooms at night, lecture or seminar rooms by day

Date of completion: 1962

Cost: Approximately £45 000 over 10 years, including treatment for extensive dry rot

Rate: Approximately £5·75 per sq. ft.

3, the entrance hall

4, the staircase

Longitudinal section. Scale 1/24in. = 1ft.

key
1, hall
2, lecture or seminar rooms by day; common rooms by night

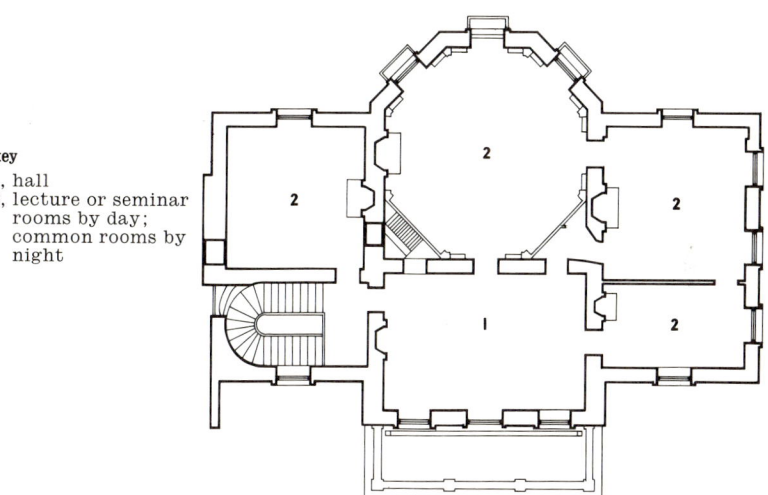
First floor. Scale 1/24in. = 1ft.

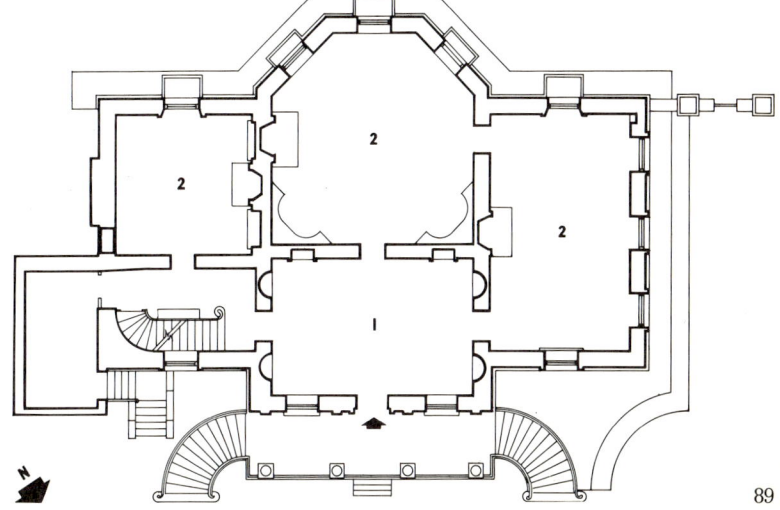
Ground floor

PRIVATE HOUSE, KREFELD, GERMAN FEDERAL REPUBLIC

Architect: None

Client: Stadtverwaltung, Krefeld

Site: 91 Wilhelmshofallee, in a residential district of Krefeld with detached houses in large gardens full of mature trees.

History: In 1928 Mies van der Rohe built two houses side by side for textile manufacturers at Krefeld, the Lange house and the Esters house. The Lange house, illustrated here, was damaged during the war and subsequently occupied by the British, who divided the music room into two spaces and made other less drastic alterations. The house was lived in by the Lange family until about 1954, after which they used it as a private museum to show their fine collection of paintings. In 1968 the family gave the house to the city, who turned it into an art gallery.

Character: The exterior is of imported Dutch brick, very precisely bonded. The roof is flat and the form is a series of interlocking cubes. Philip Johnson has said of the exterior that it has a 'Schinkelesque serenity'. On the garden side some of the character has been lost by the removal of the continuous window boxes on the two first floor terraces. The interiors are distinguished by their extreme simplicity—hardwood floors and skirtings, plain plastered walls and ceilings painted white and metal windows. The ground floor windows on the garden side were originally designed to slide downwards into the basement and to be operated electrically.

Work done: The intention was to turn the house into a gallery for changing exhibitions of contemporary art with the minimum of alterations. Some of the original fittings, like the bookcase in the main room of the ground floor, had already gone. Others, like the fitted cupboards in the bedrooms, were removed. The main terrace on the garden side, originally paved in stone, was repaved in brick. Repairs and redecorating were carried out and the servants rooms on the first floor were turned into a caretaker's flat. The exhibition areas are on the ground floor and comprise the main rooms, the terraces and the garden. The smaller rooms on the ground floor are used as offices and workshops. There is a dark room on the first floor. The remaining rooms on the first floor, the former bedrooms and bathrooms, could provide additional exhibition and storage space or two or three comfortable hotel-type suites in which artists could stay.

Date of completion: 1968

1, the house seen from Wilhelmshofallee. The exterior is of imported Dutch brick, very precisely bonded

2, the garden façade with the house and garden during the Cristo exhibition, 'wrapped floors—wrapped walkways', in June 1971

3, the living room looking towards the garden

4, another part of the living room. The left-hand door leads into the former music room, the right-hand door into the former study

key
1, exhibition room
2, roofed terrace
3, open terrace
4, workshop
5, storage
6, lavatory and cloakroom
7, garden

Ground floor plan. Scale 1 in 200

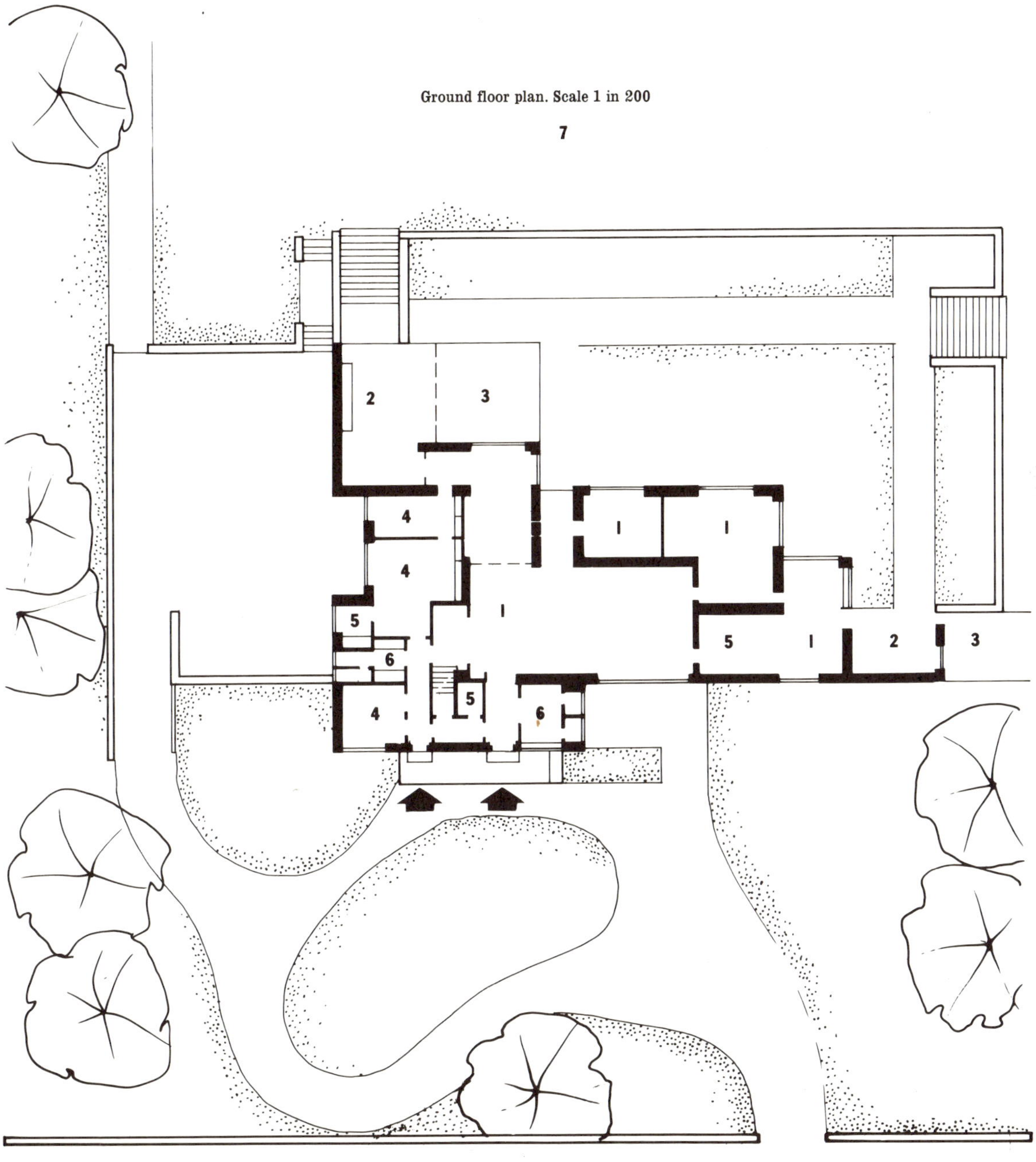

CARRIAGE HOUSE, LOCKPORT, NEW YORK

Architect: Hardy, Holzman, Pfeiffer Associates

Client: Kenan Centre

Site: The detached building stands back from the road, facing open parkland at the rear, at 533 Locust Street in the old town of Lockport.

History: Lockport grew up around the locks of the Erie Canal in the early years of the nineteenth century, and the carriage house was built in 1850. It underwent at least three major renovations before being recently bought by a group of local people who were looking for a location to start a new community theatre.

Character: There are brick bearing walls with windows and doors set in slight recesses. A hipped slate roof with a cupola at its peak and projecting eaves supported on elaborate paired brackets give the building an Italianate character. There is a modest weatherboarded extension on one side.

Work done: The intention was to provide Lockport with a small intimate theatre for drama, dance, chamber music, films and meetings. The theatre requires additional rehearsal space for which the Kenan Centre are now looking.

The original structure has largely been retained and repaired. A cantilevered 'thrust' stage was constructed out of timber framing, raised above the existing floor level and finished in pressed wood chippings to absorb sound and provide a comfortable surface for performers. Multi-coloured seating has been arranged on three sides and on four or five levels around the stage. The seating is built up, like the stage, on timber framing. Above the seating hangs round enamelled air duct to which fluorescent lighting is fixed. Rods, suspended from the open roof structure, carry adjustable fittings for the stage lighting. The large cupola and all existing sashes were repaired and reglazed. Back-stage facilities have been provided by forming dressing rooms at one side of the stage (the other side being reserved for storage) and by making use of the extension as an entrance for performers.

Accommodation: Auditorium with 156 seats, 'thrust' stage 24ft. deep by 14ft. wide with space at back and to one side for storage, screen and projection facilities, dressing rooms for men and women, side entrance for performers

Date of completion: September 1969

Cost: $40 000

Rate: $18 per sq. ft.

1, the carriage house is set well back from the road and faces open parkland at the rear

2, multi-coloured tiered seating wraps around the thrust stage

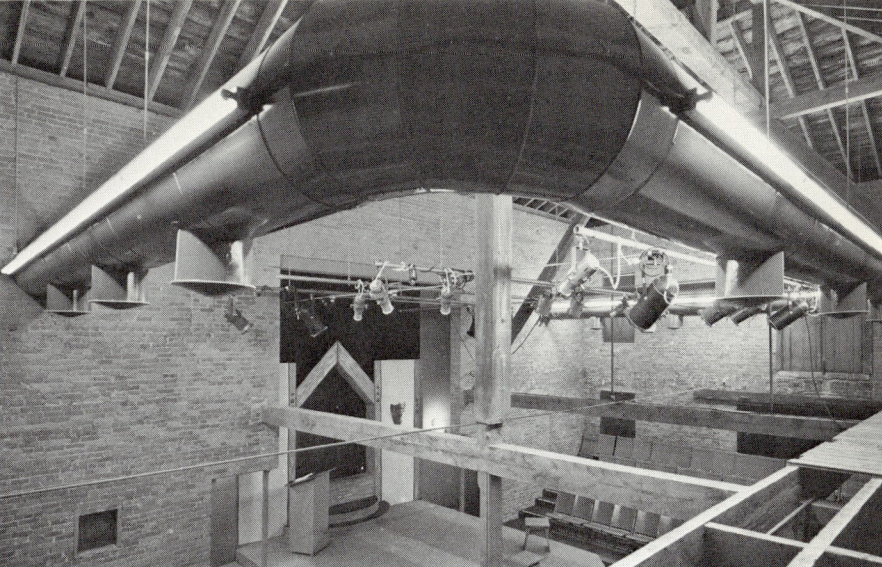

4, over the seating hangs a round enamelled airduct to which fluorescent lighting is fixed

3, rods suspended from the open roof structure carry adjustable table fittings for the stage lighting

5, the interior of the weatherboarded extension (seen right in 1) which serves as an entrance for performers

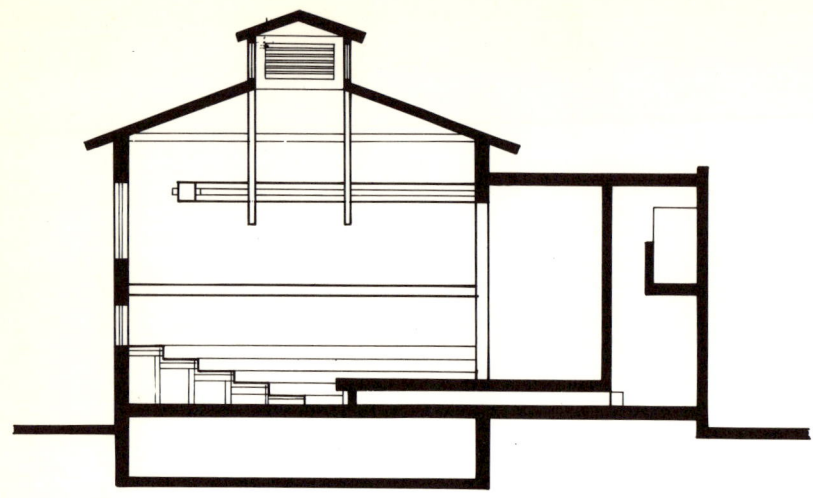

Cross section. Scale 1/16in. = 1ft.

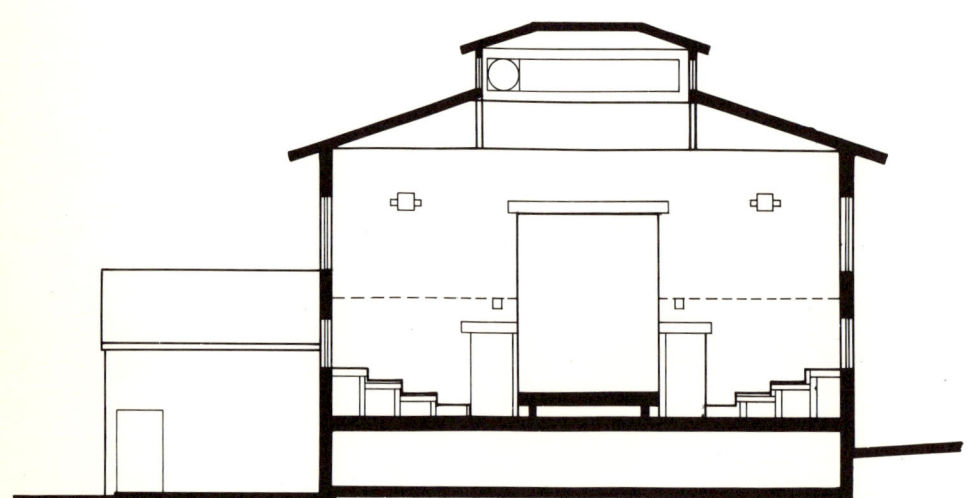

Longitudinal section. Scale 1/16in. = 1ft.

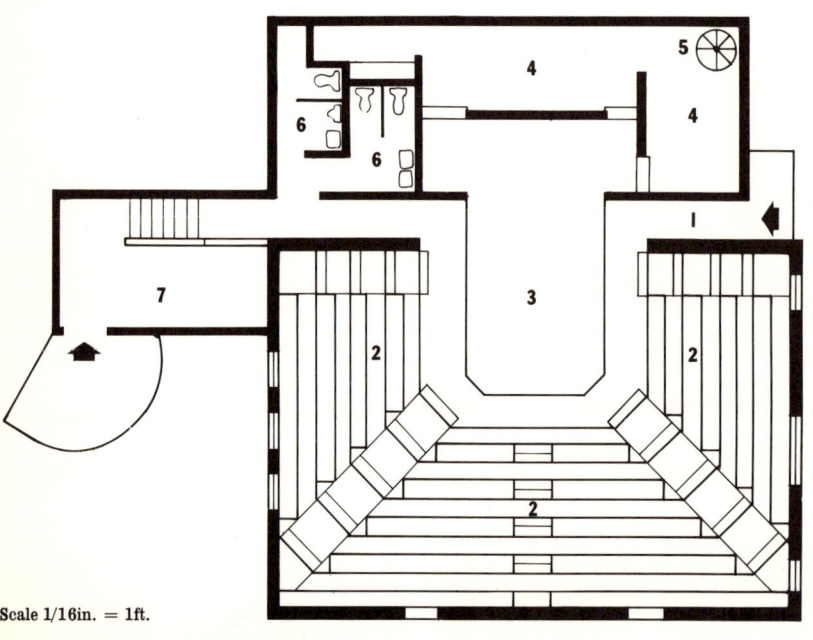

Plan. Scale 1/16in. = 1ft.

key
1, entrance to auditorium
2, raked seating
3, 'thrust' stage
4, storage space
5, circular stair to above stage structure
6, dressing room
7, performers' entrance

COMMERCIAL BUILDINGS, BOSTON, MASSACHUSETTS

Architect: Hardy, Holzman, Pfeiffer Associates

Client: A. Johnson

Site: Nos. 35 and 37 Winchester Street in a central district of Boston of mixed commercial and residential use, but which has recently been re-zoned for eventual residential use only. It is up-and-coming and may one day rival the fashionable Beacon Hill area. The site is L-shaped with no. 37 occupying the full depth of the block and having vehicular access and a garage at the rear. The two buildings have a basement, ground and first floor.

History: Both buildings are about one hundred years old. No. 37 was originally a carriage house and more recently a theatre supply company. No. 35 was a small commercial building which had been gutted by fire.

Character: Both buildings have a brick street facade with plate glass shop windows and entrances on the ground floor. On the first floor of no. 37 are wide mullioned windows with some brick relief decoration. Inside are rough brick walls and a timber floor and roof structure.

Work done: No. 37 was converted for the client into a two-bedroom house on two floors (the basement not being used) and no. 35 into his guest house.

Despite the fire, the roof and first floor timber structures of no. 35 survived and were trimmed for a large industrial skylight and an open well respectively. A new ground floor, some 4ft. above street level, repeats the trimmed line of the floor above so that the skylight can illuminate the basement living room. The new structure throughout is in timber, with floors finished in oak boarding (the basement floor in green terrazzo), ceilings in fir boarding and walls in gypsum board. Brick walls were left rough. No. 37 makes use of the same materials but has a diagonal plan in an existing rectilinear container. In both houses the space revolves around the staircases, emphasising the vertical dimension. In no. 37 the living room, the inner part of which is open to the roof, is lighted by skylights. Both houses have gas-fired warm air heating. Above the first floor, the facades remain unaltered except for new windows; on the ground floor the plate glass shop windows and entrances were bricked up and new openings formed.

1, 35 and 37 Winchester Street after conversion. The plate glass shop windows on the ground floor have been bricked up and new openings formed. No. 35 provides a guest house for the owner who lives in no. 37

2, the entrance hall of no. 35 from which steps lead down to the living room and kitchen or up to the study

Accommodation: No. 35 basement—living room, lavatory, kitchen, boiler room
ground floor—entrance, study
first floor—bedroom, bathroom
No. 37 ground floor—entrance, cloakroom, living room, kitchen, garage
first floor—two bedrooms, two bathrooms, study

Date of completion: 1968

Cost: No. 35, $21 000
No. 37, $32 000

Rate: $30.00 per sq. ft.

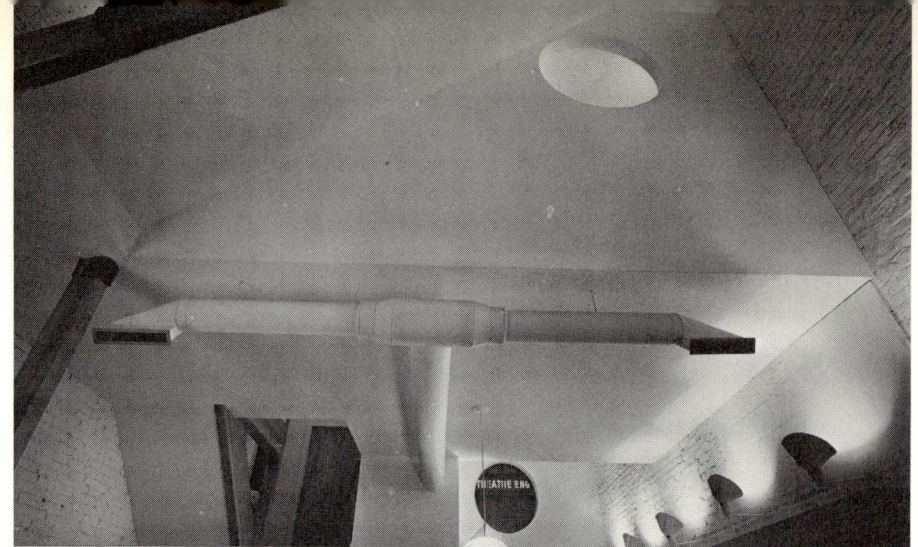

3, 4, two views looking upwards from the living room in no. 35. Both show the circular opening in the study wall and the underside of the staircase which leads to the top-floor bedroom. 4 also shows the timber-boarded back wall and the industrial skylight which illuminates the living room down in the basement

5, view down to the living room in no. 35 through the circular opening in the study wall

6, the two round windows on the street façade of no. 35 (seen in 1) seen through another circular opening in the study

 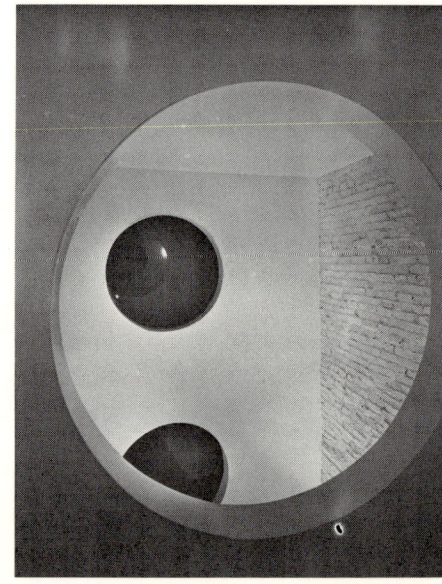

96

7, 8, the central living area of no. 37 is defined mainly by diagonal walls and balustrades at different levels which makes it a very complex space and difficult to understand. 7 is a view looking towards the walls which divide the living area from the bedroom and garage on the street front. 8 shows the other end of the living area and is taken from the top of the steps seen in 7

9, looking upwards to the skylights and boarded ceiling over the living area

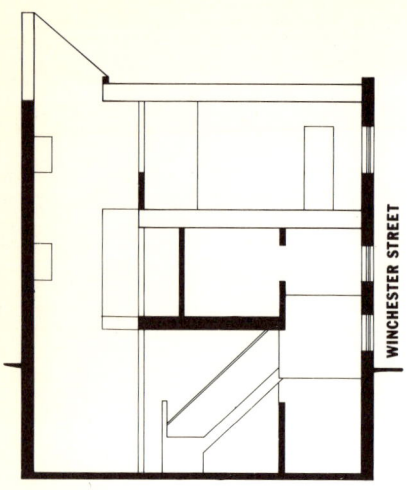

Section through No. 35. Scale 1/16in. = 1ft.

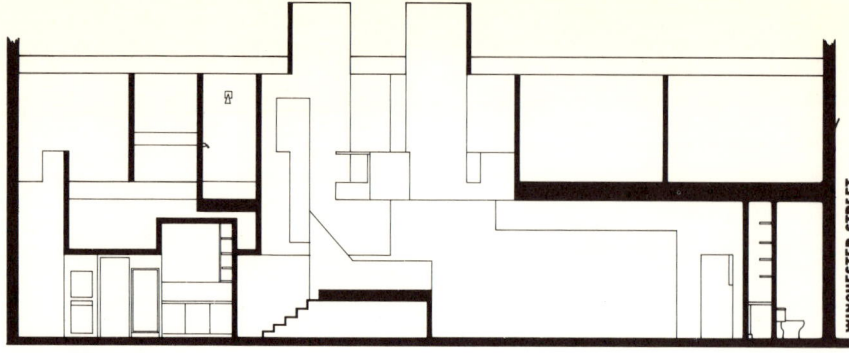

Section through No. 37. Scale 1/16in. = 1ft.

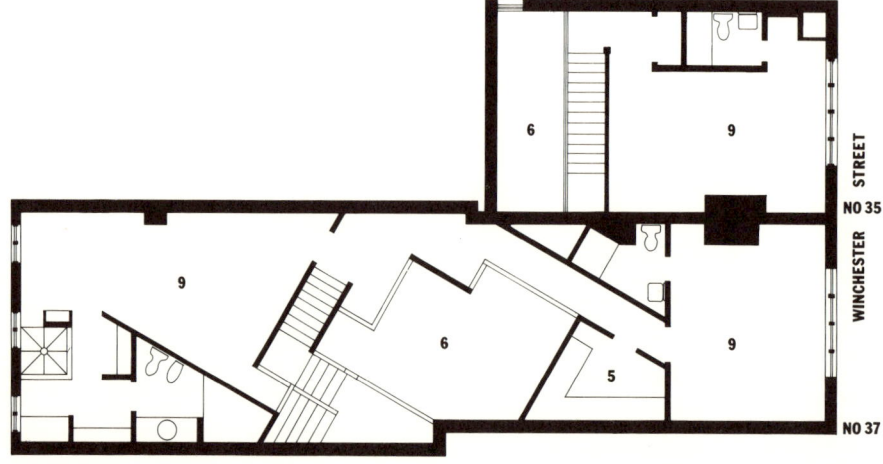

First floor plan. Scale 1/16in. = 1ft.

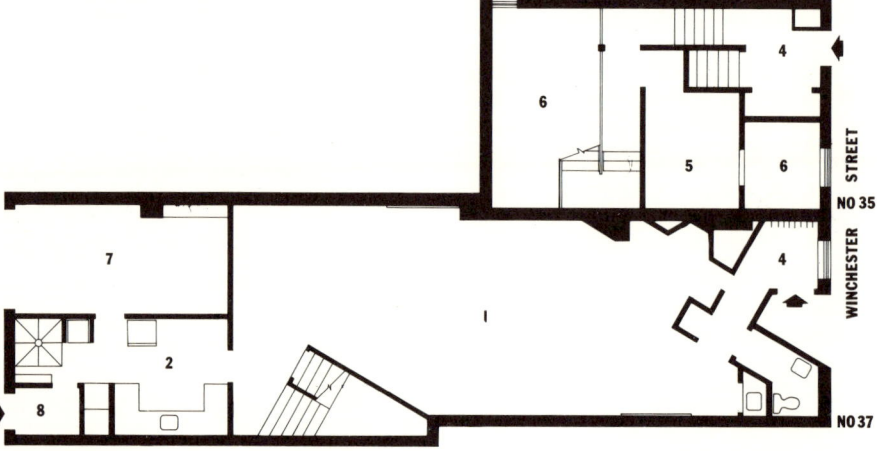

Ground floor plan

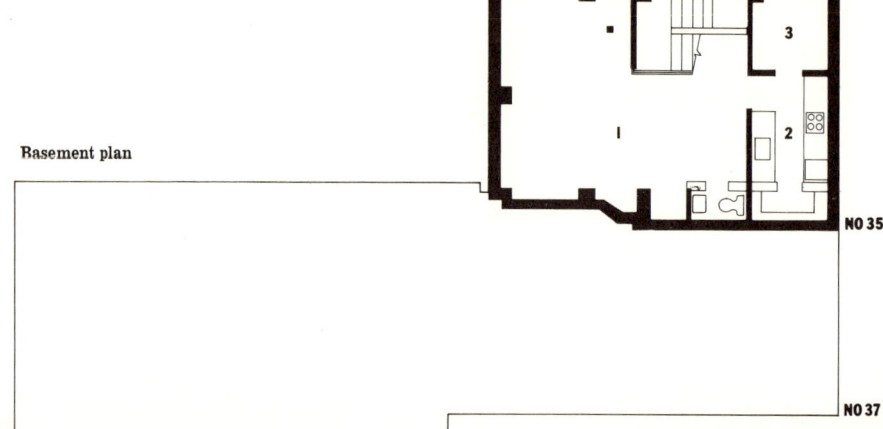

Basement plan

key
1, living room
2, kitchen
3, boiler
4, entrance hall
5, study
6, void over room below
7, garage
8, back entrance
9, bedroom

GOTHIC TEMPLE, STOWE, BUCKINGHAMSHIRE

Architect: Hugh Creighton

Client: Landmark Trust

Site: A rural site on a hilltop in the eighteenth-century gardens at Stowe, near Buckingham.

History: Built about 1740 by James Gibbs for General Sir Richard Temple, the first Viscount Cobham of Stowe (1675–1749). Its Gothic style is rather in advance of the eighteenth-century Gothic revival and is a demonstration of defiance to Walpole, who, as it seemed to Cobham and his friends, was allowing the British flag to be dragged in the mud by Spanish warships, which attacked British ships even in peacetime. The Gothic style was thought to have originated with the Anglo-Saxons from whom all true Englishmen were descended and was the obvious choice of style for a demonstration of patriotic feelings. Gibbs's original drawings for the building are in the Ashmolean Museum at Oxford.

The temple was used for a great many years as an armoury, first by the Duke's Buckinghamshire Yeomanry and then by Stowe school. The school leased the temple free to the Landmark Trust, who have had it repaired and restored, and it is now available to the public to rent as a holiday house.

Character: This surprisingly large and bold folly is made of Northamptonshire ironstone which is orange in colour. It is triangular in shape with pentagonal turrets at each corner. It has a pitched roof with Gothic gables and on each facade it has three pointed openings on each of its two floors with plate tracery in the upper windows. Inside, the rooms have moulded stone pilasters and plaster vaults, and the main vault of the central space is painted with elaborate heraldic achievements, against a background of simulated gold mosaic. At the top of the staircase there is a belvedere with stone seats and a fine view.

Work done: The temple was in a derelict state when work was first undertaken: there were rifle racks all round the gallery, the roof leaked and most of the windows were bricked up. A lot of stonework repair was needed. The two cupolas and the pinnacles and parapet of the tower were taken down and rebuilt, also many of the battlements, and the whole generally patched and pointed. All the windows were renewed and some new ones put into previously blank openings. The roof was re-slated and the main plaster dome refixed to the timbers. The heraldic painting was restored and largely repainted by Michael and Benjamin Gibbon. The interior was cleaned down, painted and fitted out for living in (including water, electricity supply and drainage).

1, of the three facades (the building is triangular on plan) this is the only symmetrical one, the third point of the triangle being marked by a higher tower with pinnacles (just visible above the castellated gable). The temple is built of Northamptonshire ironstone which is orange in colour

Accommodation: Ground floor—kitchen, bathroom, living room
First floor—two bedrooms

Date of completion: 1971

Cost: £28 000 (part of the cost was met by a grant from the Historic Buildings Council)

2, the central space which has been converted into a living room, rises the full height and has a gallery at first floor level. Its vaulted ceiling, 3, is painted with heraldic emblems on a background of simulated gold mosaic

4, the gallery at first floor level seen from one of the turret rooms

5, the kitchen has been fitted into the ground floor space on one of the turrets. The wall and ceiling decoration is plaster

6, view through one of the quatrefoil openings in the tower which houses the staircase

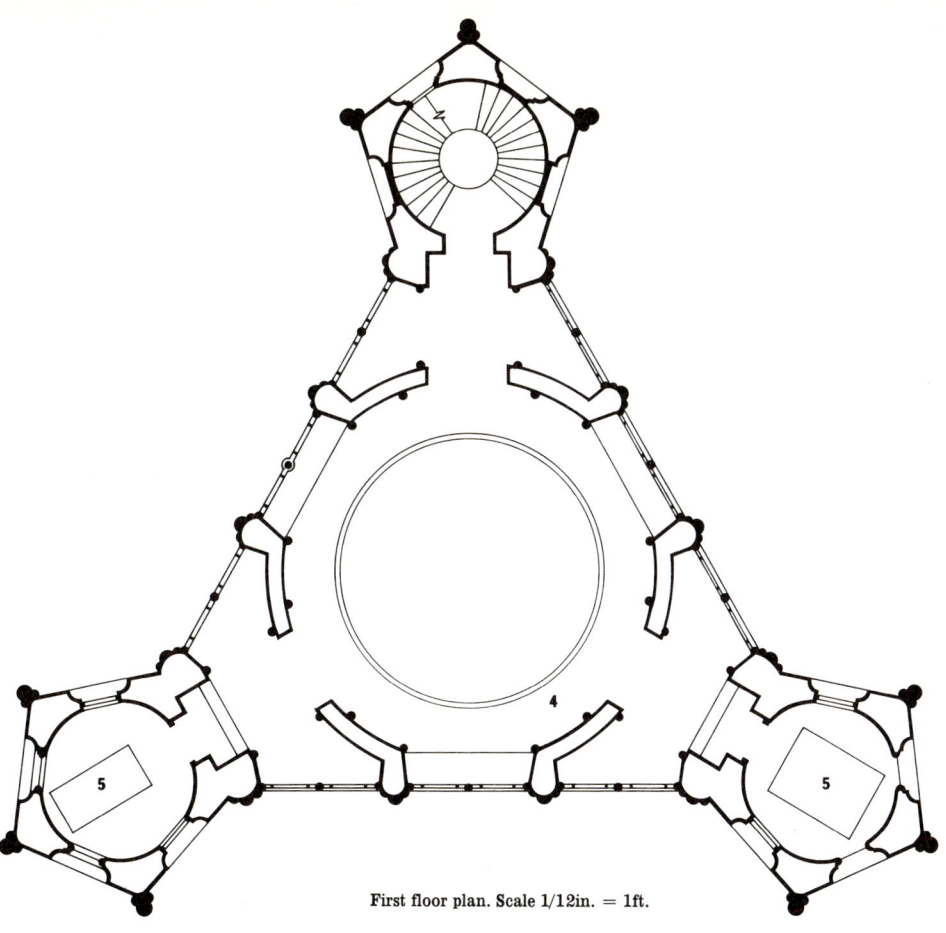

First floor plan. Scale 1/12in. = 1ft.

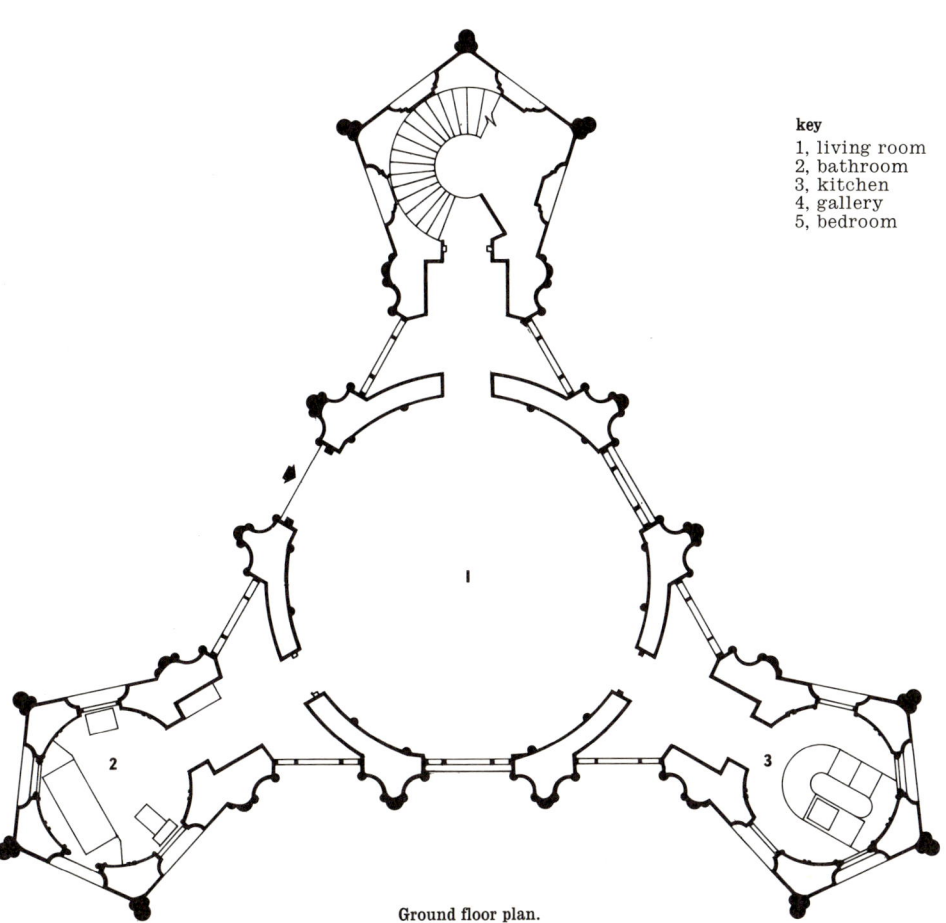

key
1, living room
2, bathroom
3, kitchen
4, gallery
5, bedroom

Ground floor plan.

DOVECOT, TIXOVER GRANGE, RUTLAND

Architect: Roman Halter and Associates

Client: Spastics Society

Site: A group of outbuildings including a dovecot, belonging to Tixover Grange, a house situated one mile off the A1 and six miles south-west of Stamford close to the village of Doddington. Trees and rolling fields divided by stone walls surround the property.

History: Tixover Grange dates from the nineteenth century, but the dovecot and the outbuildings belong to a seventeenth-century manor house on the same site. Bought by the Spastics Society, the buildings have been converted over the years into a boarding school for severely disabled children and comprise dormitories, classrooms and laboratories. A library and staffrooms were built on a site among trees some sixty yards west of the old building.

Character: A small cylindrical stone building 7ft. in diameter internally, with a conical slate roof crowned by a timber glover which provided entry for the doves. The interior of the dovecot was a single space with crumbling stone walls and an open roof structure of rotting timbers. The other outhouses and the Grange itself are also built of stone and slate.

Work done: The intention was to convert the dovecot into a tuckshop and to make it the link between the old and the new buildings. The brief required additional dormitories and a clubroom-cum-gym. The latter is built up against the old stone wall of the original kitchen garden. The area around the dovecot, as well as the link corridors, provides space for tricycling, which is a useful form of mobility for spastics.

The conversion of the dovecot was part of the contract for the new dormitories and was carried out by the same builder at low rates. Some roof members were replaced; others were strengthened by gusseting with new pieces of wood. The resulting structure full of criss-cross members was stained black and stands out against the white walls which have been repaired, rendered and painted. The roof timbers outside the dovecot, which radiate from its wall like spokes from a wheel, help to support the dovecot's roof structure. Inside the dovecot, at a child's waist level, there is a counter (with drawers underneath), and against the remaining part of the wall a timber seat with a cupboard under. A doorway with adequate headroom was formed, a new stone floor laid, and a serving hatch cut, opening out on to the covered space from which the link radiates.

Accommodation: Tuckshop

Date of completion: 1968

Cost: £525

1, the circular dovecot has been incorporated into a group of new buildings which includes a gym (left) and a passage (right) forming a link with the old buildings
2, inside, the area around the dovecot provides space for tricycling—a useful form of mobility for spastics. The doorway and the service hatch into the dovecot are new

3, the open roof structure of the dovecot which was repaired and stained black

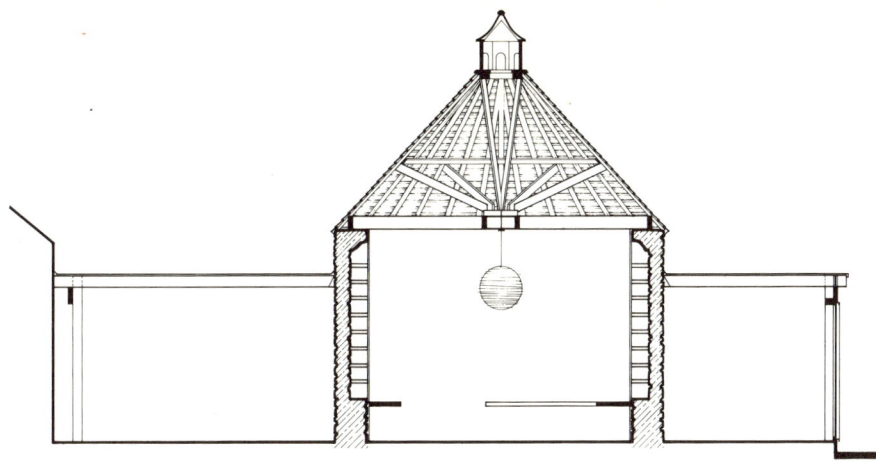

Section through tuckshop. Scale 1/10in. = 1ft.

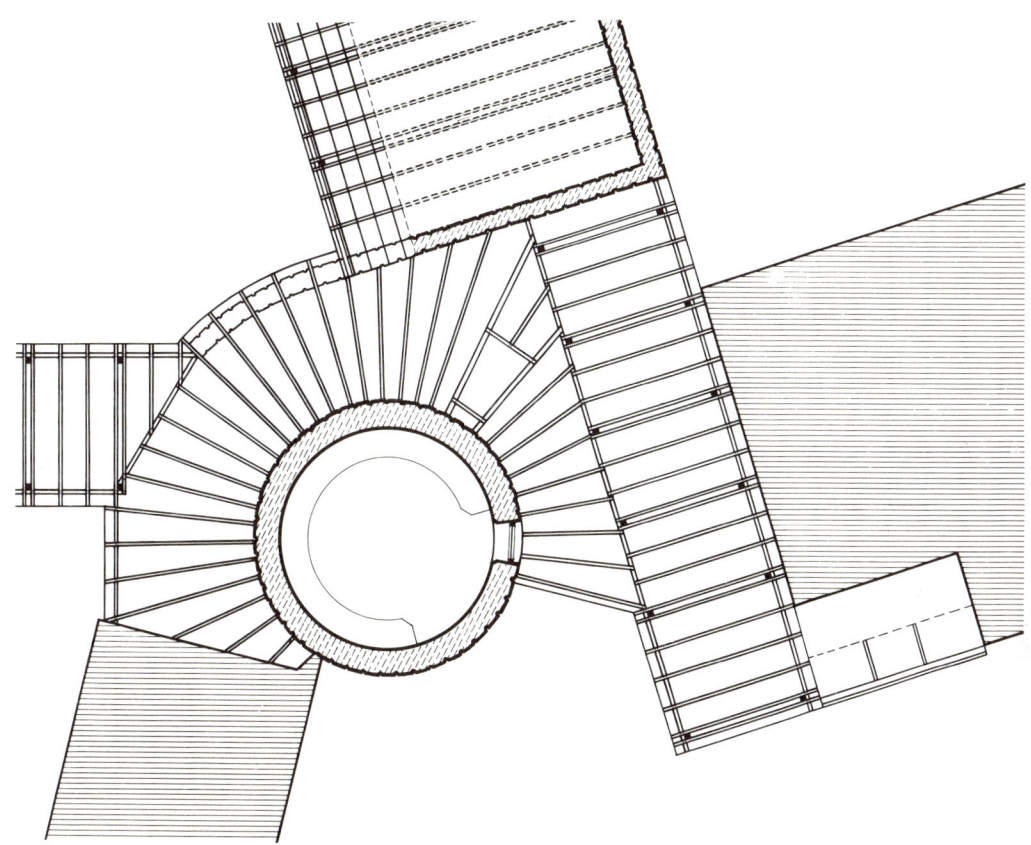

4, the gym which has been built up against the old stone wall of the original kitchen garden

Plan of tuckshop. Scale 1/12in. = 1ft.

Section through gym. Scale 1/10 = 1ft.

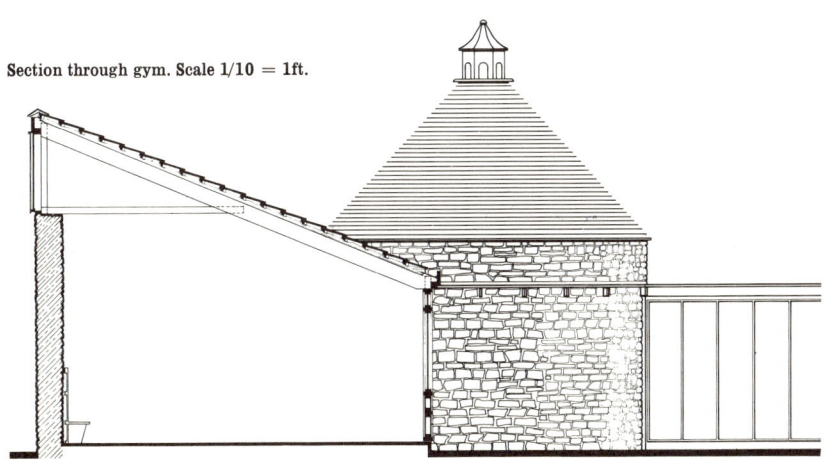

DOVECOT, BICESTER, OXFORDSHIRE

Architect: Albert E. Smith, Oxfordshire County Architect

Client: Oxfordshire County Council

Site: The dovecot is part of Old Palace Yard, a one-and-a-half acre site in the centre of Bicester which includes an old house, now converted into four flats. The site, which is dotted with a large number of mature trees and surrounded by a stone wall, was acquired by Oxfordshire County Council from Bicester Urban District Council and was developed with an old people's home, a branch library, a health clinic, a pair of nurses' houses, a police inspector's house, as well as 20 bungalows and six semi-detached houses for the urban district council.

History: On the site stood a monastery which almost certainly provided the materials for a house built shortly after the dissolution of the monasteries. The foundations of this monastery were exposed during the construction of the old people's home. The dovecot may have been built at the same time as the house and its vast stables, which stood in the enclosed yard within living memory.

Character: A small building, square on plan, with walls of random rubble and a pyramidal roof of tiles. The upper parts of the walls are punctured on three sides with a random pattern of small square openings which formed the original dove nests. On the fourth side there are doors at ground and first floor level. The latter used to be reached by a steep flight of timber steps. Internally the building has an upper room—the original dovecot—and a lower room for storage.

Work done: The intention was to convert the upper floor into a meeting room and to preserve the building as far as possible in its original state. That is why no windows were inserted and why, instead, a number of the dove nests were extended through the wall and fitted with coloured glass blocks or hit-and-miss ventilators. The roof structure and covering were renewed and properly insulated with glass-wool and, to provide more daylight, a perspex flèche was fitted on its apex. The underside of the roof was lined with timber boarding. The floor was renewed with 9in. by 2in. joists, glass-wool insulation, ½in. plywood and a cork tile finish. Built-in seating was provided. Two new door frames and mahogany framed doors were fitted in the existing openings, and a new reinforced concrete staircase was cantilevered from the walls of the dovecot. Brick paviours were laid around the foot of the building.

Accommodation: Ground floor—store
First floor—meeting room

Date of completion: 1967

Cost: £1700

Rate: £4·25 per sq. ft.

1, the dovecot with the new reinforced concrete staircase leading to the upper floor which has been converted into a meeting room. The random pattern of dove nests has been preserved by extending the nests through the wall and filling them with coloured glass blocks or hit-and-miss ventilators. The perspex flèche on the apex of the pyramidal roof replaces the original glover and provides the interior with additional light

2, another view of the dovecot shown in relation to some of the council housing which now occupies the site of Old Palace Yard

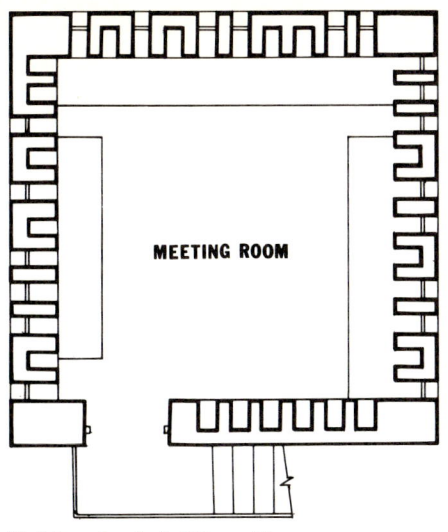

First floor plan. Scale 1/8in. = 1ft.

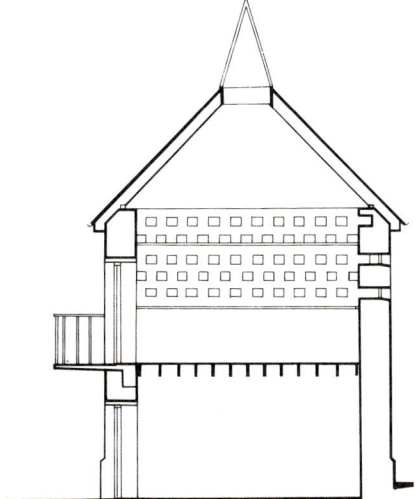

Section. Scale 1/16in. = 1ft.

3, the meeting hall was provided with built-in seating, a patterned floor of vinyl tiles and a timber-boarded ceiling

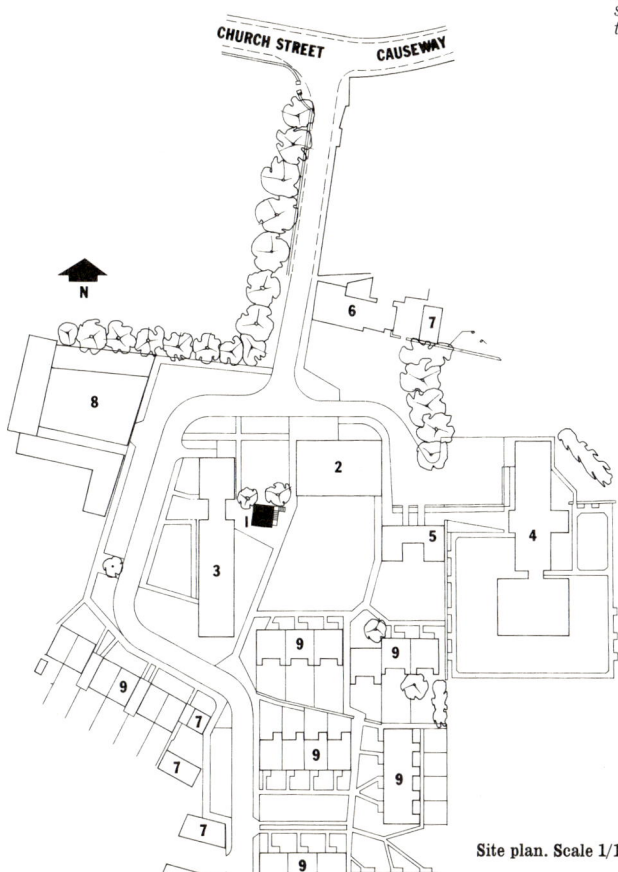

Site plan. Scale 1/160in. = 1ft.

key

1, meeting room (formerly dovecot)
2, library
3, clinic
4, old people's home
5, nurses' houses
6, existing building converted to staff flats
7, garage
8, existing stables (future church hall)
9, council housing

Schools

In England a building type which presents no problem when it comes to finding a new use for it is the Victorian village school. The schoolroom will provide a living room of ample dimensions, and the smaller rooms (the head teacher's quarters, usually an integral part of the same building) can be converted to bedrooms and utilities. The result is a house with a volume well in excess of what the client could normally afford in building a new house and, one need hardly add, with a good deal more character. A good example is the school at Haynes in Bedfordshire, illustrated in this chapter. A building of considerable charm, perhaps designed by a talented pupil of Butterfield, it had reached a serious state of dilapidation which would almost certainly have led to its demolition if the present owners had not seen its potential as a spacious family house. Prospective buyers, however, should be warned that many nineteenth-century schools were built on land which was given privately and with the provision that the site reverted to the original owners or their descendants if the school closed. This problem over reversionary rights, which existed in the case of the school at Haynes, can be resolved by finding an insurance company to cover the risk.

When a school is very small and consists only of a schoolroom, like the example at Rampton, an extension will have to be built to provide bedrooms and bathrooms. Like Warren Platner at Princeton (page 85), Keith Garbett makes no concessions to the old building with his flat roof, shiplap boarding and general character of a caravan perched in the back garden. No doubt the fact that the extension is invisible from the road had something to do with so uncompromising a solution, but it is carried out with as much conviction as the alterations to the back elevation of the old building are carried out with sympathy. At Hunton Bridge, a much larger school hall which already had a narrow back extension has been converted into a house and office without any new building or external alterations and with the minimum of internal work. To retain the existing spaces and to save money, the architect-owner was prepared to make sacrifices which most clients would not even consider. Thus the master bedroom is on an existing gallery overlooking the double-height living room, and another bedroom is under the gallery, screened only by bookcases, cupboards and a curtain.

The Board Schools, which were built in towns after the
1870 Education Act, present a different problem. The move
to the suburbs is bound to lead to the closure of this type
of school. Often quite large, with spacious classrooms and
plenty of room to expand, they should be retained as schools
where their geographical situation still makes them viable.
Northamptonshire County Council have shown the way to
prevent the demolition of a school at Wellingborough by
converting it into a youth club and social centre, a use
which they feel may turn out to be socially productive.
The double-height hall makes an admirable space for dances
even if the extreme length of the plan creates difficulties of
supervision for the leader. Some of the spaces are used for
hobbies and semi-educational activities so that the new use
is well suited not only to the form but to the spirit of the
old building.

BOARD SCHOOL, WELLINGBOROUGH, NORTHAMPTONSHIRE

Architect: John Goff, County Architect

Client: Northamptonshire County Council

Site: An urban site on Rock Street in a somewhat run-down part of Wellingborough, the kind of district most in need of a social centre, not only for the young, but also for the old.

History: Built in 1873 (when the town's population was under 10,000) as the Broad Green Girls School, it must have been one of the first Board Schools built outside London under the 1870 Education Act. It became a girls' and infants' mixed school probably around 1900, a mixed junior school after the last war, and finally closed in the mid-sixties.

Character: A single-storey building on a characteristic E plan, but later additions obscured this. The walls are of brick and covered with a tiled pitched roof. Windows and doorways are of neo-Gothic design with stone surrounds. Inside, the timber roof trusses are exposed, and the walls were originally plastered and painted.

Work done: The original E plan was freed from additions and, because this made the outside of the building look patchy, it was painted olive green. Internally the roof trusses and cross walls supporting purlins have been retained and expressed. As the number of cross walls was reduced—to form the hall, for instance—the purlins had to be strengthened with steel angles, and in one case a truss was moved to a new position to replace a cross wall. The buttressing effect of the E plan encouraged the architects to remove the tie bars from the trusses. This enabled them to insert a new upper floor (RSJs and timber joists) over half the building, supported on the external walls (whose foundations were found to be adequate) and on new internal loadbearing partitions. In addition to the open staircase an escape staircase, of timber construction but fully enclosed, was required by the fire officer. The structural work also included a shallow flat-roofed addition, between two legs of the E plan, to form an entrance and an extension to the somewhat narrow hall.

The original combined drainage system was retained and augmented, but a completely new oil-fired central heating system using radiators and fan convectors (built into brick walls) had to be installed. Ventilation is by extract fans controlled from central points. To retain the character of the building externally those windows which had to be blocked up have been left with their stone surrounds and a 4½in. recess. The original pair of entrance doors on the street side has been made into windows.

1, part of the street facade with the original pair of entrance doors made into windows

2, the youth club comes alive at night when the two-storey high hall provides an excellent space for dances and other social activities. A gallery has been inserted at the far end to provide a club room

3, on one side the hall was extended at ground floor level to provide circulation space, and the brick wall pierced with arches

Floor finishes are semi-sprung hardwood strips in the hall, concrete or epoxy resin in the workshops, vinyl asbestos tiles elsewhere on the ground floor and flexible vinyl tiles on ¾in. chipboard on the first floor, with nylon carpeting in selected areas on both floors. Suspended ceilings are timber in the ground floor reception area, plastic-faced plasterboard in the lavatories and changing room areas, and fibre tiles elsewhere.

Accommodation: Ground floor—reception, double-height hall with movable stage, activity room, double-height practical workshop, offices for group leader and district organiser, cloakrooms, lavatories, changing rooms with showers First floor—club room which forms a gallery to hall, library/committee room, coffee bar with kitchen and servery, art and craft room, dark room

Date of completion: 1970

Cost: £43 500, including furniture and equipment but excluding external work

Rate: £4·65 per sq. ft. (£50·05 per m²)

4, the first floor club room which forms a gallery to the hall

key
1, reception
2, boys' cloakroom
3, music/recording
4, store
5, youth leader
6, district organiser
7, wc
8, activity room
9, machine shop
10, practical workshop
11, chair store
12, hall/general recreation
13, movable stage
14, stage unit store
15, stage equipment
16, girls' cloakroom
17, boys' wcs
18, girls' wcs
19, powder room
20, boys' changing room and showers
21, girls' changing room and showers
22, upper part of hall
23, clubroom
24, library/committee room
25, coffee bar
26, servery
27, kitchen
28, art and craft
29, dark room
30, balcony
31, upper part of workshop

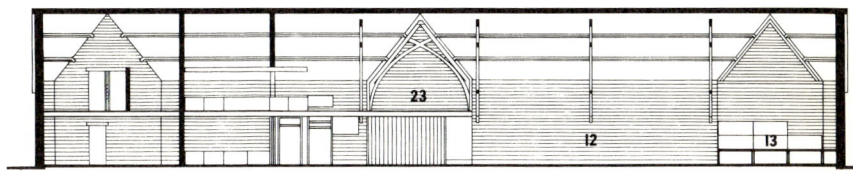

Section

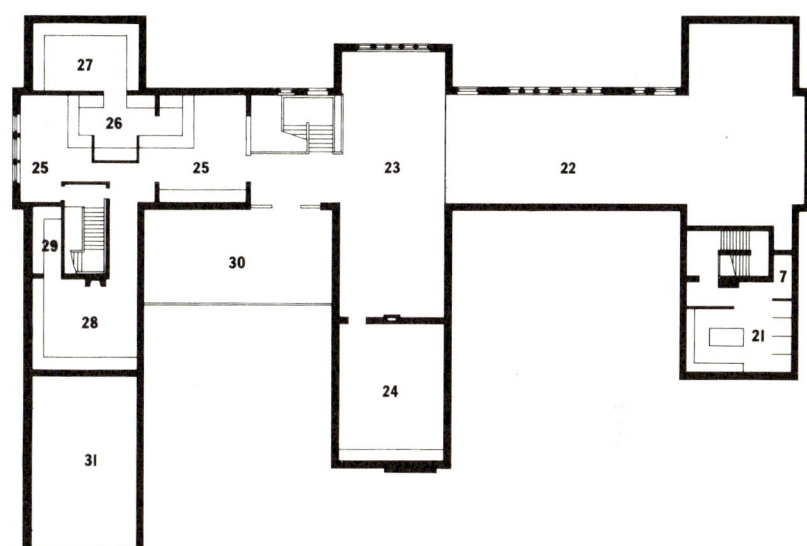

First floor plan. Scale 1/32in. = 1ft.

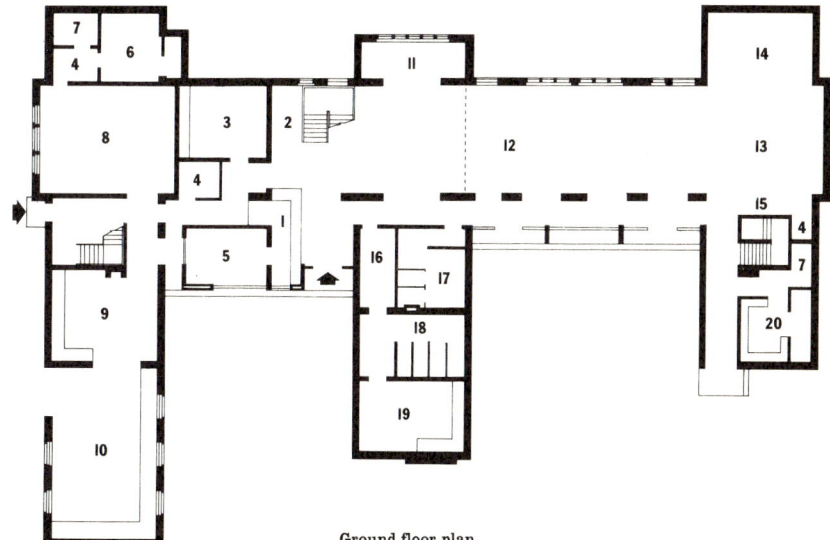

Ground floor plan

VILLAGE SCHOOL, HAYNES, BEDFORDSHIRE

Architect: Dawber, Fox & Robinson

Client: Mr. and Mrs. Christopher Robinson

Site: On the edge of the sprawling village of Haynes, one-and-a-half miles from the centre, a fact which contributed towards the unsuitability of the building for continued use as a school. The church and vicarage and the local mansion, Hawnes, are nearby to the north. The school stands in a garden with a large pond.

History: In 1849, Thomas Cubitt's firm began work on the south and east fronts of Hawnes, and in 1850 Lord John Thynne, whose family were the owners of the mansion, restored St. Mary's Church and built the school to the designs of Henry Woodyer, who may have been a pupil of Butterfield. The school was used until 1932, when it was closed down following an inspector's report on the unsatisfactory heating and sanitation. When the present owners (an architect and an interior designer, both partners in Dawber, Fox and Robinson) bought it in 1968, it was in a seriously dilapidated state, even though for some years the church verger had been living in the schoolmaster's cottage, which is an integral part of the school, and had been using the schoolroom as a store and workshop.

Character: A two-storey brick building of irregular shape with sharply pitched tiled roofs and gable ends. The schoolroom is double height with a huge south-west facing window crowned by a pointed relieving arch; the infants' classroom was also double height originally. The roof structure is exposed inside, trusses in the old schoolroom being shaped into pointed arches and braced longitudinally with a charmingly decorative result. Other neo-Gothic features include pointed arches to doorways and a rose window in one of the gables.

Work done: Major repairs had to be carried out to the roof and chimneys including the replacement of gutters and downpipes; new soil drainage, with connection to the main sewer, had to be laid; the damage done by rising damp in the cottage necessitated new plaster in the lower part of the walls; and a damp-proof course was applied throughout by a pressure-injected silicone liquid.

The double-height schoolroom, with its open roof truss, has become the living room, with a new gallery that serves as a studio area and also provides an essential link between the first floor of the cottage and the main bedroom, which has been formed by inserting an upper floor into the former double-height infants' classroom.

Other structural work included the demolition of lavatories and outbuildings; the construction of an entrance

1, the school from the south with Hawnes in the background

2, another view from the south with the pond in the foreground

3, the porch and front door to the former cottage continues to fulfil the same function

4, from the garden on the west side, with the former cottage on the left and the projecting gable-ended schoolroom in the centre

drive and double garage with material from the demolition; and the construction of a small bedroom over the cottage kitchen within a tile-hung gable re-using old tiles.

There is a new electrical installation and an oil-fired central heating system. Finishes include a pine-boarded kitchen, white-painted brickwork in the living room and sitting room (where worm-infested panelling had to be taken out) and wax polish on cleaned-down Columbian pine beams, doors, windows and skirtings. The sanding and sealing of the original schoolroom floor was done by the owners as was all the garden work, including removing all the rubbish and cleaning the pond.

Accommodation: Ground floor—hall, living room, dining room, kitchen, study, sitting room, playroom and a small bathroom with a shower
First floor—four bedrooms, bathroom and living room gallery, used as a studio

Date of completion: 1970

Cost: £9500, excluding cost of purchasing the building

Rate: £3·21 per sq. ft. (£34·55 per m²)

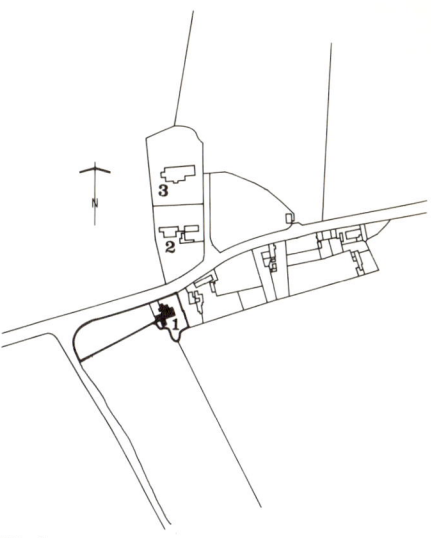

Site plan

key
1, school
2, vicarage
3, St. Mary's Church

5, the main bedroom formed out of the upper part of the infants' classroom
6, 7, the living room formed out of the old schoolroom. The gallery provides an essential link between the main bedroom and the first floor of the cottage

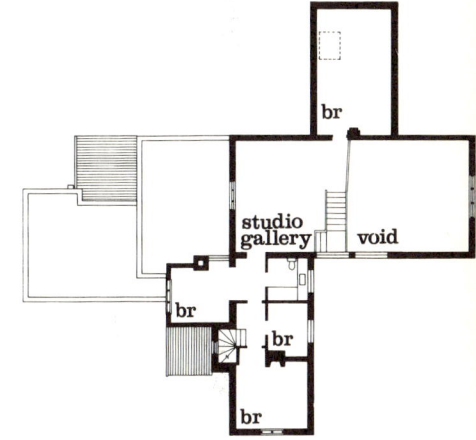

First floor plan. Scale 1/32in. = 1ft.

Ground floor plan.

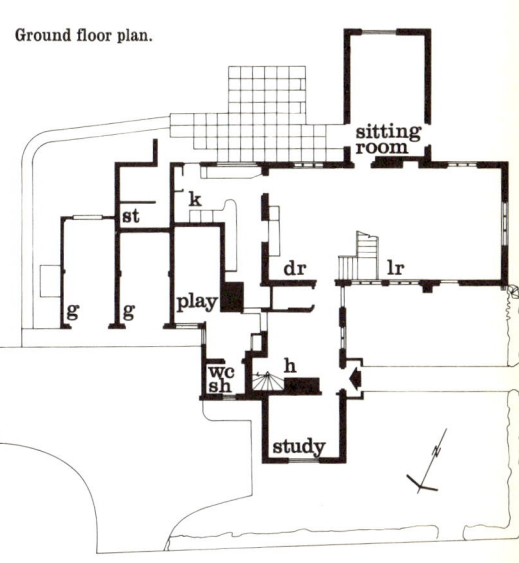

111

ST. PAUL'S HALL, HUNTON BRIDGE, HERTFORDSHIRE

Architect: Holscher & Tye

Client: Alan Tye

Site: A detached building fronting on to the main street of the village of Hunton Bridge, next to the King's Head public house and near the old St. Paul's School, which was the chief user of the hall.

History: The larger part was built around 1870 and a flat-roofed extension to the west added at a later date when the hall became too small. The building combined the functions of a school and village hall. When St. Paul's school moved to new buildings in the mid-1960's, the hall fell into disuse. Alan Tye, who wanted to buy and convert the hall into a house and office for himself, took some time to persuade the planning authority that such a change of use was practicable. In the meantime the condition of the building deteriorated and its market price went down to £4500, Tye finally getting it for £4000 in 1968. It would have been simpler and more profitable to have demolished it and built seven terrace houses. But by then Tye had been granted permission by the planning authority, who imposed the condition that the office space should not exceed 3000 sq. ft., a limit which in retrospect seems absurdly high in the context and which greatly increased the value of the property. Tye's office is in fact little more than 500 sq. ft.

Character: A two-storey hipped building with a tiled roof and brick walls painted white. The flat-roofed extension of the same height has a small parapet capped with tiles. Both parts have a cornice of brick dentils and three-light windows with flat arches giving the building a wholly domestic look. In fact what looks like a two-storey house from the outside is a double-height hall inside, the original hall being divided from the extension by rolling shutters that provided maximum flexibility in its many uses.

Work done: The conversion, which was carried out on a minimum budget, retained the original spaces and consisted mainly of painting. The match-boarding on the walls and ceilings as well as the rolling shutters between living room and office were kept and repaired. Part of the old stage was re-used as a base for a large mattress on the sleeping gallery, while a child's bedroom over the play area was given a simple trap door and ladder access. Another child's bedroom and a dressing room were formed under the sleeping gallery out of bookcases, hanging cupboards and a curtain. There is an efficient (and expensive to run) off-peak electric heating installation consisting of ducted warm air circulated by fan. The only lavish touch is the bathroom—a timberboarded ceiling, a cork

1, What looks like a two-storey building from the street is in fact two two-storey high halls divided by rolling shutters

3, the living room formed out of the longer of the two halls, with the old gallery used as a sleeping area

2, the studio seen from the living room, with the rolling shutters open

floor, ceramic wall tiles to hide the plumbing, translucent sheets of perspex to hide the ugly existing windows, and fittings by Adamsez for whom Tye and his partner Holscher are design consultants. When the client acquired the building, there was only a tiny piece of land at the back, but he has since been able to buy an adjoining plot of land which provides a small garden.

Accommodation: Basement—wine cellar Ground floor—office/studio, dining room, living room, bedroom and dressing room with sleeping gallery over, utility room, kitchen, play area with bedroom over, reached by trap door

Date of completion: 1970

Cost: £2000 for conversion

Rate: £0·95 per sq. ft. (£10·23 per m²)

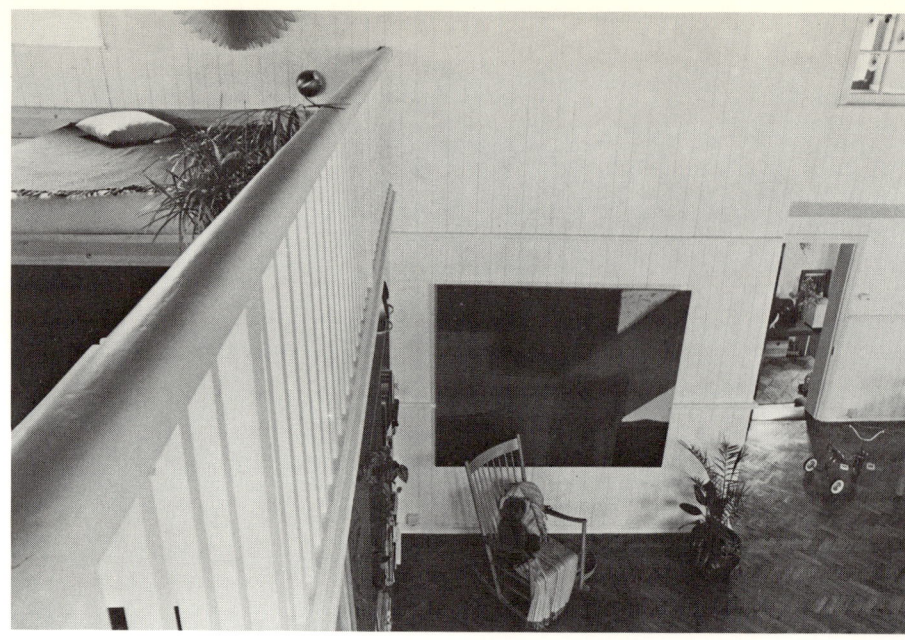

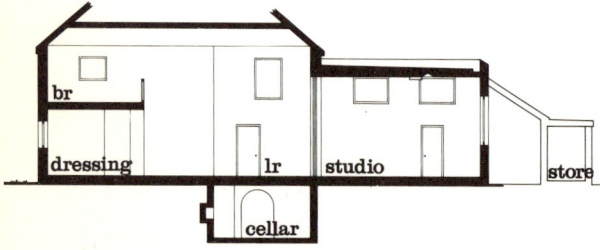

Section. Scale 1/24in. = 1ft.

4, looking down to the living room from the sleeping gallery

5, the sleeping gallery

6, the kitchen seen from the play area

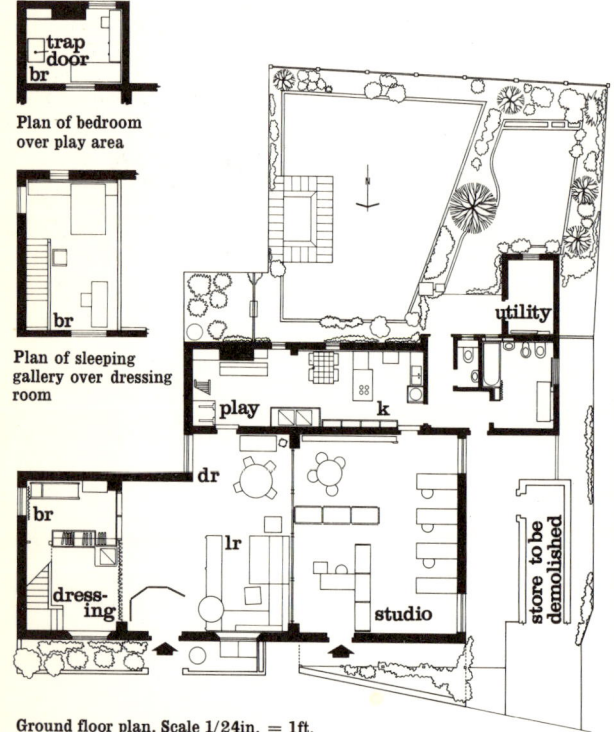

Ground floor plan. Scale 1/24in. = 1ft.

114

VILLAGE SCHOOLROOM, RAMPTON, CAMBRIDGESHIRE

Architect: Keith Garbett

Client: Mr. and Mrs. A. M. Boyce

Site: A quarter acre site at the Cottenham end of Rampton, opposite the church on the High Street.

History: This building, a schoolroom, was opened as a National School in 1845, and closed down in 1964. It lay empty until the present conversion was started in 1971.

Character: The schoolroom was a simple double-height hall, in local brick, with a steep slate roof, an entrance porch on one end and a brick barrel vaulted store (thought once to have contained the local jail pre-dating the school) at the other. The windows were large and originally in diamond panes, and there was a small belfry over the porch. The site was fronted on the street by iron railings and a small tarmac playground, with lavatory stalls and an air-raid shelter at the back. The rest of the site, which contained a chestnut and other smaller trees, was overgrown.

Work done: The main factors governing the proposed work were a limited budget and a requirement by the client, who is an industrial designer and skilled joiner, that he collaborate on the interior design and execute many of the interior finishings. In converting the building to residential use, it was decided to preserve as far as possible the original appearance, because of its character, but at the same time to exploit the internal volume and shape and to provide additional accommodation in an extension.

The shape of the schoolroom and existing additions was retained and repaired with minimum change to the three exposed street sides (the porch became a larder and the jail the main entrance). The back elevation was considerably altered by the new extension and also by the introduction of a dormer window, with full glazing below (to light the new gallery and ground floor). The great care taken to preserve all trees controlled to some extent the dimensions of the extension.

The schoolroom itself was subdivided by a two-level gallery reached by means of a ladder-type stair, all in timber. A suspended boarded ceiling was added over part of the schoolroom. Externally the single-storey extension is in stained shiplap boarding over a timber frame. The interior is a mixture of timber boarding and plasterboard.

Heating of the schoolroom is by electric underfloor heating and a Pither stove, with the flue connected to the existing chimney. Provision in the extension has been made for an oil-fired boiler.

Accommodation: Schoolroom
ground floor—entrance, living area, dining and kitchen area with larder
lower gallery—bathroom and dressing area
upper gallery—sleeping area
Extension—garden room, two double bedrooms, garden courtyard, bathroom and large garage/workshop/studio

Date of completion: April 1972

Cost: Contractor's final account figure, £5200
Client's expenditure, materials (no labour) £740, direct subcontractors £660, equipment £250, furnishings, etc., approximately £500

1, the schoolroom from the street side circa 1910

2, the schoolroom today with the new extension on the left. The appearance of the old building on the street side has not been altered. The view shows the old store, thought once to have been the local gaol, converted into the main entrance

115

3, the garden facade was considerably altered to allow for the new extension and also by the introduction of a dormer window with full glazing below. The extension, with its flat roof, shiplap boarding and character of a caravan perched in the back garden, makes no concession to the old building

4, the schoolroom subdivided by a two-level gallery reached by means of a ladder-type stair

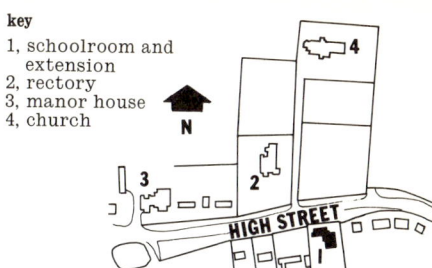

key
1, schoolroom and extension
2, rectory
3, manor house
4, church

Site plan. Scale 1 in 5000

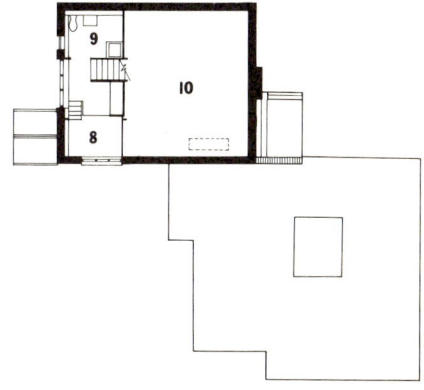

First floor plan. Scale 1/24in. = 1ft.

5, the kitchen and dining area under the staircase and gallery. In the background on the left is the new opening which connects the schoolroom with the new extension

6, view from the schoolroom looking into the entrance hall (left) and through the opening into the new extension (right)

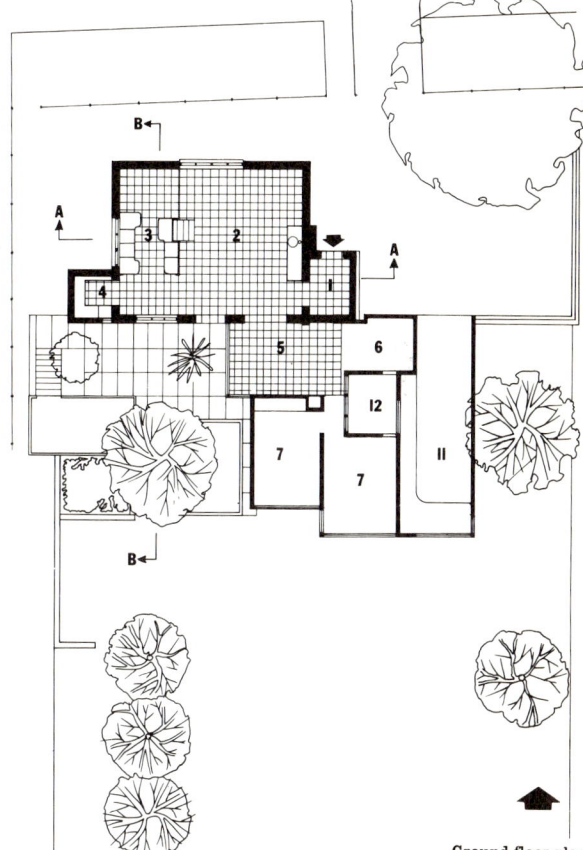

key
1, entrance hall (schoolroom)
2, living room (schoolroom)
3, kitchen-dining room (schoolroom)
4, larder (schoolroom)
5, garden room (extension)
6, bathroom and wc (extension)
7, bedroom (extension)
8, bedroom (schoolroom)
9, shower and wc (schoolroom)
10, void over living room (schoolroom)
11, garage (extension)
12, walled garden

Ground floor plan

Section AA. Scale 1/24in. = 1ft.

Section BB. Scale 1/24in. = 1ft.

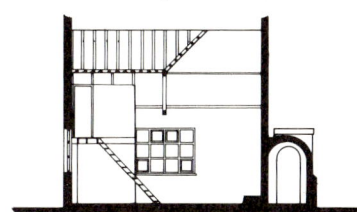

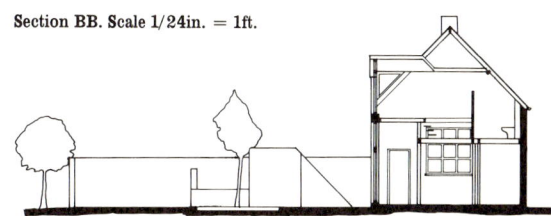

117

Corn exchanges

With corn exchanges one leaves the functional tradition and the vernacular in architecture and returns to the monument. This is particularly true of the corn exchange at Bishop's Stortford with its island site, cruciform plan and temple fronts on each of the four elevations. Its value as a focal point at the intersection of the *cardo* and *decumanus* of the town is immeasurable, and its preservation, even at the cost of having to accommodate an unsuitable new use, marks the triumph of the local will over the misguided decisions of the local authority.

Whether the monumental qualities of a corn exchange survive intact must depend ultimately on the relationship of the corn exchange with the surrounding buildings. Britain's 1967 Civic Amenities Act recognised the collective value of buildings and demanded of local authorities the designation of conservation areas. Corn exchanges tend to be in central areas which have often been so designated, and it is unlikely, for instance, that the pre-eminence of the corn exchange facade in the Tuesday market at King's Lynn for all its vulgar swagger will ever be challenged. Much the same is true of Sudbury, where a similar facade now provides entry to a branch library whose popularity rose by sixty per cent within six months of its occupying the old building.

Corn exchanges survive in many country towns, often crying out for new uses. Buildings with large halls like these are scarce and therefore valuable. In the nineteenth century, country towns often had several of them. Canterbury, for instance, had a theatre, a guildhall, a corn exchange and a philosophical and literary institution (with a lecture room holding two hundred), none of which has survived in use. Ely only recently allowed its corn exchange to be demolished to make room for a shopping development and found itself in need of a hall until the conversion of the maltings provided one. Even a university town like Cambridge does not have a satisfactory concert hall, and it is to the credit of the former city architect that he commissioned Arup Associates to examine the feasibility of converting the corn exchange which had in the past been used for concerts. At Ipswich the corn exchange is now being converted into a multi-purpose hall. Saffron Walden would have lost a vital part of its identity if the corn exchange, now the most important building in Market Square, had been demolished

Essex County Council, who are the trustees for a fine Victorian reference library, intend to use it as part of the county library and make it a centre for Victorian studies. Banbury's corn exchange, which is one of the grandest in the country with its giant order of paired Corinthian columns, is to be preserved and incorporated in a central area development whose commercial bias is unlikely to enhance its setting. At present a public house and a flat for the publican, it is a classic example of misuse. Corn exchanges like churches are essentially great halls and any new use must recognise this basic fact. That is why of the examples illustrated one applauds the solution at Sudbury or Cambridge and accepts only as a last resort that of Bishop's Stortford, which is trying, in morphological language, to make a honeycomb out of a shell.

CORN EXCHANGE, SUDBURY, SUFFOLK

Architect: Jack Digby, West Suffolk County Architect

Client: West Suffolk County Council

Site: The corn exchange is situated in the centre of Sudbury, facing on to the market place. To the west runs Station Road, which gives access to the staff car park at the rear of the building.

History: Built in 1841 and designed by H. E. Kendal, it was falling into disrepair by the early 1960's and was in danger of being demolished to make way for a shopping centre. At a public inquiry in 1962 it was described as the most important building in the town, next to the three medieval churches. As a result of this inquiry, the county council put a preservation order on the façade and five years later bought it, together with a small plot of land behind, for use as a branch library to replace the town's old and inadequate one.

Character: The corn exchange is a splendid early Victorian neo-classical stucco building. The facade is colonnaded with four giant Tuscan columns supporting a pronounced pediment and crowned with a group of resting corn-reapers sculpted in Coade stone by F. L. Coates of Lambeth. The central entrance arch is flanked by full-height windows with intricate glazing patterns. The interior originally consisted of an aisled hall with tall cast-iron columns supporting a continuous clerestorey over the central aisle. Cast-iron roof lights provided daylight and the south end was dominated by a huge, highly decorative arched window.

Work done: A new mezzanine floor has been inserted over both aisles, and 'floated' on a light steel structure so as to interfere as little as possible with the character and spatial proportions of the building. Two free-standing open staircases lead up to this floor. The steelwork supports the bookstacks which are kept clear of all walls, floors and ceilings. The separation of new and old is emphasised by the indirect lighting of the side walls, and the bright floodlighting of the ceiling over the central aisle helps to stress the original form and height. Existing roof lights have been retained after shot blasting and reglazing. Adjustable spotlights have been provided for extra flexibility. Afrormosia is the predominant wood used for the joinery work. The mezzanine staircase balustrade is protected by plate glass panels and the boarded soffit has been treated with a white wood preservative.

1, Colonnaded with four giant Tuscan columns supporting a broken cornice, the facade is a characterful expression of Victorian prosperity

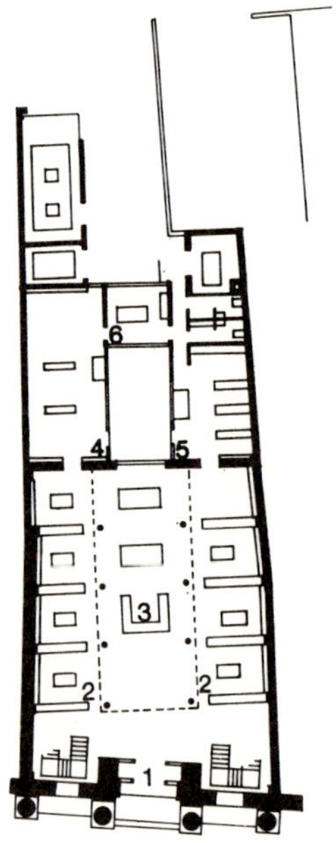

ground floor plan section
key
1 entrance
2 landing
3 counter
4 children
5 workroom
6 librarian
7 reference

Walls and ceilings are painted off-white and the nylon carpet is grey.

The facade was restored, the stucco overhauled and renewed as necessary, and the crude entrance doors replaced by a new aluminium-framed glazed lobby.

The existing outbuildings at the rear were demolished to make way for the new children's library and offices which are planned round a small courtyard. The large south window has been extended down to the ground to provide a view into the court from the interior of the library. The mobile library is also housed at the rear, together with staff parking. To open up the rear, it was necessary to demolish a house in Station Road that bridged the access drive.

The library is heated by a pressurised system with fan convectors in the circulating areas, and high-level radiators running full length below the clerestorey to eliminate downdraughts. The success and popularity of the conversion has been enormous: borrowers increased from 7000 to 11 000 within six months of opening.

Accommodation: Basement—store, connected to the control desk by a spiral staircase
Main hall—adult sections, control desk
Mezzanine—reference sections and exhibition space
Outbuildings—children's library, offices, mobile library and staff car parking

Date of completion: July 1968

Cost: Building contract, £35 282
Acquisition cost, £17 200 (The Ministry of Housing made a grant of £1500.)

Rate: £97 per m^2, not including area of basement. This rate compares favourably with the cost of providing a comparable new library.

2, Sudbury's High Street: the Corn Exchange in its setting

3, the interior is divided into a nave and two aisles. a mezzanine floor has been inserted over the aisles and entrance area

4, view of the counter from the mezzanine floor

CORN EXCHANGE, CAMBRIDGE (project)

Architect: Arup Associates

Client: Ian Purdy, Cambridge City Architect and Planning Officer

Site: In the centre of Cambridge, bounded by Corn Exchange Street to the east, Wheeler Street to the north and Parson's Court to the west. To the south is the New Museums building and on the other side of Corn Exchange Street the Lion Yard development (public buildings, shops, offices and car park), both of which are by Arup Associates. The corn exchange is a rectangle with the long axis running north-south and with the entrance at the north end in Wheeler Street. The proposals will allow it to benefit from the car park and pedestrian deck which will bridge Corn Exchange Street and lead directly to a new public entrance at the south end on the upper foyer level.

History: Built in 1874–75 to the designs of a local architect and engineer, R. R. Howe, the building replaced an earlier and smaller exchange on a neighbouring site. In addition to its main use as a corn exchange, it has provided the setting for many concerts, from the opening ceremony to the Celebrity Subscription Concerts in the 1920's, which numbered Fritz Kreisler among the performers. Recently the building has been used for pop concerts, exhibitions, wrestling, roller skating and badminton. The original study for its conversion was proposed in 1971 by the then city architect, Ian Purdy. The building has been listed by the Department of the Environment.

Character: The existing structure consists of yellow brick walls with piers supporting iron arches which support in turn a timber roof structure covered in slate. The long elevation on Corn Exchange Street has large window openings with round diaper-brick arches and two-light windows with rosettes above. The upper storey has three small round-headed windows to every one of the floor below. The elevation to Wheeler Street is more domestic, with a central gable over the entrance flanked by dormers and round-headed windows of simpler design.

Work proposed: The intention is to provide a concert hall seating 1500 but also to house as many other activities as possible provided these do not adversely affect the performance of music. Preliminary calculations indicate a first class acoustic for large orchestras, small groups and soloists, due to the combination of a long reverberation time (2·0 seconds at the average of 500 Hz to 1000 Hz to 3·3 seconds at 125 Hz) and short first reflections. The architects believe that not only Cambridge, but Britain as a whole, will gain a concert hall of international stature.

1, the long east facade on Corn Exchange Street. At the south end a new entrance will be formed at first-floor level which will link with the elevated pedestrian deck of the adjacent New Museums building and, by means of a bridge, with the Lion Yard development on the other side of the street

2, the interior showing the structure of iron arches supporting a glass roof

To provide the foyer space now lacking, the existing annex in Parson's Court will be replaced by an extension taking up the sites of both the old annex and Parson's Court. This will mean demolishing buildings west of Parson's Court to form a new cul-de-sac for servicing the building and for maintaining access to the existing examination halls. The new foyer space will link the north and south entrances and a side stage, built over the lower foyer, will allow direct delivery of scenery via a dock in the new cul-de-sac. This is why the main stage, pivoted to allow a rake and extendable by means of a lift (which can drop to form an orchestra pit or an extension to the auditorium), has been planned at the Wheeler Street end.

With recording companies in mind, only the back part of the auditorium will be raked. A deep gallery at the south end and four shallow galleries along the west side, accessible from the upper foyer level and constructed in a mixture of precast and in situ concrete, will make up the full complement of 1522 seats, 1230 of which will be on the main floor level below. The auditorium will have full air conditioning, whereas other areas that are only occupied for short periods at a very high density will have an extract plant with a high and low duty to deal with the large variation in ventilation needs.

In view of the many possible uses of the hall, an extensive lighting system, together with its control panels, is recommended. Lighting galleries along the side walks will be installed to provide a comprehensive range of options for such lighting. The lighting control system will be placed in a lighting box at high level on the west wall giving a clear view of the stage and auditorium. The installation will also include a sound system for amplification, effects and internal communications.

The new extension will be clad externally in yellow brick to match the existing bricks, and the exposed roof structure in the southern part of the foyer will be supported by timber trusses to conform in spirit with the construction of the main hall.

Accommodation: Lower foyer level—public entrance from Wheeler Street, box office, foyers, cloaks and lavatories, bars, auditorium, understage area, stores, plant room
Main floor level—public entrance from pedestrian deck, foyers, auditorium, stage, scene dock, artists' entrance
Upper foyer level—upper foyer, bar, galleries to auditorium, backstage accommodation

Date of completion: Scheme design was submitted to the city in April 1974. Placing of contract subject to decisions of new county authority.

Cost: Estimated to amount to about one-third of the cost of a new concert hall with similar seating capacity and comparable facilities.

key
1, Corn Exchange
2, New Museum's building
3, Lion Yard development
4, Fisher House
5, Guildhall
6, head post office
7, St. Andrews the Great
8, St. Mary the Great
9, St. Edward, King and Martyr
10, Arts Theatre
11, St. Bene't's

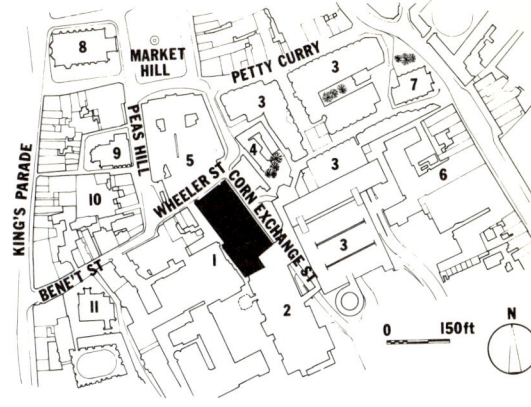

Site plan

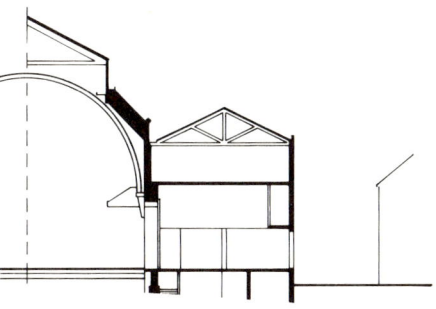

Section AA

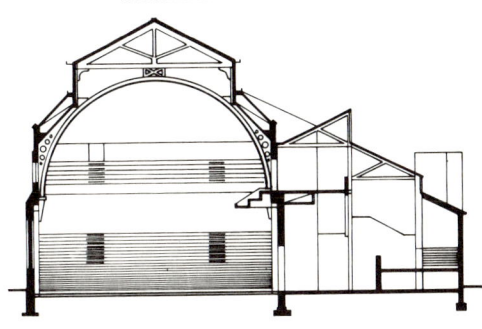

Section BB

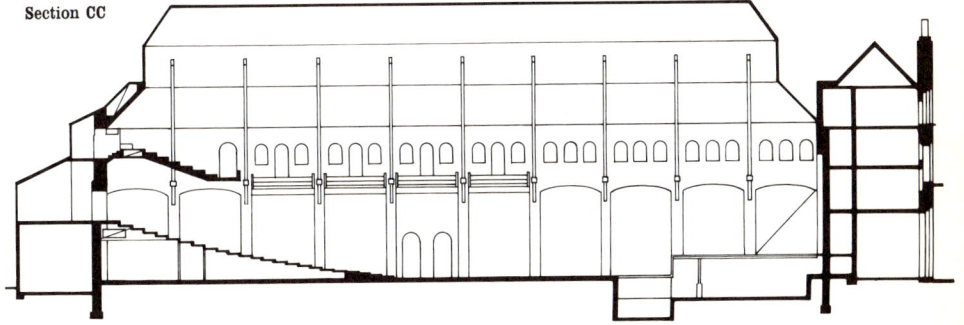

Section CC

3, a drawing of the interior during an orchestral concert. The conversion envisages only the back part of the auditorium raked and additional seating on shallow galleries along the west side

key
1, public entrance
2, box office
3, foyer
4, bar
5, cloakroom
6, lavatories
7, store
8, auditorium
9, lift
10, under stage
11, artists' entrance
12, plant
13, stage
14, scene dock
15, upper gallery
16, side galleries
17, backstage accommodation
18, cooling tower

Main floor level

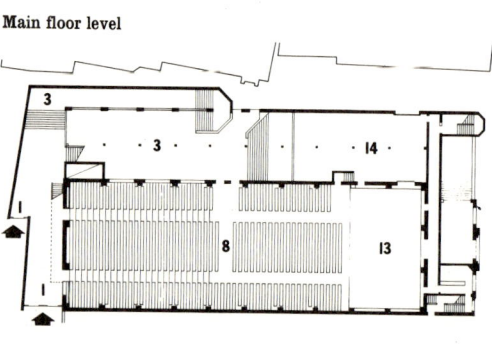

Upper foyer level

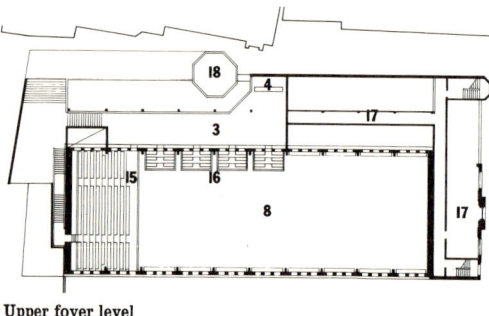

Lower floor level

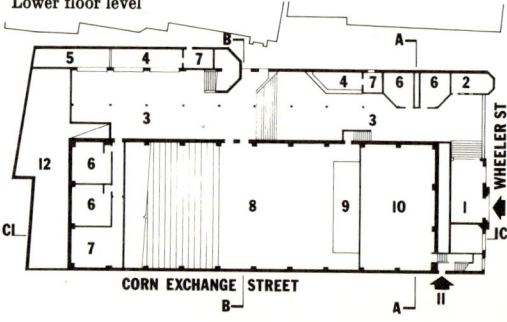

CORN EXCHANGE, BISHOP'S STORTFORD, HERTFORDSHIRE (project)

Architect: Ronald Cox Associates

Client: G. C. Harrison and M. S. Lucas

Site: In the market place in the centre of Bishop's Stortford, at the junction of the High Street, Wind Hill, North Street and Market Street. It closes the vista along North Street, for which it provides the natural focus. The site slopes sharply towards the river to the east.

History: The building was erected in 1828 to a design by Lewis Vulliamy. The ground floor was used as a corn exchange until the 1950's while the upper floors were used by the Conservative Club from 1883. Since 1959 when Hertfordshire County Council acquired it, it has been used as salerooms, a boxing arena and an exhibition space, but it was allowed to fall into disrepair. The building is included in the Statutory List of Buildings of Architectural and Historic Interest (Grade II), but this did not stop more than one proposal for demolition. Local interest prevented this and recommended that the building be put to community or cultural use. For financial reasons this proved impossible, so permission was finally granted for conversion to commercial and office use. Harrison and Lucas bought the building in March 1972

Character: The corn exchange is a focal point in Bishop's Stortford town centre. It dominates the surrounding buildings in the square but is in fact much smaller than its grand classical style might suggest in photographs, containing less than 6000 sq. ft. of floor area. Its main entrance, on the north side, consists of a columned portico surmounted by a tympanum with a clock and an allegorical sculpture. The fabric is brick faced with Roman cement. The original building included a semicircular exchange yard, one of the remarkable features of the building, reconciling it to the steeply sloping site. A pointed glazed roof erected over this yard in 1884 obliterated the view of the north portico. At the same time the removal of the lanterns at each corner of the ground floor and of the north axial entrance to the exchange yard and the remodelling of the interior destroyed the symmetry and much of the character of the design. In 1898, the single-storey portion to the south was demolished and replaced by a stucco-covered market building, which was later converted for use as a bank.

Work proposed: The design envisages the demolition of the glazed rotunda and, in the main building, the insertion of an additional office floor at second floor level, the conversion of the first floor to office use, and the division of the ground floor into three units for use by a building society, insurance agents and estate agents. The adjoining bank

1, a contemporary lithograph of the Corn Exchange. The view is of the north facade with its Ionic portico and shows the semicircular exchange yard before it was covered by a glazed roof

2, the same view taken in 1971 showing the exchange yard covered with a tall glazed roof which obscures the north portico. This will be removed in the alterations and an open terrace formed a little below the top of the surrounding wall

3, view from the south-east

unit was later also purchased by the client and is now being repaired and converted for use by the building society. The curved retaining wall to the north will be set back to allow for pavement widening and will provide an open terrace at first floor level which will form the approach to the main office entrance in the north portico. The terrace is approached from an open staircase on the west side and its level has been kept as low as possible to preserve views of the north portico.

The dangerous state of the building made it essential to start repairs in November 1972, before planning approval was obtained. It has been found necessary to rebuild the parapets, reslate the roof, and renew the leadwork. Little of the original Roman cement remained in a sound condition, and the building has been re-rendered in a compatible lime-cement mortar, which will be painted 'magnolia' on completion.

Bad subsoil conditions and the weakness of the building's foundations necessitated the removal of existing timber floors and cast-iron columns (which were not original) and their replacement by hollow tile floors on a reinforced concrete frame over piled foundations.

Date of completion: 1975

Cost: Approximately £100 000

Rate: £12 per sq. ft.

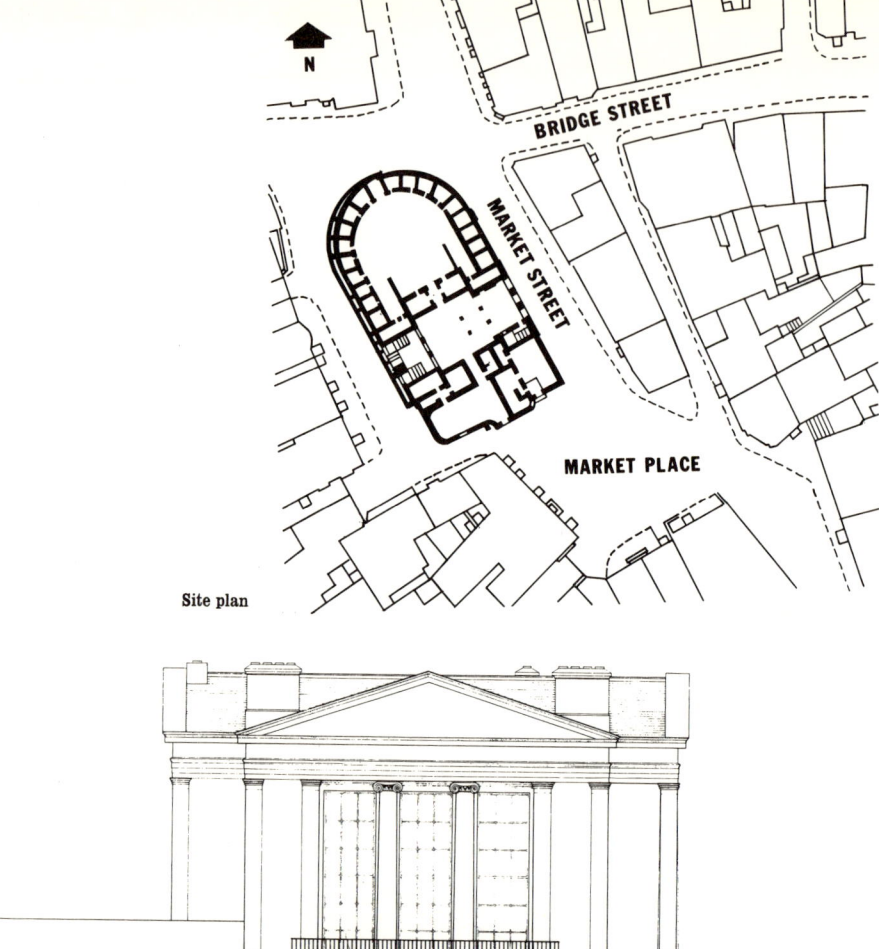

Site plan

4, east elevation (measured and drawn by R. W. Howard, R. A. Lee and G. H. Yandell, 1967. University of Cambridge, School of Architecture)

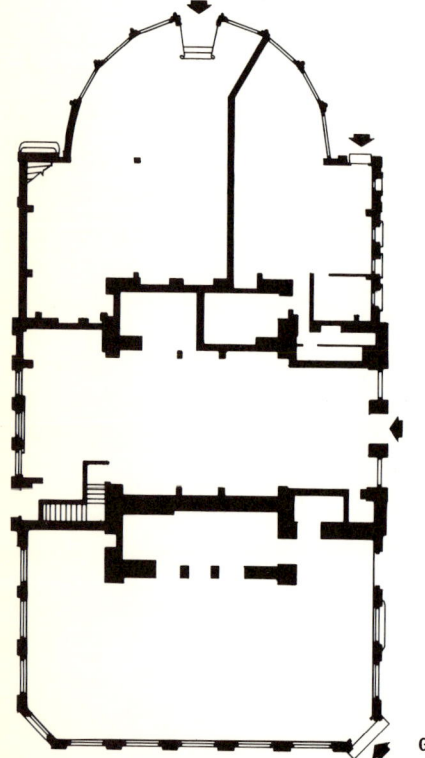

Ground floor plan

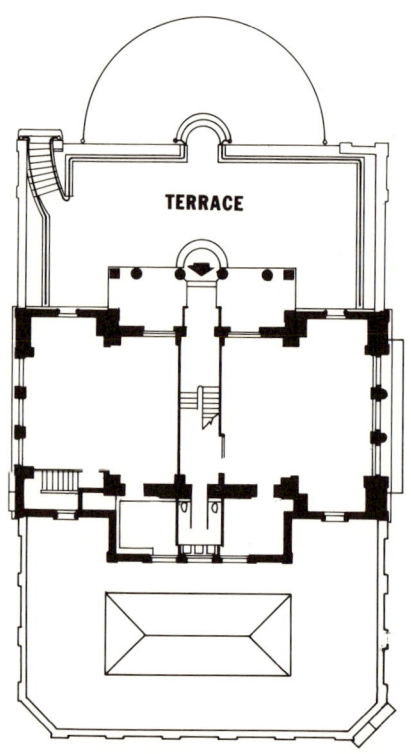

First floor plan

Barns and Granaries

Like churches and corn exchanges, barns are shells enclosing large single volumes, but the shell is an unadorned structure meeting the demands of function in a simple and direct manner. Because barns are intended for the storage of goods, they tend to have no windows, openings being limited to large doors at ground level and sometimes cantilevered structures housing hoisting machinery with loading doors at high level. Barns are associated in people's minds with the countryside and three of the examples in this chapter are indeed set in isolated rural surroundings. The remaining two examples, however—the barn at East Hendred and the granary at Blakeney—form part of a built-up street; and if the sheds of builders' yards and other light industry were to be included, the importance of these unassuming buildings in the context of the typical county town would require no further emphasis.

With the exception of the granary at Blakeney, all the barns illustrated are weatherboarded or shinglefaced structures, over a masonry base. Internally the exposed timber framing and roof structure have usually been retained, but with modifications imposed by the need for thermal insulation. In most cases the weatherboarding or roofing material had to be taken down and a layer of insulating material applied before being fixed back. Most often, as can be seen best at East Hendred, the smooth inner surface is painted white to emphasise and enhance the skeleton timber structure. At Great Barrington in Massachusetts stringent fire regulations resulted in smooth interior walls of gypsum board with only the roof trusses remaining exposed.

Great Barrington offers an example of a compact group of farm buildings where the domestic scale of the farmhouse stands side by side and in harmony with the more industrial scale of the barns and silos—a happy relationship which is found whenever the two follow the same functional principles. The conversion into a school with a curriculum based on dance, theatre and music has done nothing to disturb this relationship. On the contrary, the new boiler house, with its tall, free-standing chimney, continues an honest tradition. While the house has suffered little change in its conversion to office use, the two main barns have undergone transformations which reflect the forceful personality of the architect. One barn now houses an art gallery and studios, the other a theatre; both are now crested with strangely angular dormers and one, the theatre block, has been extended eccentrically by having a diagonal axis driven through its formerly sedate rectangular volume.

Less wilful but more memorable is Sverre Fehn's brilliant conversion at Hamar in Norway. Plenty of space and the need to allow the continuation of archaeological excavations that could be seen by visitors led to an ingenious solution based on ramps and bridges. There is complete separation between the new reinforced concrete internal structure and the existing external structure. Thus an old shell has been used to create within it a sequence of spaces which are unmistakably of today and could not have been conceived except with the aid of modern structural methods and materials. But the relationship is completely successful because the new work follows the same functional principles as the old.

The barns at East Hendred and Knebworth preserve their identity as barns, both inside and out. This is all the more remarkable at East Hendred, where conversion to a private house might so easily have resulted in a complete change of character. It did not because of the double-height living room with its exposed timber wall and roof structure and because of the careful window detailing which manages to conceal the wood frame behind the weatherboarding. The windows on the roadside, moreover, are small and random, so that in its village setting the barn appears almost unaltered.

The Knebworth barns offer an example of an almost ideal new use: restaurants for visitors to Knebworth House. The great seventeenth-century oak-framed buildings would seem to provide exactly the right character for the convivial occupation of eating in company. Yet there are two reservations. The fire officer will, as he has here, demand the subdivision of the space into compartments within which a fire can be contained; and barns are rarely in the central position that makes them suitable for public restaurants—which at Knebworth meant bodily moving one barn and dismantling and re-erecting the other. Even so, the cost suggests that there is nothing prohibitive in an exercise which is common enough in other countries, and Knebworth may indeed provide a valuable example for the National Trust or other bodies who have the problem of feeding large numbers of visitors in places where the construction of new buildings might be undesirable.

Finally the two-storey granary at Blakeney must be mentioned as the odd man out. Built of brick externally and of long rectangular shape stepping down towards the sea front, it lent itself to lateral subdivision and conversion into flats and shops. Its walls were dotted with small openings and its scale was always more domestic than industrial. Nevertheless the new timber detailing has a tough nautical character which has prevented the building from becoming overdomesticated.

FARM BUILDINGS, GREAT BARRINGTON, MASSACHUSETTS

Architect: Hardy, Holzman, Pfeiffer Associates

Client: Simon's Rock Girls School

Site: A farmhouse, barns, silos and outbuildings on an open site near the junction of Hurlburt and Alford roads, with vehicular access from Hurlburt Road. There are trees to the south and a brook running east-west to the north. The ground slopes gently down to the brook and there are good views to the west.

History: The house and barn date from the eighteenth century, accretions and other outbuildings from the nineteenth and twentieth centuries. The theatre block was a dairy barn with a hay loft, horses were stabled in the art block, and pigs were kept in one of the other buildings.

Character: A group of farm buildings typical of New England, dominated by a tall central two-storey barn with a hipped roof (made of Jamesway trusses, a patented system of construction for farm buildings) and two cylindrical silo adjuncts at the west end. The walls are generally red cedar shingles or weatherboarding and the roof is red cedar shingles. The structure is timber and is exposed to view internally.

Work done: The purpose was to create an environment with dynamic qualities for a school whose teaching is based on dance, theatre and music. The farmhouse became the administration building with the minimum of alterations. Two outbuildings were converted into music and recreation blocks by being subdivided into small classrooms. The main work consisted of converting the large barn into a theatre and the other main barn into studios and a gallery for art teaching.

The existing ground floor structure was mainly concrete slab and this was levelled to provide 7ft. 6in. to the underside of the existing beams. New concrete slabs were laid for the extensions to the theatre block and for the terrace, steps and floor of the new building for the mechanical plant, which has been neatly tucked into the fall of the ground north of the theatre block. The ground floors of the theatre block are finished in polished concrete, all other floors in English oak. Generally the existing upper floor structure in timber was retained, but a new timber structure to support the raked seating of the auditorium had to be provided, and the existing floor of the art block was trimmed and cut back to form a double-height space.

The new external walls of the extensions to the theatre block were constructed in timber framing with red cedar shingles to match existing ones and plywood sheets inside. The cavity was filled with granular insulation. Existing walls and ceilings were lined with gypsum board, and all new internal

1, view from the south-west showing the music teaching block (left) and the theatre block with its angular extension flanked by the two silos which now accommodate fire-escape staircases

2, looking down from the upper-level gallery in the art block. The tall structure on the left encloses a new staircase

3, the theatre looking towards the stage and the angular extension which provides an entrance for the performers

129

partitions were timber stud faced with gypsum board (⅝in., one hour fire rating). The new walls of the mechanical plant building were 12in. concrete. The new staircases (the two in the silos of the theatre block and the second one in each of the other buildings were required for fire escapes) were constructed conventionally in timber. Existing openings in walls were mainly repaired and glazed; some were closed. Elsewhere walls were trimmed to form new timber doors and windows.

All new roofs (new boiler house, extensions to theatre block, roof lights) are of timber construction covered in red cedar shingles. The existing roofs of the theatre and art blocks were trimmed and new roof lights formed. The very tall metal flue of the new boiler house was steadied by tie rods fixed to the existing buildings.

Accommodation: Theatre block
ground floor—entrance hall, lavatories/dressing rooms, shop, office
first floor—multi-purpose hall with stage and raked seating over storage space
Art block
ground floor—gallery (part double-height), studio
first floor—upper level gallery, studio
Music block—two floors of eight small classrooms (12–18 girls per classroom) for music teaching
Recreation block—two floors of eight rooms (11–16 girls per room) for recreational activities
Administration—re-use of existing farmhouse
Boiler house—new building

By 1975 the art block will be extended to the north and a new drama centre built, overhanging a pond formed out of the existing brook.

Date of completion: 1966

Cost: $126 862

Rate: $12 per sq. ft.

4, a closer view of the stage, behind which steps lead down to the performers' entrance

5, the studio on the upper level of the art block with one of the new skylights

key
1, administration
2, theatre
3, art
4, music
5, recreation
6, future art centre
7, future drama centre
8, pond
9, footbridge
10, brook

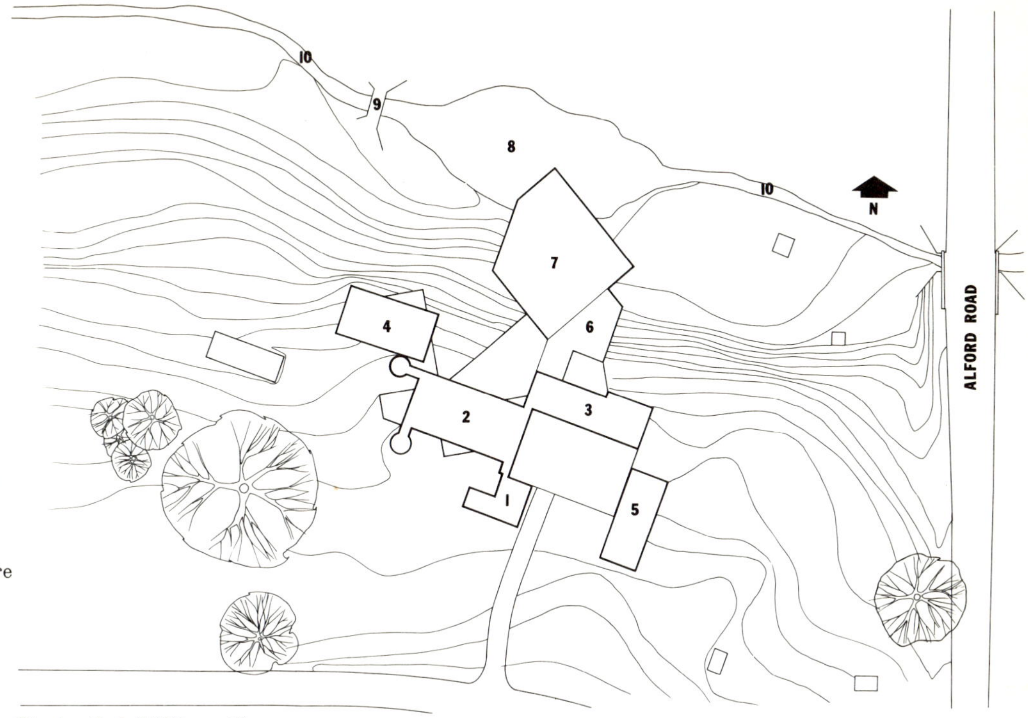

Site plan. Scale 1/112in. = 1ft.

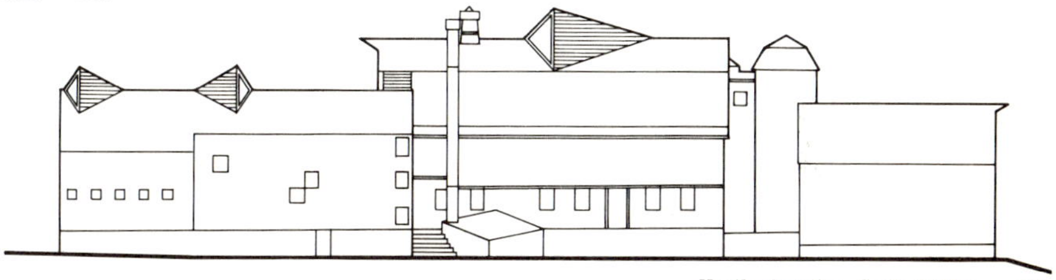

North elevation. Scale 1/48in. = 1ft.

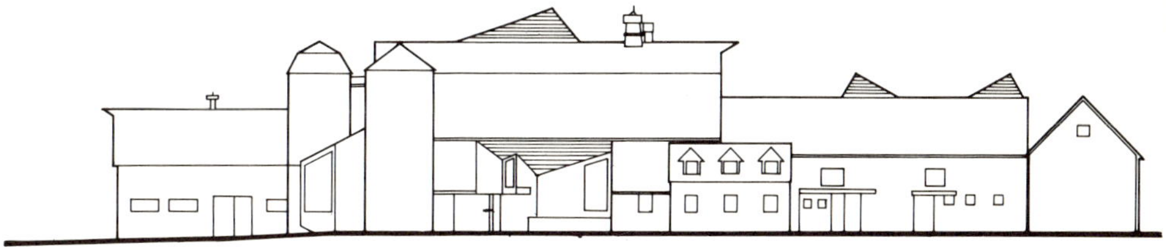

South elevation. Scale 1/48in. = 1ft.

key
1, entrance
2, performers' entrance
3, theatre workshop
4, dressing room
5, office
6, art gallery
7, studio
8, stage
9, raked seating over storage space
10, void over art gallery on ground floor
11, boiler house

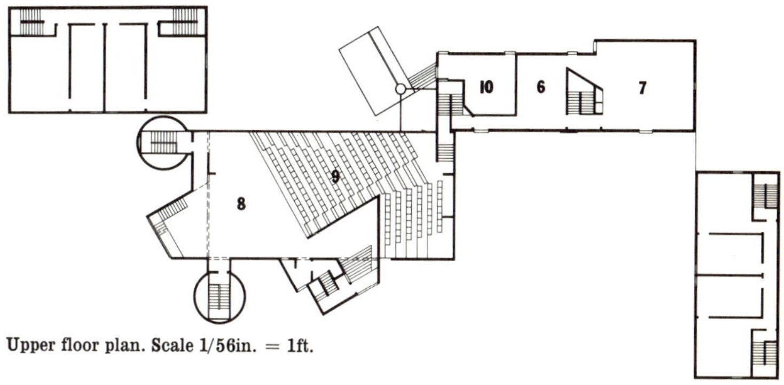

Upper floor plan. Scale 1/56in. = 1ft.

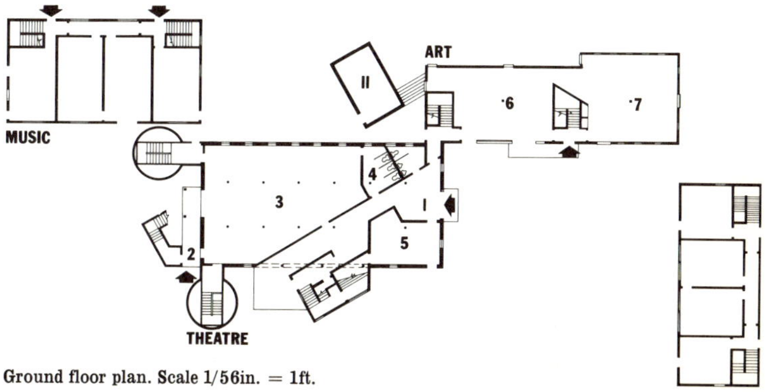

Ground floor plan. Scale 1/56in. = 1ft.

BARNS, HAMAR, NORWAY

Architect: Sverre Fehn

Client: Hedmarksmuseet og Domkirkeodden

Site: The U-shaped barn, surrounded by fields and trees, stands on ground sloping down to the west. In the courtyard formed by the three wings, excavations of earlier buildings provide archaeology in action as a living exhibit.

History: The agricultural barns are of medieval origin and formed part of the Bishop's Manor at Hamar. The north wing was the stables.

Character: The massive stone walls and extensive weatherboarding with only a few small openings, and the hipped pantile roof without dormers or gables, gave the buildings an impressive and forbidding appearance. Inside, vast single spaces were crowned by open timber roof trusses in a rotting state.

Work done: The intention was to create an archaeological museum which disturbed the old structure as little as possible and which allowed the continuing excavations to form an important part of the museum. It will accommodate collections which, due to shortage of space, cannot be on view; it incorporates a modern storage system which will enable it to receive new objects in the future; and it includes a lecture hall and space for temporary exhibitions. The roof was renewed with laminated timber trusses, purlins and boarding, and the old pantiles were re-used. The main entry was formed in the south-west corner by means of an external concrete ramp which starts near the north wing and rises in a long curve over the excavations in the courtyard. There is also an entrance below this at ground level, which leads to a circular concrete ramp connecting all three levels. In the north wing both internal and external concrete ramps connect the different levels, and in the north-west corner another circular concrete ramp performs the same function.

The link between the north and south wings is a concrete bridge at middle level, passing over excavations which extend under the west wing. This bridge also serves three separate volumes—special exhibition areas of in situ finds—in the form of concrete boxes lifted off the ground on single, central columns and top lit by translucent pantiles. Throughout, the new internal structure, which is all reinforced concrete, is kept away from, and remains independent of, the old structure.

Accommodation: North wing—interconnected levels for use as a folk museum, with a stepped area connecting the two levels, which can be used for informal discussions; lavatories in the north-west corner at middle level; storage with access from the

1. the barns before conversion. The massive stone walls and the timber superstructure is of medieval origin

2, the south wing after conversion. The large window reveals the raked lecture hall

north at ground level
West wing—devoted to the Middle Ages with excavations and other exhibits visible from the bridge, three separate volumes for special exhibits
South wing—entrance, lavatories, stores, lecture hall for 200 on ground floor; administration, library, lecture hall and link to west wing on middle floor; entrance from ramp, temporary exhibition space and lecture hall on upper floor

Date of completion: 1973

Cost: 5·8 million Norwegian kroner

3, the concrete ramp which starts near the north wing and rises in a long curve over the excavations in the courtyard to the main entrance in the south-west corner

5, the bridge passing over excavations in the west wing. The concrete boxes to the right and left are top-lit rooms for housing and exhibiting in situ *finds*

4, the circular concrete staircase in the south-west corner which serves the three levels of the museum. On the top level the staircase connects with the ramp shown in 3, and on the middle level with a bridge which extends through the whole length of the west wing

6, the north wing; formerly the stables and now a folk museum. The roof timbers throughout were rotten and have been renewed with laminated timber trusses and purlins. The old pantiles were re-used except where roof lights were needed

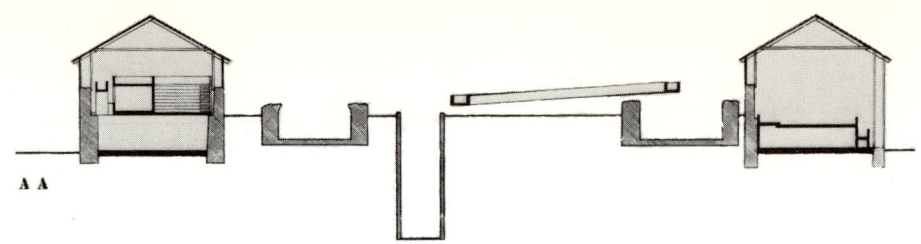

Section AA

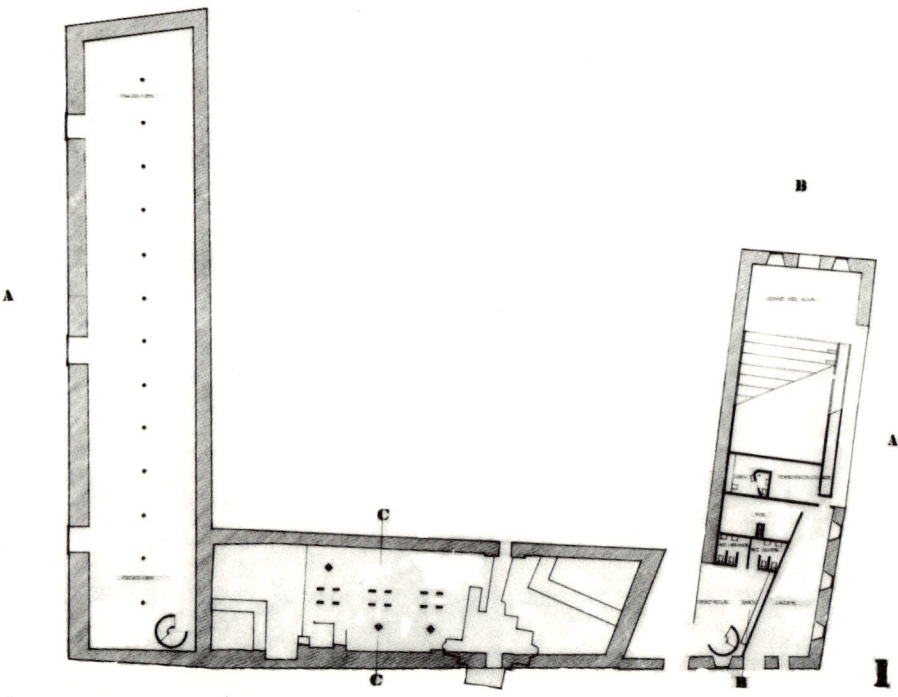

Ground floor plan

7, an original medieval opening in the stone walls has been treated with due reverence. The plain sheet of glass also provides a bonus by reflecting the landscape and curved ramp

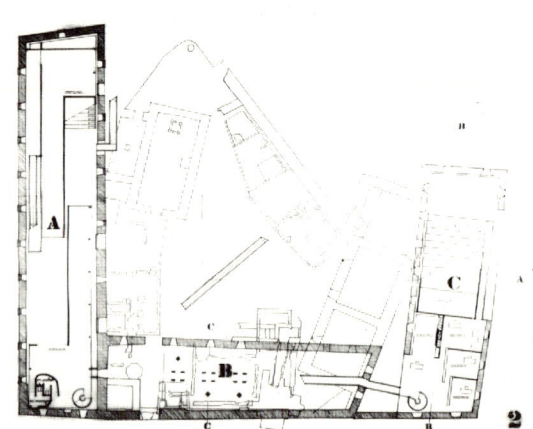

First floor plan

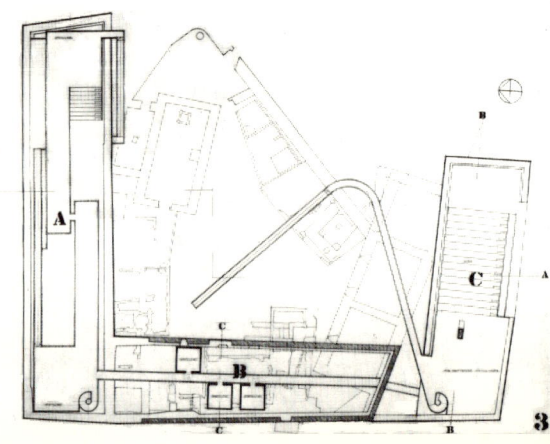

Second floor plan

BARN, EAST HENDRED, BERKSHIRE

1, the barn from the road before conversion and, 2, after conversion. The thatched roof and weatherboarded walls still predominate over the random pattern of small windows, leaving one in no doubt that this was once a barn

Architect: Irena Mardi

Client: Mr. and Mrs. Bruno Schlaffenberg

Site: The barn is part of a continuous row of buildings on the west side of Chapel Square in the village of East Hendred. The site extends at the back to form a considerable garden.

History: Originally part of the King's Manor, the barn is one of the few remaining timber and thatch buildings in the village dating back to the seventeenth century. It is a Grade II listed building and the conversion received a Civic Trust commendation in 1968.

Character: A structure of elm posts, ties and braces sits on a rubble stone base and supports a lofty elm roof structure of trusses, purlins and rafters. The external walls are weatherboarded timber stained black and the roof is thatch.

Work done: To provide bedrooms, an upper floor was inserted into approxi-

mately half the interior space. The ground floor is on two levels and was formed out of 2in. concrete blinding, a damp-proof membrane and 2in. paving bricks. The dividing walls on the ground floor are 4½in. brick on concrete footings and one of these walls has been taken up through the first floor to provide lateral bracing. The new first floor structure is timber boarding over joists and the dividing walls are 4in. stud partitions.

To preserve the character of the building, the street facade has only a few small openings. The exceptions are the front door and garage door, both of which cut into the stone plinth. The unobtrusive quality of the windows at the front and back is due partly to their random size and pattern (they were, in fact, carefully placed to admit sunshine into specific areas throughout the house) and partly to the use of glass louvres for ventilation, which made it possible to hide the window frame behind the weatherboarding, no opening sash being required. The elm roof trusses were expertly restored, any new sections being jointed to the old with traditional timber dowels.

Over the bedrooms a flat ceiling was formed out of timber rafters and 2in. woodwool slabs. To insulate the outside walls the weatherboarding was removed and polythene sheeting fixed over the existing timber framing. The spaces between were fitted with 2in. rockwool, plasterboard and skimcoat painted white. Besides installing all the services—drains, water, electricity, gas—a gas-fired central heating system with a continuous coil of pipes along the perimeter of the building threading through skirting radiators was also provided. As individual radiators cannot be turned off with this system, two circuits have been installed which can be used separately or together. Heating pipes, electrical flex or sliding door gear remain unconcealed, and new elements like the staircase and fireplace are contemporary in design and made of steel, concrete or timber.

Accommodation: Ground floor—garage, cloakroom, kitchen/dining area, living room
First floor—three bedrooms, bathroom, lavatory and gallery (overlooking double-height living room)

Date of completion: May 1967

Cost: £5278

Rate: £3·52 per sq. ft. (£37·89 m²). The cost must be seen in relation to the fact that the client was her own architect and consciously made a number of omissions a layman client would be unlikely to agree to. She was also prepared to undertake a considerable do-it-yourself programme after the builders had left.

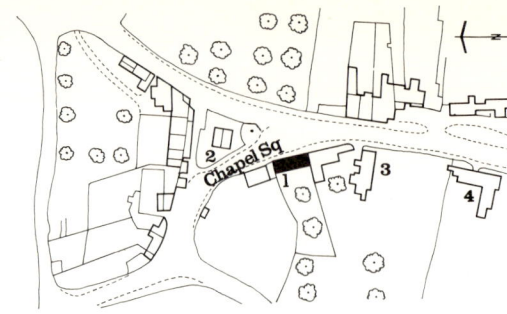

key
1, barn
2, Jesus Chapel
3, King's Manor
4, Abbey Manor

Site plan

3, on the garden side the openings are larger, but their vertical proportions express the framed construction behind the weatherboarding

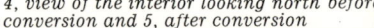

4, view of the interior looking north before conversion and 5, after conversion

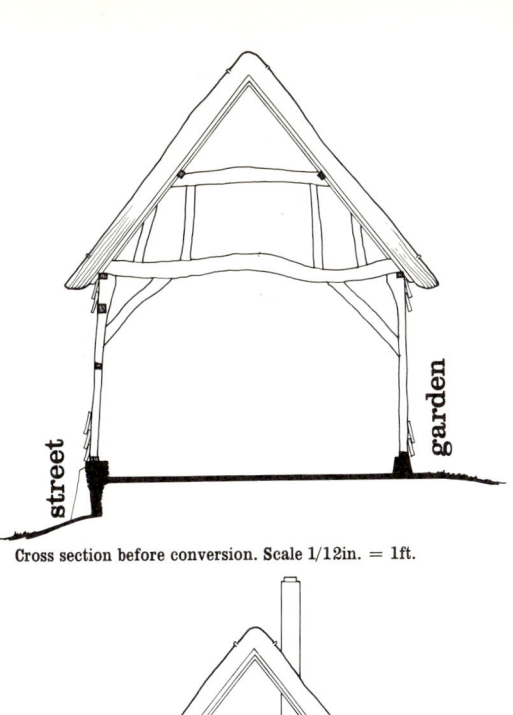

Cross section before conversion. Scale 1/12in. = 1ft.

Cross section after conversion. Scale 1/12in. = 1ft.

Plan

5, a discreet roof light emphasises height and draws attention to the roof timbers

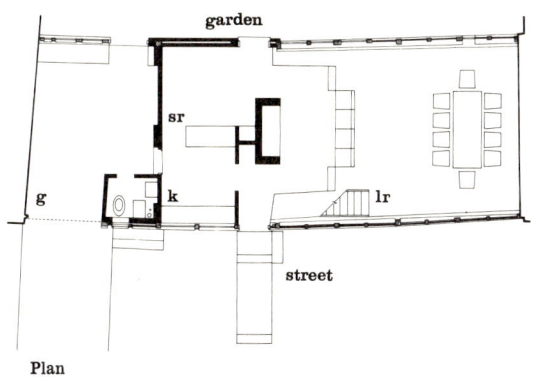

6, the southern half has been divided by an upper floor which is reached by means of an open-riser staircase

7, detail of the elm structure on the gallery overlooking the living room

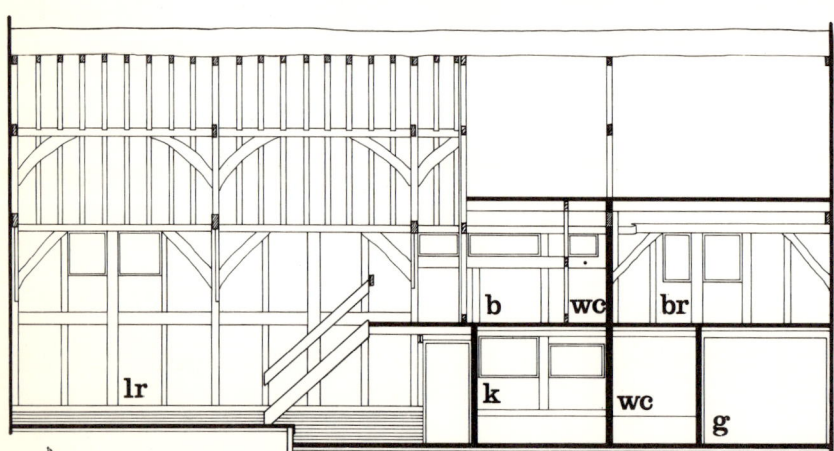

Long section looking east. Scale 1/12in. = 1ft.

GRANARY, BLAKENEY, NORFOLK

Architect: Feilden & Mawson

Client: W. Deterding

Site: The gable end of a long rectangular building faces the mud flats and marshes on the north coast of Norfolk where the sea once came. At high tide the mud flats become rivers. On the east side runs the High Street. On the west side the building faces a cul-de-sac and a hotel (also owned by the client). The site slopes down towards the marshes.

History: Built about 1750 as a warehouse for deep-sea shipping before the harbour silted up, it later became a boat storage shed and store for bait diggers.

Character: Externally, brick and flint walls with an irregular pattern of small windows and large loading door. The pitched roof of pantiles steps up with the slope and is broken on the east side by a projecting timber gable supporting a hoist. Internally the walls are faced in flint, contrary to the local tradition which uses flint for the exterior and brick for the interior. The upper floor is open to the roof, which is a simple structure of triangular trusses with ties halfway up and purlins to support the rafters.

Work done: The building was to be converted into five flats and two shops. Cross walls in 9in. and 13½in. brick on concrete footings were constructed for fire protection and to provide the necessary division between the flats. External walls below ground level were tanked with asphalt. Above ground level, new openings were formed for doors and windows with brick arches and surrounds and new timber windows inserted. The level of the ground floors was raised for the shops by backfilling with rubble, and lowered for the flats to provide 7ft. ceiling heights. New 4in. site concrete with a damp-proof membrane was laid throughout and the shop floors were finished with quarry tiles. The other floors were left with a 2in. screed ready to receive the tenant's choice of finish. Existing timber floors were repaired and trimmed to receive new staircases. The roofing tiles and battens were completely stripped, the timbers trimmed for new dormers and the tiles rehung on new battens over felt and insulation board. Internal divisions between flats were 3in. stud partitions.

Accommodation: South half—three flats each with two bedrooms and a box room on the ground floor; main entrance (from projecting balcony reached by steps), bathroom, kitchen and living room on the first floor; gallery over roughly half the area overlooking the double-height living room on the second floor
North half—two shops and an entrance to two flats, as well as the two bedrooms and bathroom of one of the flats, on the ground floor; the living room and kitchen of one flat, and the dining

1, the long rectangular granary with its stepped pantile roof seen from the east side before conversion and, 2, after conversion into shops and flats

3, the weatherboarded loading hatch has been preserved, and the detailing of the new timber features is robust and appropriately functional

room, kitchen, bathroom, two bedrooms and living room of the other flat on the first floor; open galleries overlooking the double-height living rooms on the second floor

Date of completion: 1966

Cost: £23 880

Rate: £3·16 per sq. ft., flats
£3·69 per sq. ft., shops

4, looking down the street towards the distant mud flats

5, from the cul-de-sac on the west side. The granary faces a hotel which is in the same ownership

6, 7, the interior before conversion when it was used as a boat storage shed, and, 8, after conversion showing one of the open galleries overlooking the double-height living room

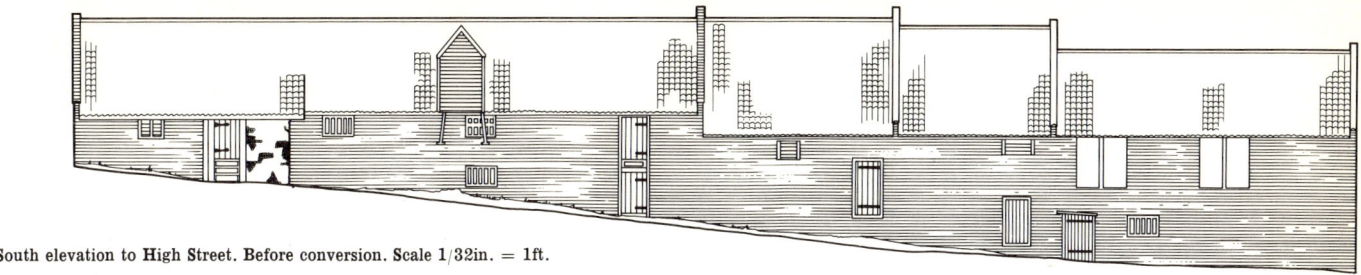

South elevation to High Street. Before conversion. Scale 1/32in. = 1ft.

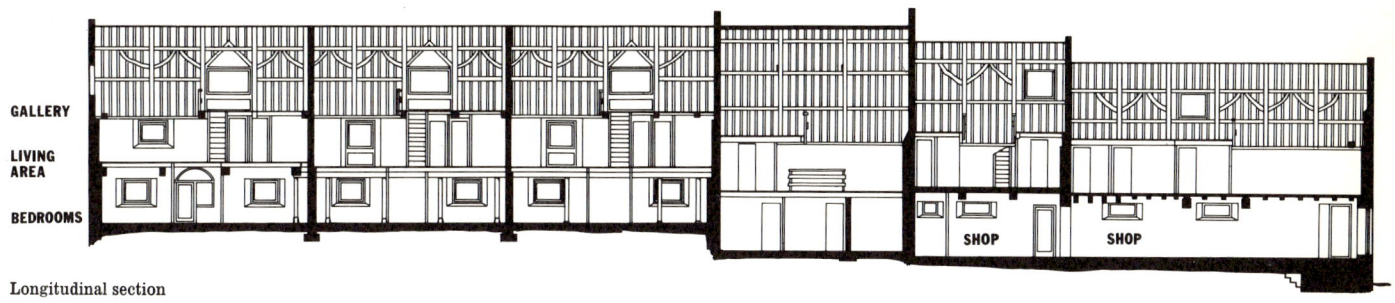

Longitudinal section

key

1, shop
2, lavatory
3, hall
4, bathroom
5, bedroom
6, boxroom
7, kitchen
8, living room
9, dining area

Upper floor plan

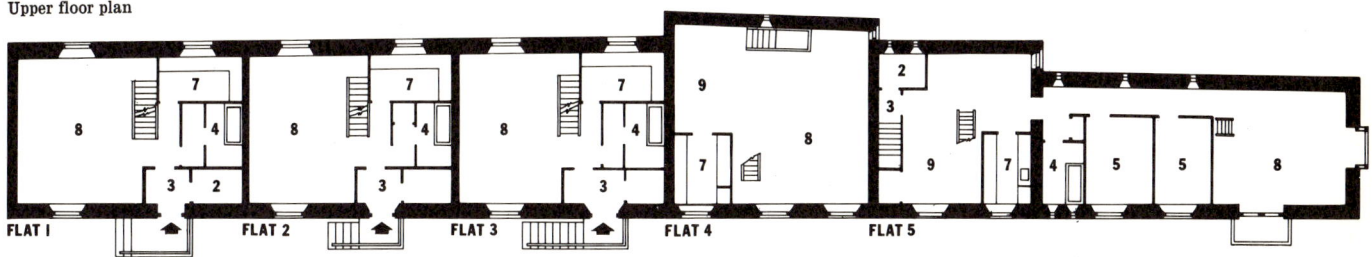

Lower floor plan

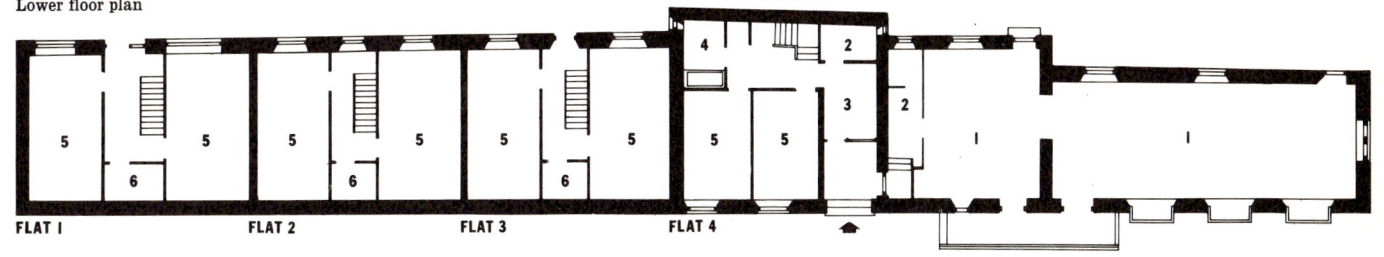

BARNS, KNEBWORTH HOUSE, HERTFORDSHIRE

Architect: Donald W. Insall & Associates

Client: Lytton Enterprises Ltd.

Site: Dominated by Knebworth House in its 250 acre park, the Knebworth barns stand discreetly on the edge of the formal garden, screened by imposing trees. When Knebworth Park was declared a country park in 1971, a major condition of approval of this designation was that access to the park should not be from local roads, which would be heavily overloaded, but directly from a roundabout on the A1 motorway, about one mile from Knebworth House. Two and one-quarter miles of new and remade old drives now lead from the roundabout to the house and barns.

History: Knebworth House, originally completed in 1540, was substantially altered in the early nineteenth century when it was given its present romantic, battlemented, pinnacled and gargoyled facades. In 1970, 8000 people visited Knebworth; in 1972, 17 600. This great increase in the number of visitors made it necessary to provide better refreshment and lavatory facilities.

The site chosen was at a nodal point where the new drive now delivers visitors outside a former entrance to the formal garden. Any building on this site, within view of the house, demanded sensitive treatment. Various building forms for the new building were being considered, but while discussing the future of some of the estate outbuildings, attention was drawn to two barns. After an investigation of the problems and costs involved, both barns were moved to form the two main refreshment halls for visitors to the house and park.

Character: The two barns, Manor Barn and Lodge Barn, are early seventeenth-century oak-framed buildings. Both barns had handmade tiled roofs and were weatherboarded externally with tarred or creosoted horizontal boards. In both cases the tiles were retained but the weatherboarding was renewed. The building consists of a barn on either side of a central kitchen with access to lavatories which are also accessible from the park. The new parts of the building took on the character of the barns and thus are also weatherboarded and have pitched roofs covered with handmade tiles.

Work done: Different solutions were found for moving the two barns. Manor Barn was five-eighths mile from its proposed new site and the route was reasonably flat over parkland. The barn had recently been re-roofed and it was hoped, rightly as it turned out, that no work would need to be carried out on the roof, should the barn be bodily moved to its new site. Manor Barn was braced by fixing Bailey bridging around the walls and scaffolding inside the barn; it was then jacked up off the ground and let down on to sixteen pairs

1, Lodge Barn on its original site. This was dismantled and re-erected

2, Manor Barn, which was much nearer the new site, being moved bodily. It was jacked up on wheels and drawn across flat parkland by a steam plough

3, the barns re-erected and grouped together on the new site seen from the north. The two gabled portions are new additions and provide lavatory accommodation (left) and a kitchen between the two barns. The steep roof of Manor Barn can be seen behind

of wheels. A steam plough, which proved to have better anchorage than a caterpillar-tracked bulldozer, drew the barn across the park to its new site. Lodge Barn was too far away from its new site to be moved there bodily. This aisled barn was therefore unpegged, taken apart and reconstructed on the new site. The oak timbers of both barns were in sound condition and only minimal repair was necessary before timber treatment against beetle and fungicidal attack.

To conform to local authority regulations, each barn had to be compartmented and finishes had to provide a half-hour fire protection. The roof of Manor Barn was entirely undisturbed by the move, but fire protection and thermal insulation were provided by plastering between the rafters. On the outsides of both barns were fixed 1in. woodwool slabs which were plastered internally and weatherboarded externally; 1in. woodwool slabs were also laid on the rafters unplastered. The floor of Manor Barn is carpeted on screed and the floor of Lodge Barn, which is used for dancing, is of woodblocks on screed. The buildings are centrally heated.

All the year round the barns are let out for private dances, weddings, or banquets; 350 to 400 people can be accommodated in them at one time. During the summer season, when the house and park are open to the public, Manor Barn is a waitress-service restaurant and Lodge Barn is self-service.

Date of completion: December 1971

Cost: £60 000, excluding fees

Rate: £8·25 per sq. ft.

4, Lodge Barn after re-erection seen from the west. The weatherboarding was renewed but the old roofing tiles were re-used. The old barn doors have been replaced by French windows

5, Manor Barn from the south-east

North elevation

West elevation of Lodge Barn

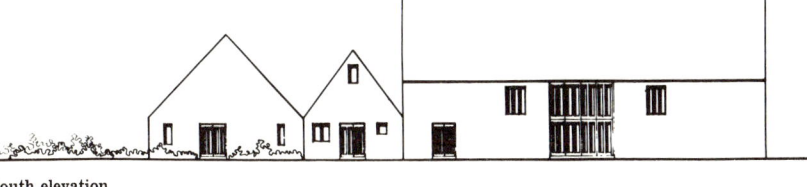

South elevation

East elevation

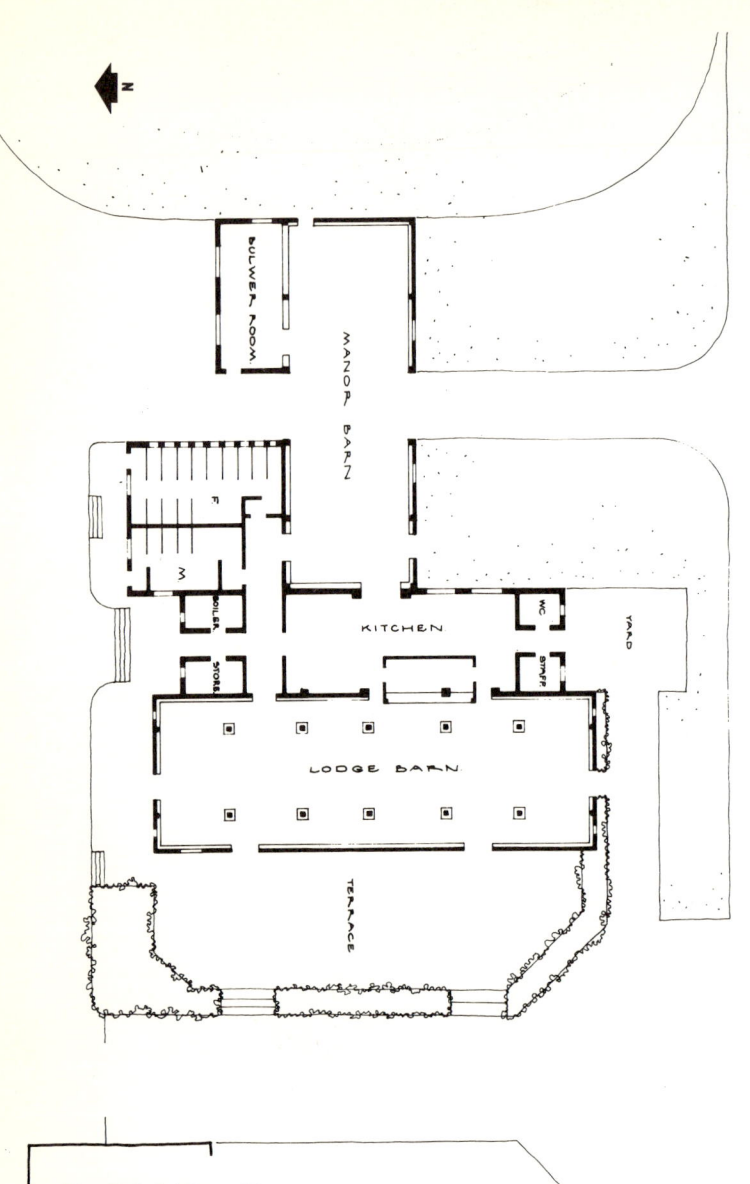

Plan. Scale 1/36in. = 1ft.

6, Manor Barn before conversion and, 7, after conversion into a waitress-service restaurant

8, Lodge Barn is aisled and has been converted into a self-service restaurant

Aerial view showing barns in relation to Knebworth House and St. Mary's Church. The A1 runs east of the park and house.

145

Mills

A clear distinction must be made between textile mills, a product of the Industrial Revolution, and water mills, which belong to an earlier tradition and were used for grinding corn. Textile mills are really factories for spinning and weaving wool, cotton, flax or silk, and the word *mill* was borrowed only because the early examples, like water mills, were driven by water power. The two textile mills illustrated in this chapter belong to a later age. Both represent the wool industry which was first centred in the west country and later developed in Yorkshire. But whereas the mill in Wiltshire was built when the local industry was in decline, and its use for spinning wool was short-lived, the mill in Yorkshire continued in use until 1970. Like their Georgian predecessors, both mills are large, multi-storey and industrial in character. Just as the mills were assimilated into the landscape when the need for water power kept them in the rural surroundings of river valleys, so they were assimilated into an urban setting after their move to the towns, where the supply of labour was plentiful.
In each case it was the combination of traditional forms with natural materials—stone, slates, bricks, tiles—and the punctuation of the large expanse of walling by windows of Georgian proportions—a unit of human scale—which made this assimilation possible. Where a whole industrial community was established, as at Styal in Cheshire (1784) or New Lanark on the Clyde (1784), the large size of the mills could more easily be related to the worker's cottage via the intermediate size of schools, chapels and other community buildings.

The whole of Styal has belonged to the National Trust since 1939 and the mill has recently been restored, though no use has yet been found for it.* While the future of Styal is thus reasonably safe, that of New Lanark has until recently been under serious threat. The imminent redundancy of the three mills—one has stood empty for some time—and the semi-derelict condition of the fine community buildings require the injection of public money and positive conservationist action by government and the local authority. The recent feasibility study by the county council and the Scottish Development Department gives hope that such action may now come about.

Of course redundancy in textile mills is not new. The woollen mill at Bradford in Wiltshire was adapted to the

---

*In an article entitled 'A Mill and its Master' (*Country Life*, December 28, 1972), John Cornforth suggests that the mill might be converted into a museum of the local textile industry—that Styal could do for Manchester and the cotton trade what the Du Ponts and the Du Pont company have done for Hagley or, one might add, what Bradford Corporation are doing at Moorside Mills for the textile industry in Yorkshire (see p. 165).

manufacture of rubber soon after it was built. At Norwich, the yarn mill beside the Wensum has for a long time been a printing works. Many textile mills have continued in some kind of industrial use, not always to the advantage of the original structure; this is the case with two out of the three mills at New Lanark. More recently there have been examples of woollen mills converted to battery-hen and mushroom farms.

Such new uses can hardly be recommended. One would rather single out the conversion into flats of a woollen mill in the Stroud valley, the use of Jackson's Mill by various departments of the University of Manchester Institute of Science and Technology, or the adaptation of the famous Marshall's Mill at Leeds as the headquarters of a large mail-order business. The two examples illustrated, conversions into open offices and a museum of industrial archaeology, demonstrate all the problems. Windows are always large, so that there is never any need to alter the exterior. The difficulty arises with the interior space, which consists invariably of open floors supported on rows of timber posts or, later, cast-iron columns. A hybrid structure of iron supports and timber beams continued to be used despite fire risks, as is evident from both the late examples illustrated. At Bradford in Wiltshire false ceilings, which conceal the floor structure, were required by the fire officer, who nevertheless allowed the iron columns to remain unprotected. Because the standards expected by office workers today are quite different from the standards imposed on mill workers in the past, the rough stone walls have been plastered and the coarse-grained floor timbers carpeted. While much of the robust character of the interiors has inevitably been lost, the relatively small area of each floor has not made it necessary to placate the fire officer by closing off the open areas required for offices.

Multiple subdivision required for conversion into flats or houses is more acceptable in the early all-timber structures. Once cast-iron columns come into use, especially when these are combined with a fireproof floor construction of iron beams supporting brick segmental vaults, subdivision can quickly make nonsense of the structure (see page 240). At Moorside Mills in Bradford (Yorkshire), relatively infrequent subdivision and less need for intensive cosmetic treatment (walls have been sandblasted to expose the brickwork) have resulted in much of the old character being preserved.

Water mills are smaller than the large textile mills, but many are large enough to have been converted in the past to other industrial uses including spinning and weaving. Often they are too large to convert into a single private house, and both the examples illustrated here, which have been adapted to residential use, have been divided into several units.

The situation of water mills beside rivers makes them at first sight attractive as potential living accommodation. But corn-grinding was a commercial activity that took place inside the building with the exception of loading and unloading, for which a yard was provided on the roadside.

Water mills rarely have much land besides the land the buildings stand on, and people living in converted mills, especially when there are several families living in flats, have found this constraint both physically and psychologically disagreeable.

Often the complex form of a water mill reflects quite faithfully its various functions: the projecting timber structure high up in the roof, like a cantilevered dormer, which houses the hoist; the lofts behind it which store the grain; the grinding chamber underneath into which the grain is delivered through chutes; the building alongside into which the milled flour passes for storage in bags; and the miller's house, sometimes attached, sometimes separate. Windows, too, have their functional *raison d'être* and appear random in size and arrangement. Materials are white-painted weatherboarding in East Anglia and the Home Counties, stone and slate in the north and west of England. This chapter includes two of each, all of them converted with understanding. The mill at Chipping in Lancashire lost its interior character when it became a cheese dairy and the machinery was removed. The new modern interiors, though admirable in themselves, have little to do with the spirit of the old mill. They should be compared with the interiors of Ellingham Mill in Suffolk, also a conversion to residential use, where there was plenty left worth saving and where the loft especially retains much of its original character.

The tide mill at Woodbridge and Arlington Mill in Gloucestershire are both converted into museums. In addition to exhibiting local life and industry, both mills display their machinery, and in the case of the tide mill it is hoped eventually to make its uniquely complete machinery operational. Obviously there is a limit to the number of water mill museums that a country can hold, and one accepts that other uses, especially domestic ones, will have to be found for the many redundant mills all over the world. But one remains grateful that these two mills, both in their way exceptional, have been preserved to demonstrate one of the most ancient and ubiquitous of industrial processes.

ABBEY MILL, BRADFORD-ON-AVON, WILTSHIRE

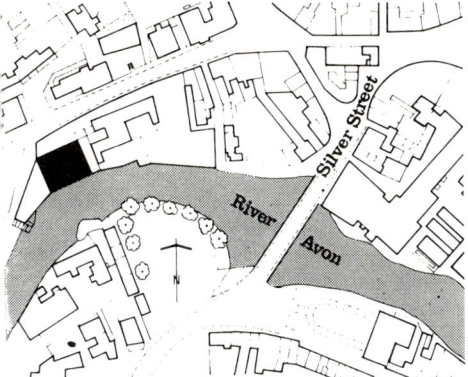

Site plan

Architect: Thurlow, Lucas & Janes

Client: Avon Rubber Company

Site: Abbey Mills is a collection of old factory buildings fronting on to the River Avon and backing on to Church Street.

History: Today, Bradford is famous for its Saxon church and fourteenth-century tithe barn, but its prosperity dates from the eighteenth century when it became a centre of the cloth-making industry in the west country. The main five-storey mill of the Abbey Mills complex was built in 1875 when the industry was in decline, and its use as a woollen mill was short-lived. It was taken over by the rubber industry before the end of the century. In 1967 the present owners, who were using both the mill and another building upstream as factories, decided to concentrate production in the latter and convert the mill into offices. The mill has been listed by the Department of the Environment.

Character: An impressive pile of Bath stone, with all of five storeys rising sheer from the river bed. The tall, pointed arcading containing individual windows, and the cornice of blind, corbelled arcading give the building an almost Richardsonian grandeur. Internally each floor is an open space 80ft. by 60ft., with cast-iron columns supporting the timber floor structure. The walls are exposed rubble stonework.

Work done: The shape of each floor suited landscaped offices but the construction posed serious problems. The timber staircase and hand-operated goods lift in the corner projection had to be replaced with a reinforced concrete staircase and an automatic passenger lift, the projection as a whole becoming a protected shaft. The existing emergency staircase on the outside of the building was renewed, chipboard was laid over the old floorboards to give greater fire resistance, and a suspended ceiling was installed to house the light

1, view from the river and, 2, view from the street. Built as a woollen mill in 1875, it has been converted into offices without any alterations to the fenestration. Whether across the river or from the street, the five-storey building of Bath stone dominates its surroundings

fittings and sprinkler system and to provide the sound absorption needed for landscaped offices. The ceiling does not mask the pointed window arches and only partly masks the capitals of the cast-iron columns, which a lenient fire officer allowed to remain unprotected.

Air conditioning was omitted because of cost and, instead, the existing heating system—three large hot-water pipes round the perimeter walls—was re-used, and an intake and extract ventilation system installed in the space above the false ceiling. Splendid views and the possibility of obtaining ventilation through the roof determined the siting of the dining rooms on the top floor.

The floor finish throughout is a carpet, laid over a grid of special boxes which incorporate power points as well as GPO and internal telephone connections. To prevent the rough stone walls from collecting dirt, they have been plastered and painted.

The work was carried out in two phases, the first phase comprising the conversion of the three top floors while production was allowed to continue on the ground floor. The second phase consisted of turning part of the ground floor into a store and printing rooms, and the first floor into more offices.

Accommodation: Ground floor—entrance hall, store, printing rooms, lavatories
First, second and third floors—landscaped offices, lavatories
Fourth floor—staff dining room and servery, visitors' dining room, senior staff dining room, coffee room, kitchen, manager's office, female staff room, lavatories

Date of completion: Phase I, 1968
Phase II, 1971

Cost: Phase I, £62 700

Rate: £3·80 per sq. ft. (£41·20 per m²)

3, 4, office floors, which are a near square on plan, have been laid out on Bürolandschaft principles. A lenient fire officer allowed the cast iron columns to remain unprotected, and the suspended ceiling leaves the capitals exposed

Fourth floor plan. Scale 1/32in. = 1ft.

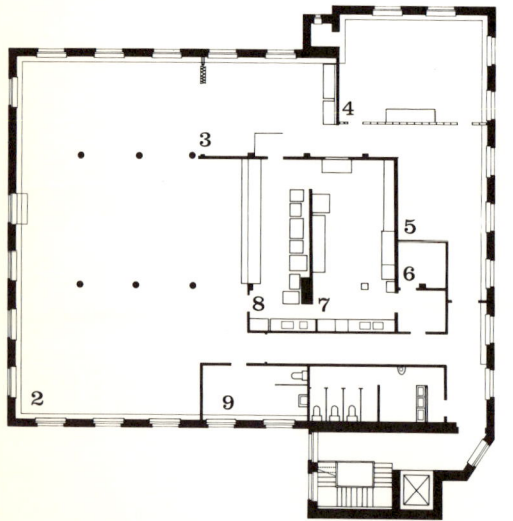

key
1, office
2, staff dining
3, visitors' dining
4, senior staff dining
5, coffee room
6, manager's office
7, kitchen
8, servery
9, female staff

Second floor plan. Scale 1/32in. = 1ft.

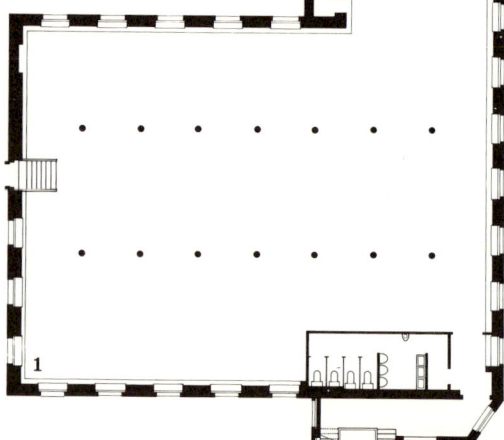

GRAIN MILL, ELLINGHAM, SUFFOLK

Architect: Fielden & Mawson
Interior design and specification, Lucy Halford

Client: Mr. and Mrs. Chester Williams

Site: The Waveney breaks into three sections at Ellingham weir (between Bungay and Beccles), and one part flows under the mill and empties into the mill pond. The river is tidal on the east side and has a rise and fall of up to two feet. The area is unusually flat and is surrounded by the Broome, Ellingham, Banstead and Geldeston water marshes, which are crossed by dykes.

History: Although a mill on this site is recorded in the Domesday Book, the present building is largely a Victorian structure. Traces of fifteenth- and sixteenth-century woodwork have been found, including a mullioned window on an inside wall separating the mill from the miller's house. The foundations are of Tudor brick. The mill was working as a grain mill up to about 1964.

The entire site was bought in 1965 and divided into two parts, Mr. and Mrs. Chester Williams buying the north section (second and attic floor only) from the new owner. A few years later they acquired the first and part of the ground floor and they use the mill both as living accommodation and as a gallery for art exhibitions.

Character: Like many East Anglian mills it is largely constructed of clapboard and brick on the outside. Lucams for hauling up or lowering sacks of grain and small-paned windows are characteristic features. The flooring on the first, second and third floors is timber on stout joists. The first and second floors are supported by round cast-iron columns and RSJs (introduced into the building around 1947 because of the weight of the grain). The attic/studio floor at the top has a fine sweeping timber raftered roof with a number of valleys. Large beams are tied into it and supported by timber posts. Access to the building was by very steep and small ladder stairs. The whole space, about 1500 sq. ft. on each floor, was unencumbered except for holes for funnels and shafts.

Work done: To maintain the industrial character of the building, as little work as possible was carried out. The major job was one of insulation. All the pantiles had to be removed, felt roofing laid, and woodwool slabs, pre-painted white, fixed to the existing softwood rafters. All outside walls were repaired where necessary, lined with a thermal blanket and faced internally with plywood.

Timber and iron-bolted ladder-type staircases were inserted from ground to second floor with a short flight to the studio/attic. Most of the floors are original timber, sanded and sealed. The joists were left exposed and all

1, the mill from the road side (north-east), with the waters of the Waveney flowing under the mill and road into the mill pond (left)

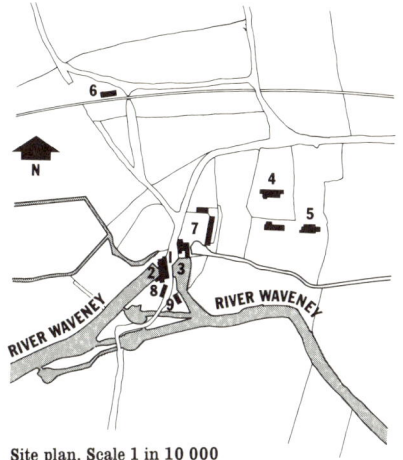

key
1, miller's house
2, mill buildings
3, mill pond
4, St. Mary's Church
5, rectory
6, railway station
7, farm
8, storage building
9, cottage

Site plan. Scale 1 in 10 000

151

timber was treated against infestation. The partitions are mainly timber stud, filled with fibreglass and faced with a softish kind of hardboard which in turn is covered with a rough paper-backed hessian, which was left natural or painted white. The hallway entrance was faced with tongue-and-groove pine panelling, and all doors, similarly faced, were flush with it. The west elevation was altered to allow larger windows and a balcony with folding doors.

Heating in the sitting/dining room is by one night storage heater and a Pither stove; in the studio by two night storage heaters and a Pither stove; elsewhere by plug-in fan heaters. Lighting throughout is with spotlights. The studio has a continuous track for adjustable fittings in the apex of the roof.

Two bathrooms and a room with a washbasin and lavatory were installed. All metal work was painted matt black; the walls were generally painted with white emulsion. Timber work was either left as found or sealed, in the case of furniture and floors. The furniture, except for the chairs, was specially designed and made of pine, mostly 2in. thick so that it maintained the robust and workmanlike feeling of a grain mill.

Accommodation: Ground floor—room belonging to River Board Authority, lumber room, potting shed
First floor—exhibition gallery, two bedrooms (also occasionally used as exhibition space), bathroom, kitchen
Second floor—entrance, two double bedrooms (one with its own adjoining washbasin and lavatory), kitchen, dining room-cum-living room, bathroom (outside front door)
Third floor—studio, small bedroom, bathroom

Date of completion: 1968

Cost: £6114, excluding decoration, floor coverings and furniture

Rate: £2·04 per sq. ft.

2, the mill from the south-east seen across a branch of the Waveney which connects with the mill pond in front of the mill

3, view from the south-west across the arm of the Waveney which leads to the mill and under it into the pond on the other side

4, on the river side new balconies have been cantilevered out at first and second floor level

5, 6, the art gallery on the first floor where exhibitions are held annually. The cast iron columns and beams have been left exposed and painted black

7, the new open-riser timber staircase between the first and second floors

8, the living-dining room on the second floor where the timber beams, as well as the cast-iron work, have been left exposed. The walls are unplastered brickwork painted white

9, the attic which has suffered the least change of character

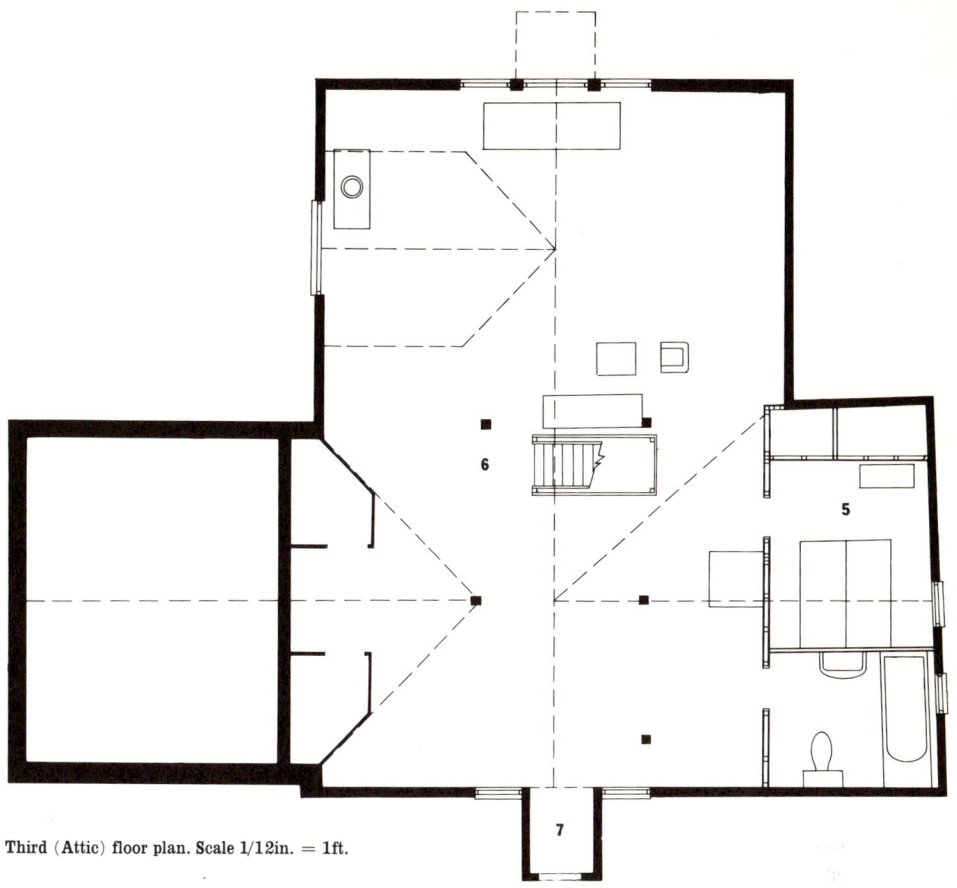

Third (Attic) floor plan. Scale 1/12in. = 1ft.

key
1, entrance hall
2, living-dining room
3, new balcony
4, kitchen
5, bedroom
6, studio
7, lucam

Second floor plan.

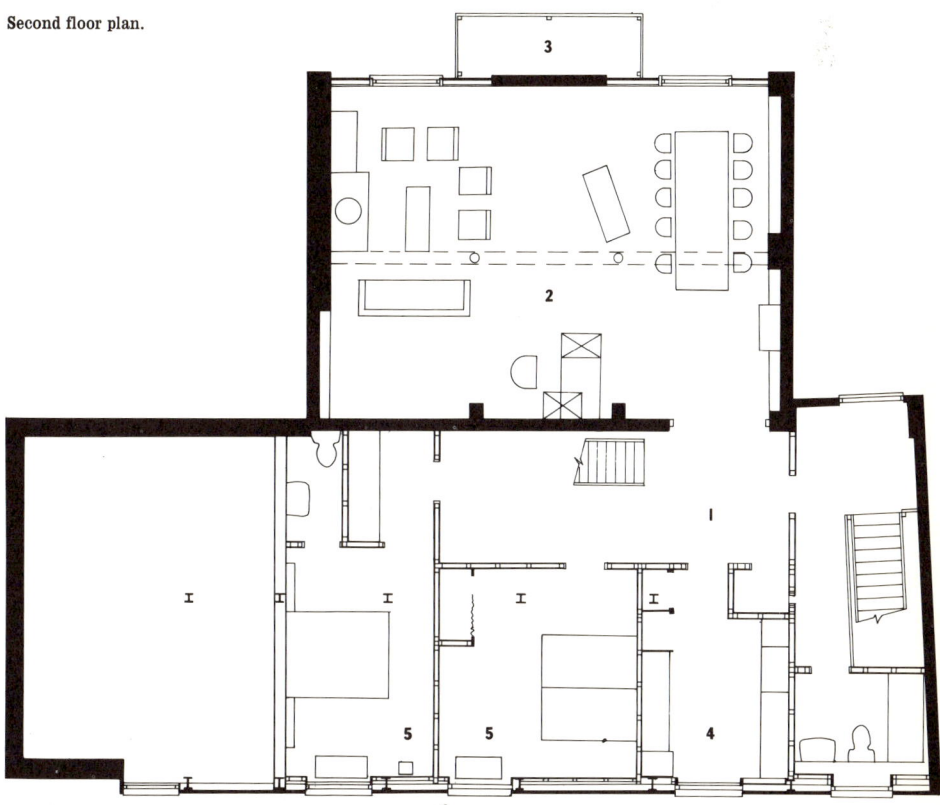

WOLFEN MILL, CHIPPING, LANCASHIRE

Architect: Raymond Burton

Client: Mr. and Mrs. Raymond Burton

Site: An old mill and cottage in some seven acres of woodland, lake and trout stream, designated an area of 'outstanding natural beauty'. One mile away is the village of Chipping, which has been the subject of a conservation area study. The area around is almost entirely rural, Chipping itself providing the centre for a large farming community. The mill is twelve miles north of Preston near the forest of Bowland and within twenty minutes' drive of the M6, M61 and M62.

History: Originally (in the fifteenth century) a small water-powered corn mill on Lord Derby's estate of Wolfen Hall. In the cotton era it was enlarged and turned into a flyer-and-spindle works serving the local mills, but still using water power to drive the machinery, which included the third largest mill wheel in Lancashire. The General Strike of 1929 closed the works but the building, after remaining empty for a few years, was further enlarged and started up again as a Lancashire cheese dairy. This closed in 1969 when the present owners bought it together with the cottage and the land.

Character: A two-storey building with walls of random rubble, timber windows of nearly square proportions and roofs of slate. Except for the north-east side and the free-standing cottage, the original L-shaped structure had been largely enveloped by later additions. The interior was in a semi-derelict state; the great wheel had gone by 1930 and little of any value remained.

Work done: The architect-owner required a family house, a small amount of office space for himself and a large studio for his sculptor wife. The intention was to provide freely planned open spaces where all activities could take place simultaneously, with wall and floor areas treated as simply as possible for displaying modern sculpture and paintings.

The brick addition on the east side dating from the mill's use as a cheese dairy, the adjoining external staircase, the asbestos lean-to between the cottage and the mill and the brick loading stage were all demolished. Two double-height volumes were created in the middle of the building, one as an entrance hall merging into a dining area and kitchen, the other as part of the studio which extends under the living room. Both have galleries on the upper level and both are top lit by extensive new skylights. The hall has a new timber staircase leading to the gallery. The first floor and roof structure over the studio and living room had to be renewed, the span of the floor being broken by an RSJ and the roof rafters supported on

1, the mill before conversion and, 2, after conversion. The new windows have a functional character which recalls the industrial origins of the building

prefabricated lattice purlins spanning 29ft. The original slates were re-used and elsewhere the roofs were repaired with matching second-hand slates.

The existing entrance was used on the south side to provide a self-contained guest area. There, too, the first floor structure had to be renewed. Some window openings were blocked up; others were unblocked. Altogether some thirty-six new timber window frames were provided, most of which were top-hung single-light casements, the others traditional double-hung sashes with glazing bars. New services were installed including hot-water coils in the ground floor. The roof was insulated throughout with fibreglass quilt and the ceilings finished in plasterboard and plastered. New partitions are timber stud lined with plasterboard and plastered, and all stone walls are plastered. Ground floors are finished with a buff clay tile and upper floors with tongue-and-groove boarding. A glazed screen divides the living room from the staircase and gallery.

The work was carried out in two phases, without a general contractor but with direct trades contracts directly under the management of the architect. The second phase, completed a year after the first, converted the old boiler house of the mill into a self-contained living unit. An upper floor was put in and the cottage provided with a living/dining room, kitchen, two bedrooms and a bathroom.

Accommodation: Mill
ground floor—entrance, living area entered from courtyard, dining area, kitchen, pantry, cloakroom, utility room, guest bed-sitting room, two sculpture and painting studios
first floor—upper part of entrance, living/working area and gallery, living room, children's bedroom/playroom, double bedroom, bathroom
Detached cottage—boiler house, stores, garage

Date of completion: Mill, 1970
Cottage, 1971

Cost: Mill, £12 558
Cottage, £2233
These costs were partly met by a discretionary improvement grant of £1000 for the mill and £750 for the cottage.

Rate Mill, £2·80 per sq. ft. (£30·15 per m²)
Cottage, £3·06 per sq. ft. (£32·93 per m²)

key
1, mill building
2, cottage
3, yard
4, shed
5, demolished water treatment plant
6, mill pond

Site plan. Scale 1 in 2500

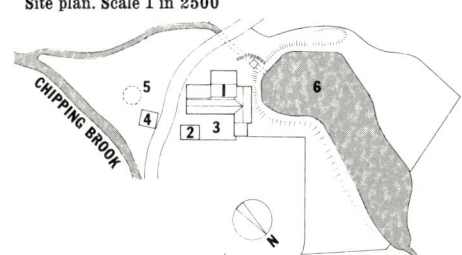

3, the hall is a double-height volume with a gallery and a skylight. This view shows the dining area on the ground floor, with the kitchen, 4, tucked away to the left, and the gallery giving access to the bedrooms on the first floor

4, looking into the kitchen from the dining area

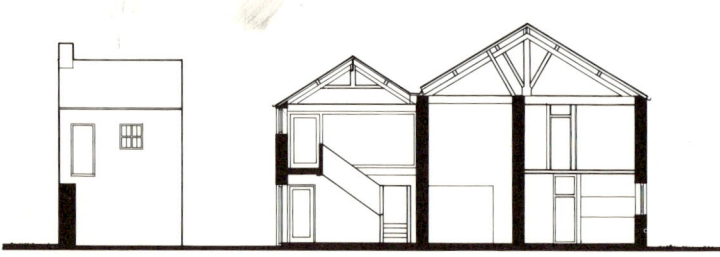

Section BB. Scale 1/24in. = 1ft.

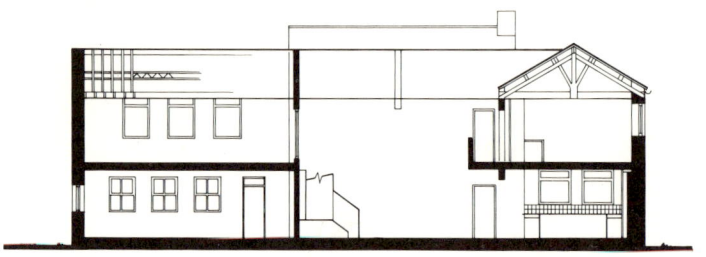

Section AA

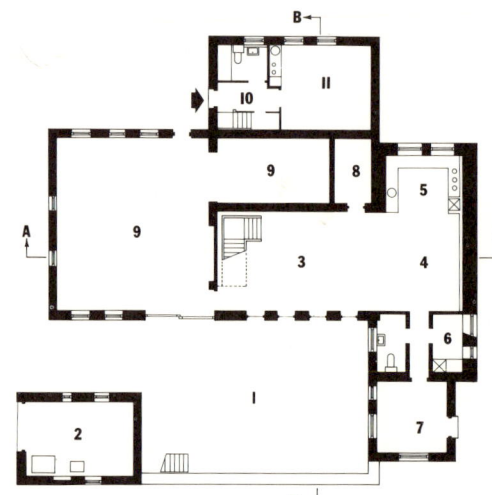

key
1, yard
2, garage and boiler
3, entrance hall
4, dining area
5, kitchen
6, utility
7, playroom
8, larder
9, studio
10, lobby
11, spareroom

Ground floor plan. Scale 1/32in. = 1ft.

5, another view of the double-height hall looking through the laylight into the first floor living room

6, the living room on the first floor has white walls and ceilings, and timber-boarded floors

7, view from the first-floor living room into the double-height hall

8, part of the studio extends the full height of the building and is top lit

ARLINGTON MILL, BIBURY, GLOUCESTERSHIRE

Architect: Peter Falconer and Partners

Client: David Verey

Site: Mentioned by Pope, 'discovered' by William Morris and popularised by Arthur Gibbs in *A Cotswold Village*, Bibury, with its Saxon church, seventeenth-century manor house, picturesque river and water mill is one of the most beautiful villages in England. The mill stands by a stream, an arm of the River Coln which runs just to the east past the Swan Hotel. Past the mill on the south side runs the Cirencester road, and on the north side a small garden of triangular shape is bounded by dry stone walls to the west (on the other side of which is an orchard with beehives) and the stream to the east.

History: Although a mill was probably established here already at the time of the Domesday survey, the present building appears to date from the seventeenth century, the projecting cottage being added early in the eighteenth and both restored in 1859. It was always a corn mill, though in the seventeenth century and earlier it was also a fulling mill for the cloth which was made in the nearby Arlington Row cottages. When the cloth industry moved in the eighteenth century to the Stroud valleys, where there was a better water supply, the mill reverted to its original use, and in the nineteenth century it was the largest and busiest mill in the district, power having to be augmented with a steam engine and the building strengthened. In 1859 new millstones were inserted and, to meet the increased weight, girders, cross ties and external buttresses were added. The ground and first floors were strengthened by iron columns and fish-bellied girders. In 1914 the mill machinery was dismantled and sold as scrap. The building was used as a trout farm until 1949. It was bought by its present owner in 1965 and subsequently converted into a museum.

Character: A four-storey building of Cotswold stone with gable ends and a large number of buttresses at the river end. There is a two-storey cottage projecting on the road side and another two-storey cottage abuts the west gable. All parts have an attic in the roof space, lit by dormers or windows in the gables. Internally the character is determined by the exposed timber floor structure supported on the lower floors by a mixture of cast-iron and timber columns, by the rough timber boarding on the floors, by the stone walls left bare or coarsely plastered and above all by the original grinding stones (first floor), chutes and storage bins (attic) and mill-race (ground floor). The attics, too, have their timber roof structure exposed.

Work done: The intention was to convert the building into a museum but at the

1, view from the road showing the mill in the centre with a two-storey cottage abutting at right angles and the caretaker's house (formerly the miller's house) joined to the mill on the left

2, view from the mill stream—an arm of the river Colne. This end of the mill has a large number of buttresses that rise almost the full height of the walls

same time to preserve as much of its character as possible. A new entrance to the museum was formed in an existing window opening at the side of the cottage. A new timber staircase was inserted in the mill from the ground floor to the attic. Existing partitions were removed and new ones formed to divide the main floor space and to provide lavatories (second floor). Machinery from another mill was installed with the exception of the water wheel. General repairs and some decoration were carried out. It is hoped to open the loft over the second cottage for exhibition purposes in the near future.

Accommodation: Cottage ground floor—entrance room with open fireplace and displays of cooking implements and taxidermy
first and attic floors—Victorian and Edwardian furniture
Mill ground floor—local pottery (for sale), mill machinery, mill-race, miller's office, display of farm carts, sleigh, winnowing machine, etc.
first floor—display of old farming implements, mill machinery and grinding stones (one pair working), exhibition of Arts and Crafts movement and furniture designed by Gimson and Ashbee
second floor—farm utensils, tools, children's toys, ecclesiology
Mill loft—hoist mechanism in situ, bins and chutes

Date of completion: 1965

Cost: £10 000

3, part of the mill-race at the mill stream end of the ground floor
4, a display of farm carts in the central part of the ground floor

5, the new timber staircase on the first floor

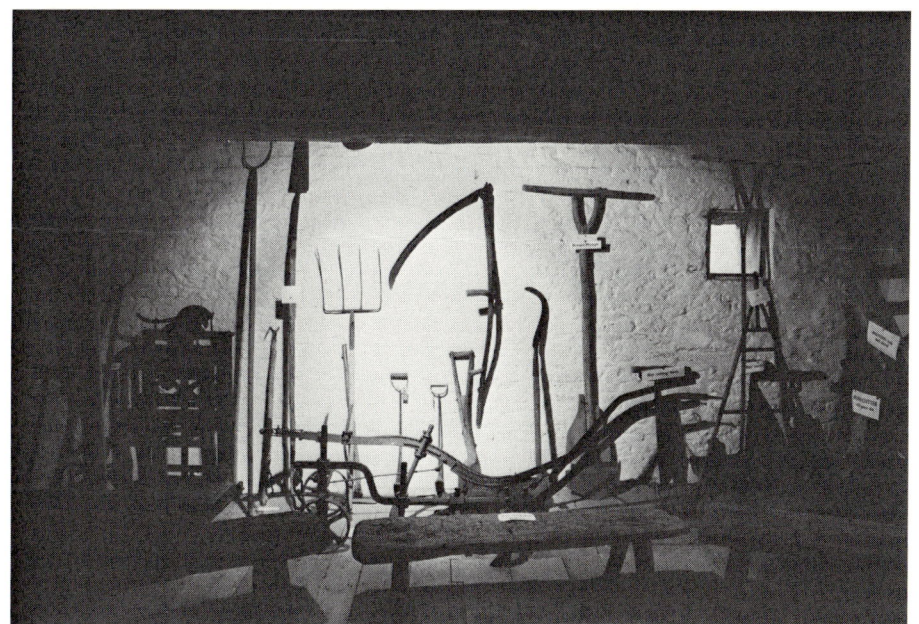

6, display of old farming implements on the first floor

7, the bedroom in the cottage displaying Victorian and Edwardian furniture and furnishings

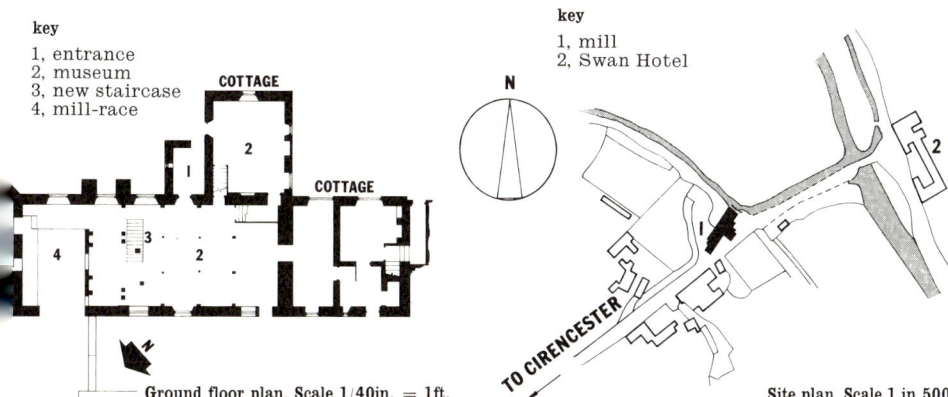

key
1, entrance
2, museum
3, new staircase
4, mill-race

Ground floor plan. Scale 1/40in. = 1ft.

key
1, mill
2, Swan Hotel

Site plan. Scale 1 in 5000

161

TIDE MILL, WOODBRIDGE, SUFFOLK

1, the tide mill before restoration when the whole building was covered in corroded corrugated iron sheeting which concealed decayed weatherboarding

Architect: Donald W. Insall & Associates

Client: Woodbridge Tide Mill Trust Ltd.

Site: The mill stands prominently on the shore of the River Deben, amidst Woodbridge harbour's maritime bustle. On the far side of the Deben, the wooded banks are a rural backcloth for the mill. Coastal barges no longer moor beside the quay, but the river is still used for yachting.

History: A tidal mill on the site of the existing mill has been continuously recorded since 1170. The present building dates from the eighteenth century, and full working by water power continued until 1957 when the main wheel shaft broke. The stones were for a time driven by a diesel motor but after the sale of the millpond, which is now a yacht marina, milling ceased and commercial use was abandoned. Total dereliction would have ended the mill's long history had it not been purchased by Mrs. R. T. Gardner for preservation in 1968. The Woodbridge Tide Mill Trust was set up and the mill was presented to the trust. A repair programme was then put in hand.

Character: With its prominent position, tall proportions and high wagon roof, the tide mill is one of East Anglia's best-known landmarks. Until recently the corroded red-painted corrugated-iron sheeting over the building, which covered decayed weatherboarding, constituted much of its character. It is the only tide mill in England in which all the machinery survives. There are three main floors, each floor dividing into four bays, the eastern end bay on each floor being devoted to the machinery. Structurally the mill is a simple box-framed timber building on a brick plinth. The main timbers are of pitch pine.

Work done: The intention was to bring the building back into working order to provide a working demonstration of

2, the tide mill after restoration with the corrugated sheeting removed and the weatherboarding renewed and painted white

3, the restored tide mill from the River Deben

4, the interior before restoration showing the lifting gear (left) used for putting the mill stones in place

a tidal mill and to provide space for exhibitions about rural life, especially about Woodbridge and the River Deben. The structural condition of the mill was extremely hazardous. The eastern foundations, much affected by tidal erosion, were slipping into the mill-race and the building was leaning eastwards. In addition it was bulging outwards in all directions because of the weight of the tiled roof and the extreme weakness of the beetle-and-rat-infested timbers. To stabilize the structure, the posts, renewed where necessary, were tied to the beams with metal straps. The posts were set on a new timber base-plate over a continuous reinforced concrete ring-beam which spreads the load over the foundations. The exact make-up of the foundations is not known but they must largely consist of water-logged material. Below the ring-beam the brick plinth was then rebuilt as necessary, and at the same time plywood sheets were laid over the existing rafters to stiffen the roof.

The mill was now structurally stable and, after timber treatment against beetle and fungicidal attack, the finishing skins could be applied to the framework of the building. The corrugated-iron sheathing was removed together with the remains of the old weatherboarding which was found underneath. Because the mill was to be open to the public as a working museum, the local authority required a fireproof internal lining to the walls. They also required that each floor should be compartmented. Before fixing new white-painted weatherboarding to the outside face, the stud walls were lined externally with asbestos boards. The new elm second floor was also laid on asbestos boards, and the spaces between the joists of the ground floor ceiling as well as the underside of the roof were plastered. The whole of the inside of the building, plasterwork and timber, was then limewashed as it had been originally. The roof was covered with handmade pantiles and all the sash windows were renewed.

Of the machinery, most of the iron fittings were rusted with disuse and the water wheel was so decayed that complete rebuilding together with a new drive shaft was necessary. The rest of the machinery needed only minor repair and was mostly left in the mill while the building was being repaired, although the millwright, Derek Ogden, removed some of the machinery before work began, to reduce the load on the structure. This machinery was repaired in his own workshops and now all the machinery, as well as the water wheel, is again in full working order.

Future work includes an iron stair at the west end of the mill (on which the local authority insists before allowing the public access to the upper floors) as well as the reinstatement of the southern lean-to and of the water wheel roof. Because the seven-and-a-half acre mill pond is now a yachting marina, the tidal flow of the river can no longer be harnessed to drive the water wheel. An alternative form of water power may eventually be found which will set the machinery in motion.

Date of completion: May 1973

Cost: £29 439, excluding fees and cost of repairs to machinery of £11 500

Rate: £8·50 per sq. ft.

key
1, tide mill
2, mill pond (now mud)
3, ferry quay
4, railway station

Site plan. Scale 1 in 12 500

5, the interior after restoration. It shows how the asbestos sheets behind the timber-framed walls, required by the fire regulations, are almost indistinguishable from the old weatherboarding seen in 4

6, a beam and post before restoration and, 7, after restoration

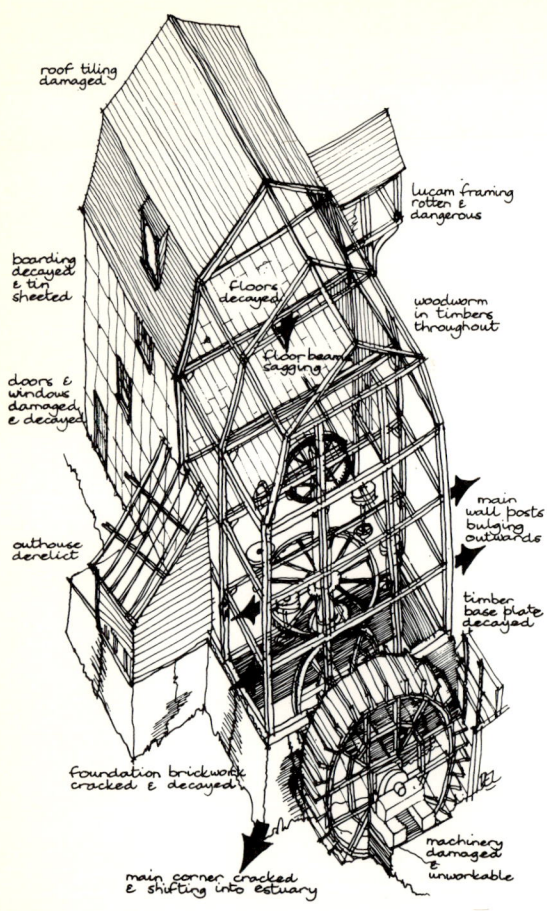

Isometric drawing showing structure and machinery of mill.

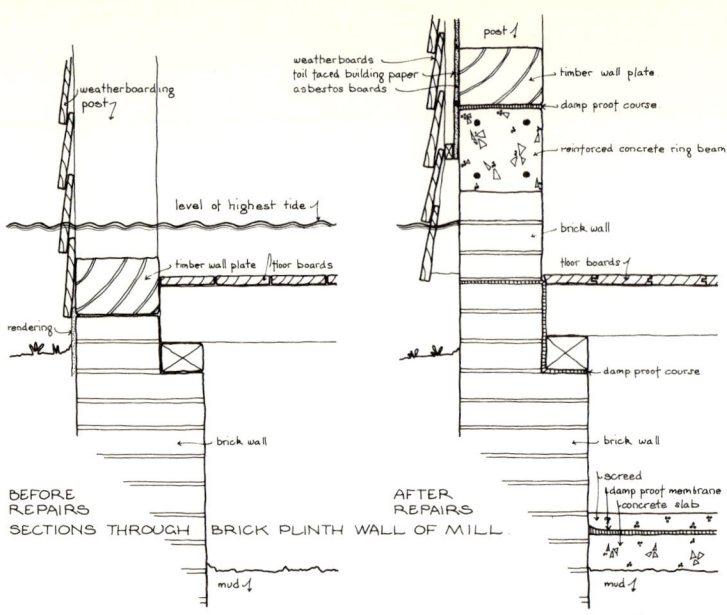

Before repairs: Sections through brick plinth wall of mill before repairs (left) and after repairs.

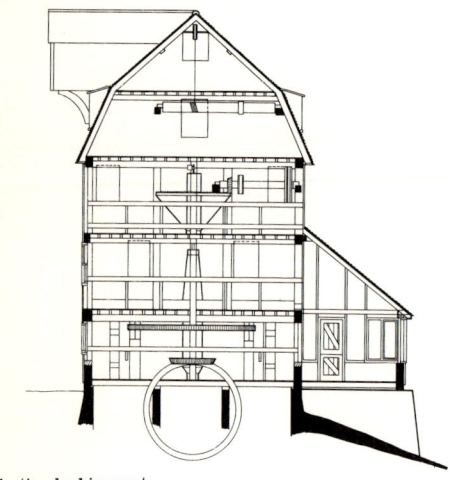

Section looking east

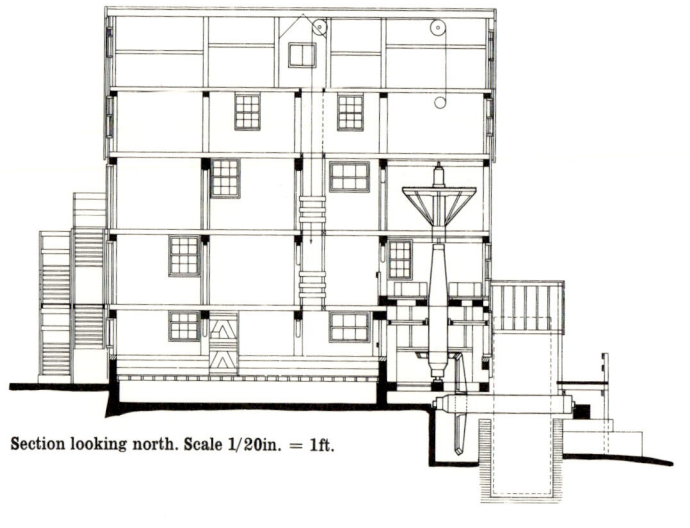

Section looking north. Scale 1/20in. = 1ft.

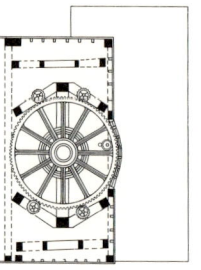

Upper part of ground floor plan.

Ground floor plan.

MOORSIDE MILLS, BRADFORD, YORKSHIRE

Architect: Owen Perry, Bradford City Architect

Client: Bradford Corporation, Bradford City Art Gallery and Museums

Site: The site is in the Eccleshill district of Bradford, and large enough for car parking and a limited amount of future development. Access is from two entrances in Moorside Road. The fields surrounding the mill do not belong to the Bradford Corporation, and the field to the north has been developed with housing, detracting from the mill's rural setting.

History: Built in the late nineteenth century as a worsted spinning mill, it continued in operation until April 1970, and was bought by Bradford Corporation in October of the same year with the intention of converting it into an industrial museum with special emphasis on the textile industry.

Character: An austere four-storey stone-faced structure with a parapet. The flat silhouette is broken by chimneys, a clock tower and a water tower. The industrial character of the building is further emphasised by the regular pattern of large timber windows along each of the four storeys on the north and south elevations. The main building is surrounded by outhouses, which included a boiler house now demolished. Another separate building is Moorside House, the former mill manager's residence.

Work done: The limited amount of money made available up to March 1971 was used in the construction of a car parking area and access roads, the work being carried out by the city engineer's direct labour force. The mill pond was also drained and cleared out and the old boiler house demolished.

During the following financial year (1971–72) a new allocation of money made it possible to begin the conversion of the mill manager's house, which involved only general repairs, the replacement of some modern fittings with contemporary ones and the installation of new services including central heating.

Since the vendors had dismantled the heating installation of the main building, a new central heating system became a matter of priority and has now been completed. At the same time certain areas including the basement were fitted out as workshops so that the museum technicians could become operative as soon as possible. A sample area of internal wall was successfully cleaned by sand-blasting, exposing attractive brickwork. Some areas will be decorated in a traditional manner, for example, the third floor, which will be partitioned to provide offices and studios both for the Industrial Museum

1, view of the worsted spinning mill from the south. The boiler house and chimney (left) have been pulled down. The low block (right) is the former garage which will be used for the display of large transport exhibits

2, view from the north with the single-storey workshop, the future transport gallery, extending to the right

3, view from the entrance with the garage block (left) and the two-storey mill manager's house which will be converted into a typical late Victorian middle-class dwelling

staff and for the museum service staff who deal with the whole of Bradford's Museum Educational Service and Design Department. Storage, lecture and display areas for educational purposes will also be provided on this floor.

A new fire escape and tram and trolley bus shed are to be erected on the north side of the main building. Otherwise all repair work, including the renewal of the patent glazing which covers the forecourt to the garage block, has now been completed. The housing of exhibits in the various galleries has been proceeding steadily under the direction of the Keeper of Archaeology and Industrial Archaeology, Stuart W. Feather.

Accommodation: Main building
basement—workshops, stores
ground floor—gallery introducing museum collection, temporary exhibition space, motive power gallery, printing machinery and carpet loom gallery, transport gallery (in former single-storey workshop)
first floor—galleries displaying woollen and worsted textile machinery
second floor—galleries displaying non-worsted textile machinery, future expansion
third floor—offices, studios, archive store, study rooms, library, lecture room
Mill manager's house—museum of typical late Victorian middle-class dwelling
Engine house—display of beam engine
Garage block—display of large transport items
Mill canteen—café and tea garden
Small outbuildings—public lavatories

Date of completion: December 1974

Cost: Site and buildings, £25 000
Alteration and repair work, £155 000 expected total

4, early 20th century worsted textile machinery on display in one of the first-floor galleries

5, a twin-cylinder steam pump of 1870 in the 'motive power' gallery on the ground floor

6, the temporary exhibitions area on the ground floor

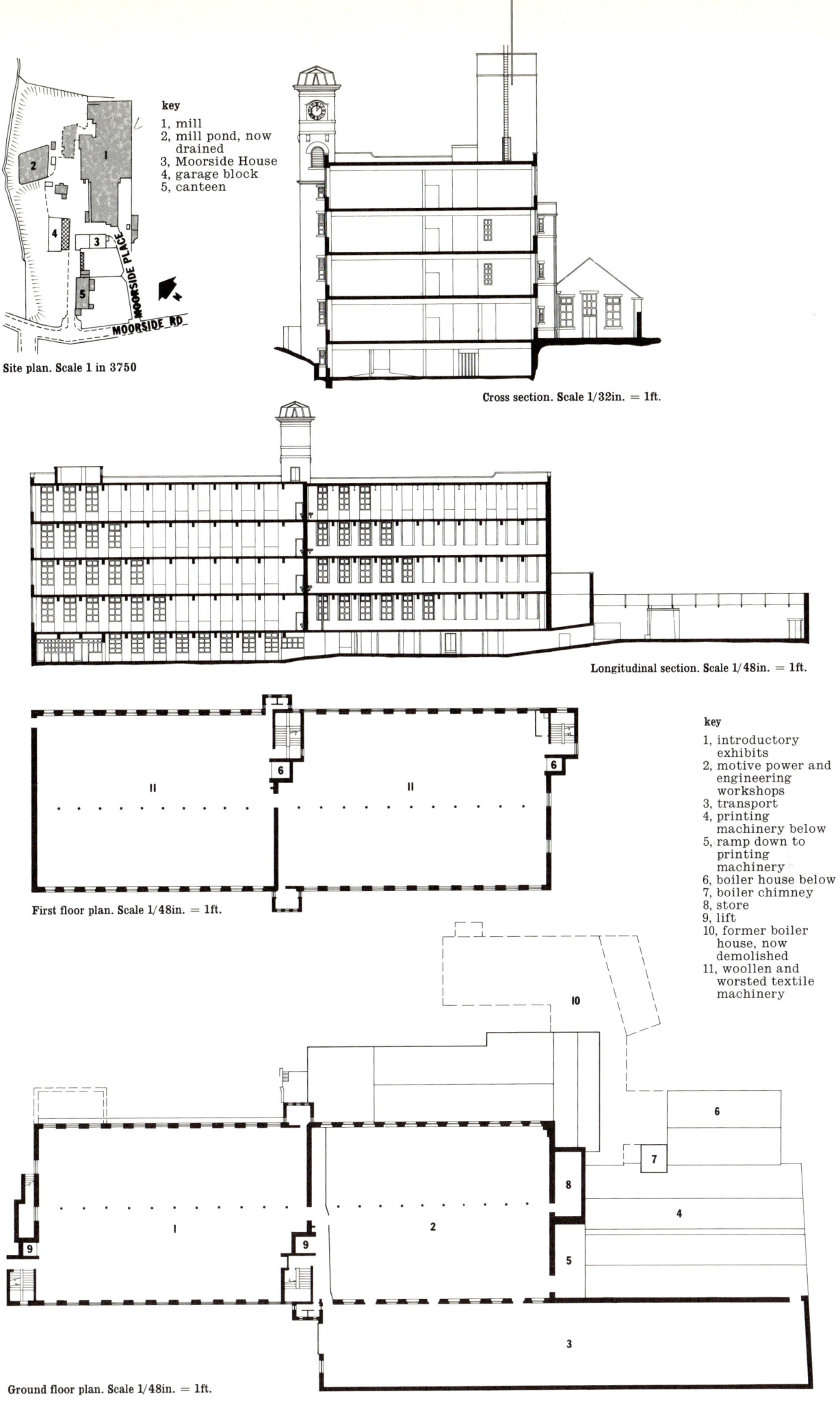

Site plan. Scale 1 in 3750

key
1, mill
2, mill pond, now drained
3, Moorside House
4, garage block
5, canteen

Cross section. Scale 1/32in. = 1ft.

Longitudinal section. Scale 1/48in. = 1ft.

First floor plan. Scale 1/48in. = 1ft.

key
1, introductory exhibits
2, motive power and engineering workshops
3, transport
4, printing machinery below
5, ramp down to printing machinery
6, boiler house below
7, boiler chimney
8, store
9, lift
10, former boiler house, now demolished
11, woollen and worsted textile machinery

Ground floor plan. Scale 1/48in. = 1ft.

Maltings and Breweries

For economic reasons to do with the Industrial Revolution—cheap labour on the one hand and heavy taxation on barley and hops on the other—brewing ceased to be a private activity and became wholly industrialised during the first half of the nineteenth century. There are three types of buildings associated with brewing; the brewery itself, which is usually a complex group of buildings and includes, in addition to the main space required for transforming the raw materials into beer, a bottling store, workshops, offices, vehicle sheds and stables; maltings, where barley is converted into malt and which sometimes form part of a brewery but are often an independent group; and oast houses, where hops are dried. The first two are represented in this chapter.

Turning oast houses into private dwellings has been a popular activity for a long time. There is no shortage of examples of the small hop farm where two or three drying kilns now serve as bedrooms and bathrooms, though never without the addition of windows to a structure that was intended to have none. The danger is that the rarer examples of large groups—ten or more cylindrical kilns with their conical roofs and wooden cowls—will disappear from the Kentish countryside for want of finding a suitable use. There is no ready answer to this problem and, as far as is known, there are no converted examples. Perhaps the agricultural college at Wye or the University of Kent at Canterbury could acquire such a group and find a use for it.

The brewery at Freshford is typical of an industry which belonged essentially to the small county town. Its great mass is broken up into several units and tucked well into the hillside so that it integrates easily with the scale of the surrounding domestic buildings. It becomes part of that urban 'grain', referred to in an earlier chapter, which is capable of absorbing spaces of almost any size and which here absorbs the brewing hall, an exceptionally large and impressive space that has been converted into an architects' drawing office with the minimum of change.

Of the three types of buildings associated with brewing, maltings have probably received the most attention from conservationists in recent years. As late as 1958 Sir James Richards was able to write: 'In the whole wide range of anonymous industrial architecture, maltings are probably the buildings whose beauties have been least noticed. They have neither the rural charms of water and windmills nor the romantic associations of the pioneer textile mills.'

In the same book the author illustrated the maltings at Snape in Suffolk, which 'is not only one of the finest specimens of its kind, but shows how work of several different periods maintains a unity of character when it all follows the same functional principles'.* Nine years later the malt house at Snape opened as the main concert hall for the Aldeburgh Festival. It received wide acclaim and other maltings followed—Ely, Bishop's Stortford, Farnham—all of which are illustrated here. In every case the malt house is converted into a hall—a single volume in other words—which means gutting the building of its multi-layered floor structure. Headroom on each floor of a malt house is usually six feet or less and is expressed externally by parallel rows of small louvred openings. To respect these openings—to make use of them as windows, say—any conversion must do away with all the floors or with every other floor. Far more important than the floor structure are the pyramidal kiln vents which provide maltings with their characteristic silhouette. Both at Snape and at Ely this feature has been preserved (or renewed) and ingeniously adapted, in the one case for ventilation and in the other for the boiler flue.

The situation of the maltings at Beccles on the edge of the town beside the Waveney made them particularly suited to conversion into dwellings. It proves once again that domestic scale is not incompatible with industrial size and that the Victorian builders, in continuing a Georgian vernacular, not only placed dwellings and industrial structures harmoniously side by side, but made it possible for a later generation to extend the life span of a redundant industrial building type by a fundamental change of use.

---

*Sir James Richards *The functional tradition in early industrial buildings.* London 1958 and 1968, Architectural Press.

OLD BREWERY, FRESHFORD, SOMERSET

Architect: Leonard Manasseh & Partners

Client: Leonard Manasseh & Partners

Site: The property, which is in the heart of Freshford, consists of several linked buildings facing east on to a cul-de-sac that runs north off the top of Church Hill. The old brewery itself forms the main central bulk, with its lower part dug into the hillside. At the north end there is a three-storey cottage and at the south end another three-storey block (probably the former brewery offices) abutting a double-fronted house which in turn abuts adjoining property. The entrance, at high level, is from Dark Lane into a yard west of the buildings.

History: The present buildings are probably no older than the eighteenth-century (with nineteenth-century additions and alterations), though the site may have been used for brewing ale since much earlier times. The buildings ceased as a brewery some time before the Second World War and were used as a bookstore during the war. After many years of disuse, the buildings became derelict and were put up for sale. They were bought by the present owners in 1964 because they were cheap and attractive as well as a way of providing a country office for a practice which had been working for some time in the Bath-Bristol area.

Character: An imposing mass of buildings with walls of dressed stone, and a dominating feature of the small Somerset town. The 80ft. chimney, which gives the buildings their industrial character, was the present owners' main reason for buying the property. The central part—the old brewery itself—consists of a lower barrel-vaulted hall and vast two-storey-high hall above with windows on two levels set in deep reveals. In this, the rough stonework of the walls and the timber structure of the floors remain exposed. The cottage at the north end was in a ruined state (with a demolition order on it) and consisted of a single space on each of the three floors, connected by a circular wooden staircase.

1, the entrance block before conversion and, 2, after conversion

3, the main entrance door is part of a continuous opening which rises through two floors

Work done: Originally only the entrance block to the brewery on the yard side and the cottage were converted. The entrance block formed a small architects' office, and the cottage was used by the London partners when working at Freshford. Except for new floor finishes (quarry tiles downstairs, carpet upstairs) and some painted matchboarding to the lavatory, the existing stone walls and suspended floor structure of the entrance block were left exposed. The roof was insulated and finished with plasterboard and plaster, leaving the trusses and purlins exposed. A new ladder-type timber staircase with a simple steel handrail connected the two floors. The cottage was repaired and completely modernised. New services were installed in both the cottage and the entrance block. The original iron cramps of the chimney had rusted and their expansion was forcing the stonework apart. The cramps were removed, the displaced stones put back and galvanised steel straps fitted to replace the old cramps.

More recently the office was expanded into the upper part of the brewing hall. For reasons of economy and in order to preserve the space as a whole visually, it was not partitioned or divided. Central heating was installed in the form of a gas-fired industrial heater (with outlets for future ducting should it become necessary to subdivide the space). The existing brewery chimney, lined with stainless steel, became the boiler flue. Pin-up boards placed vertically between windows concealed lighting and telephone conduits to each work station. The boards were covered in sacking bleached by the staff themselves. The existing floor was levelled off with a latex screed left uncoloured. Fibreglass insulation was laid on the ceiling rafters, and new windows, some opening and some glazed, were fixed direct into the stonework.

Future intentions include providing the brewing hall with direct access from the street by means of the existing stone stairs extended with a circular concrete stair. The lower hall could become two or three 'duplex' flats with sleeping galleries inserted beneath the vaulted ceiling, an art gallery or small museum, or a workshop-cum-offices for an industrial designer. The three-storey structure between the brewery and the double-fronted house would make a fine house with terraced gardens, or two flats, one approached from level 3 and the other from level 1.

Accommodation: Entrance block
level 3—reception area, lavatory
level 4—office, tea kitchen
Cottage
level 2—entrance, living room
level 3—kitchen
level 4—bedroom
Brewing hall—office

Date of completion: Entrance block, 1970
Cottage, 1971
Brewing hall, 1973

Cost: Entrance block, £2435
Cottage, £1440 (50 per cent recovered with discretionary improvement grant)

4, the reception area on the ground floor. The staircase leads to the first-floor office

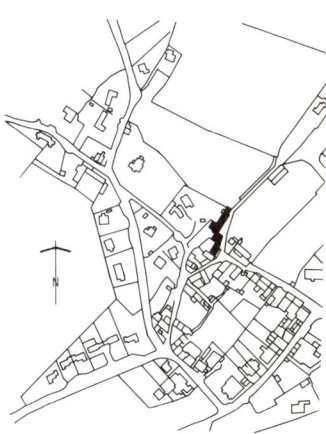
Site plan. Scale 1 in 7500

5, the first-floor office with roof trusses and stone walls left exposed

7, the superimposed windows set well forward in the thick stone walls of the upper hall

6, the upper hall of the brewery (level 3) which the architect hopes to use as a drawing office

Fittings in cottage, £200
Brewing hall, £2000, including repairs
and reconditioning of furniture

Rate: Entrance block, £3·70 per sq. ft.
(£39·83 per m²)
Cottage (based on £1640), £3·64 per sq. ft.
(£39·18 per m²)

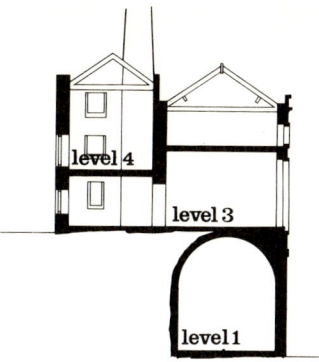

Section AA. Scale 1/32in. = 1ft.

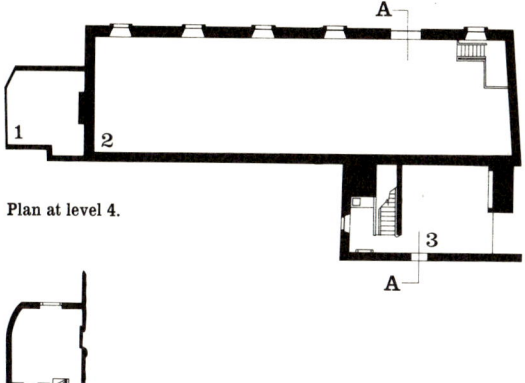

Plan at level 4.

Second floor plan of cottage

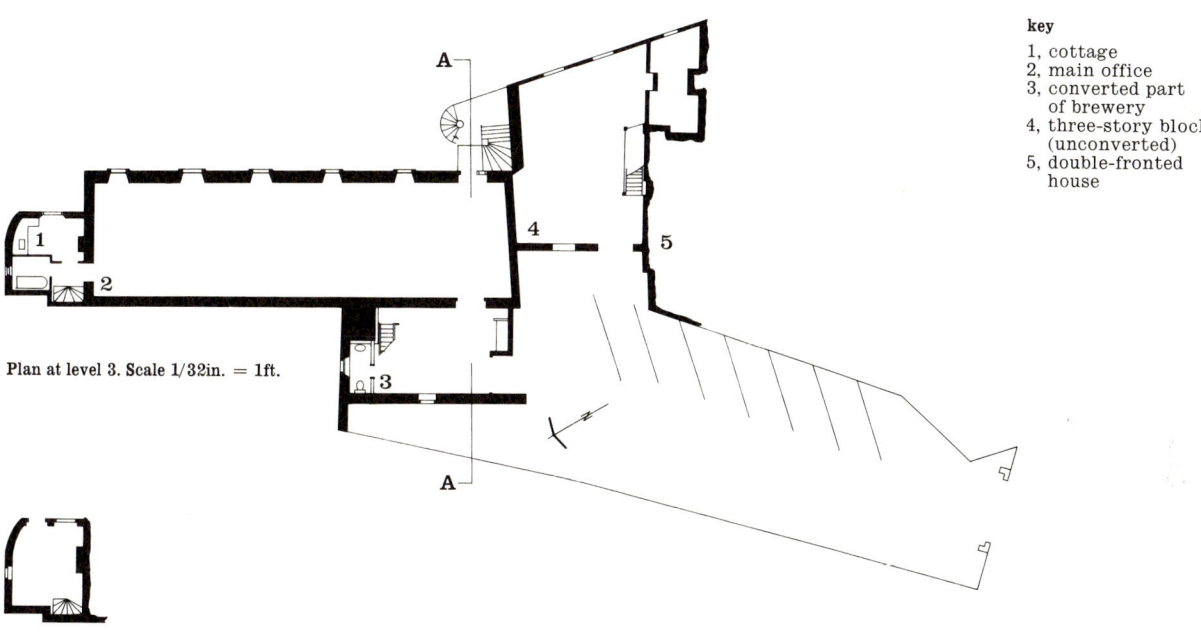

key
1, cottage
2, main office
3, converted part of brewery
4, three-story block (unconverted)
5, double-fronted house

Plan at level 3. Scale 1/32in. = 1ft.

Ground floor plan of cottage

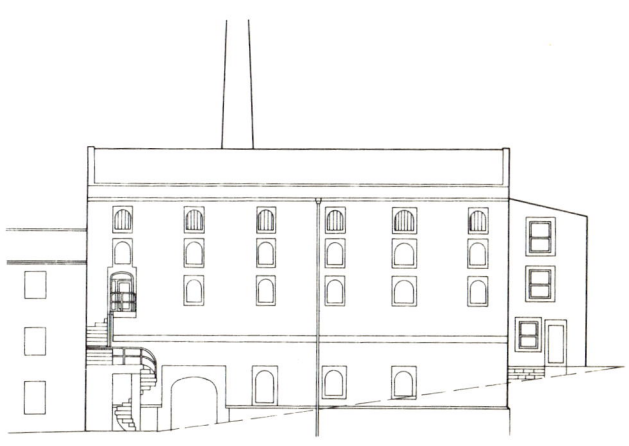

South elevation and section through three-storey block

East elevation

MALTINGS, SNAPE, SUFFOLK

Architect: Arup Associates

Client: Aldeburgh Festival of Music and the Arts

Site: Snape maltings lies on the road between Snape village and Orford. It is bounded on the north by the River Alde and on the east by marshland. This most famous of nineteenth-century maltings in the functional tradition lies just south of Snape bridge and, despite its name, actually lies within the parish of Tunstall.

History: The construction of the Snape maltings was begun in the mid-nineteenth century by Newson Garrett—shipowner, grain transporter, Lloyds agent and mayor of Aldeburgh—and two of the later buildings carry the dates of 1894 and 1953. After the maltings changed hands in 1964, the maltings process ceased, and the buildings were used for grain drying and storage. The large malt house, because of its divisions with charging floors and hoppers, was lying disused at the back of the site, overlooking the marshes, when it caught the eye of the Aldeburgh Festival as a possible concert hall. It was surveyed and shown to be suitable for conversion to an auditorium accommodating just over 800 people, a full-scale orchestra and a choir.

Character: A complex of malt house, storage sheds, turning bays, and kilns, the maltings are traditional mid-nineteenth-century industrial buildings. They are built with red bricks from the local Snape brickworks, with timber floors and deep timber roofs in the local shipwright tradition. The roofs were originally finished with Welsh and Italian slates and the turning bays and low buildings with red clay pantiles. But when repairs were necessary, roof slates and tiles were replaced with asbestos slates or sheeting which rapidly grew moss and fitted in well with the industrial scale of these buildings. This method of roof covering —for construction as well as repair— was maintained throughout the nineteenth century and right up to the building added in 1953. Although this last building is in reinforced concrete, it still fits in with the Snape tradition because it has an asbestos roof and it has been carried out in a simple, unselfconscious way.

In the main malt house—135ft. long and some 80ft. wide—the kiln drying took place, and the building was divided with longitudinal walls and cross walls forming hoppers and charging floors and had a deep two-way spanning roof of steel and timber.

Work done: The preliminary survey showed that although the foundations and brickwork were in tolerably good condition, the roof timbers had virtually turned to charcoal and would have to be removed. To create the maximum size auditorium, the main longitudinal

1, view of the maltings from the north-east across marshland and the River Alde

2, sculpture by Henry Moore near the entrance to the foyer

3, view from the north-west with the foyer and concert hall block on the left and on the right unrestored buildings whose roof is covered with corrugated asbestos sheets

key
(existing conversion dark tint)
 1, private entertaining space (warden's flat in phase 1)
 2, workshop and storage space (multi-purpose space in phase 1) warden's office on ground floor
 3, management offices on ground floor; single studio on first floor and roof
 4, exhibition space/entrance hall; library and manuscript store on first floor and roof
 5, public wcs on ground and first floors; private flat on first floor
 6, rehearsal room
 7, rest rooms, kitchen, public wcs on ground floor; exhibition space on first floor
 8, storage on ground floor; artists' studios on first floor
 9, warden's residence and garden
 10, small rehearsal rooms and studios
 11, workshop and studio
 12, new car park
 13, new pedestrians' courtyard
 14, possible new stables
 15, possible new paddock
 16, George Gooderham (Investments) Ltd

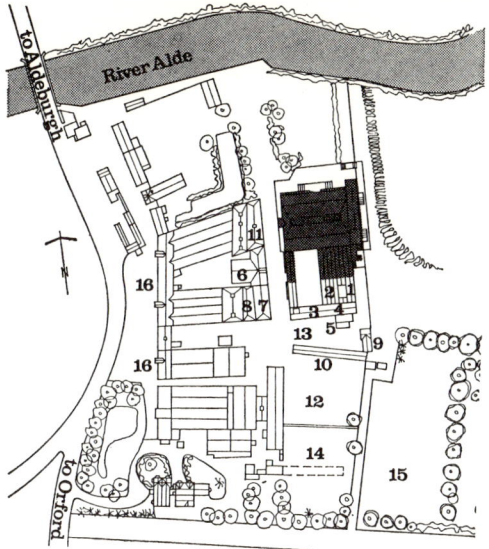

Site plan

4, the foyer—a single space 135ft. long by 19ft. wide—gives access to the rear of the auditorium (via the steps in the foreground) and to the restaurant at the rear end. Here, as in the auditorium the bricks were sandblasted

walls dividing the kilns from the drying room were removed, together with all the internal structures, cross walls and hoppers down to the kiln floor. The roof was entirely removed. This left an auditorium of 135ft. by 60ft. in plan and a foyer the full length of the auditorium and 19ft. wide. A new roof was designed keeping the basic shape of the old roof but moving the ridge over to the new centre line of the auditorium. The height of the walls and of the roof was increased to give the required volume for the acoustic design and a flat top similar to the old design was introduced to receive ventilators based on the design of the old smoke hoods. A simple roof truss with a cross brace centre piece with struts of Columbian pine and ties of 1in. diameter high-tensile steel with bottle screws was used. The walls were stiffened with new piers and arches, and tied together with a new reinforced concrete beam at eaves level. The rear floor was raked and constructed in in situ reinforced concrete, and the lavatories, cloakrooms, heating and air-handling chamber and the electrical switchgear were placed beneath the rake.

The foyer, which gave access to the rear of the auditorium at the west end and to the restaurant at the east end, was a single space 135ft. long by 19ft. wide. A stage, the full width of the auditorium and 40ft. deep, was supported on screw jacks at the east end of the auditorium. This gave conductors and producers the ability to choose a rake between the horizontal and a 2ft. drop at the front. An orchestra pit was formed, projecting 10ft. from the front of the stage and extending right to the rear of the stage, giving conductors the ability to vary the placing of the orchestra in relation to the stage. Orchestra pit covers were provided together with a removable front to the stage for concert hall use. The 824 seats designed for the auditorium were made of cane with ash frames. The auditorium floor was finished with hardwood strip and with cork under the seating. The foyer was finished in red pamments.

The building to the north of the malt house was converted into dressing

5, 6, the auditorium was created out of the large kiln structure overlooking the marshes. All intermediate floors and dividing walls were removed, and a new roof structure was designed. The back part of the floor was raked and the space underneath used for lavatories and cloakrooms

6, looking up the rake to the back of the auditorium

7, the restaurant on the first floor of the east wing overlooking the marshes. Underneath are the artists' dressing rooms

rooms at ground level giving direct access to the stage, and a restaurant and kitchen at first floor level. The original structure was retained here and was cleaned and redecorated, and new windows built into the east wall of the restaurant and dressing rooms. A recording room and BBC control room was built adjacent to the dressing rooms, and the whole auditorium was wired back to this recording room to provide all the necessary facilities for modern professional stereo recording and transcription broadcasting. On the south side of the auditorium, 20ft. of the turning bays was converted into an additional access to the auditorium and also to the side of the stage. A viewing room for the artistic director was also provided on the east side of the building. Access for vehicles to the south side of the stage was provided together with a loading bay at stage level.

After two years of intensive use, the concert hall was burnt down on the first night of the June 1969 festival. A contract was immediately let for rebuilding the hall. Plans had already been drawn up for extensions in the turning bay for improving the dressing rooms and access to the stage, and for providing parking for BBC and recording vans; and studies had already been made for building a warden's flat on the site. These plans were included in the rebuilding of the auditorium. Other alterations included a change in the design of the opera lighting control board, enlargement of the kitchen, the removal of the recording room to the south side of the building and the installation of mechanical apparatus to remove the orchestra pit covers. Future plans include the provision of a small hall or rehearsal hall and accommodation for students for study weekends.

Accommodation: Ground floor—auditorium, stage, foyer, cloakroom, lavatories, offices, recording room and tape room, various control rooms, dressing rooms, exhibition space, store rooms, kitchen, warden's flat, chorus room
First floor—upper foyer, lighting control room, restaurant and upper kitchen, upper part of warden's flat, office, store, exhibition space, upper chorus room

Date of completion: First completion, 1967
Second completion plus extensions, 1970

Cost: 1967 scheme, building, £127 000
Opera lighting and controls, £25 000

Rate: £180 per seat

8, a cantilevered loading hatch which has been adapted to other uses and where access is now by spiral stair instead of hoist

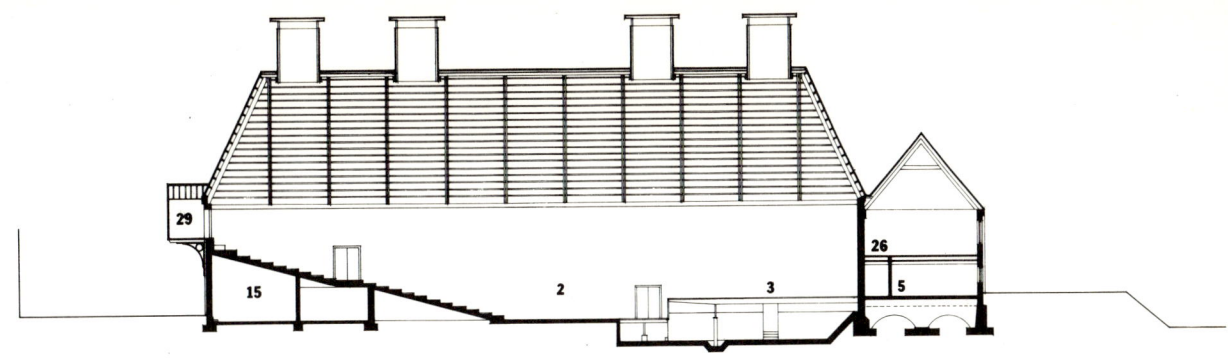

Longitudinal section through auditorium. Scale 1/40in. = 1ft.

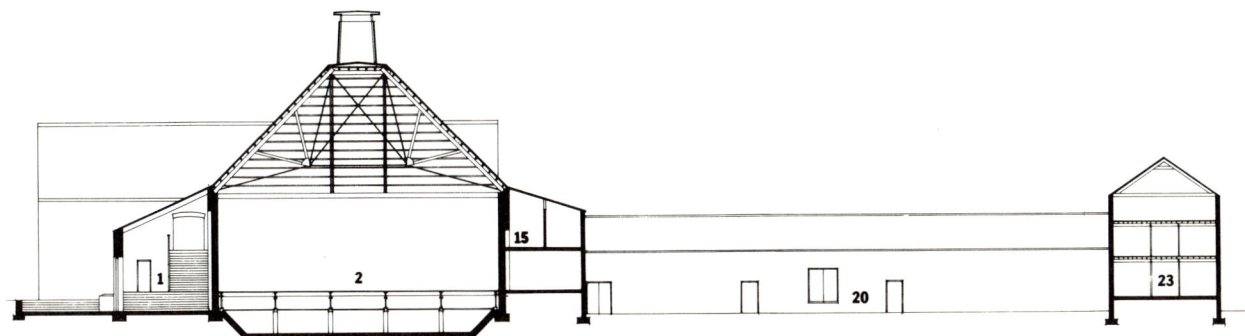

Cross section through auditorium

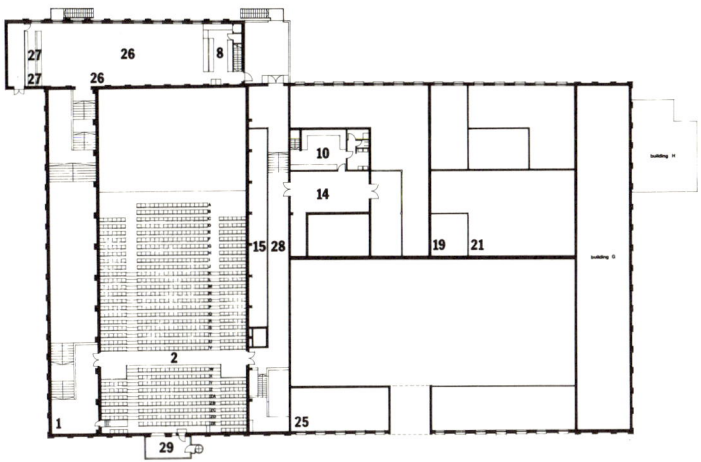

First floor plan. Scale 1/72in. = 1ft.

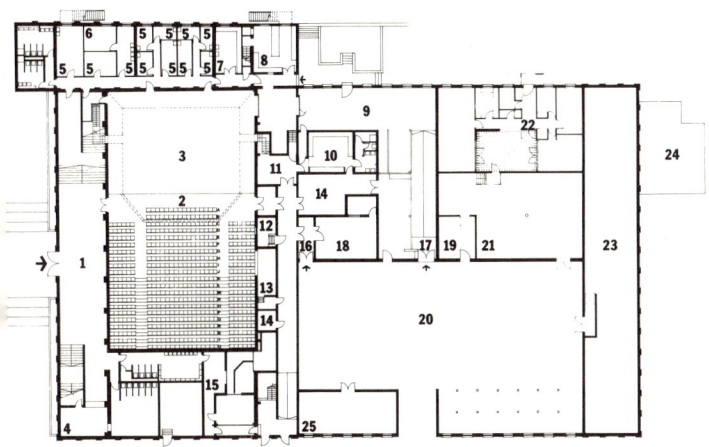

Ground floor plan. Scale 1/72in. = 1ft.

key

1, foyer
2, auditorium
3, stage
4, cloakroom
5, dressing room
6, warden's office
7, wardrobe room
8, kitchen
9, ramp and storage area
10, chorus room
11, orchestra lobby
12, stage manager
13, directors' box
14, store
15, plant
16, artists' entrance
17, delivery entrance
18, recording room
19, office
20, service yard
21, exhibition space
22, warden's flat
23, building G
24, building H
25, sprinkler tank room
26, restaurant
27, bar
28, Marland gallery
29, lighting control room

MALTINGS, ELY, CAMBRIDGESHIRE

Architect: Dennis Adams & Associates

Client: Ely City Council

Site: On the banks of the River Ouse in a part of Ely which is popular for its leisure activities and on the fringe of the shopping area. The conversion work has been integrated with a council project for a riverside walk.

History: Built as a maltings in the 1860's, it continued in the same use until 1967, when fire swept through the east wing and its owners, Watney Mann (East Anglia), decided that work on the premises should cease. Ely had been without a hall since the demolition of the corn exchange in 1963 and Watney Mann offered the maltings and land to the city for a nominal £100 provided they were converted to provide a new hall and after a feasibility study prepared by Arup Associates (the architects of the maltings at Snape) had shown that the main block could be converted into such a hall at roughly two-thirds the cost of a new building. After the conversion the main block was listed by the Department of the Environment.

Character: The buildings consisted of a three-storey main block with a kiln tower at one end and the remains of the gutted wing, which was demolished together with most of the out-buildings. Walls are of brick with diaper patterns forming string courses and window surrounds. The regular pattern of small windows was broken by the characteristic weatherboarded cantilevered structure which housed the hoisting machinery and which was unfortunately lost in the conversion. Other features such as the dormer windows, the scalloped fascias and the circular tie rod plates were retained. The most characteristic part is the kiln tower with its pyramidal slate roof and capped vent through which moisture from the drying process used to escape and which now acts as a terminal to the flue of the new boiler.

Internally the kiln tower has an ingenious light roof structure of timber combined with steel rods. Before conversion the main block had three floors, each floor barely 6ft. 8in. in height. The suspended floor structure consisted of timber joists over massive 10in. by 14in. Baltic pine beams built into the outer walls and supported on two rows of cast-iron columns. The top floor was an attic within the roof space lit by dormer windows and dotted by gantries, hoists and machinery penthouses which were removed in the conversion.

Work done: In removing the floor structure of the main block to form the new hall, it was necessary to ensure that any lateral restraint which it provided was taken up by the roof trusses. This was achieved by adding knee braces to each roof truss so that the structure as a whole took the approximate form of a

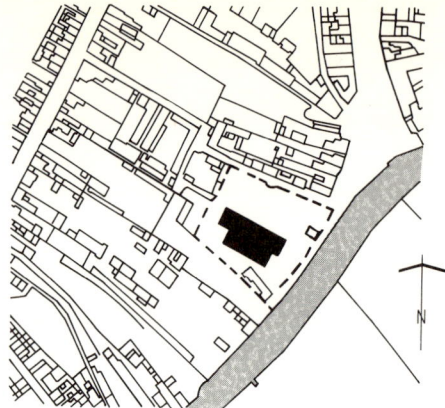

Site plan

1, the converted maltings seen across the River Ouse. The tower of Ely Cathedral is visible in the background just left of the kiln tower

2, the maltings before conversion with the kiln tower at the far end. The weatherboarded cantilevered loading hatch which housed the hoisting machinery has unfortunately been demolished

3, at the junction of the kiln tower and the three-storey main block the brick-patterned string courses ingenuously overlap. Dormer windows, scalloped fascia and capped vent have been retained, the latter as a flue for the boiler

hammerbeam roof. To avoid disturbing the brickwork, the beams were cut 12in. from each end and the stub carefully eased out later. The roof slates were lifted and fibreglass felt was fixed over the existing boarding before relaying the slates. On the inside, foil-backed plasterboard was fixed to the underside of the rafters. The pyramidal kiln tower now rises above the boiler room, stage and changing rooms.

As the main block was only large enough for the foyer, hall and stage facilities, a meeting room, bar and catering accommodation (required to make the running of the place a paying proposition) were added on the south side in the form of a flat-roofed extension in matching brickwork. At the east end new in situ reinforced concrete floors were inserted over the foyer to provide a conference room and a gallery, and over the conference room a plant room. Closely spaced windows were cut into the east gable to light the foyer and the conference room. Space heating in the hall is by warm-air ventilation combined with low-pressure hot-water skirting heating. Convectors are used elsewhere with the exception of the conference room and bar. Finishes throughout are in natural materials—oak for joinery, clay brick floor tiles, maple for the hall floor and brick walls sandblasted to remove innumerable layers of paint or, in the case of new walls, to give them the same texture as the old. The open roof trusses were cleaned and treated with a water-repellent solution to maintain the moisture content at a steady level. In the conference room and bar, walls are lined with hessian and floors carpeted.

Accommodation: Basement—boiler room
Ground floor—foyer, lavatories, hall, stage, green room; in new extension—service entrance, kitchen, stores, cloakroom, bar and meeting room
First floor—conference room, gallery, upper part of hall, changing rooms
Second floor—plant room

Date of completion: 1971

Cost: £87 000, including £100 for purchase of site, feasibility study, furniture, carpets and fees

Rate: £8·53 per sq. ft. (£91·82 per m²)

4, the east gable with the new windows lighting the foyer and conference room. On the left is the flat-roofed extension

key
1, foyer
2, hall
3, stage
4, green room
5, store
6, kitchen
7, service entrance
8, cloakroom
9, bar and meeting room
10, terrace

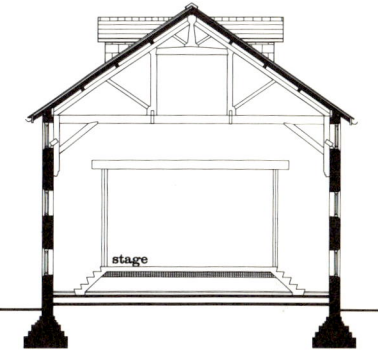

Cross section through hall. Scale 1/24in. = 1ft.

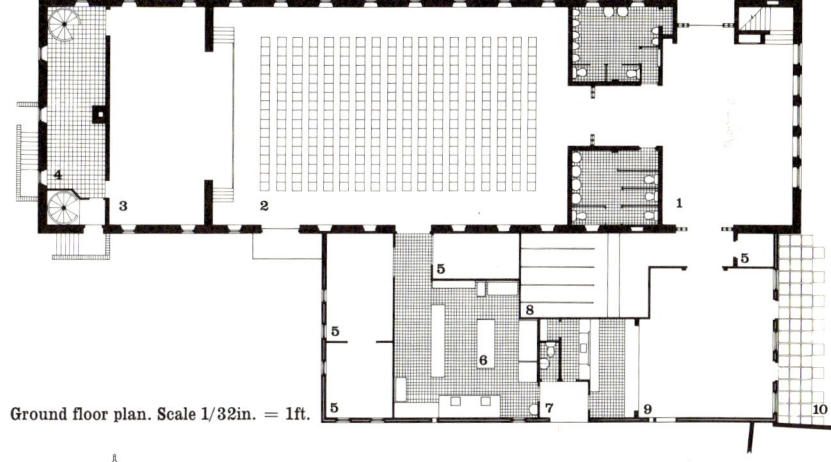

Ground floor plan. Scale 1/32in. = 1ft.

5, the three-storey main block converted into a multi-purpose hall. The Baltic pine roof trusses have been reinforced with kneebraces

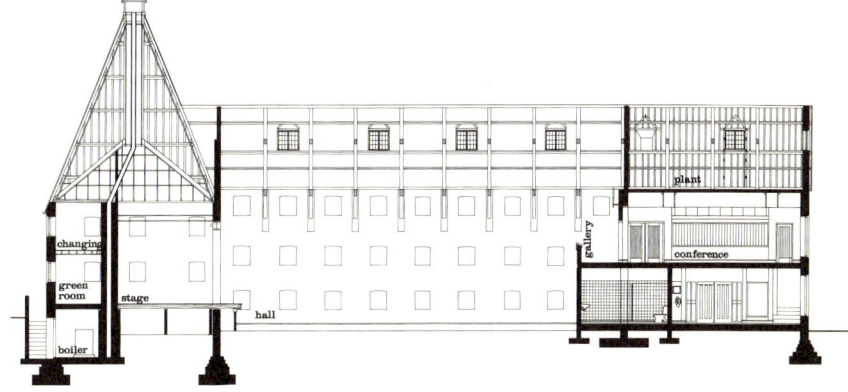

Long section. Scale 1/32in. = 1ft.

TAYLOR'S MALTINGS, BISHOP'S STORTFORD, HERTFORDSHIRE (project)

Architect: Boyd Auger

Client: Hertfordshire and Essex Malthouse Trust Ltd.

Site: Three almost parallel malt houses on one-and-three-quarter acres extending from Southmill Road to the River Stort. Beyond the river is an area of potential development, including space for a large car park adjacent to the railway station. The site is south-central in the steadily growing Eastern Arts Association area, where there is already a population of over one-and-a-half million.

History: The buildings, previously known as Taylor's maltings, date from the early nineteenth century when advantage was taken by Joshua Millar of the newly navigable River Stort for establishing large-scale premises for industrialised malting. Traditionally known as Millars I (the north block), Millars II (the south block) and Millars III (central block), all are listed Grade II and were actively malting until 1968. In 1969, Ted Smith —scientist and musician, formerly head of biological research for the British Antarctic Survey and conductor of the Edinburgh University Musical Society—conceived the idea of a major regional concert hall and arts centre. He formed the Hertfordshire and Essex Malthouse Trust, which acquired the site for £30 000, and as director he has already established an arts centre of national as well as regional importance. The staff has expanded to include an administrator, development officer (concerned with revenue and capital fund raising), publicity and catering officers, resident stewards, full-time joiner and decorators and several 'artists-in-residence', including a professional drama company.

Character: Built of red brick, weatherboarding and tiled and slated roofs, the maltings are characterised by a spectacular skyline dominated by six kiln vents and by gabled projecting grain hoists. The massive central building presents an almost blank face to the road, relieved by circular symmetrical tie bar plates. At the approach to the Millars I building there is a two-storey, eighteenth-century style cottage with gable roof and irregular facade. The interiors of the malt houses are typical, with heavy timber floor and roof supports, the couching room floors covered in immense slate flags or quarry tiles and separated by frequent cast-iron stanchions.

Work done: As the buildings had been well maintained in operation until 1968, they were in good condition when purchased by the trust. The Millars I building has been converted, using a substantial proportion of voluntary

1, view of the maltings from the south across Southmill Road. The dominating central block—Millars III—will be converted into a concert hall. The weatherboarded block on the right—Millars II—has been partly converted to include a suite of sound-proofed music practice and teaching rooms and, 2, a dance/drama studio

key

MILLARS I
1, manager's house
2, studio
3, gallery
4, bar
5, restaurant with exhibition space under
6, coffee shop (now demolished but to be rebuilt)

MILLARS III
7, orchestra room and workshops with dressing rooms over
8, concert hall with 1400 seats maximum
9, new building integral with bridge over river

MILLARS II
10, dance studio (ground floor); five small practice rooms above hall for main theatre
12, dressing rooms both floors

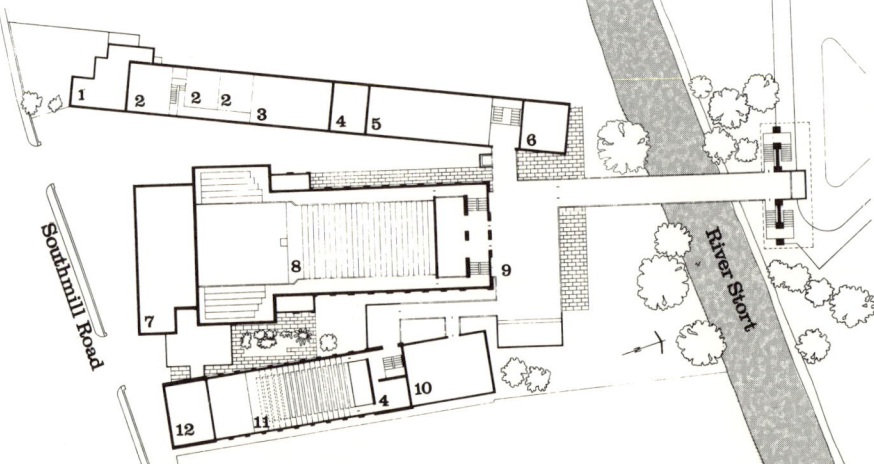

Plan. Scale 1 in 1200

labour, to provide two spacious galleries/auditoria, dressing rooms, studios, offices and a bar restaurant. Millars II already includes six soundproof music studios and a dance and drama studio theatre, and is destined to include a film theatre. At this stage a sum of £120 000 has been raised through fund raising, and an average of one hundred concerts and fifteen exhibitions are presented each year. Classes in a variety of arts and crafts are provided and the premises hired by a range of local organisations.

The Millars III concert hall will hold 1400 people, and, as its success for both performances and recording will depend on its acoustic properties, a research programme, using a detailed one-tenth scale model, has been carried out in the school of Architecture at Bristol University. Results, which can be evaluated both objectively through instrumentation and subjectively using tape recordings, have confirmed the basic tenets of design in terms of soundproofing, reverberation times and internal configuration.

Accommodation:
Millars I—art gallery (25ft. by 75ft.), studios for artists and craftsmen, bar and restaurant, stores and offices
Millars II—film theatre (340 seats) usable as small theatre and also as facsimile rehearsal facilities for main concert hall, music studios, recital, dance and drama studio, dressing rooms, workshop
Millars III—main concert hall (1400 seats), offices, dressing rooms, workshop, control rooms
New buildings—(providing site access from river approach) river bridge, foyers, exhibition areas, box office, heating and ventilation plant

Date of completion:
Millars I (Phase 1), 1972
Millars II (Phase 1), 1973
Millars II (Phase 2), 1974
Millars I (Phase 2), 1975
Millars III, 1978–80

Cost: £350 000

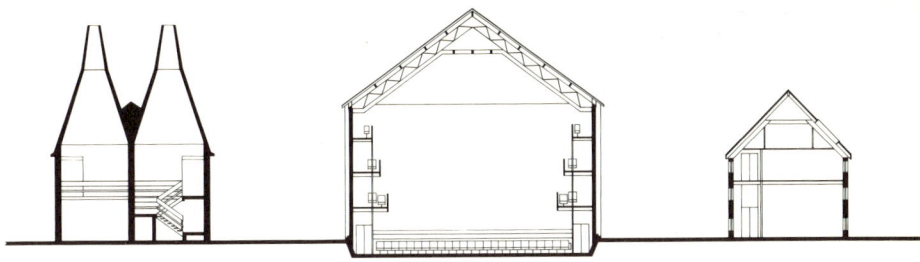
Section through site looking south. Scale 1 in 500

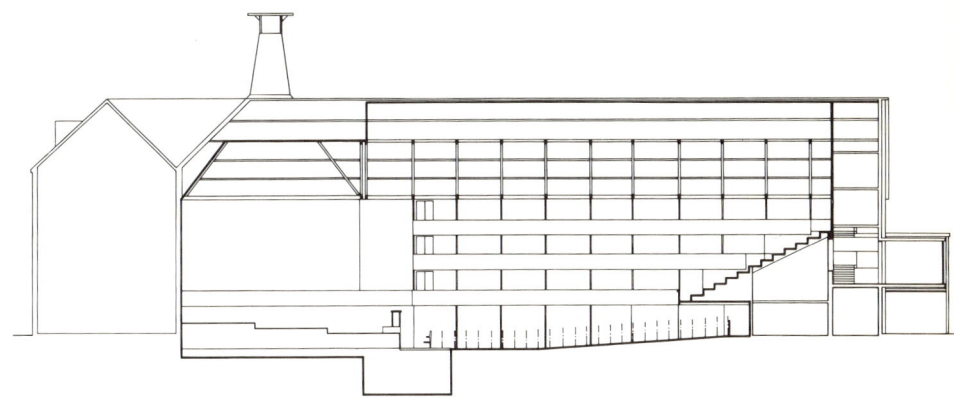
Section through concert hall (Millars III). Scale 1 in 500

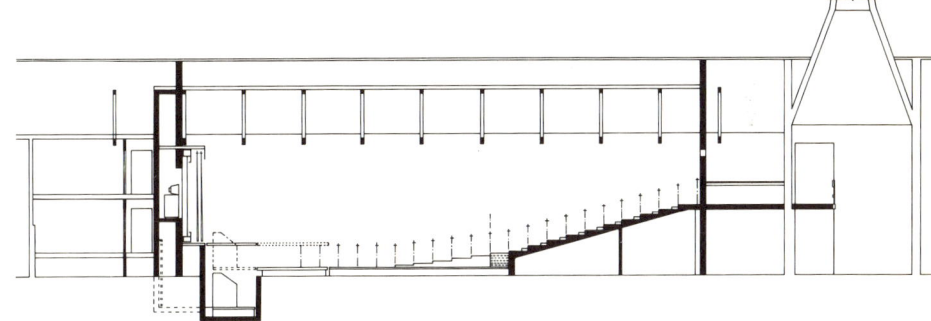
Section through small theatre (Millars II). Scale 1 in 600

3, view of the maltings from the river side

4, the north block, Millars I, has all been converted for temporary use and includes an auditorium/gallery, 5; a rehearsal room, 6; a bar, 7; and artists' studios

MALTINGS, BECCLES, SUFFOLK

Architect: Feilden & Mawson

Client: Fitzwalter Wright (Property) Ltd., Norwich

Site: The maltings are situated on Fenn Lane at Beccles and run down to the river and yacht station at the north end. They look out north and west over the River Waveney and the adjacent marshes. The River Waveney at this point is part of the Broads complex and is well used by holidaymakers for sailing and cruising.

History: The maltings are about one hundred and fifty years old, being built in the 1820's. This part of Suffolk was in the centre of the barley-growing district and the corn was transported from the farms by wherry (a form of sailing barge) along the river system to the various maltings. This particular maltings had its own loading dyke, enabling craft to discharge their cargoes directly into the building.

The building was last used as maltings in the 1930's, after which it became a seed warehouse until the 1950's. From that time it was unused and fell into a state of disrepair. The Beccles Borough Council then bought the property with a view to demolishing and enlarging a caravan site. The local amenity society asked for alternatives to demolition and a feasibility study by Feilden and Mawson suggested that a conversion to flats and commercial units could be more profitable than the caravans. The borough council then accepted the study and started work on the conversion; however, after a period of time the financing became difficult. Fitzwalter Wright (Property) Limited then stepped in and took over the project.

Character: This is typical of many maltings in East Anglia. Built of local red brick with red pantiles, the window openings are relatively small with arched heads at ground and first floor and with square heads where the openings are hard up under the eaves. The whole complex is dominated by the kiln chamber roof, which is a pyramid shape some 28ft. square at the base, rising at an angle of 60°. Internally timber floors are supported on 10in. by 10in. beams spanning 30ft. with a centre support.

Work done: The scheme is divided into two parts, both around existing internal courtyards. At the north end a restaurant and pub and two staff flats with beer store are grouped around a brick paved courtyard, and the remaining flats are entered from a quieter courtyard to the south. Each flat has a mooring for boats on the adjoining dyke. The building governed to a degree how the conversion took place, and because of the complexities of the existing plan, no two flats are alike. Wherever possible, existing walls were used as compartment walls, giving the necessary fire resistance between flats.

1, the model showing the conversion of the maltings into a restaurant and flats. The view is from the north with the single-storey public lavatory block in the foreground. Behind is the old yard which now provides access to the restaurant and two of the flats

2, the kiln tower at the north end before conversion and, 3, after conversion into a restaurant and bar

The internal finishes are simple, being white-painted brickwork or wood-float render with the roof timbers exposed and the insulation material over the top of the rafters; both internally and externally the joinery finish is a stain rather than paintwork to cut out as far as possible the maintenance problem.

Date of completion: December 1973

4, entry into the first-floor restaurant, 'the loaves and fishes', is from an external staircase and balcony, detailed robustly in timber

5, view from the east down the River Waveney. It shows the kiln tower converted into a restaurant with its capped vent carefully preserved. To the right stretches a wing of two-bedroom flats, the second bedroom being accommodated in the roof space and lit by large new dormer windows

6, inside the restaurant the roof structure has been left exposed. New insulation board has been fixed between the rafters

7, under the restaurant, on the ground floor, the bar tries to recapture a traditional atmosphere with bentwood furniture and 'lincrusta' wallpaper on the ceiling

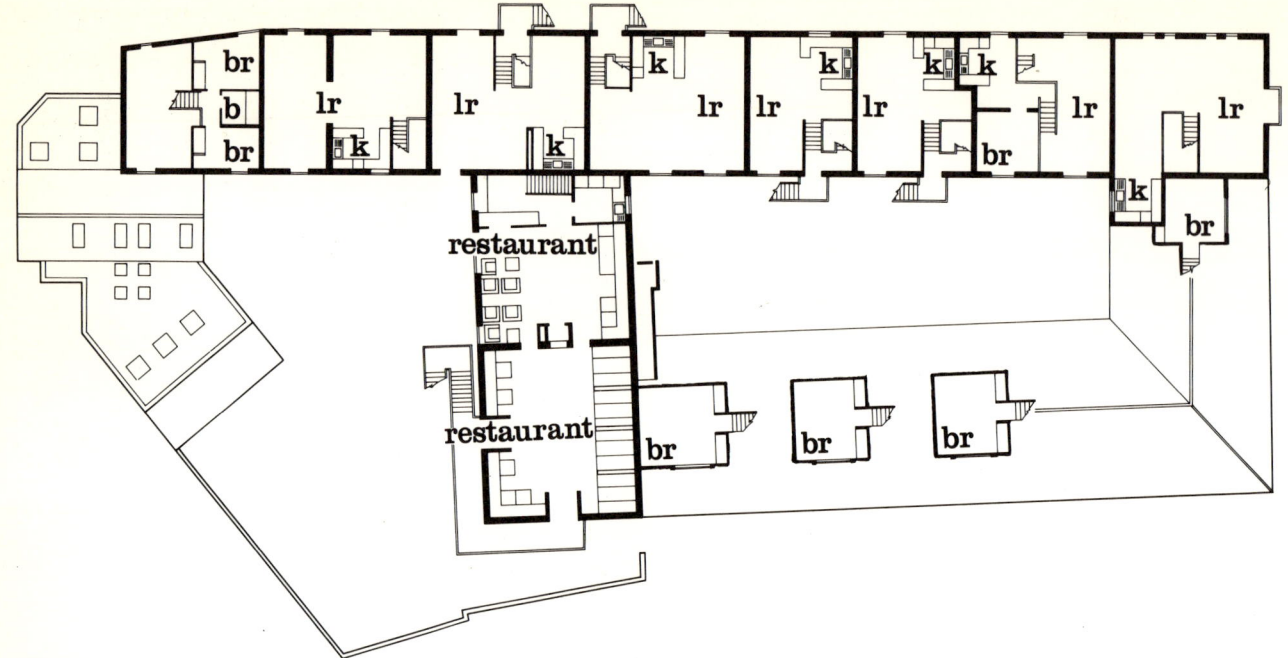

First floor plan. Scale 1/24in. = 1ft.

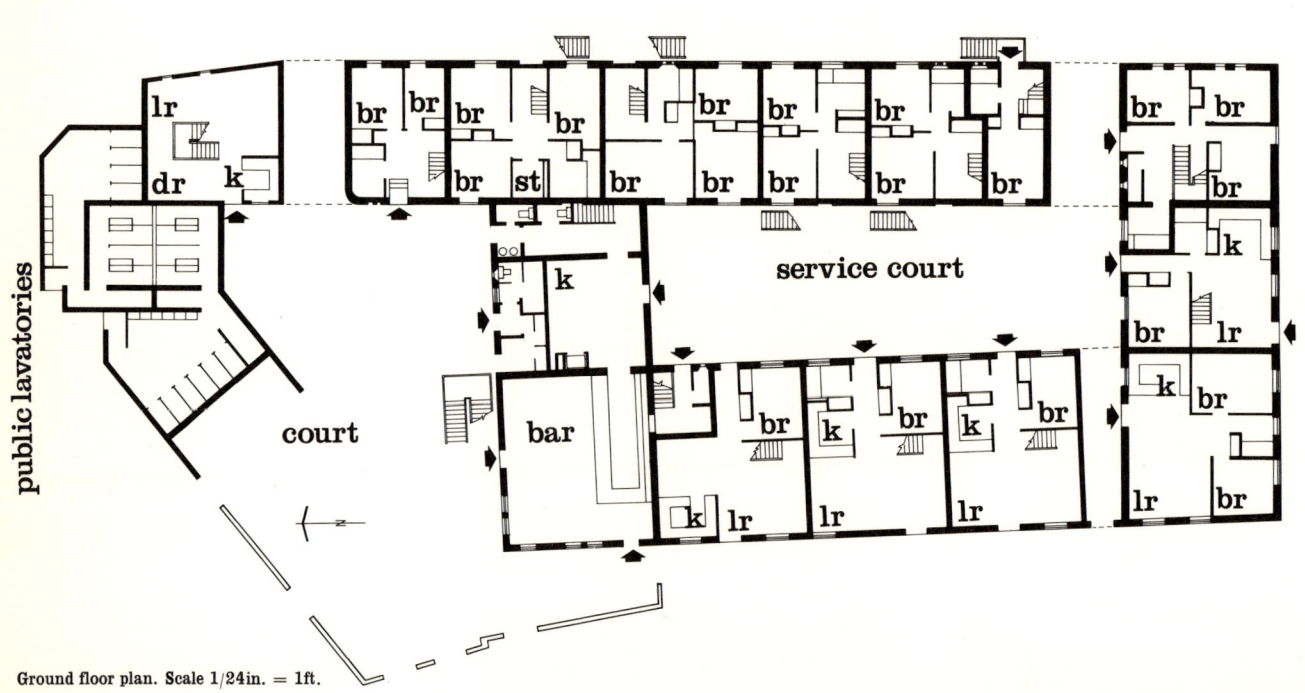

Ground floor plan. Scale 1/24in. = 1ft.

MALTINGS, FARNHAM, SURREY (project)

Architect: Kenneth Adams & Partners

Client: Farnham Maltings Association

Site: A roughly L-shaped group of buildings in the centre of Farnham with short frontages on to Long Bridge and Red Lion Lane, the main frontage facing north on to the River Wey. The site includes a two-acre meadow to the west. Originally nine cottages facing south on to Bridge Square and Red Lion Lane were part of the site. The vehicular entrance is between the cottages through a gap which leads to a courtyard.

History: Of the present buildings on the site, some probably date from the mid-nineteenth century, though the group as a whole is stylistically of the late nineteenth century. In the mid-1960's the site was the subject of several planning applications for high-density residential development. The threat to demolish the maltings led to the formation, in 1968, of an action committee (under the auspices of the Farnham Society) to convert the buildings into much-needed accommodation for cultural activities, Farnham having over two hundred societies and only two inadequate halls and the local schools to meet in. An encouraging feasibility study by the county council failed to persuade the town council to become involved financially so that the committee had to raise by appeal the £30 000 which the owners, Courages, were asking. The cottages were then sold for £12 000, and in May 1969 the Farnham Maltings Association Ltd. was incorporated as a nonprofitmaking body enjoying the status of a legal charity. At the same time outline planning consent was obtained for a community centre, two halls, other community uses and a car park.

Character: The red brick buildings with gables and slate roofs are of a robust industrial character. Small window openings with flat brick arches punctuate the walls which on the river side rose sheer out of the water until a year or two ago when the river was re-routed some 12ft. away and a flood platform constructed. Much of the brickwork is divided into recessed panels. Some of the roof is in characteristic pyramidal form capped by vents.

Work proposed: While preparing for the formidable task of raising money to convert the buildings, the association encouraged their use for a number of activities such as markets and fêtes, which provided the regular income needed to pay for insurance premiums, maintenance work, etc. Volunteer labour cleared and tidied the large hall area, the courtyard and the approach from the temporary footbridge (bought from a shipyard for £35 but subsequently disposed of).

The project consists of three main parts: (1) a large general-purpose hall

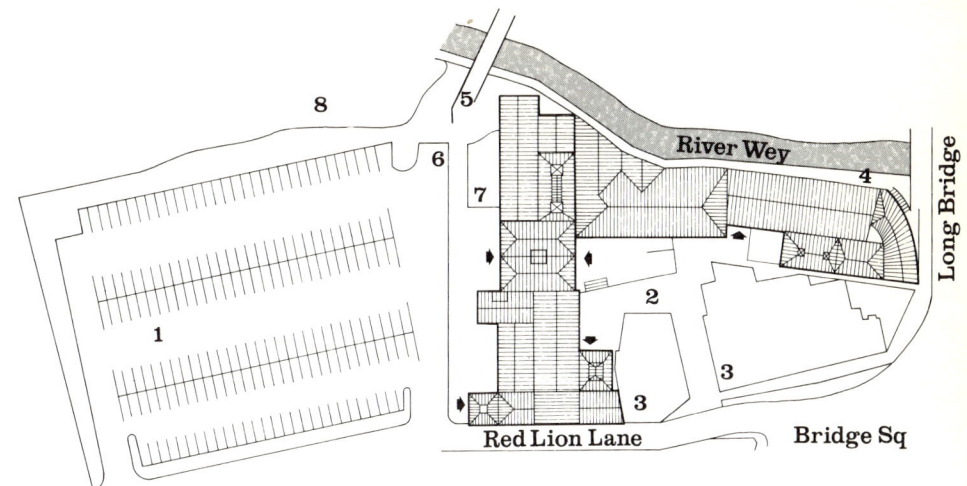

Site plan.

key
1, car park
2, courtyard
3, existing cottages
4, new flood platform and riverside walk
5, temporary footbridge (now removed)
6, off-loading bay
7, service yard
8, meadow

1, the courtyard in use by one of the markets which provided the association with an income, but which had to be stopped due to the structure's non-compliance with the Building Regulations

2, the maltings along the River Wey before the recent realignment and deepening of the river to prevent flooding

with its related accommodation in the centre, (2) a community centre in the south-west wing and (3) an adult education centre in the east wing, which has been incorporated in agreement with the county council, to whom it will be leased. The general-purpose hall with its related accommodation will form the first phase of the work.

Date of completion: First phase, 1975
Second phase, possibly 1980
Third phase, not yet estimated

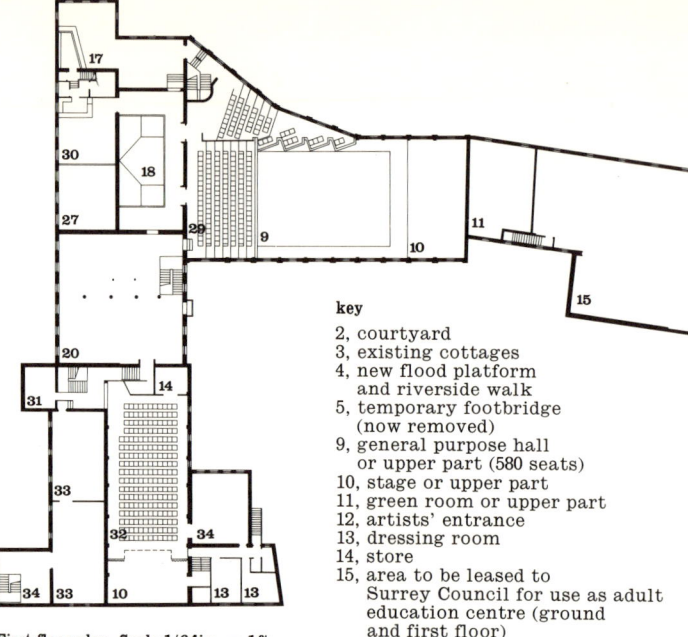

First floor plan. Scale 1/64in. = 1ft.

key
2, courtyard
3, existing cottages
4, new flood platform and riverside walk
5, temporary footbridge (now removed)
9, general purpose hall or upper part (580 seats)
10, stage or upper part
11, green room or upper part
12, artists' entrance
13, dressing room
14, store
15, area to be leased to Surrey Council for use as adult education centre (ground and first floor)
16, promenade
17, bar
18, foyer or upper part
19, stillage
20, assembly and general purpose area
21, raised terrace
22, oil storage
23, manager
24, cloakroom
25, nursery
26, entrance to nursery
27, committee room
28, stage door to hall on first floor
29, balcony
30, coffee bar
31, boiler room
32, general hall (200 seats)
33, nursery
34, unspecified

3, young voluntary labour at work

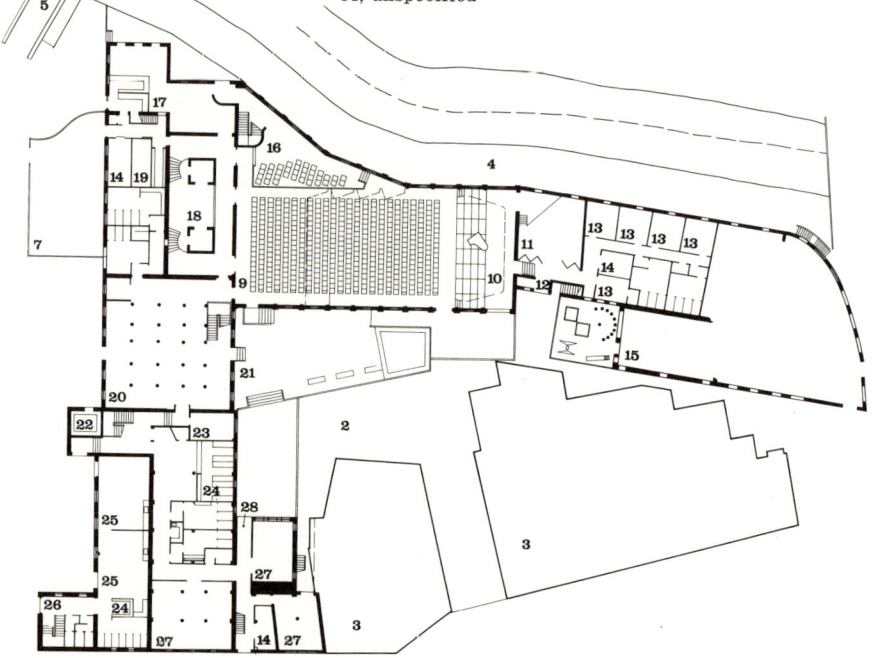

Ground floor plan

West-east section. Scale 1/40in. = 1ft.

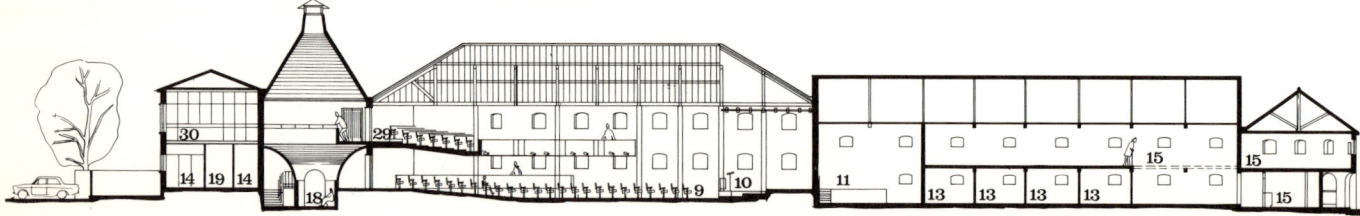

Warehouses and other industrial buildings

Unlike the preceding chapter in which four out of the five maltings illustrated have been or are going to be converted into arts centres with theatres or concert halls, this last chapter is remarkable for the variety of new uses to which redundant industrial buildings can be put. Its main concern is with warehousing and associated factory buildings, all of which constitute large volumes almost invariably enclosed by brick walls. Frequently occupying whole city blocks, they make considerable impact by their sheer bulk. An essential part of their character is the fenestration, the width of the opening being determined by the span of a brick arch. To enlarge these openings by inserting steel or concrete lintels is as easy as it is ill advised, and all the examples illustrated wisely eschew this solecism. On the other hand the repetition of the same opening on a long facade like Canal Square in Washington, D.C., gives the building an indeterminate character which makes it possible to add a few bays or even a floor without causing harm. Obviously this must be done in the same style as the building unless the contrast can be expressed as a separate element, like the two additional floors over the printing works at Hanover which appear like a light roof structure over massive brick walls.

The internal character of warehouses is determined by their large open spaces and by their exposed structure of rough timber posts and beams, cast-iron columns and beams with brick vaulting, or a combination of iron and timber. The spaces are relatively low and, ironically, the constant level of floor and ceiling has an oppressive monotony comparable to today's *Bürolandschaft* office. (What used to be suitable for storing goods is now good enough for people to work in!) When a warehouse is converted into an office for a single firm, one way of breaking this monotony is by trimming the floor structure and forming wells, as the architects of the Saturday Review offices in San Francisco have so brilliantly succeeded in doing.

In Britain fire regulations make it difficult to maintain the character of the interior. They demand the subdivision of large spaces with fireproof walls and the protection of the floor structure with false ceilings, which are also useful for concealing services. We have already seen in an earlier chapter (page 149) how the cast-iron columns of Abbey

Mill at Bradford-on-Avon were allowed to remain exposed but how the false ceiling obscured the upper part of their capitals. In other countries fire officers seem to be more lenient. With the exception of the floors, the interior finishes of Canal Square are the original timber posts and beams enhanced, like the brick walls, by sandblasting.

To meet the demands for subdivision the most promising solution would appear to be conversion into flats like Oliver's Wharf at Wapping or the 'I' warehouse at St. Katharine's Dock. But this is also the way that most surely sacrifices the internal character, the occasional appearance of a cast-iron column or two in a room proving more of an embarrassment than anything else. It is not surprising, therefore, that some of the most successful conversions in Britain have been of small warehouses, like the ones at Norwich and Skipton, where in providing facilities for shops it has been possible to maintain and even improve on the open character of the spaces.

The radical solution is to gut the inside and put reinforced concrete floors within the existing shell. This at least preserves the character of the public exterior, which is often more important than the private interior. In this context the two railway examples make an interesting comparison. The Brunswick station has not only had its interior gutted and reconstructed, but its rear elevation drastically vamped up. Only the front is old, proudly declaring its respect for the past (the reverse of the eighteenth-century fashion for vamping up the front as a declaration of faith in the future). The London Round House, on the other hand, remains virtually unaltered both outside and in. The arrangements for theatrical performances are of a temporary and make-do nature, and all proposals for a permanent conversion have so far failed to materialise. In the one case we have the worldly self-confidence of a bank; in the other, the love of improvisation and fear of commitment of fringe theatre.

The examples presented in this chapter fall into two categories: groups of buildings like Ghirardelli Square or Ledoux's saltworks at Arc-et-Senans, and single buildings like the Old City Hall in Boston or the monumental ice houses in San Francisco. All the examples are urban except for one in each category—the saltworks in the first and the Landmark Trust's little mine building in the second. New uses include offices, theatres, restaurants, showrooms, shops, a yacht club, a bank, a school of architecture and housing. Such an eclectic selection makes it almost impossible to talk of the conceptual nature of converting warehouses. Given the basic rules mentioned earlier, anything is possible, the degree of success depending less on the choice than on the location, the budget, the will of the client and the skill of the designer.

Historically the examples stretch across the full span of the Industrial Revolution, from the saltworks of 1775, with their idealistic sense of order applied for the first time to industry and the worker, to the 1920's garage in Washington, built to service the last and most insidious product of that revolution which in America more than anywhere else became the symbol of worker emancipation. The chapter ends with some examples of that monument to nineteenth-century municipal pride, the pumping station. In its grandest form, as at Leicester and Sunderland, it poses a special problem because of its machinery which forms such an integral part. For this reason the best pumping stations should be restored and preserved intact as museums which could be enlarged to include other aspects of industrial archaeology. A more modest example, at Haringey on the River Lea, shows an imaginative transformation of sewage beds into a children's playground—a note of welcome altruism in the face of so much self-interest. Such exemplary reclamation of redundant municipal land should encourage other local authorities, especially those that are short of public open space, to follow suit.

SALINES ROYALES DE CHAUX, ARC-ET-SENANS, FRANCE

Architect: Chief Architect, Monuments Historiques, Georges Jouven
Architect to the Département du Doubs, Pierre Boudvillain
Interior designer, Francine Galliard-Risler

Client: Département du Doubs and five central government ministries

Site: Ten buildings surrounded by a curtain wall in a rural setting between the villages of Arc and Senans, 34km. south-west of Besançon in eastern France. The site was originally chosen because the large supplies of timber from the neighbouring forest of Chaux were considered more important than proximity to the salt-water springs at Salins where the forests had been denuded.

History: The saltworks grew from an ambitious plan by Claude-Nicolas Ledoux for extracting salt from the springs at Salins by piping the salt water 21km. along the rivers La Furieuse and Loue and by evaporating it over wood fires with the help of winds from the Jura mountains. The first stage, built between 1775 and 1779, consisted of ten buildings, one for the director, two for the administration and collection of the unpopular salt tax, two for the manufacture of salt, four for workmen of different trades—wet-coopers, farriers, carpenters and joiners—and a gatehouse. The later stages, conceived as a city around the saltworks, were never built.

The completed buildings functioned unsatisfactorily as a saltworks until 1890. In 1926 the Ministry of Cultural Affairs classified the buildings, which had become largely ruined, and the Département du Doubs took them over and carried out some essential repairs to the façades and roofs. In 1931 a decision to move a riding school into the two buildings flanking the Director's House resulted in further restoration work which saved the complex as a whole. This included work to the Director's House (which had been dynamited in 1918 by the private owners 'for reasons of safety' after the interior had been gutted by fire) and a new reinforced concrete structure in the flanking buildings to support the roof covering and tie in the external walls, which were seriously out of plumb.

Character: All the buildings were of stone, with tiled roofs. Some of them had neoclassical temple fronts, and the three-arched porticos on the two buildings flanking the Director's House (3 and 4) mastered a bracketed roof projection designed to protect the workers from the rain. As a whole the buildings combined classical grandeur with the cosier French rural tradition of large mansarded and hipped roofs. Inside, the buildings were utilitarian in character, with the exception of the

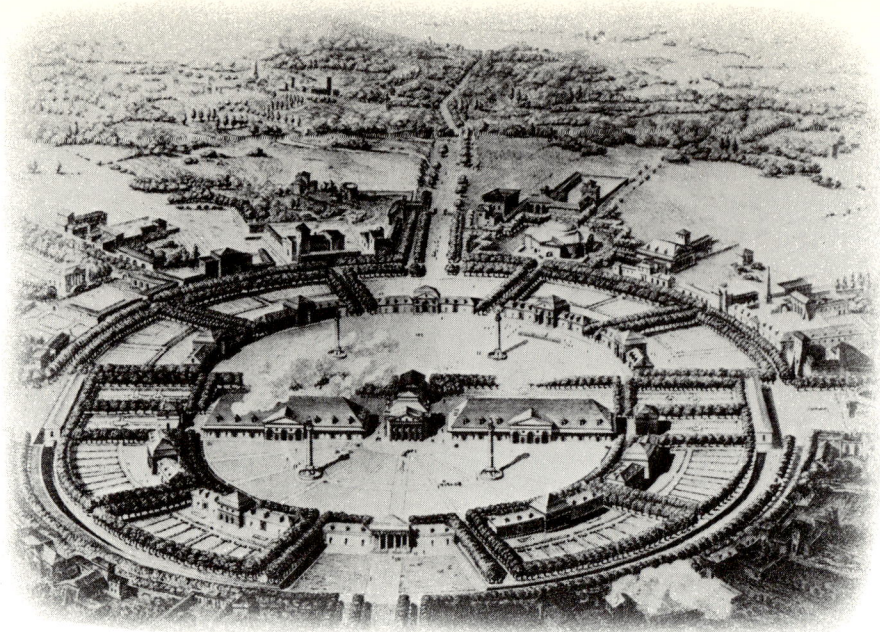

1, Ledoux's imaginary town centred around the saltworks at Arc-et-Senans and, 2, the only part which was completed (see also block plan below)

Block plan

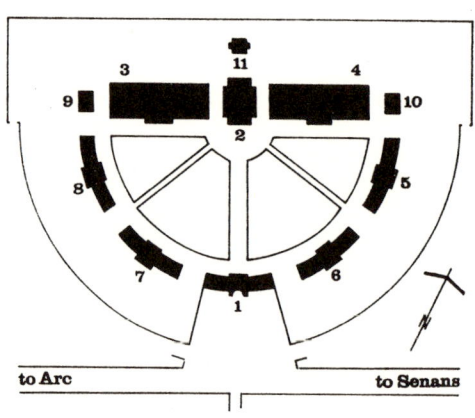

key

1, gatehouse: reception hall for visitors, flat for keeper and six rooms for visitors and students; right-hand side not yet converted
2, director's house: conference centre, temporary exhibitions and administration
3, building for the manufacture of salt; temporary theatre with 2500 seats
4, building for the manufacture of salt: future library
5, workmen's building: future accommodation for groups of students
6, farriers' building: dining rooms and kitchens
7, wetcoopers' building: permanent exhibitions
8, workmen's building: 20 duplex flats for married students
9, administration building: 15 beds for unmarried students
10, administration building: future director's house
11, stables

Director's House (2), which contained a towering central space with a grand staircase leading to a chapel (now destroyed). The workmen's buildings (5, 6, 7 and 8) each had central double-height halls with first floor galleries. The character of large barns, manifested in the two buildings flanking the Director's House, was successfully retained in the structural alterations of the thirties.

Work done: The buildings were converted to provide accommodation and facilities for an international conference and study centre devoted to research into any matters concerning the long-term future of mankind. The programme has been carried out in stages according to the amount of money available. Externally there was only strict restoration work, and no alterations were allowed.

The earlier reconstruction of the Director's House had been strictly confined to the exterior, that is, the walls and portico, the roof and lantern, and sufficient reinforced concrete tie beams internally to hold up the walls. Now the central staircase was rebuilt, the surrounding three floors inserted in reinforced concrete and modern services installed. One of the workmen's buildings (8) has been turned into twenty small duplex apartments, preserving the double-height central space for access *and* communal functions but inevitably altering the character of the flanking spaces beyond recognition. High window sills suggested a raised ground floor level inside the apartments and this still left room for a mezzanine floor (an open gallery) which extended back over the central corridor, apartment entrance and bathroom (all at the old ground floor level). Another workmen's building (7) has been converted into a permanent exhibition centre and best retains its original character.

Yet another workmen's building (5) is being converted into dormitories for students. The two corner buildings (9 and 10) have been turned respectively into 15 bedrooms for unmarried students and into the new director's house. Formerly used for administration, these were already domestic-type buildings requiring merely a straightforward rehabilitation and the installation of modern services. The building to the left of the Director's House (3) is being used as a temporary theatre after the installation of a simple stage and seating, and the one to the right (4) will be converted into a library. The surroundings have been landscaped and planted with close regard to Ledoux's intentions.

Accommodation: Gatehouse centre—reception hall for visitors
left side—two flats for staff
right side—six rooms for visitors and/or students
Workmen's buildings—twenty duplex flats, permanent exhibition centre, restaurant and club, dormitories for students
Administration buildings—fifteen bedrooms for students, director's house

3, 4, the condition of the buildings in 1926 when the French Ministry of Cultural Affairs decided to classify them as historic monuments

5, the monumental Doric portico which forms the gatehouse

6, *the wall behind the colonnade which is treated like a grotto with the entrance cut into it*

Buildings for salt manufacture—theatre seating 2000, library (for future conversion)
Director's House basement—temporary exhibitions
ground floor—work rooms, meeting rooms, temporary exhibitions
first floor—lecture room, secretary's and director's offices, foyer, bar
second floor—conference rooms and work rooms
third floor (attic)—work room
Stables—no plans for conversion

Date of completion: The conference centre opened in the summer of 1970, when work to the Director's House and to three of the workmen's buildings was completed.

Cost: Approximately 10 million francs, half subsidised by five government ministries and half by the Département du Doubs. This includes 200 000 francs for furniture and furnishings, 50 000 francs for landscaping and planting and 200 000 francs for security measures.

7, the Director's House seen through the archway of the gatehouse. Plans and interior views of the conversion are on page 196-7

8, the restored colonnade of the Director's House and one of the two flanking buildings used originally for the manufacture of salt. It will be converted into a library

195

9, one of the blind orifices oozing salt which form Ledoux's Leitmotiv *at the Royal Saltworks*

10, the stable block behind the Director's House. There are no plans for conversion at present

11, the Director's House with the great central staircase which originally led to a chapel

12, the 150-seat conference room, also on the first floor of the Director's house

13, offices on the first floor of the Director's house

14, the old salt-manufacturing building (3 on block plan, page 192) converted in 1931 for the use of a riding school and now used as a temporary 2500-seat theatre

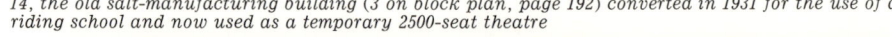

15, the sleeping gallery in one of the flats and, 16, the central hall in the old workmen's building (5 on block plan, page 192 and see detailed plans on right)

key
1, hall
2, bar
3, duplex flat
4, laundry
5, store
6, central heating
7, store
8, gallery of duplex flat
9, false ceiling
10, luggage
11, balcony at first floor

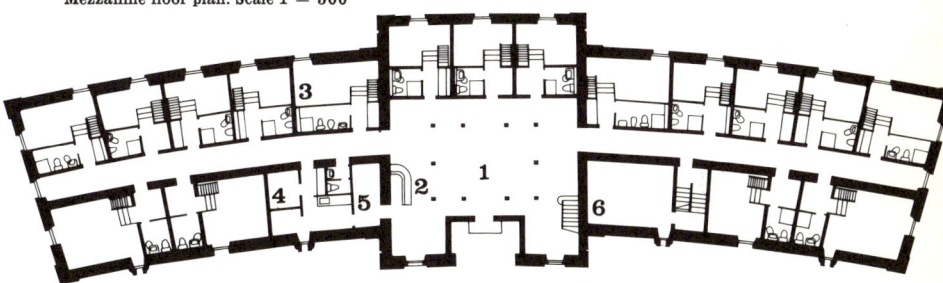

Mezzanine floor plan. Scale 1 = 500

Ground floor plan (building 8 on block plan)

17, the old wetcoopers' building which has been converted for permanent exhibitions

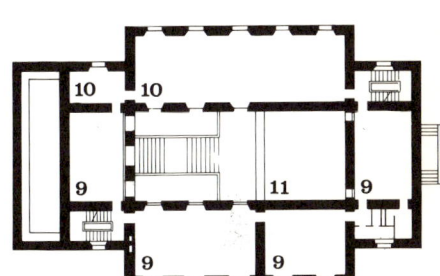

Second floor plan. Scale 1 = 450

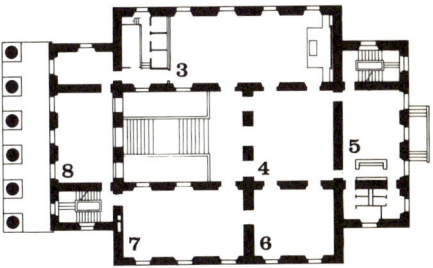

First floor plan

key
1, cloakroom
2, temporary exhibitions
3, conference room
4, hall
5, bar
6, director
7, secretaries
8, lounge
9, workroom
10, reading room
11, void

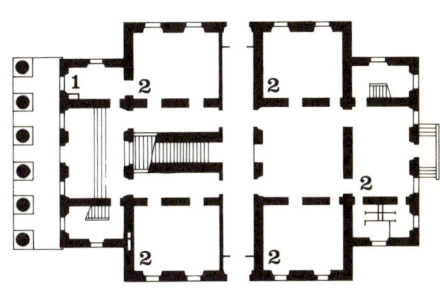

Ground floor plan (building 2 on block plan)

GHIRARDELLI SQUARE, SAN FRANCISCO, CALIFORNIA

1, drawing of the whole city block which forms Ghirardelli Square from the sea front. Seven of the original eight buildings which belonged to the Ghirardelli chocolate factory have been converted to new uses—the Apartment Building, the Clock Tower, the Mustard Building, the Cocoa Building, the Chocolate Building, the Woollen Mill and the Power House. The other buildings are new

Architect: Wurster, Bernardi & Emmons Inc.
Landscape architect, Lawrence Halprin & Associates
Design consultant, John Matthias (shops), Barbara Staufacher (graphics)
Sculptor, Beniamino Bufano

Client: William M. Roth

Site: A sloping city block on the waterfront overlooking San Francisco Bay, bounded by Beach Street to the north, Polk Street to the west, North Point Street to the south and Larkin Street to the east.

History: Built between 1893 and 1916 and designed by William Mooser, the buildings were once a complex of factory and warehouse buildings belonging to the Ghirardelli chocolate factory. The earlier Woollen Mill (1862) is the only remaining building of those purchased by Domingo Ghirardelli in 1893. It is the oldest factory in the West and was once used for manufacturing Union uniforms during the Civil War. William Roth bought the buildings for mixed public use and started work on the eastern half of the square in 1963, meanwhile leasing back the western half of the complex to the chocolate factory for five years to allow for careful planning. The only wooden building, the box factory, was demolished because of its unsound condition.

2, the Clock Tower at the junction of Larkin Street and North Point Street. The building is now used for shops on the lower two floors and for offices and a crafts museum on the upper floors

Character: The seven old buildings—the Clock Tower, the Mustard Building, the Cocoa Building, the Woollen Mill, the Chocolate Building, the Power House and the Apartment Building—are of red brick either over a heavy timber post-and-beam construction or (in the case of the pseudo-French Clock Tower) over reinforced concrete. The fact that the oldest building, the Woollen Mill, was built before the grid street pattern was established explains the different angle on which it was aligned. The only single-storey building is the Power House; the others have three or four storeys.

Work done: Exposed beams, columns, roof structures and walls were left intact wherever possible and new elements such as the glass domes, clerestoreys, gutters, bay windows were specially designed to harmonise. The structural engineer designed an exposed bracing system for reinforcement that complies with the city's earthquake code, yet maintains the spirit of the old structures.

The reconstruction work was carried out in two stages. In Stage I the first three buildings to be converted were the Clock Tower, the Mustard Building and the Apartment House. The Clock Tower was left virtually intact. The Mustard Building had horizontal lateral bracing timbers inserted below the existing floors. Shop fronts, corridors, lifts and lavatories were added. On the piazza side, a new 20ft. deep balcony provides a covered walkway and access at first floor level. Existing windows were either enlarged or converted into French windows opening on to the balcony. In the basement a furnace for a gas-fired hot-water central heating system was installed to serve both the Mustard Building and the Clock Tower. Other buildings have their own gas-fired central heating systems. The Apartment Building, former residence of chocolate factory superintendents, had structural steel introduced into the framing system below the floors to create clear spans. At street level is an entrance to the public parking garage and the two floors above have been converted to restaurant space. The terrace across the rear facade has been closed in with glass.

Eight new buildings within the square are designed to harmonise with the existing ones. The Wurster Building and Carousel Building are of reinforced concrete faced with brick; the others are of concrete and glass. A central piazza was constructed partly over a four-storey car park. The piazza's three main levels, which follow the slope of the site, are paved with fine aggregate concrete slabs set in border strips. A complex of walkways, decks, steps and ramps leads into and out of the shops and restaurants. The car park, which is under the eastern part of the piazza, houses 300 cars (required by the San Francisco Building Code) and consists of overlapping levels. It is of reinforced concrete construction, with mechanical ventilation and a fully automatic sprinkler system. At its eastern limit a four-storey high

3, detail of the Clock Tower facade on Larkin Street

4, the main entrance on Larkin Street with the Clock Tower on the left and a restaurant block on the right

5, view from Beach Street with the new Winster Building housing shops and a restaurant in the foreground. On the left is another new building—the octagonal Carousel

reinforced concrete wall supports the Apartment Building.

The buildings in Stage II comprise the Cocoa Building and Chocolate Building, which are linked with the Mustard Building by means of interior corridors. The Cocoa Building has wide balconies on its three upper floors fronting on the West Plaza and in many cases these have been glassed in to create eating areas or small shops. Once again the stairway is glazed to provide shelter. On its upper floors the Chocolate Building houses a restaurant which is two storeys in height, providing a most dramatic space with wonderful views through its great bay windows. A new one-storey building has been inserted between the Chocolate Building and the Woollen Mill. The last old building in Stage II is the Power House, which though originally designed as a night club has since been adapted into a luxurious cinema. In addition to the main piazza on Stage II, the West Plaza, there are two smaller outdoor spaces in this phase, the Lower Plaza and Rose Court at successively lower levels as the project drops down to the Beach Street level. The same type of intricate parking levels has been created under this phase of the square as was put in for Stage I.

Accommodation: Clock Tower (Stage I)
basement—storage space
ground floor—shops
first floor—shops
second floor—offices and contemporary crafts museum
third floor—radio station
Mustard Building (Stage I)
basement—boiler for heating
ground floor—shops
first floor—restaurant
second floor—theatre
Apartment Building (Stage I)
basement and ground floor—car park
first and second floors—restaurant
Cocoa Building (Stage II)
ground floor—shops
first floor—shops and restaurant
second floor—restaurant
Chocolate Building (Stage II)
ground floor and first floor—shops
second and third floors—restaurant
Woollen Mill (Stage II)
plaza level—shops
Polk Street level—shops
top floor—restaurant
Power House (Stage II)—used as a cinema
New Buildings
Wurster Building (Stage I)
street level—shops
piazza level—restaurant and shop
Carousel Building (Stage I)—shop
Bookstore (Stage I)
Garden shop and gallery of children's art (Stage I)
Children's clothes shop (Stage I)
Three shop buildings (Stage II)

Date of completion: Stage I, May 1965
Stage II, Spring 1968

Cost: $11 million, including land at $2·5 million

6, the new terrace and staircase built out in front of the Mustard Building on the plaza side

7, the Cocoa Building from the plaza side with the Mustard Building and Clock Tower in the background

8, the Woollen Mill is the oldest building on the site (1862) and the only remaining one bought by Domingo Ghirardelli in 1893

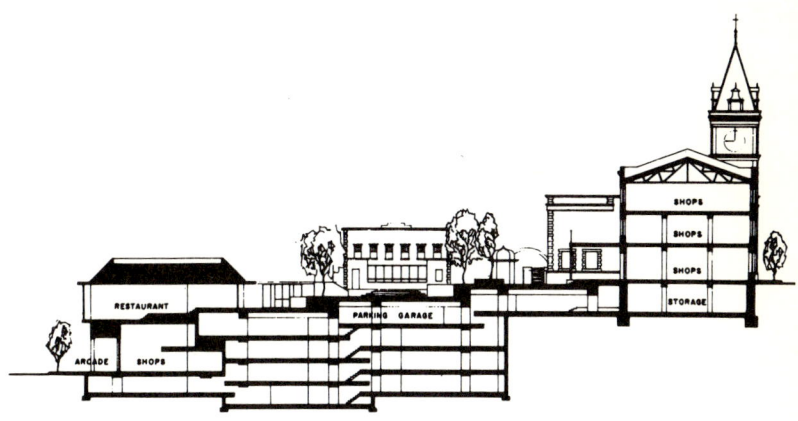

Section

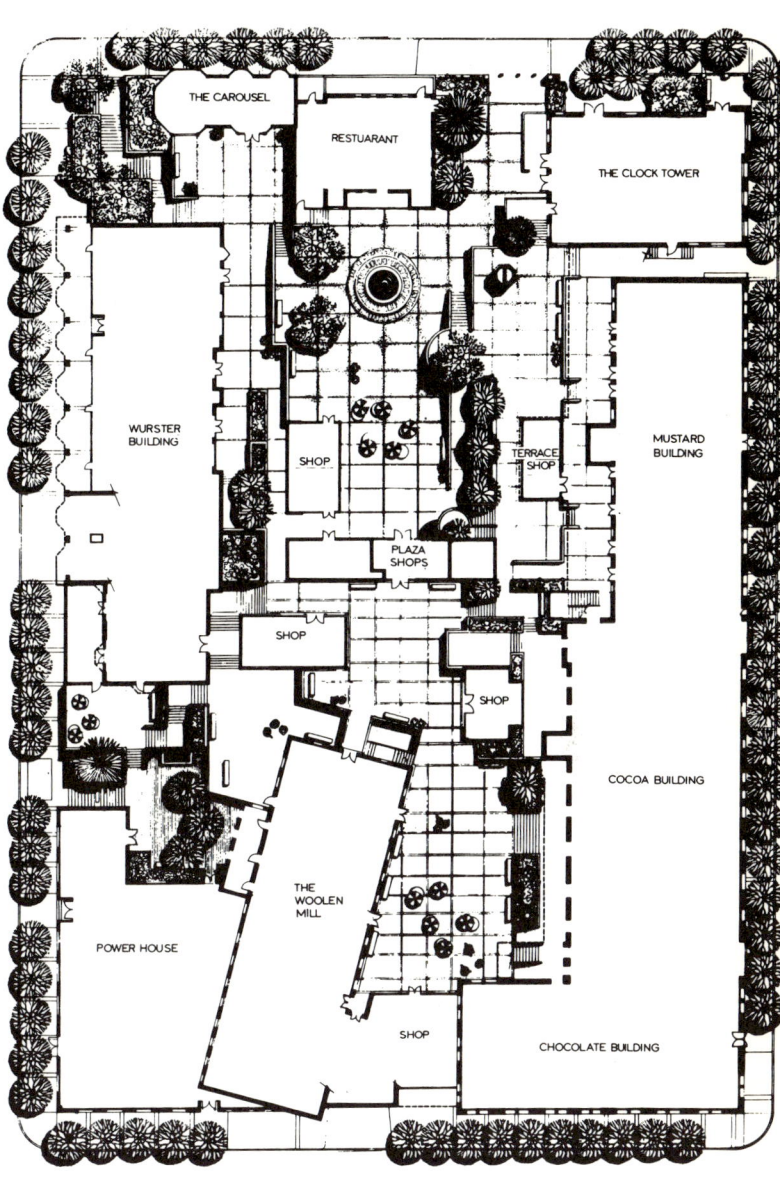

Plan

9, a craft shop in one of the rehabilitated buildings

CANNERY, SAN FRANCISCO, CALIFORNIA

Architect: Esherick Homsey Dodge and Davis

Client: Leonard V. Martin

Site: Urban site in San Francisco at the foot of Columbus Avenue overlooking Fisherman's Wharf, not far from Ghirardelli Square. It is bounded by Cannery Street to the west, Beach Street to the south, Leavenworth Street to the east and Jefferson Street to the north. One of these streets was a railway siding which ran between the cannery and a warehouse. It is now an olive grove.

History: Built in the latter part of the nineteenth century after Ghirardelli Square, the building operated as a cannery until after the Second World War. It is a San Francisco landmark spared by the 1906 earthquake and fire.

Character: The old Del Monte cannery was a three-storey brick-walled structure with repetitive bays and gabled ends. The exterior walls were supported on wood piling, still in good condition, and pierced by segmented arched windows. The interior framing consisted of heavy timber post-and-beam constructions with wood floor and roof joists.

Work done: The aim was to turn the building into a commercially viable city shopping centre with shops, a food market and restaurants divided down the middle by a pedestrian walkway. The architect also tried to generate the excitement and bustle of a market place.

The inside was completely gutted, and during reconstruction the exterior walls, which were to be retained, were held up on the inside (there was no room on the outside) by trussed braces from the original timber framework. These were removed one by one as building progressed. A walkway open to the sky was cut through the middle of the building and bordered by new brick walls to match the old. The levels of the new floors were changed only slightly from the old. The basic framing system of steel framing, wood joists and plywood sheathing was chosen to provide versatility and light weight, and to maintain the original character of the building. To comply with fire regulations, one floor level was built with a lightweight concrete floor slab cast on corrugated steel shuttering supported on steel beams.

New columns were located as close to the existing wall as possible (13 to 14ft.) to reduce the increased loads from the new construction on the old walls. The new columns were supported on drilled friction-type concrete piers extending through loose fill and bay mud into alluvial strata and bedrock. The idea of pile-driving for foundations was discarded because of possible vibration damage to the existing walls.

1, a view of the model from the Leavenworth Street side against the background of the Cannery reconstruction. This involved the complete gutting of the buildings and the propping up of the exterior walls from the inside

2, view from Beach Street with one of the entrances on the left

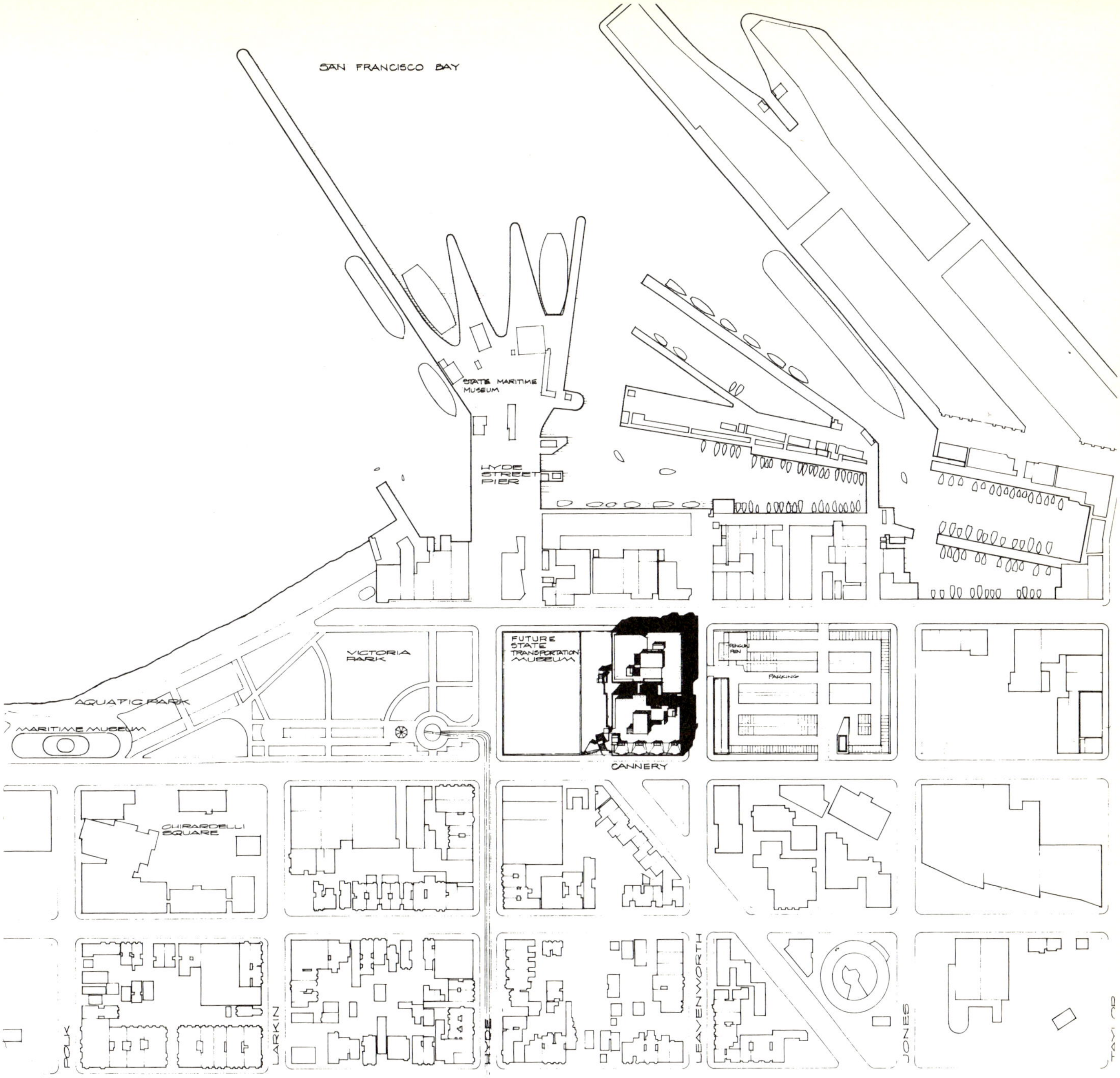

Site plan

3, view down the back of the Cannery with steps leading up to Beach Street beyond. Formerly a railway siding which ran between the Cannery and a warehouse, this sunken area is now an olive grove and forms the forecourt to the main entrance

Most of the difficult and unusual problems faced were connected with the lateral loading required in Seismic Zone 3. The lateral system of the completed building consists of horizontal plywood diaphragms and 6in. concrete shear walls cast on the inside face of the existing brick walls. The concrete shear walls cover approximately one-quarter of the area of each wall and were designed to act both alone and in conjunction with the brick walls. The diaphragms are tied to the walls with a continuous steel and wood ledger held to the walls with bolts embedded in the brick with an epoxy resin.

There is an intricate arrangement of stairways, balcony arcades, bridges, shop entrances and display windows. Part of the top floor has been opened up by a roof platform. Vertical circulation is by stairs, lifts and escalators. An external glass lift gives views over and into the building.

Accommodation: Ground floor—shops, two two-storey restaurants (one of these is the English Restaurant with seventeenth-century oak panelling and carved ceiling from the long gallery at Albyn's Hall and a Jacobean staircase from the William Randolph Hearst collection, out of store for the first time since the twenties), market, wine cellar, discothèque, services room and mail room
First floor—shops, café and gallery
Second floor—shops, two restaurants

Date of completion: 1968

Cost: $7·5 million

4, looking back towards the main entrance from one of the upper galleries

5, 6, the buildings are cleft in two by a wide walkway at ground level but connected at high level by bridges. Vertical circulation is by staircases and escalators or, inside the buildings, by lifts

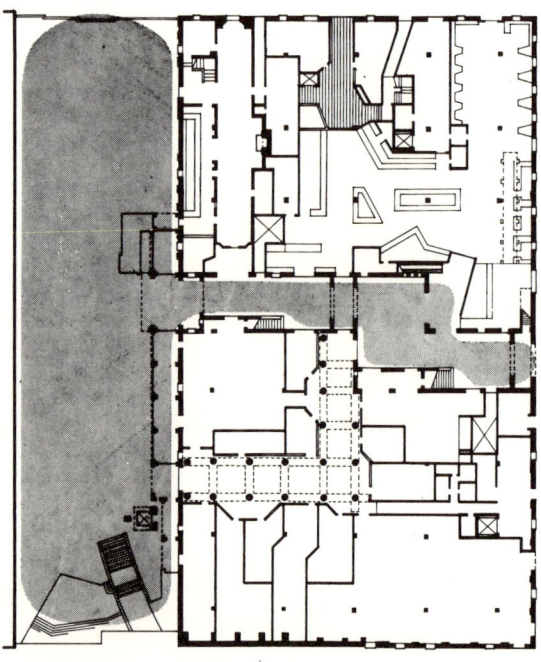

Ground floor plan

204

CANAL SQUARE, WASHINGTON, D.C.

Architect: Arthur Cotton Moore Associates

Client: Canal Square Associates

Site: In south Georgetown, bounded by M Street on the north, 31st Street on the east and the tree-lined Chesapeake and Ohio barge canal on the south. Vehicular access was restricted to 31st Street and pedestrian access to both 31st and M streets. No access was possible on the west because of private property and none on the south because of the canal. The site slopes down to the canal so that the old warehouse appeared as a four-storey building on the canal side and a three-storey building on the north side.

History: The old four-storey warehouse along the canal pre-dates the Civil War; its stone foundations were probably laid in the 1820's. Dr. Herman Hollerith, who later owned the warehouse, used it to compile the 1890 census by collating special cards with a machine of his own invention. Both the cards and the machine became the basis for the first IBM developments. More recently the building was used to store greeting cards and finally left empty and for sale, suffering vandalism and weather damage. The previous owners wanted to demolish and provide a car park, but the warehouse was declared a Class III Historic Landmark and so came under the protection of both the Washington and Georgetown fine arts commissions. The remainder of the site—a jumble of small-scale buildings including two historic houses—had become an industrial slum which included a machine shop, a fish dealer, a car wash, a funeral parlour, a furniture mart and a sprinkling of transient residents.

The intention was to preserve the old warehouse and to make full use of the high density allowed by providing 75 per cent cheap speculative office space and the remaining 25 per cent in the form of shops, underground car parking and a canal-side restaurant.

Character: The old warehouse was functional and repetitive in character, with no less than twenty-one identical window openings per floor on the canal side. The external walls of the lowest floor were stone, the upper floors red brick. The primary internal structure consisted of massive timber beams supported on a central line of timber posts (brick piers on the lowest floor) and brick projections in the external walls. The secondary beam structure was also timber and was lined on both sides with thick timber boarding.

Work done: The old warehouse was underpinned in order to construct the two floors of underground parking required by town planning regulations. On the north side a new public square

1, view from the canal of the old four-storey warehouse after conversion into restaurant, shops and offices. The structures rising above the roof line are part of the new buildings behind which enclose a courtyard on the other side of the warehouse

2, the warehouse seen from the tow-path alongside the canal. The wooden steps lead to the restaurant and café deck

was formed at the level of the lowered basement floor of the warehouse, exposing its stone foundation walls. The new openings in this wall provide access and light to the restaurant which has its main outlook on to the canal. The double-hung sashes were replaced by fixed steel windows and the floor levels were raised to accommodate steel lattice girders and services (air conditioning, electrical and telephone). The exposed timber structure and brickwork has otherwise been retained and enhanced by sandblasting. Partitions are gypsum board painted white and the floor is carpeted.

The greatest part of the development consists of new buildings enclosing the square and is sympathetic in design to the old. The fall in the ground has been used to form an upper level shopping gallery leading to a deep, narrow shopping arcade which cuts through existing buildings and connects the square with M Street.

Accommodation: Old warehouse basement or lower ground floor—restaurant and bar with outdoor deck on canal side
upper ground floor—shop and offices
second and third floors—offices
New development
first and second lower basements—underground car park
basement or lower ground floor—restaurant, shops and square
upper ground floor—shops, gallery and aracade
remaining floors (4)—offices

Date of completion: November 1970

Cost: $3 million

Rate: $17·20 per sq. ft.

3, the north side of the warehouse with the courtyard formed by new buildings on three sides. There is a shopping gallery at first-floor level which connects via a shopping arcade with M street behind

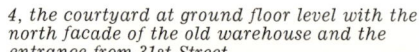

4, the courtyard at ground floor level with the north facade of the old warehouse and the entrance from 31st Street

5, the new work makes use of brick and timber to be in sympathy with the old. The night view shows the area by the two lifts looking towards the shops and steps on the north side of the court

6, the new windows and, 7, the old double-hung sashes in the warehouse replaced with fixed steel windows

8, the interior of the warehouse circa 1900 and, 9, after the recent conversion

10, a private office where the wall and ceiling structure has been sandblasted and left exposed as is the open offices

11, a perspective section of the old warehouse showing how the floor levels were raised to accommodate steel lattice girders and services, leaving the timber beams and boarding on the underside untouched

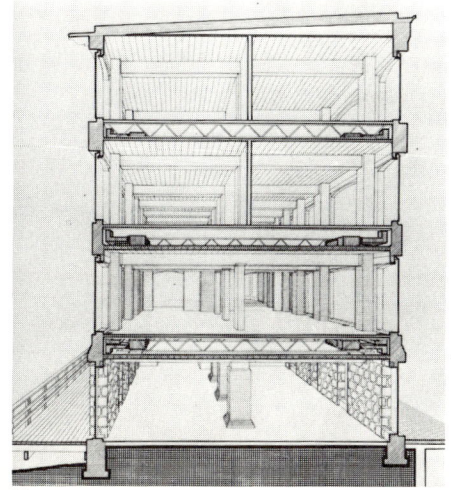

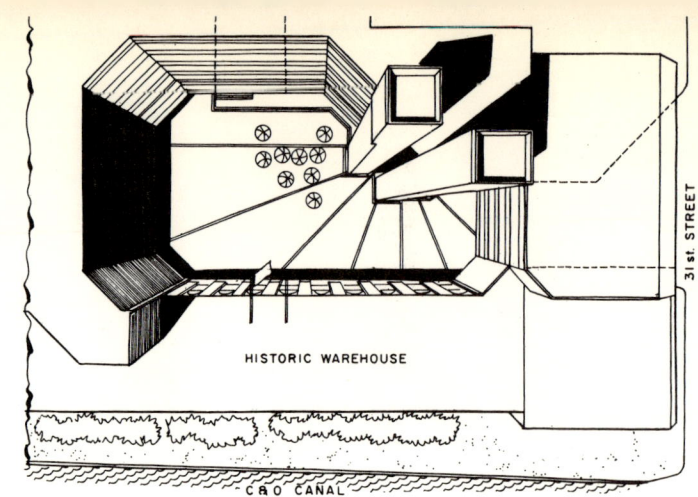
Site plan

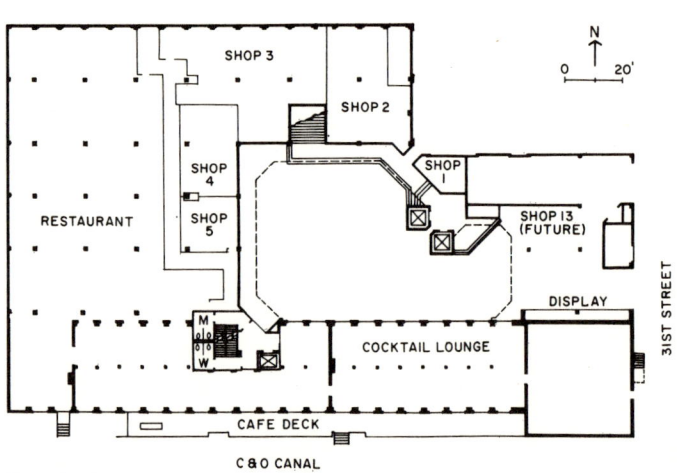
Lower level

Section

Upper level

208

WAREHOUSES, SKIPTON, YORKSHIRE

Architect: Mary D. Wales and James Wales

Site: At Skipton Wharf between the Leeds to Liverpool canal and Coach Street. Part of a conservation area, the site stands on the fringe of the business and retail district of the town, with some nearby retail premises empty.

History: The buildings were constructed in 1774 when the canal was first extended from Leeds to Skipton. They consist of two warehouses, an old stable and canal office outbuildings. The two warehouses have been semi-vacant for some twenty years and the last tenant, who had been using the ground floors for agricultural engineering, moved out a few years ago.

Character: Both warehouses have walls of random rubble and rough coursed stonework with openings of varying sizes dictated by functional needs. Corners and openings are generally framed by projecting quoins or stone surrounds, though some of the openings, of more recent date, lack this local characteristic and have ordinary lintels and sills. The roofs throughout are slate and the court between the buildings is cobbled. Internally the warehouses consist mainly of large open spaces with primary structure of cast-iron columns and beams, secondary structures of timber and open timber roof trusses. The stable block and outbuildings are of brick with arched openings on the ground floor.

Work done: The intention was to preserve the buildings and at the same time to set a new standard in a neglected part of the town. Future retail development of back land between the site and High Street will eventually link the shop and restaurant to a small-scale precinct and thence to the established business centre. The architects were asked to coordinate the design of the whole site by the main lessee, and the work was to proceed in two stages: the retail shop in the two-storey warehouse and adjoining stable block and outbuildings (Stage I), and the restaurant in the three-storey warehouse (Stage II).

Except for necessary repairs, the replacing of loading doors by windows, the installation of services and redecoration, the two-storey warehouse has been preserved intact, including even the hoists. Internally a new timber staircase has been introduced and the ground floor has been asphalted. The ceiling has been lined with timber boarding, but the main cast-iron structure remains exposed. On the upper floor the open roof truss has been enhanced by a white-painted plaster lining between purlins. The ground floor openings of the stable and outbuildings have been altered to a regular pattern of arched openings, one of which is larger and serves as a display window. Otherwise these

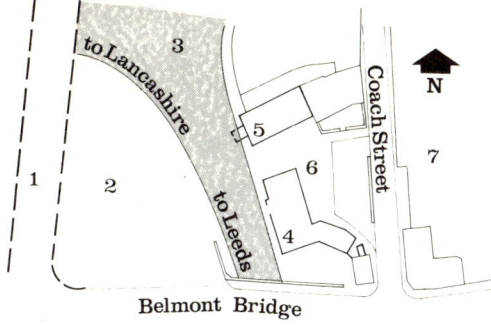

key
1, future inner relief road at high level
2, parking
3, canal basin (cruiser moorings)
4, shop for outdoor activities
5, proposed restaurant and club
6, court
7, future shopping development

Site plan. Scale 1 = 1000

The architect's sketch to show what the completed scheme will look like from Coach Street

1, the entrance to the shop from the paved court on the opposite side to the canal

2, 3, the ground floor of the shop in which the ceiling has been timber-boarded, but the cast-iron structure left exposed

ancillary buildings have been completely rehabilitated to provide an additional showroom and a changing room and staff room with lavatories. The exterior has been treated with a protective white cement paint. Heating throughout is by electricity, with 12kw. warm-air units in certain areas. Lighting in the showroom is by adjustable spotlights on tracks.

Stage I has been completed. In Stage II the three-storey warehouse will be converted into a bar, restaurant and private club for another client and planning approval has been obtained. The work will include the demolition of the corrugated-iron projection on the canal front and the erection of a new projection in steel framing and aluminium profiled sheeting. It will also include white-painted brick projections on the two long sides, one for the main concrete staircase and the other for an escape stair, storage, lavatories and additional restaurant area.

Accommodation: Ground floor—large showroom, small showroom and stores
First floor—large showroom, small showroom, staff room and lavatories, offices
Attic floor—stores

Date of completion: November 1971

Cost: £10 700

Rate: £2·40 per sq. ft.

210

4, on the upper floor of the shop the open roof truss has been enhanced by a white-painted plaster lining between purlins

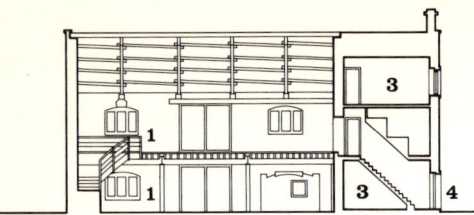

Longitudinal section of converted warehouse.
Scale 1 = 4000

key
1, large showroom
2, small showroom
3, store
4, office stock entrance

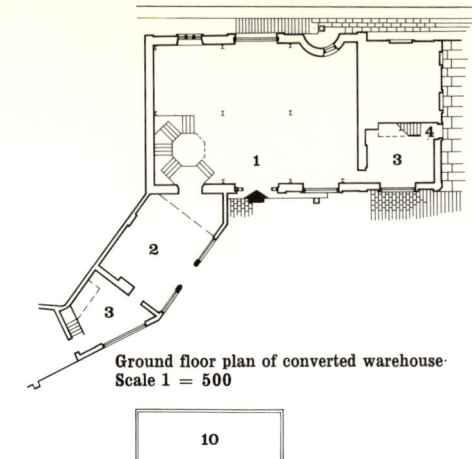

Ground floor plan of converted warehouse.
Scale 1 = 500

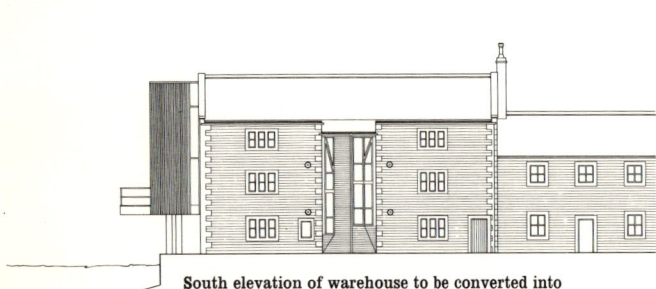

South elevation of warehouse to be converted into restaurant and club. Scale 1/28in. = 1ft.

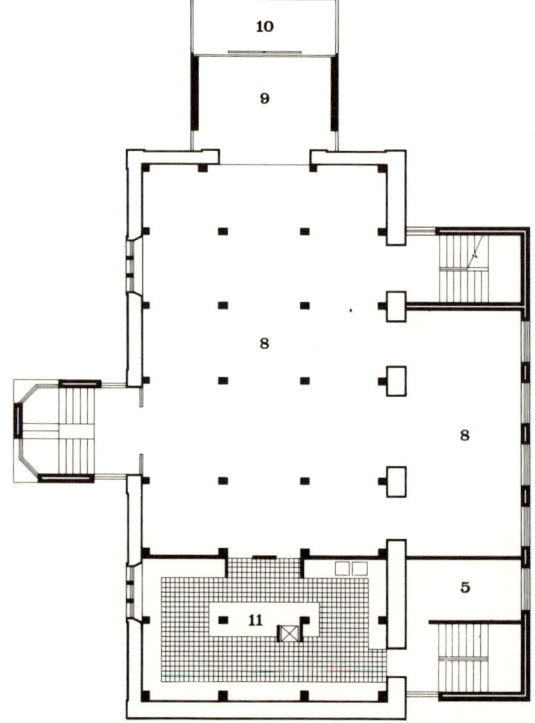

First floor plan. Proposed conversion of warehouse into restaurant and club. Scale 1/20in. = 1ft.

West elevation of warehouse to be converted into restaurant and club. Scale 1/20in. = 1ft.

key
1, cloakroom
2, lounge
3, bar
4, snug
5, store
6, manager
7, boiler
8, restaurant
9, balcony room
10, balcony
11, kitchen

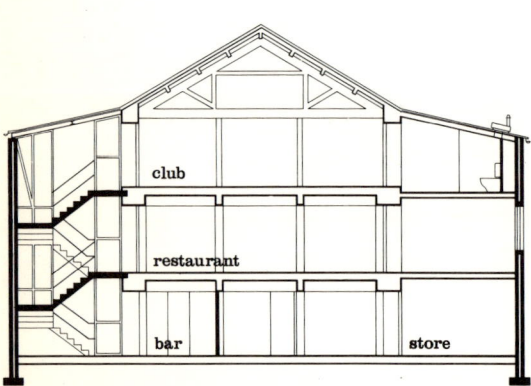

Cross section of warehouse to be converted into restaurant and club

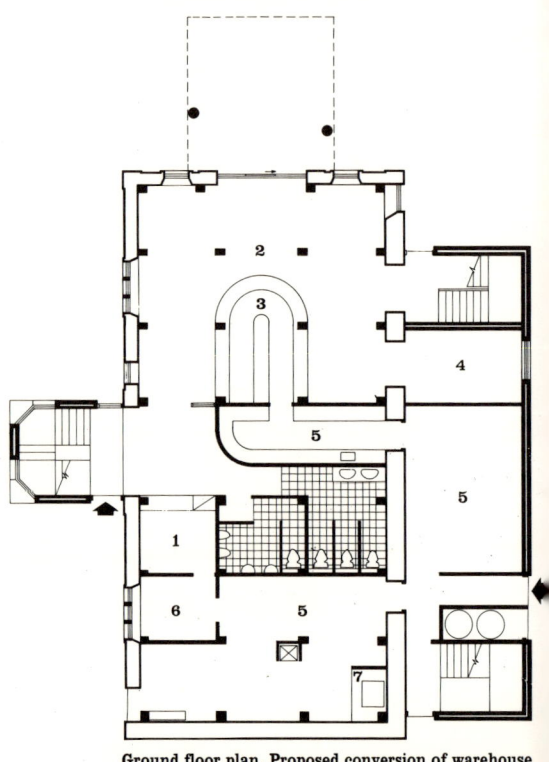

Ground floor plan. Proposed conversion of warehouse into restaurant and club.

COPPER AND ARSENIC MINE, CALSTOCK, CORNWALL

Architect: Pearn & Procter

Client: Landmark Trust

Site: The buildings of the Cotehele Consols mine stand on the west slope of a deep wooded valley which lies between Calstock and Cotehele and at whose southern end the River Tamar turns sharply towards the sea and flows under the impressive escarpment on which Cotehele Chapel stands.

History: The date of the establishment of the Cotehele Consols copper and arsenic mine has not been discovered, although records show that there was a short-lived amalgamation with the neighbouring Okel Tor mine in 1882. It is known that the Danescombe mine, which lies approximately one hundred yards down the valley from Cotehele Consols, was re-started in 1837 but the company was wound up five years later and the equipment dispersed. The Cotehele buildings, which stood in ruins when the Landmark Trust negotiated their lease from the National Trust, housed an engine, a Cornish boiler and a crushing plant, probably works remaining from the Danescombe mine that the Cotehele company made use of.

Character: The engine house is an excellent example of the simple functional architecture which was developed by the Cornish mining industry during the nineteenth century to enclose the machinery which it used. It is a tall rectangular building with walls of random masonry, and with quoins and arched window heads of brick. The gable roof is covered with slates and infilled with matchboarding around the projecting arm of the beam, which was maintained from a timber platform at the upper floor level. The design for the conversion of the building to provide holiday accommodation has attempted to achieve its objective with the least possible disturbance to the existing form and details.

Work done: A new staircase of steel strings and traditional cast-iron open chequer-type treads was placed at the north end of the building and new floors were inserted at the levels of the original platforms. A concrete slab was poured at the entrance level over the pit which housed the condenser, and this and the higher ground floor were finished with used slate flagstones.

A new flight of steps faced with used bricks brought from Newton Abbot, similar in texture and colour to the locally produced bricks of which the quoins and window arches were constructed, was formed between the boiler house and crushing plant building. This provides a dramatic approach to the engine house and gives emphasis to the vertical massing of the group.

A terrace of open timber slats was made at the top of the walls which

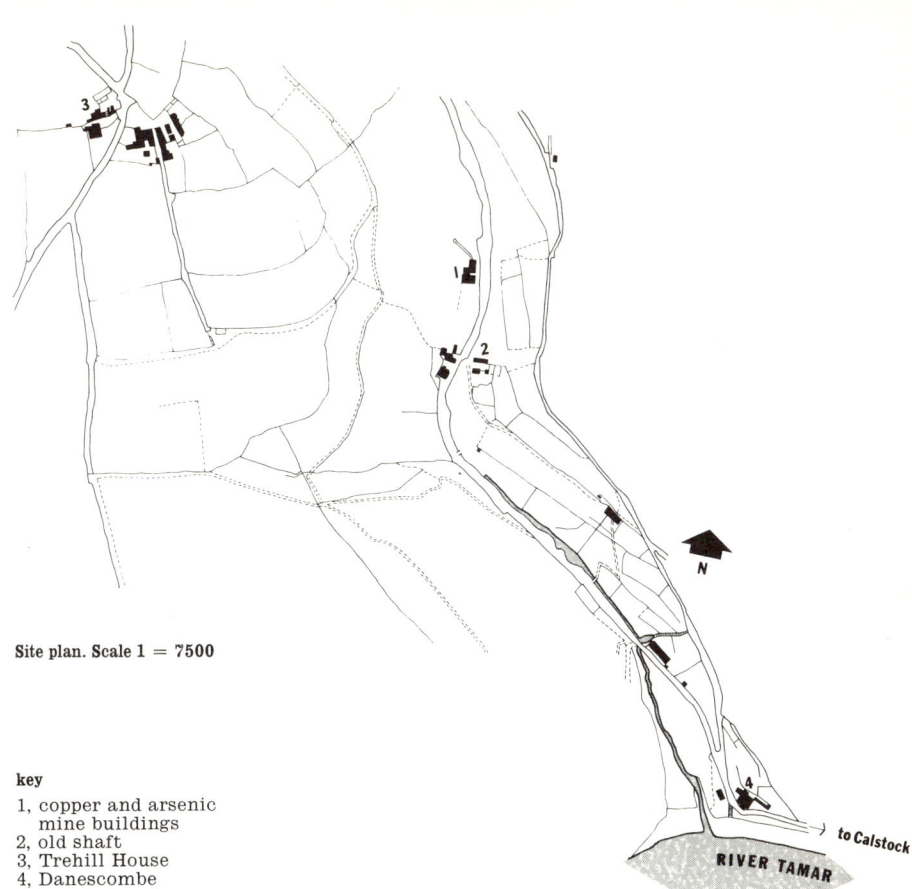

Site plan. Scale 1 = 7500

key
1, copper and arsenic mine buildings
2, old shaft
3, Trehill House
4, Danescombe Valley Hotel

1, the mine building in a ruined state and, 2, after conversion. The crushing shed in the foreground has been consolidated, but kept as a ruin

carried the axles of the winding gear and balance wheels. The terrace is surrounded with a traditional balustrade consisting of diagonal criss-cross members. This has been painted in the red-oxide colour which is still commonly used in this part of Cornwall.

The top floor bedroom window, which occupies the full width of the room, overlooks the valley to the south and is a new element made of aluminium sections with vertically pivoted opening lights. The glazing has been arranged in small pieces and allowed to overlap, as was done in early industrial buildings. The remaining windows, similar to those used on other buildings of this kind, are all of cast iron and were made at a foundry in Cornwall.

The roof trusses, of softwood, have been left exposed whilst the covering is random-width Delabole slates with a grey clay ridge tile. Heating is provided by electric underfloor panels at ground level, and by night storage units on the upper floors.

The approach to the building from the track, which lies to the west of the mine, crosses a stream by a bridge which is a simple reinforced concrete slab, wide enough and strong enough to carry two cars side by side. The surfacing material of the track is continued over the slab.

Accommodation: Ground floor—sitting room on lower level, kitchen and dining area on upper level
First floor—bedroom, lavatory and bathroom
Second floor—bedroom

Date of completion: February 1973

Cost: £27 000, including repairs to the ruins of the boiler house and crushing plant building

3, the converted engine house with the remains of the crushing shed on the right. The structures are of random masonry and brick quoins. The roof of the engine house is slated and the gable infilled with weatherboarding. The walls in the front, which housed the axles of the winding gear and balance wheels, now support a timber slatted terrace

4, the kitchen/living room on the ground floor

5, The kitchen/living room on the ground floor. The floor structure and cast iron staircase are new

6, the second floor bedroom where the roof structure has been left exposed to give added height

7, the second-floor bathroom

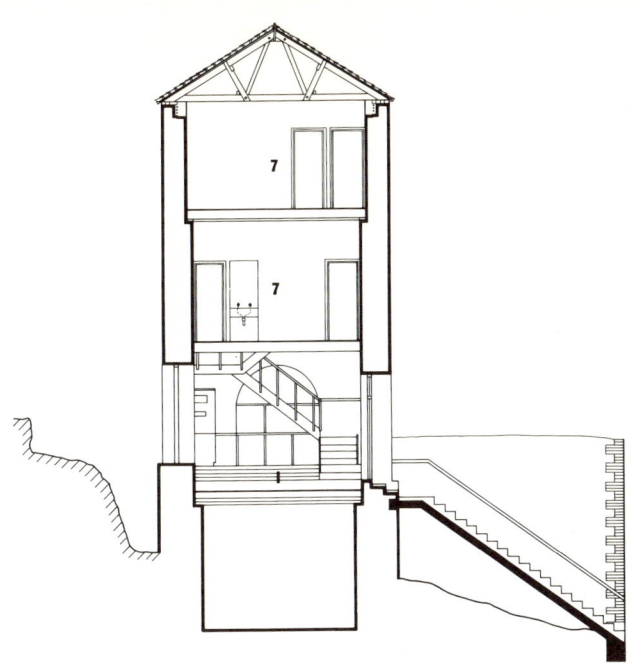

Cross section. Scale 1/16in. = 1ft.

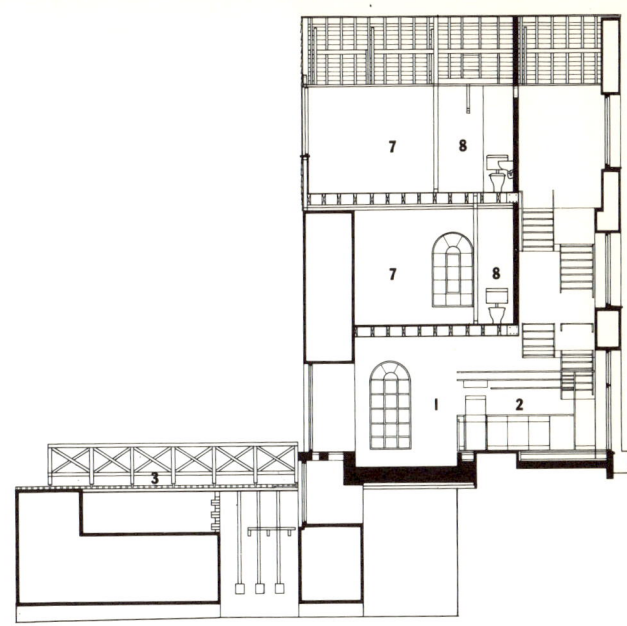

Longitudinal section. Scale 1/16in. = 1ft.

key
1, living area
2, dining-kitchen
3, terrace over pit which housed axles of winding gear and balance wheels
4, ruins of crushing plant building
5, ruins of boiler house
6, new bridge
7, bedroom
8, lavatory

8, one of the semicircular-headed windows which give so much character to the building, before restoration

Ground floor plan. Scale 1/20in. = 1ft.

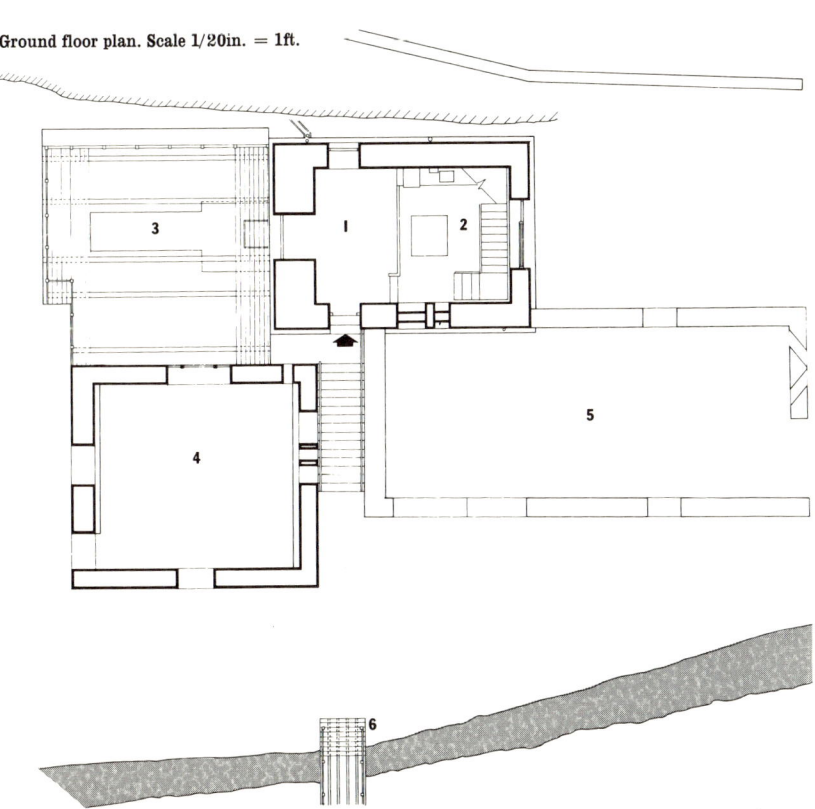

217

ICE HOUSES, SAN FRANCISCO, CALIFORNIA

Architect: Wurster, Bernardi & Emmons Inc.
Landscape architect, Lawrence Halprin & Associates

Client: North Waterfront Associates

Site: On North Waterfront of San Francisco, bounded by Union Street to the north, Battery Street to the east and Sansome Street to the west. The two ice houses were divided by Gaines Street, which ran between them. Windows on the Sansome Street and Battery Street sides are open to views of the Bay and Telegraph Hill.

History: Built in 1914, they were once two warehouses for ice and cold storage. This area below Telegraph Hill has most of the surviving old waterfront warehouses of the city.

Character: The ice houses are built of red brick. They have regular repetitive bays of decorative vertical insets, pierced at infrequent intervals by small windows. The seven-storey Ice House I is bigger and more complex in structure than Ice House II, which has five floors.

Work done: The intention was to provide wholesale showroom spaces for manufacturers of interior furnishings, altering the interior and exterior structure as little as possible.

A large number of new openings have been made in the external walls but there is little fundamental change in structure. The subdivision of each floor into compartments for letting has taken away from the interior much of its industrial character. To conform with earthquake regulations, the building had to be braced laterally, which was done by installing 1⅛in. plywood sheathing (in two layers), heavily nailed to X frames bolted to the existing masonry walls. The mezzanine and top floors of both buildings are composite floors of concrete fill on metal decking supported by a steel frame, also bolted to the masonry walls. An uncompromisingly modern glass and steel structure makes a bridge between the two buildings. Extending from the first to the fifth floors, it links the slightly different levels of the two ice houses and provides an entrance to the two buildings. One of the floors on the bridge has been used as a lunch room from time to time, with a buffet on the elevator lobby of that floor. The offices in the building are limited to those used by staff administering the building itself.

Ice House Alley, which used to be Gaines Street, runs underneath into Union Plaza, a landscaped courtyard on the lower level of Union Street. Two passenger lifts and a goods lift were installed in Ice House I and new reinforced concrete staircases constructed to meet fire regulations.

1, the ice houses before conversion and, 2, after conversion. The cornice has been broken by new windows and some of the tall brick panels have been glazed

Date of completion: March 1969

Cost: $4·4 million

Rate: $19·50 per sq. ft.

3, a detail of the brick facade varied and relieved by the graceful arched windows and vertical brick panels

4, the entrance from Sansome Street into Ice House 1

5, part of the interior used as a furniture showroom. The timber structure, floor boards and bare brick walling have all been preserved

Section looking south.

First floor plan

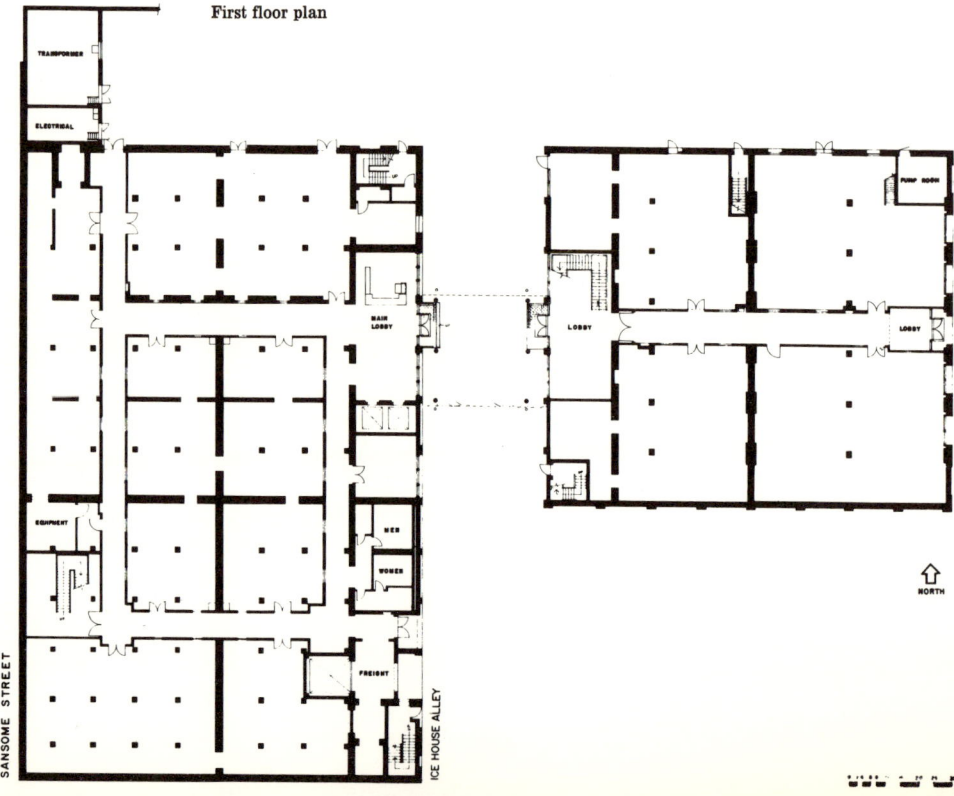

WAREHOUSE, SAN FRANCISCO, CALIFORNIA

Architect: Bull, Field, Volkmann & Stockwell
Architect in charge, John Louis Field

Client: Musto Estate Company

Site: Near the corner of Battery Street and Pacific Avenue with access from both streets. The building is L-shaped, with a courtyard in the angle of the L facing Pacific Avenue. The surrounding area, which is not far from the waterfront, retains many old buildings which house mainly offices and shops. The site is half on the rock of the original shoreline and half on the filling done by the early settlers.

History: Built as a warehouse with some office space in the early part of the century, it retained its use for some years until a sweet manufacturer took it over. When the nearby renovations of old buildings for wholesale showrooms, like the ice houses, began to develop a need for neighbouring warehousing, the building was again used as a warehouse as well as for furniture manufacturing.

Character: A three-storey brick and timber structure, with a striking facade on Battery Street which consists of seven wide window bays divided by slender rusticated brick piers cut horizontally by a cornice at first floor level. The rear facades facing the courtyard, now called Musto Plaza, are plain brick walls pierced with regularly spaced, flat-arched window openings. The interior is mainly large open spaces with the heavy timber structure of posts and beams exposed.

Work done: Openings in external walls were generally retained, except for two windows at the rear on the ground floor which were blocked up to provide adequate bracing against earthquakes. The other windows on the ground floor were lowered to floor level and some made into doors. All external doors and windows were renewed with dark glass in dark anodised frames to emphasise the clarity of the masonry openings. The building was bisected by an arcade which links the Battery Street with the Musto Plaza entrance and provides access to the new lift and staircase. An additional staircase for alternative means of escape was also installed. Musto Plaza itself was paved and planted to form an off-street public amenity. The far side was closed off with a high concrete wall. The arcade and landings on the upper floors divide the building in two and provide six separate letting areas.

On the top floor, new timber beams well below the ceiling beams were added for aesthetic reasons and to brace the thin columns on that floor. The old ceiling beams were braced by the addition of two new beams bolted at either side of the existing ones. The old beams were jacked back into a straight line, so as not to build in the deflection

1, the striking facade on Battery Street which consists of seven wide window bays divided by slender rusticated brick piers cut horizontally by a cornice at first-floor level

2, the courtyard facing Pacific Avenue which has been paved and planted to provide an off-street public amenity

3, the ground-floor windows on the courtyard side were lowered to floor level and some made into doors, 4

5, the arcade at ground-floor level which bisects the building and links the Battery Street entrance with the courtyard on Pacific Avenue

caused by overstressing. New skylights were formed and the existing roof structure was covered with plywood and new built-up roofing felt. As bracing against earthquakes, the existing floors were also covered with plywood and on the two lower floors the walls were braced with heavy diagonal timbers, required in this building because of the exceptionally large openings in the outside walls.

The lighting throughout is a mixture of suspended paper lanterns and fluorescent strips. The new air-conditioning system is sometimes concealed, sometimes exposed, depending on whether fire regulations permitted the timber structure to remain exposed or not.

Date of completion: February 1970

Cost: $435 000

Rate: $11·00 per sq. ft.

6, the architects' office on the top floor where new skylights have been formed and some of the old timber structure has been left exposed

7, view of the courtyard from an upstairs window

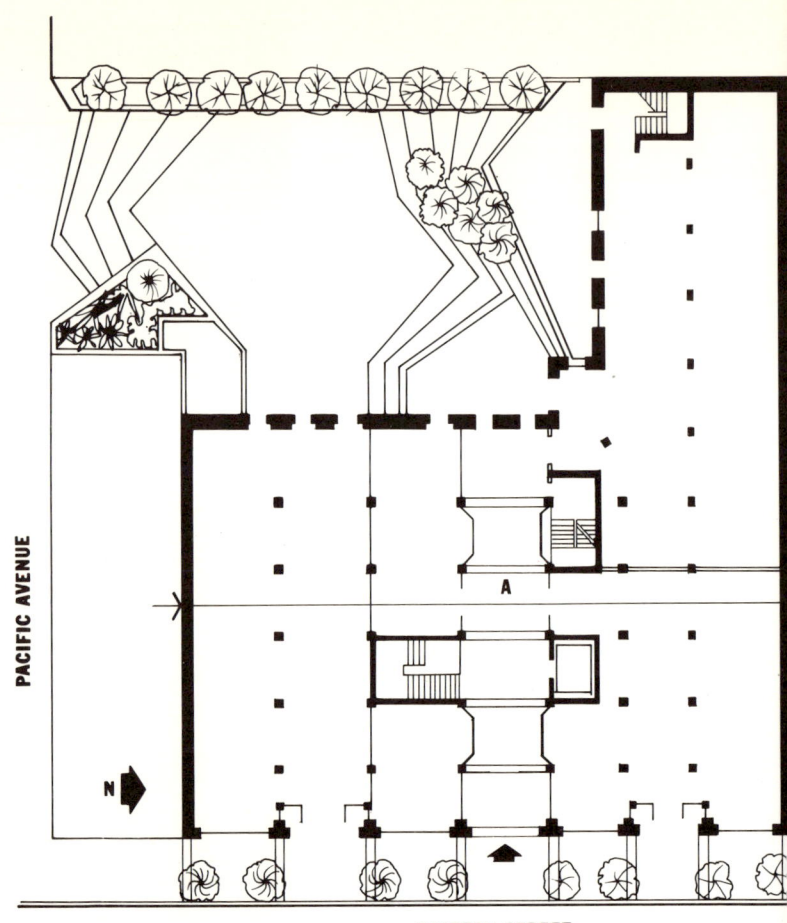

Ground floor plan. Scale 1/32in. = 1ft.

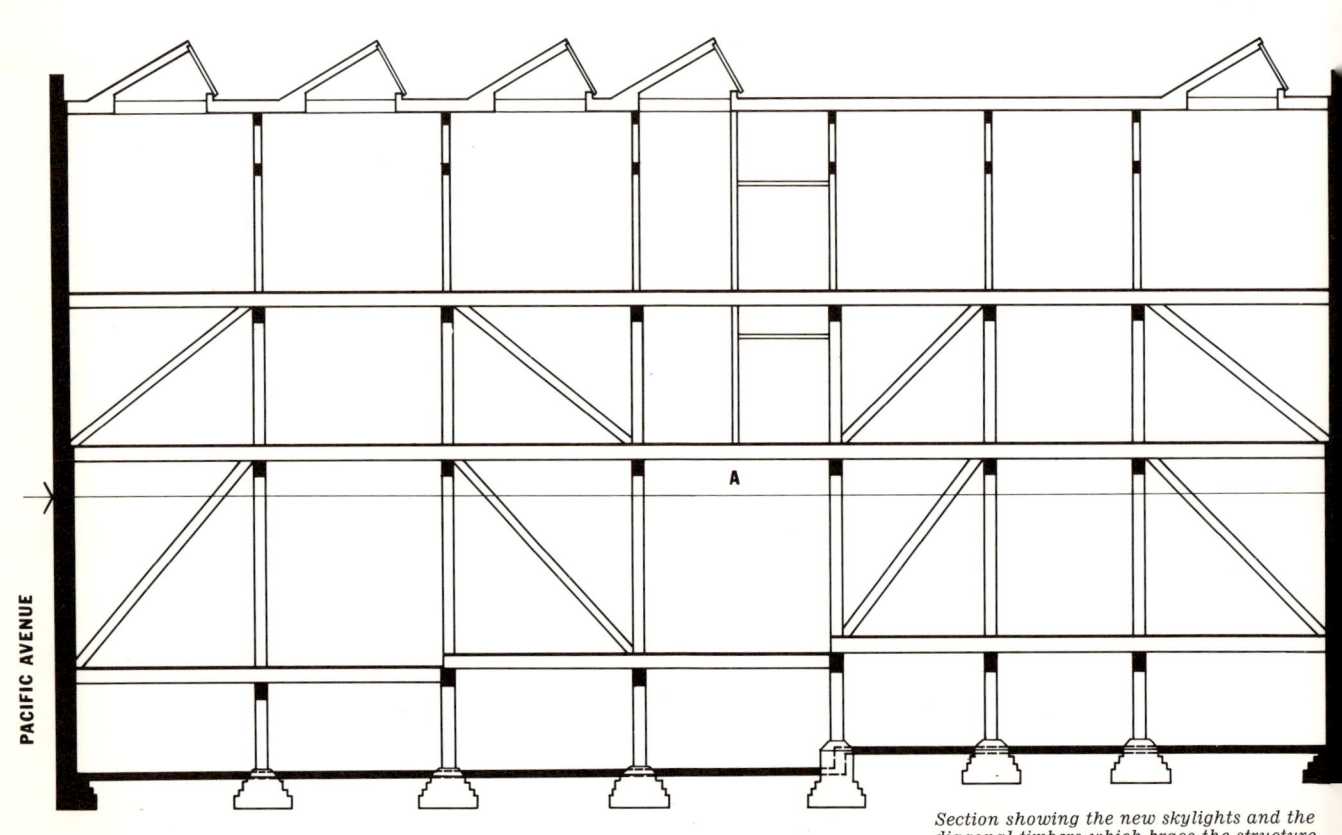

Scale 1/16in. = 1ft.

Section showing the new skylights and the diagonal timbers which brace the structure against earthquakes

WAREHOUSE, SAN FRANCISCO, CALIFORNIA

Architect: Bull, Field, Volkmann & Stockwell
Architect in charge, Daniel G. Volkmann

Client: Saturday Review Industries

Site: The building is situated in the San Francisco Barbary Coast area, among what used to be warehousing for the shipping industry. In the last ten years this area has been totally converted into offices and shops, the majority of which are occupied by or deal with the design and furnishing trades, and is now usually referred to as the Jackson Square area.

History: Built in 1907, the building was used as a Chinese cigar factory, a restaurant, and a souvenir warehouse. The architects originally designed the conversion for the periodical *The Saturday Review*, but it was subsequently taken over by a law firm who made only the most minor changes.

Character: The three-storey warehouse is of a massive brick and timber construction, with repetitive window bays. Inside, the brickwork and timber ceilings are exposed.

Work done: In order to preserve the existing character of the neighbourhood, as well as the building itself, exterior treatment was limited to restoration work, sandblasting, the lowering of some window sills, a new entrance, a new pavement and tree planting.

The redesign of the interior created many offices around a series of central spaces open either up to the roof or down to the level below. The existing structure was generally retained and sandblasted clean. Skylights were put into the roof and light wells were cut through existing floors to bring light into the interior of the building. From the reception area on the first floor it is possible to look up through the entire height of the building. Artificial lighting on the second, third and fourth floors is by fluorescent fixtures recessed between old wood joists, and on the first floor, where ceilings are too high and cut-off angles inadequate for fluorescent lighting, the architects used pendant lights with paper shades.

A new recessed wall with tall windows, as well as an entrance, was created on the ground floor, which was the limit of exterior treatment or change. Windows were also inserted on other floors. New free-standing curving walls of gypsum board in white or in Douglas fir plywood contrast with the old heavy timber construction. Exposed spiral duct-work is painted in bright colours—yellow, orange, red, violet and dark blue—two colours being used on each floor, and sprinkler pipes, window frames, etc., are painted dark blue throughout. To comply with earthquake regulations, six steel trusses were erected inside the external

1, the early 20th century warehouse stands at a street corner in the Jackson Square area of the city

2, perspective section down the length of the building with the street front on the right. It shows how the architects have opened one floor to another so that full height and depth of the building can be glimpsed from a number of positions

walls and lateral bracing was achieved by overlaying each floor with a plywood diaphragm attached to the trusses. Glass separation and a sprinkler system take care of the fire risk in the vertical shafts. Heating is by a boiler and air conditioning is by a unit, both of which are on the roof. Air circulates by means of fan-coil units. Floors are carpeted throughout.

Date of completion: December 1972

Cost: $950 000

Rate: $34·50 per sq. ft.

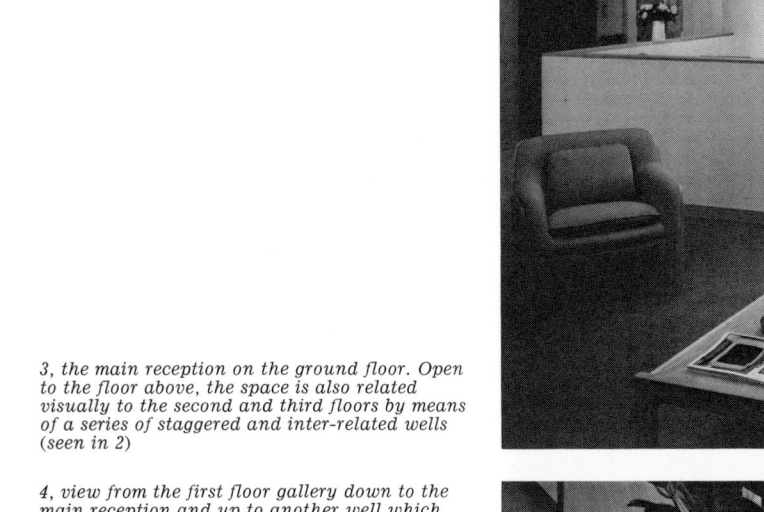

3, the main reception on the ground floor. Open to the floor above, the space is also related visually to the second and third floors by means of a series of staggered and inter-related wells (seen in 2)

4, view from the first floor gallery down to the main reception and up to another well which extends through to the third floor and the skylights. The higher well had to be glazed to comply with fire regulations

5, the curved corridor at the back of the ground floor which leads to the double-door, 7, of the main conference room

6, the reception desk at the back of the second floor which stands in the well seen through the glass in 4. The exposed duct-work is everywhere made into a dominant feature by being painted in bright colours

8, round viewing hole in one of the free-standing curved partitions which define the main reception area on the ground floor

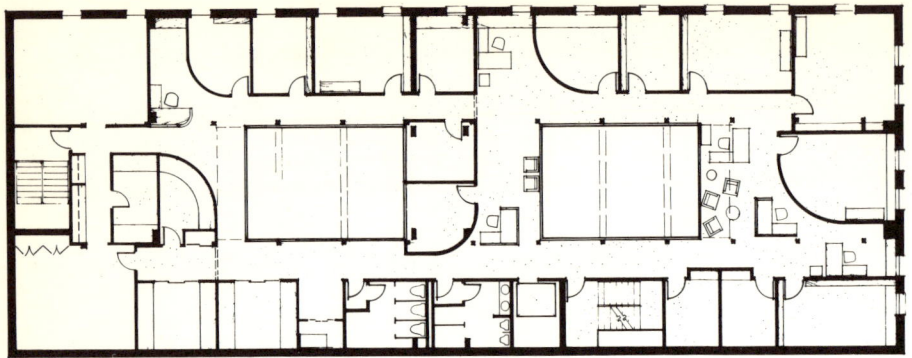
Third floor plan. Scale 1/32in. = 1ft.

Second floor plan
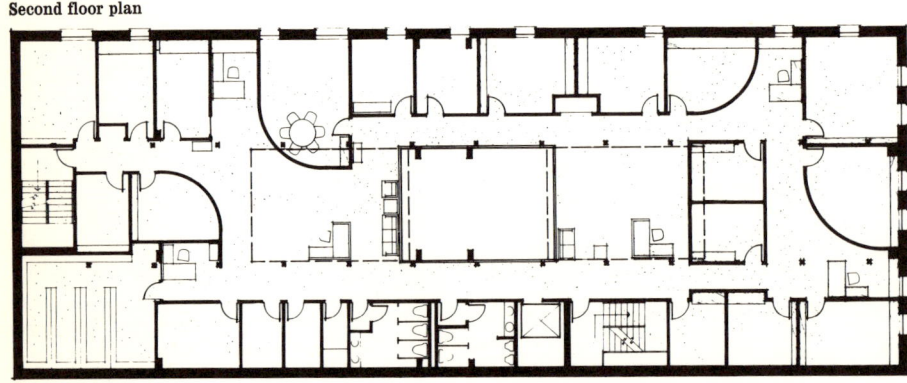

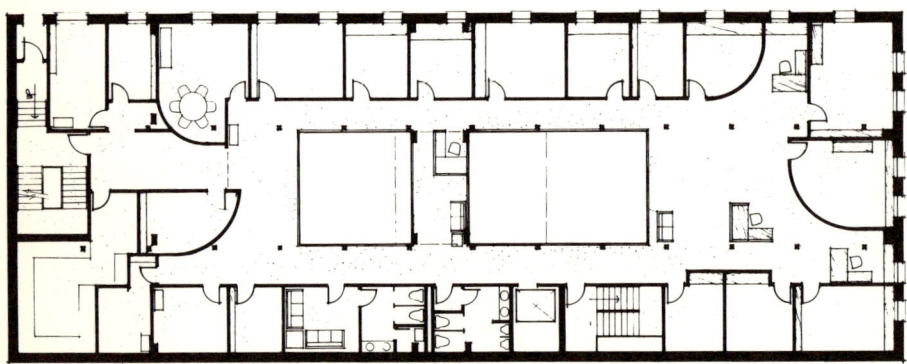
First floor plan

Ground floor plan
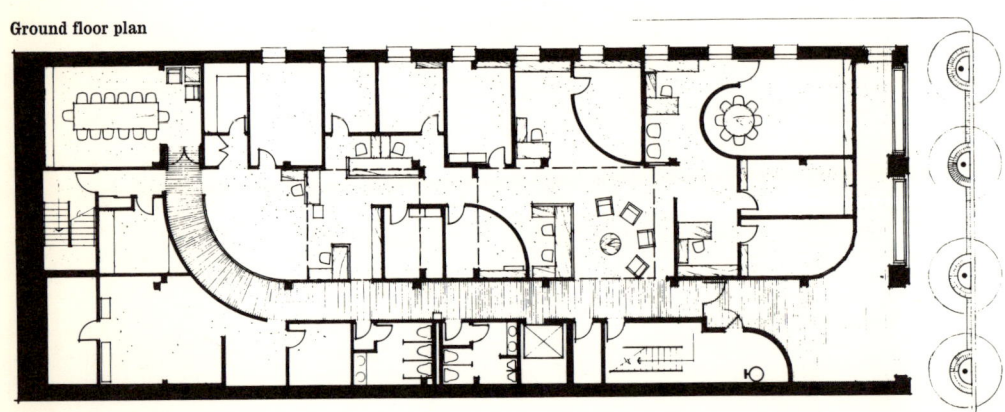

COMMERCIAL BUILDINGS, SAN ANTONIO, TEXAS

Architect: Ford, Powell & Carson

Client: The Stockman's Corporation

Site: The buildings are located in the centre of San Antonio. The front of the buildings faces Commerce Street and the rear opens on to the Paseo del Rio, a landscaped walkway along the bank of the San Antonio River.

History: One of the buildings was erected in 1867 as a shop for Diedrick Heye, a German-born master leather craftsman who made fine saddles, bridles and harness required for ranching and trail driving. More recently it was used as a laundry and tailor's shop. The right-hand building, constructed about the same time, was originally a restaurant, but recently was used as an office and warehouse for a wholesale jewellery company. The original facade had undergone several changes, the last being a 1940 modernistic plaster and glass-block front.

The two buildings were bought by the Stockman's Corporation, a group of twenty San Antonio businessmen and South Texas ranchers, for conversion to a restaurant seating 450 people, with a 'frontier' atmosphere in good taste and without extravagant details or rich materials.

Character: On the street side, two two-storey buildings side by side, one of which has a richly ornamented brick cornice supporting a quaint pediment. The first floor windows are arched and divided by pilasters which become piers on the ground floor. The projecting canopy and shop fascia suspended by four chains fixed to the brickwork has unfortunately been lost in the conversion. At the rear, the buildings had a utilitarian character and because of the falling ground were three storeys high.

Work done: In order to accommodate the new use of the buildings, the existing floors were removed and the interior completely redesigned, with three levels of dining and bar areas clustered around a four-storey-high entrance. New floors are of reinforced concrete supported by joists. The original stone walls were strengthened with concrete columns. Interior brick walls were sandblasted to remove old paintwork and left their natural colour. New electrical and air-conditioning systems were installed.

All furnishings and finishes were chosen to evoke the atmosphere of the West, such as the old stained glass and bevelled glass windows, the hand-woven wool saddle blankets (which are not only decorative but also provide acoustic insulation in the large dining room) and the specially designed pierced brass and copper gazebo in one of the bars. Finishes include cedar beams, handmade Mexican bricks, end-grain wood block flooring, oak and saddle leather.

1, the street facade of the left-hand building before conversion

2, the street facade of both buildings after conversion. The changes include new window frames, opening up the single-storey structure on the left to provide an entrance from the side and the removal of the projecting canopy and shop fascia

Accommodation: River level—dining and saloon areas including the Rider Room and Trail Bar, service kitchen, lavatories
Street level—Medina Bar, Stockman dining room, main kitchen
Upper level—private and public dining area

Date of completion: December 1971

Cost: $750 000

Rate: $42 per sq. ft., including building, kitchen equipment and all furnishings

3, the sharp fall in the ground level makes the building into a three-storey structure on the side of the San Antonio River. Here the external walls have been rebuilt and the proportions radically changed

4, the river facade before conversion

5, 6, the River Room looking up to the main entrance area and the bridge. The furnishings and finishes were chosen to evoke the atmosphere of the American West

7, view from the stairs in the Medina Bar looking down into the Rider Room

key
1, Trail Bar
2, Rider Room
3, service kitchen
4, terrace
5, unexcavated
6, River Passage
7, Medina Bar
8, Stockman dining room
9, River Room
10, main kitchen
11, void over Rider Room
12, waiting
13, the Board Room (private dining area)
14, void over Trail Bar
15, void over Medina Bar
16, lavatories
17, bakery

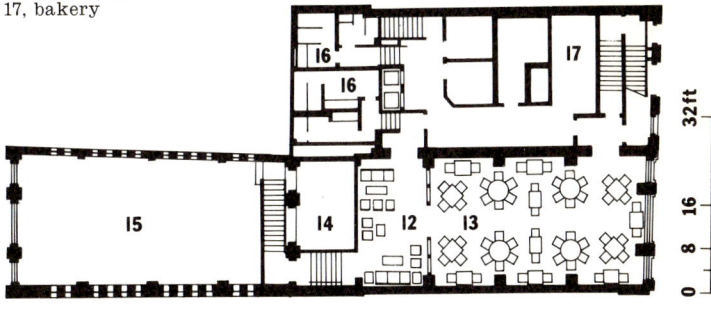

Plan above street level

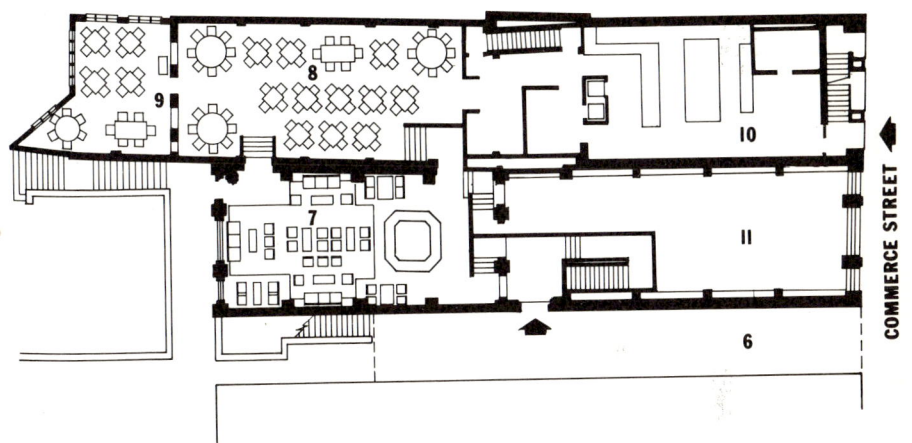

Plan at street level

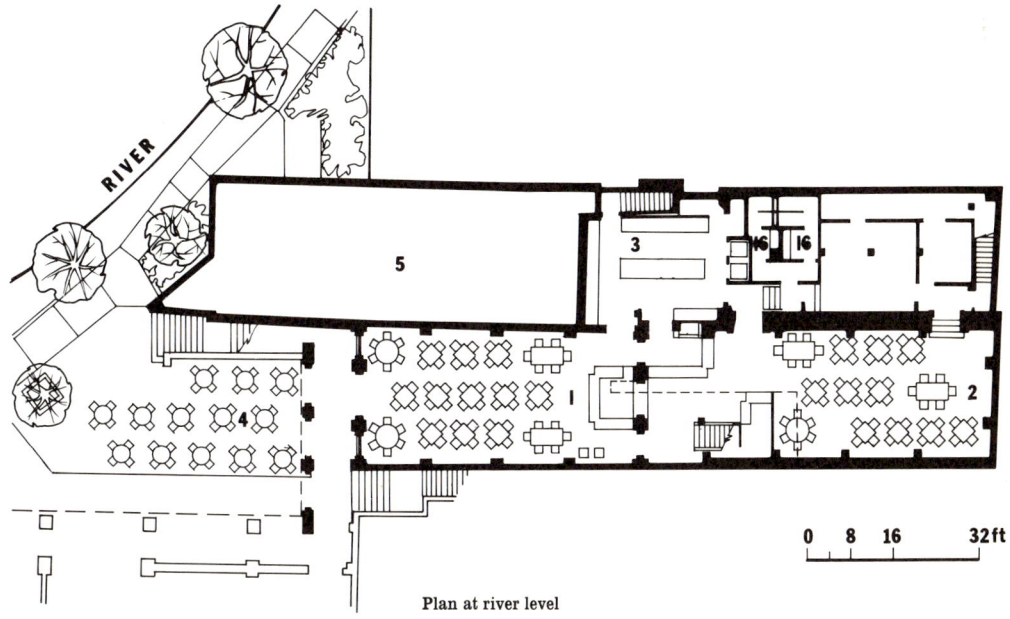

Plan at river level

CAR SHOWROOM AND GARAGE, WASHINGTON, D.C.

1, built as a car showroom the building continues to be used for parking on its upper floors. The basement, ground floor and part of the first floor have been converted into three cinemas and a restaurant. The entrance to the cinema foyer is from Jefferson Street (left)

Architect: Bull, Field, Volkmann & Stockwell
Architect in charge, John Louis Field
Graphics, Reis and Manwaring

Site: On the corner of M and Jefferson streets in lower Georgetown, one block away from Canal Square.

History: Built between the two world wars as a car showroom and garage, the building was later converted into a car park, the upper levels of which were reached by ramp from an entrance in Jefferson Street. The most recent conversion provides three small cinemas and a restaurant, keeping most of the upper levels as a car park.

Character: A three-storey flat-roofed brick building, with a basement, whose external walls are rendered up to first floor level. The windows, typical of their period, are large and horizontal with metal frames. A reinforced concrete structure of columns, beams and floors enabled the interior to provide large open spaces undivided by supporting walls.

Work done: Part of the ground floor was subdivided with concrete walls to form three small cinemas symmetrically disposed about an entrance foyer which formerly provided access to the car ramp. Where the walls separate auditorium areas from each other, there are two block walls with air space between. These have been sealed with a caulking compound at their perimeter to avoid transmission of any noise between cinemas. A new flight of steps in the foyer makes up the level between street and ground floor, the latter being ramped up the back row of the seating so as to provide a raked floor inside the theatres. A new concrete staircase leads from the foyer to the first floor, where a central projection room is flanked by men's and women's lavatories. A suspended ceiling in the foyer and back part of the theatres provides space for the mirrors which serve for the cinema back-projection.

Part of the basement has been converted into a restaurant and kitchen accessible from M Street. Part of the ground floor was removed over the restaurant, which has become double

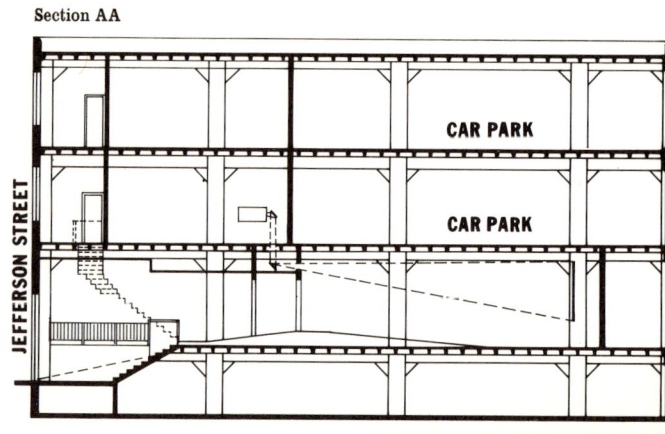

2, the foyer has a reflective ceiling with a zig-zag pattern of lights which provide a festive air. The floor slopes up to the cinema doors to allow for the raking floors of the auditorium

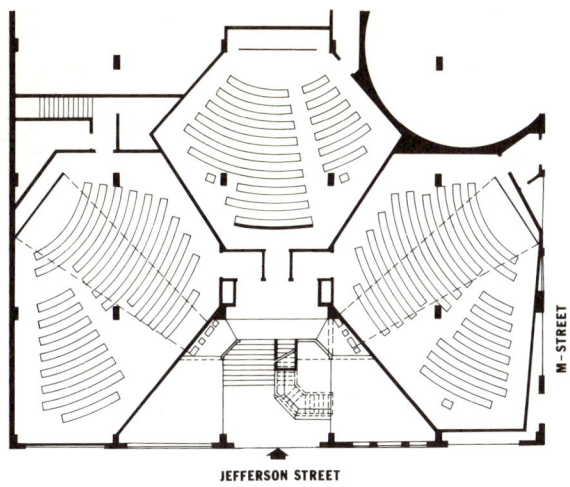

Ground floor plan. Scale 1/48in. = 1ft.

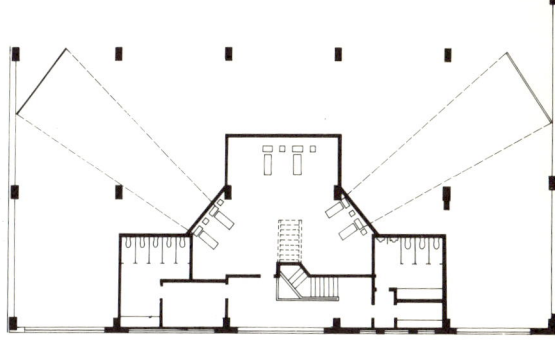

First floor plan. Scale 1/48in. = 1ft.

height. The second floor and the remaining space on the other floors continue to be used as a car park; a new access and a new ramp connecting with the old one in the rear corner of the building have been formed on M Street. To attract the passer-by, the windows at ground floor level have been used to display 'light' sculptures as signs advertising the cinemas, which are called Cerberus 1 2 3.

Accommodation: Basement—restaurant, kitchen and ancillaries
Ground floor—foyer, three cinemas with 135, 180 and 190 seats respectively
First floor—projection room, men's and women's lavatories

Date of completion: January 1970

Cost: Cinemas only, $225 000

Rate: $24·50 per sq. ft.

3, one of the cinemas

4, a new concrete staircase leads from the foyer to the first floor where a central projection room is flanked by lavatories

PRINTING WORKS, HANOVER, GERMAN FEDERAL REPUBLIC

1, the building after being struck by bombs in 1943

2, the building restored and with a new, light upper storey of studios added. The continuous band of recessed glazing provides a clear break between the old and the new

Architect: Friedrich Spengelin and Horst Wunderlich

Client: The *Land* of Lower Saxony

Site: On the corner of Nierburger and Schlosswender Strasse in the centre of the city, roughly halfway between the old city and the Palace of the Guelphs to the north. The latter is now occupied by the Technical University, of which this building forms a part.

History: The printing works were built towards the end of the nineteenth century as a three-storey block over a basement with a five-storey block on the corner and along Nierburger Strasse. In the thirties the building was taken over by the Technical University and converted to house the Faculty of Building and Architecture. In 1943 an incendiary bomb caused considerable damage to the five-storey block, which was subsequently levelled off to three storeys, like the rest of the building, before the recent addition over the whole building of an uncompromisingly modern mansard roof creating space needed to accommodate the increase in architectural students. The new premises are a temporary measure until the new building for the Faculty of Architecture is completed in the late seventies.

Character: Red brick, German neo-Gothic style with the truncated end block (originally five storeys and turreted and embattled like a castle) set forward from the long wing fronting Schlosswender Strasse. The long wing is divided into bays by buttresses and horizontally by string courses which become more elaborate with every storey. The ornate cornice of tall niches crowns three tiers of windows, the bottom window filling a whole bay and the first and second floor windows being divided into two and three respectively. The interior of the building was originally undivided space with cast-iron columns at regular intervals, but its conversion to a university faculty in the thirties involved much partitioning.

3, the top-storey addition is built of steel and clad in copper

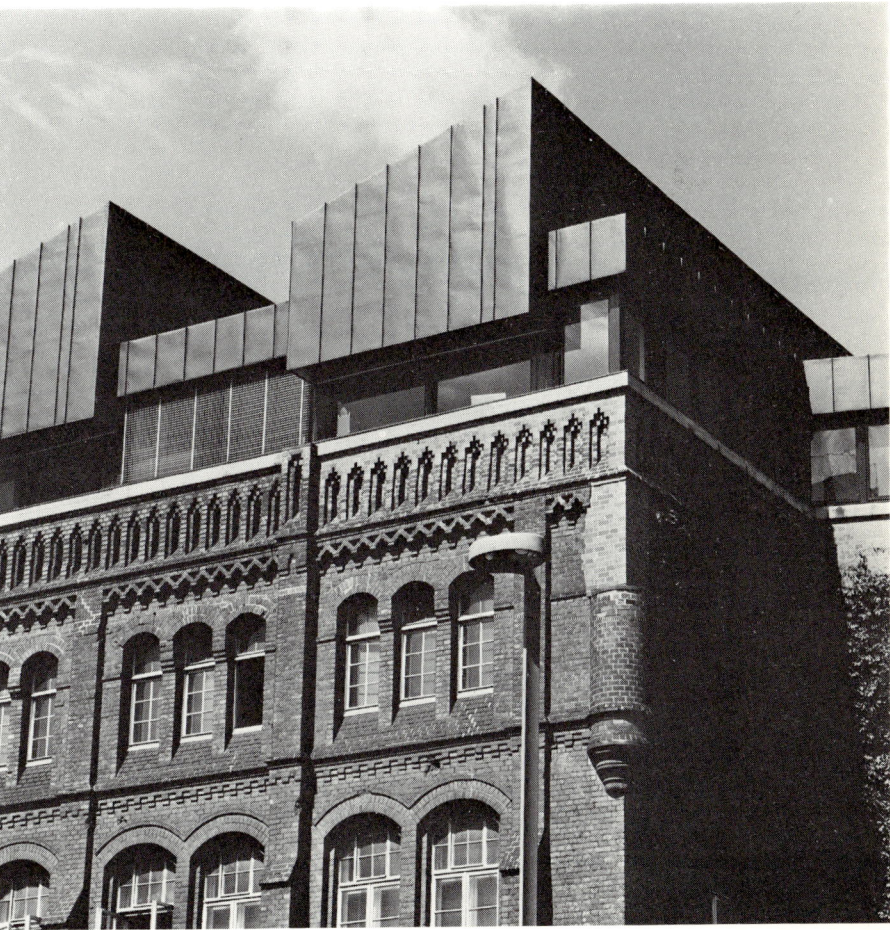

Work done: A series of light steel trusses span the full width of the building and are supported on the outside walls so as not to put additional loading on the cast-iron columns of the old building. The mezzanine floor structure of the studios, also in steel, is suspended from the roof trusses. The exterior is clad in copper and the interior mainly in wood, though the floors of the reading room and kitchen are tiled and the ceilings of the end block plastered.

Accommodation: End block lower floor—seminar room, teachers' rooms, lavatories
upper floor—small library, reading room, kitchen, courtyard and visiting teacher's flat
Long wing divided into 12 spaces with four mezzanines, providing space for 160 students

Date of completion: 1965

Cost: 1·2 million DM

Rate: 775 DM per m²

4, the new studios on the top floor for the Faculty of Architecture. The long space is broken by four mezzanine floors, 5, which extend across the full width of the building and give it its interesting silhouette (seen in 2)

6, the reading room is next to a small library and kitchen and can be used for tea breaks as well as study

7, the sitting room in the visiting professor's flat which gives on to a private courtyard

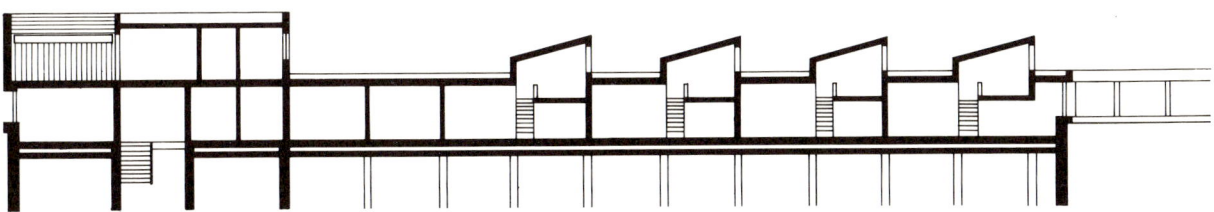

Section through new mansard roof. Scale 1 = 400

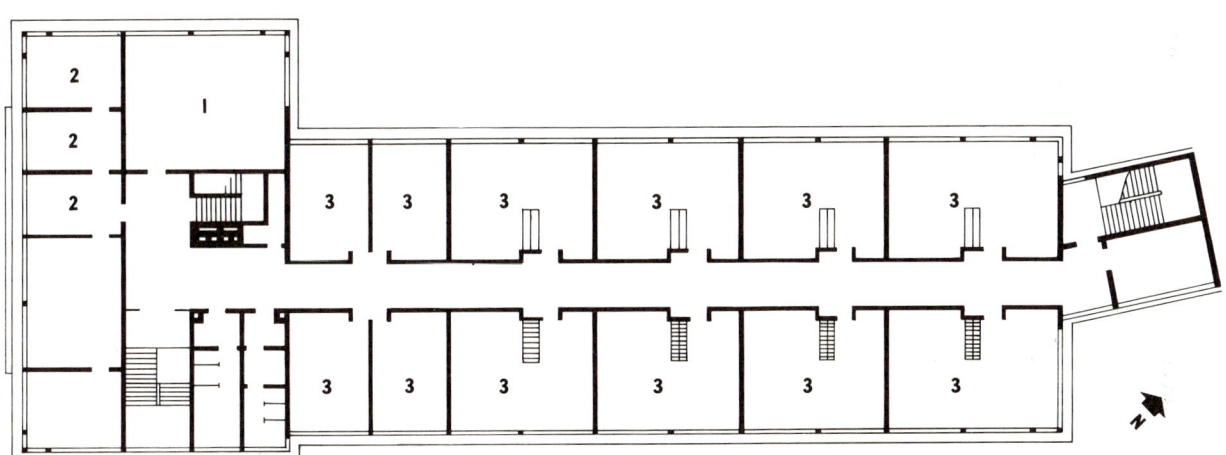

Main floor plan. Scale 1 = 400

key
1, seminar
2, teacher's room
3, studio
4, reading room
5, library
6, court
7, tea-making
8, visiting teacher's flat

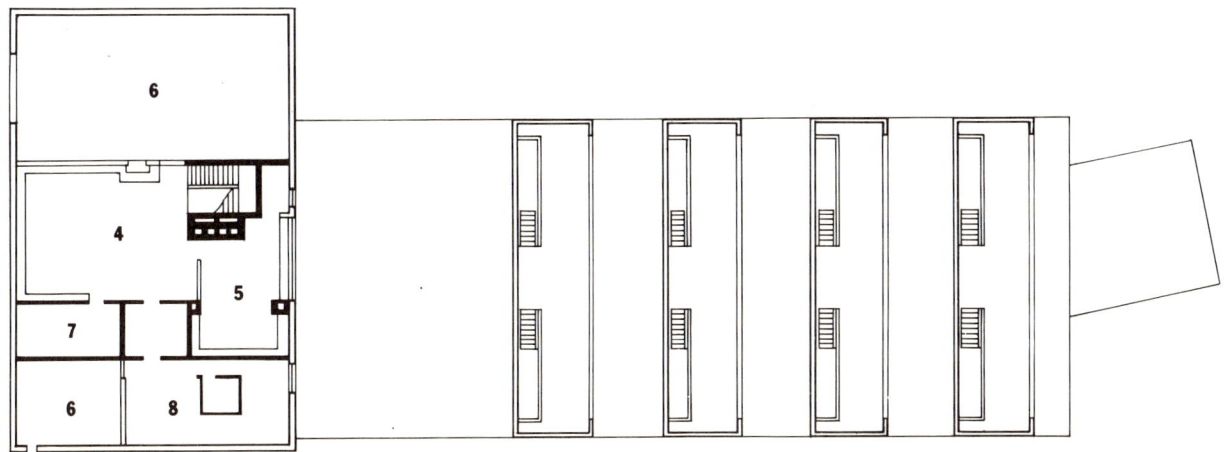

Mezzanine floor plan

'I' WAREHOUSE, ST. KATHARINE DOCKS, LONDON

Architect: Renton, Howard, Wood Partnership
Structural engineers, Ove Arup & Partners

Client: Taylor Woodrow Property Company

Site: Site has the Tower of London on the west, the Thames to the south and London Docks to the east. 'I' warehouse is situated on a spit separating the east dock from the west dock and is T-shaped following the shape of the spit. It is surrounded on three sides by water.

History: Telford and Hardwick's St. Katharine Docks (1824–29) were the fourth docks to be built after 1799 around water basins controlled by locks and thus unaffected by tides. The warehouses were built right against the water's edge (an innovatory feature) and raised on cast-iron columns to facilitate the transfer of goods from ship to warehouse. The docks were divided into two to extend the length of the quay and were preceded by an entrance basin enabling ships to come in and out at all tides. 'I' warehouse was the last of the nine warehouses to be built and is of a less substantial construction and a less functional design than the others.

The docks were closed in 1968 and sold to the GLC for £1 800 000. The GLC instigated a competition for their redevelopment stipulating that, among other things, as many listed buildings as possible were to be kept, and offices were not to be included. Meanwhile they let the building to a group of artists who found the environment stimulating. The Taylor Woodrow Property Group, together with the Renton, Howard, Wood Partnership and Ove Arup and Partners, won the competition and started work in 1970. So far the Tower Hotel, the 'I' warehouse and the St. Katharine dock house are completed.

Character: The 'I' warehouse is of yellow brick with repetitive four-storey bays of semicircular brick arches at mezzanine and top floor level. It has an Italianate 'campanile' and pedimented gables at the ends of the building. Its pitched roof is concealed by a parapeted cornice. Floors are of fireproof jack-arch construction on riveted iron I-beams which are supported on circular cast-iron columns. Floors are covered with grey quarry tiles.

Work done: The intention was to convert the top three floors into flats and the lower floors into a yachting centre with shops. The vaults in the basement are being made into a restaurant.

Because of the fireproof construction of the floors, it was possible to retain them as they were, but the required number of escape stairs had to be

1, the 'I' Warehouse seen across the east basin of St. Katharine Docks

2, 3, the long south facade facing the entrance basin to the docks. Some of the windows have been enlarged downwards to form openings for recessed balconies

inserted. At ground level, the columns supporting the building were sprayed with fireproof paint. Shops have been inserted on the ground floor by recessing the glazing line. Some windows had to be enlarged because warehouse windows tend to be too small for residential needs. These were enlarged downwards to form openings for recessed balconies. On the top floor, a part of the roof over each flat is cut back to make a space open to the sky (compare with Orto del'Abbondanza p. 77; this is not visible, thanks to the parapet. Skylights were also let in. Unfortunately, for economical reasons, partitions do not always follow the line of the I-beams and sometimes cut across the jack arches. Doors and window frames are of traditional design. The campanile contains water tanks and the ventilation extract for the bathrooms, concealed by a louvred screen. One hoist shaft contains a water tank and the other a lift.

Work is progressing on the conversion of 'G' warehouse and on GLC and private housing on the south quay of the east dock.

Accommodation: Basement—club, restaurant, kitchens, boiler room and storerooms
Ground floor—double-height entrance hall, shops
Mezzanine floor—caretaker's flat, club and bar for Cruising Association
First, second and third floors—flats, each with its own balcony overlooking the marina and river

Date of completion: April 1974

Cost: £785 000 (contract sum)

3, a closer view of the south facade

4, the pedimented east gable with the Italianate campanile rising behind. Besides the clock, it now houses water tanks and the ventilation extract for the bathrooms

5, the mezzanine above the ground floor which will house offices and a club and bar for the Cruising Association. These open floors provide the best views of the jack-arch construction on cast iron beams and columns

6, 7, a typical flat with recessed balcony on the first and second floors

8, a flat on the top floor. The oculus and French windows are in the gable end and can also be seen in 4

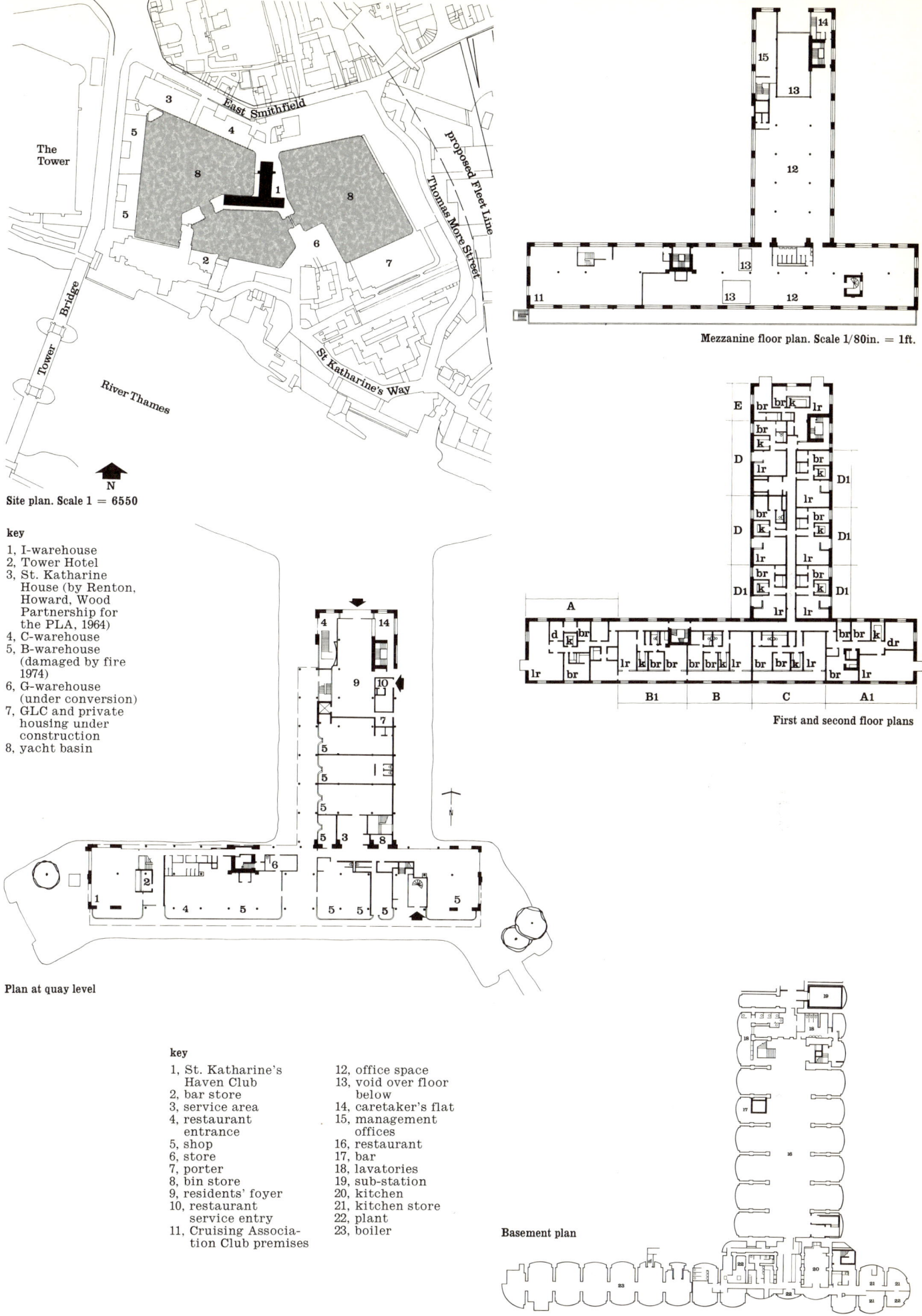

WAREHOUSE, OLIVER'S WHARF, WAPPING, LONDON

Architect: The A. J. Goddard Partnership

Client: Oliver's Wharf (Holdings) Ltd.

Site: Oliver's Wharf is situated on Wapping High Street, adjacent to the entrance to the old London docks and to St. John's Church and Wapping Pier Head. To the north lies the old church yard of St. John's, now a small park surrounded by a high wall, and to the south the lower pool of the River Thames. Fine views of the river, especially towards Tower Bridge and the City, are gained from the west side of the building.

History: Oliver's Wharf was built in about 1870 as a tea warehouse, and it was used as such until 1969, when, with the closing of the London docks, trading ceased. The building was obviously of a prestige nature, as the standard of construction and detailing is considerably higher than one would normally associate with a warehouse. Twenty-three people joined together as a company and in February 1971 bought the building to convert into flats, planning permission for which had already been obtained. All that remained to be done was to comply with the London Building Acts and with the requirements of the Historic Buildings Division of the Greater London Council. These negotiations took about three months, during which time negotiations were also carried out with contractors.

Character: The building is six storeys high with the main structural walls of London stock brick construction and with stone dressings to archways and window openings. There are also stone courses and some carvings, although these are very worn. The building is essentially a rectangle 70ft. by 150ft., divided into four equal-sized compartments, each compartment forming a flat. There is a staircase in the middle. To one side there is an annex four storeys high, 16ft. wide and 60ft. long. The floor-carrying structure is of cast-iron columns, decreasing in diameter at each floor level, supporting heavy beams. These in turn support heavy joists and boarding. The roof is also of timber construction with trusses carrying a slate roof. The original windows to the building were built up from standard steel sections, but provided no opening facility.

Work done: Planning arrangements were generally dictated by the GLC 'means of escape' regulations. Because the existing staircase in the centre of the building was not considered acceptable, it was necessary to introduce a new staircase to serve all floors, with a direct escape route at ground level to the street. A second staircase was required to serve the annex. At each floor level a series of lobbies were devised to provide two escape routes from each flat. Fire separation

1, a panoramic view across the Thames with Tower Bridge on the extreme left and Oliver's Wharf warehouse on the extreme right

2, the warehouse seen from the old church yard, now a small park surrounded by a wall

between flats was achieved with ⅜in. plasterboard to the underside of the existing floor joists. A 'waiver' was obtained to retain the existing cast-iron columns, except that at the garage level it was necessary to fireproof these.

Sound insulation between flats was achieved by floating a completely new floor over the existing floor, with fibreglass quilt separating the two units. A large number of new window openings were formed in the flank walls of the building and these were fitted with standard steel windows in a hardwood subframe. It was necessary to replace the existing metal windows with new steel units, also in a hardwood frame. New plumbing and electrical systems were installed throughout the building, and a new lift was provided within the existing shaft. Mechanically ventilated service areas were located in the middle of the building, and at ground floor level a garage was provided. Entrance areas and a colonnade leading out to the river are planned but are incomplete.

Each flat had a standard layout, and the contractors were required to give a breakdown of the overall building costs, including the price for the basic work to each flat. In this way it was possible for each individual to vary his layout or to carry out a completely different scheme and, of course, pay the difference in cost between the new project and the basic scheme.

Each of the twenty main flats (there are three small flatlets) is approximately 2500 sq. ft. in area. Bedrooms are generally located along the flanks of the building, since they are required by 'means of escape' regulations to have direct access to the fire lobby. The living accommodation is thus located on the main ends of the building, overlooking either the river or the park. Average living area size is 36ft. by 20ft.

3, the end of the Georgian terrace (seen in 4) with the warehouse behind

4, the warehouse seen from the river with a handsome Georgian terrace on the left and the tower of St. John's Church on the right

Accommodation: Ground floor—entrance hall, dustbins, garage, colonnade on river side (unallocated space)
First, second and the third floors—five flats on each floor
Fourth and fifth floors—four flats on each floor

Date of completion: September 1972

Cost: Approximately £200 000

Rate: £2·00 per sq. ft., excluding extra interior work by individual owners

5, 6, 7, inside the building, the structure—cast iron columns, timber trusses and brick walls—exposed. The flats on the top floor have the added advantage of being open to the roof space

8, another flat on the top floor similarly open to the roof space

Site plan. Scale 1 = 7500

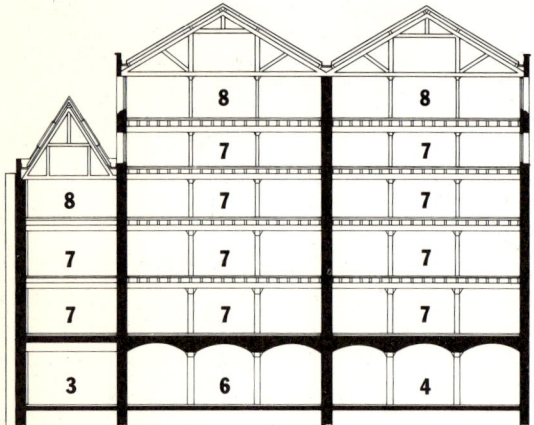

East-west section. Scale 1/48in. = 1ft.

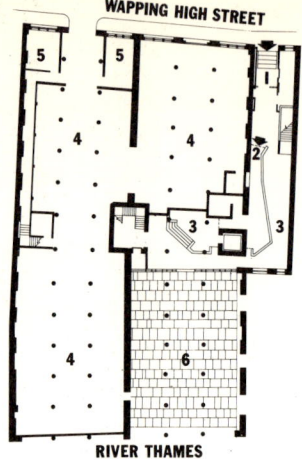

Ground floor plan

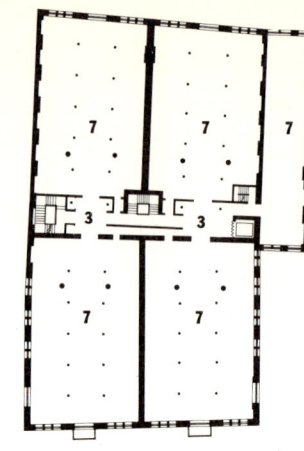

First floor plan. Scale 1/64in. = 1ft.

key
1, entrance to flats
2, ramp up
3, hall
4, cars
5, dustbins
6, colonnade open to river (unallocated space)
7, compartment for standard or special flat layout
8, maisonette

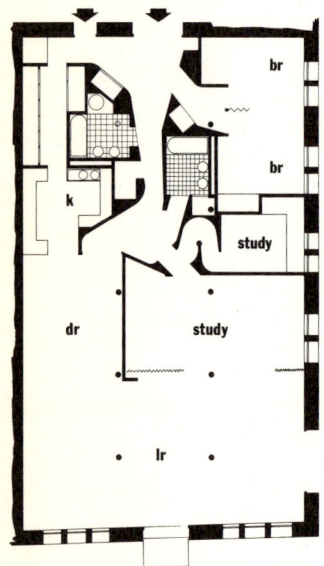

Special plan for flat facing river. Scale 1/24in. = 1ft.

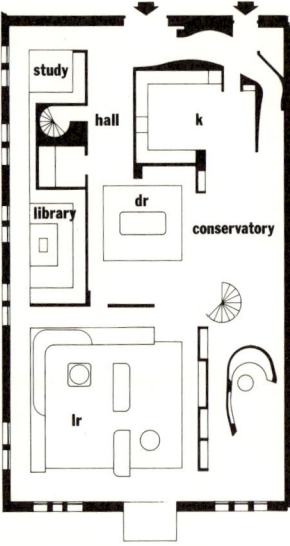

Special plan for maisonette on 5th floor facing river. Lower floor

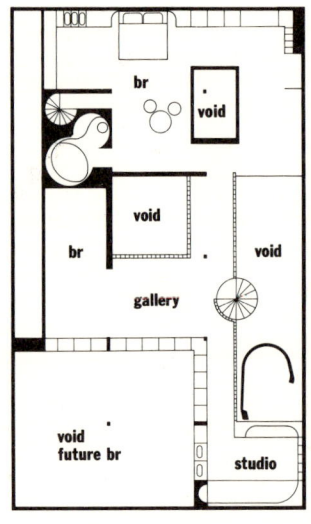

Special plan for maisonette on 5th floor facing river. Upper floor. Scale 1/24in. = 1ft.

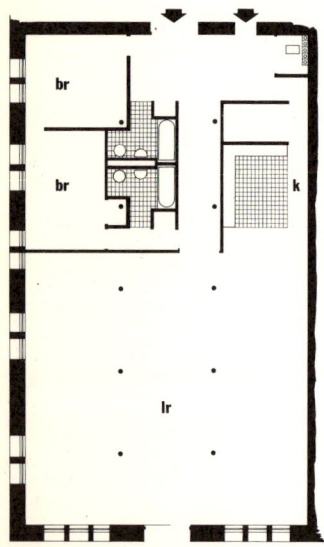

Standard plan for flats facing river

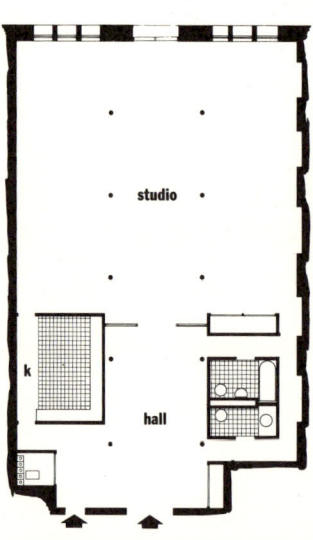

Standard plan for flats facing High Street

SEED WAREHOUSE, NORWICH

Architect: Michael and Sheila Gooch

Client: Chapman & Pape

Site: Bedford Street is the eastern continuation of Pottergate, once the street of the potters and one of the oldest streets in Norwich in an area full of historic buildings. Never a main shopping centre, it has become a street of mixed uses—specialist shops, restaurants, pubs, warehouses, etc. The converted seed warehouse (no. 5) stands on the north side of the street, on the corner of School Lane.

History: The warehouse, occupied by the seed merchants Daniels Brothers at least as far back as 1883, may have been built by them in the 1860's. A vaulted brick undercroft of late medieval date has been preserved from the remains of some old houses the warehouse was erected over. In 1939 Daniels formed a retail shop on the ground floor and inserted a new shopfront within the existing brick openings. A few years ago Daniels moved out to a site adjoining their nurseries in the western suburbs of the city and sold the warehouse to developers who intended, but failed, to rebuild a large block of property in this area. Early in 1971 the warehouse was bought by the present owners with the intention of converting it into a store selling well-designed household furniture and goods.

1, the warehouse after conversion into a store selling household furniture and goods. The previously painted brick walls have been re-painted brown. The old function of the building is still evident from the central openings (formerly loading doors) and from the little pediment above which provided a fixing for the hoist

2, the store on a dark winter's afternoon

3, the showroom on the ground floor with the new staircase in the background. The woodblock floor was existing and only had to be sanded and polished

Character: Externally the warehouse had the character of domestic Georgian, with sash windows and semicircular-headed openings on the ground floor. But the function of the building was apparent from the central loading doors at each floor level and from the little pediment above, which provided a fixing for the hoist. Internally the open floors revealed an all-timber structure of eight pine posts at each floor level supporting massive pine beams across the full width of the building. The roof, also of timber, was a type of queen post construction leaving a central area of the attic floor unencumbered by supporting structure. Walls were partly plastered, partly brick and painted.

Work done: To satisfy the city engineer and fire officer regarding fire protection and means of escape, the exposed timber structure was treated with fire-retardant paint, the ceilings between main beams were covered with ¾in. plaster and an alternative means of escape was provided between the second and ground floor in the form of a brick shaft and a concrete staircase. An existing staircase from the undercroft was made to connect with this shaft. As a result of these provisions, new open stairs in steel and timber down to the undercroft and up to the first and second floors were accepted. At ground floor level a service entrance already existed on the side of the escape stairs, leaving a recess which was partitioned off to form a stock room and fitting room. The existing lavatory accommodation on the first and second floors was re-used. On the ground floor the 1939 shop front, service doorway and windows were removed, the window sills lowered and new plate glass doors and windows in Columbian pine fitted. Other work included sanding and polishing the existing wood block floor at ground level and painting all internal walls and ceilings white and the previously painted exterior brickwork brown.

No work has yet been carried out to the undercroft and attic floor, but the company has plans to extend the shop as soon as this becomes commercially viable.

Accommodation: Ground floor—showroom, stockroom and fitting room
First and second floors—showroom and lavatories

Date of completion: January 1972

Cost: £8970, excluding decoration, electrical work and floor coverings

Rate: £1·23 per sq. ft. (£13·30 per m²)

4, one of the semicircular headed openings on the ground floor which were lowered and fitted with new timber frames and plain sheets of glass

5, the new open-riser staircase of steel and timber at first-floor level

6, the late medieval vaulting in the undercroft into which the shop may eventually extend

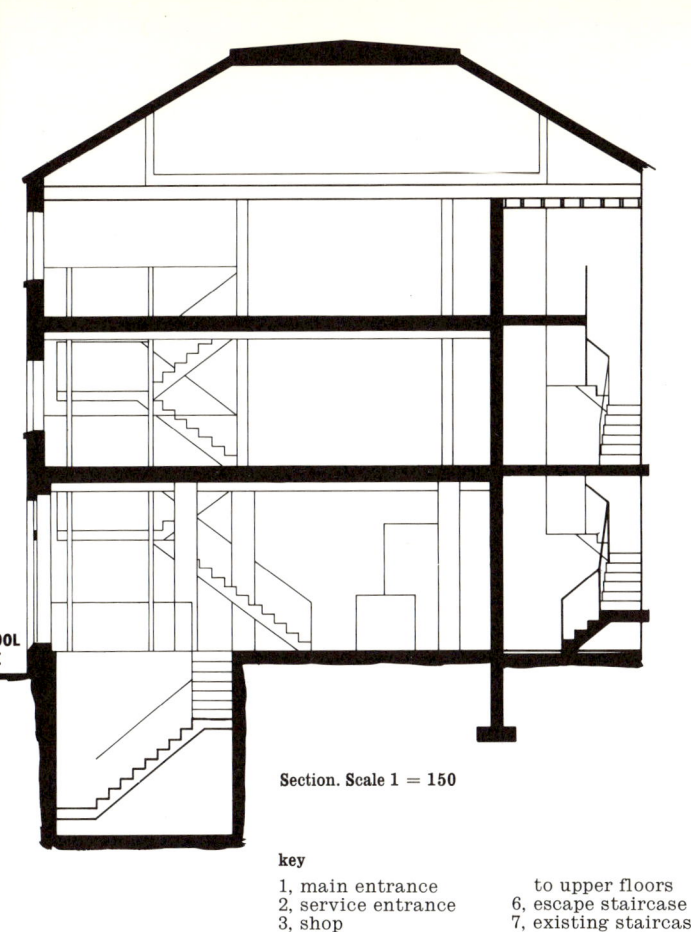

Section. Scale 1 = 150

key
1, main entrance
2, service entrance
3, shop
4, staircase to basement
5, new main staircase to upper floors
6, escape staircase
7, existing staircase
8, stockroom
9, fitting room
10, showroom

Second floor plan

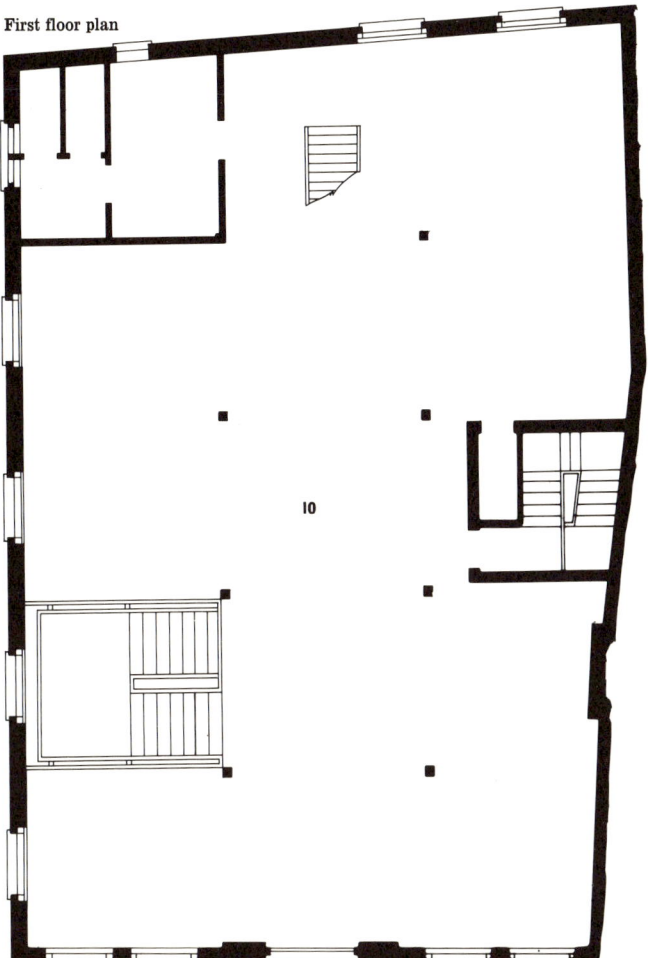

First floor plan

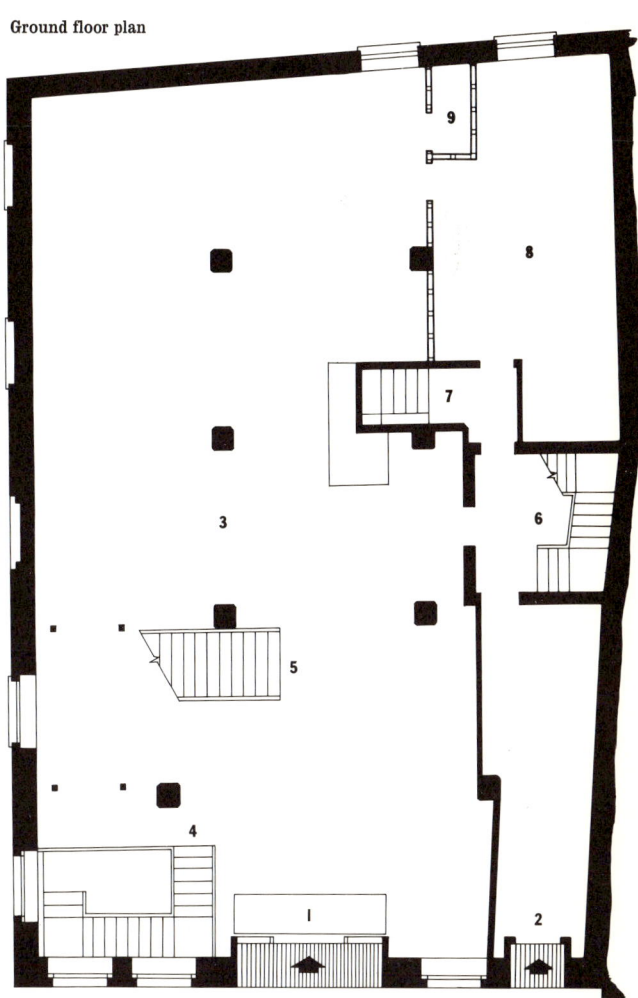

Ground floor plan

BEDFORD STREET

SCHOOL LANE

OLD CITY HALL, BOSTON, MASSACHUSETTS

Architect: Anderson Notter Associates

Client: Old City Hall Landmark Corporation

Site: Old City Hall faces south on to School Street and stands behind King's Chapel with the cemetery on the west and City Hall Alley on the east. It is situated in the centre of Boston's business and new skyscraper district where land costs and office rents are highest.

History: Based on the winning design by Gridley J. F. Bryant for a competition limited to six architects in 1860, the building was finally erected (1862–65) in partnership with Arthur Ailman. It replaced an older building (a courthouse which had been remodelled for use as a city hall by Bryant), part of which still stood on the site and whose ashlar facing was reused on the basement of the new building. Although the competition design was simplified, the final cost of the building was more than three times the original estimate, the architects' fees being a mere 2 per cent of the total. The only serious change which the building suffered between its completion and the recent conversion was the introduction in 1873 of an additional floor in the double-height mayor and aldermen's room on the second floor, for by that time the building was too small. Not until 1912 was a separate annex built. The erection of a new city hall, completed in 1969, might have resulted in demolition but for a mayor who in 1968 offered the old building for sale with preservation restrictions on the exterior. It was then that the Landmark Corporation was formed under the presidency of Roger Webb, who was responsible for finding a viable economic solution for its conversion and new use.

Character: The building of white granite in Second Empire style was modelled, so the architect tells us, on Visconti and Lefuel's new Louvre in Paris. The most characteristic part is the central projecting portion on School Street, which is three storeys high like the wings on either side, but has in addition a tall slate-covered mansard in the form of an umbrella vault. It also has a three-storeyed portico, supported by pairs of columns, which forms the main entrance, and balconies on the upper floors. The strong modelling of this principal facade can be appreciated because the whole building was set back with a forecourt in which two bronze statues (of Josiah Quincy and Benjamin Franklin) flank the entrance.

Before the recent conversion the magnificent double staircase of iron, rising through five storeys, had survived in its original state except for the insertion of two lifts within its well. The landings were carried on

1, view of the main south facade facing School Street. The conversion into restaurants, shops and offices has not materially affected the exterior—an uninhibited design of 1860 in Second Empire Style

2, the new banking hall on the first floor. The arched window openings are lined with oak cast-iron columns clad in oak, the fluted columns standing in pairs and having rich Roman Ionic capitals carrying entablatures. The other important space which had survived was the double-height council chamber on the third floor. It had galleries on three sides which did not project into the space but occupied the space over adjoining rooms. The walls and dome overhead were supported on ten Composite columns.

Work done: Because the intention was to convert the building into marketable commercial space, much of the grand and spacious quality of the interior has been lost. The central staircase was demolished and a conventional fire-proof core of lifts, lavatories, ducts and escape staircases built into the space. The council chamber has been subdivided into two floors of offices. Generally the interior was gutted (except for the load-bearing walls) and new reinforced concrete floors inserted to meet fire regulations. The floors were left open so that they can be subdivided as required by individual tenants. The arched windows, formerly divided by a transom and a mullion, were reglazed with single sheets of glass to emphasise the contrast of solid and void. Internally they were lined with oak. In some areas arched openings, reflecting the window shape, were worked into the partitions. The mechanical units of the new central heating and air-conditioning system were concealed behind grilles. All interior finishes are new and the granite on the outside has been cleaned.

Accommodation: Ground floor—restaurant, café, kitchens
First floor—bank, offices, retail shops
Second, third, fourth and fifth floors—offices

Date of completion: 1971

Cost: $1·84 million, including the tenants' work

Rate: $20 per sq. ft.

3, the offices on the upper floors where the windows have been cut in half by the new floor structure, a feature which is hardly visible from outside

4, internally, arched openings reflecting the window shapes have been formed in some of the partitions between offices

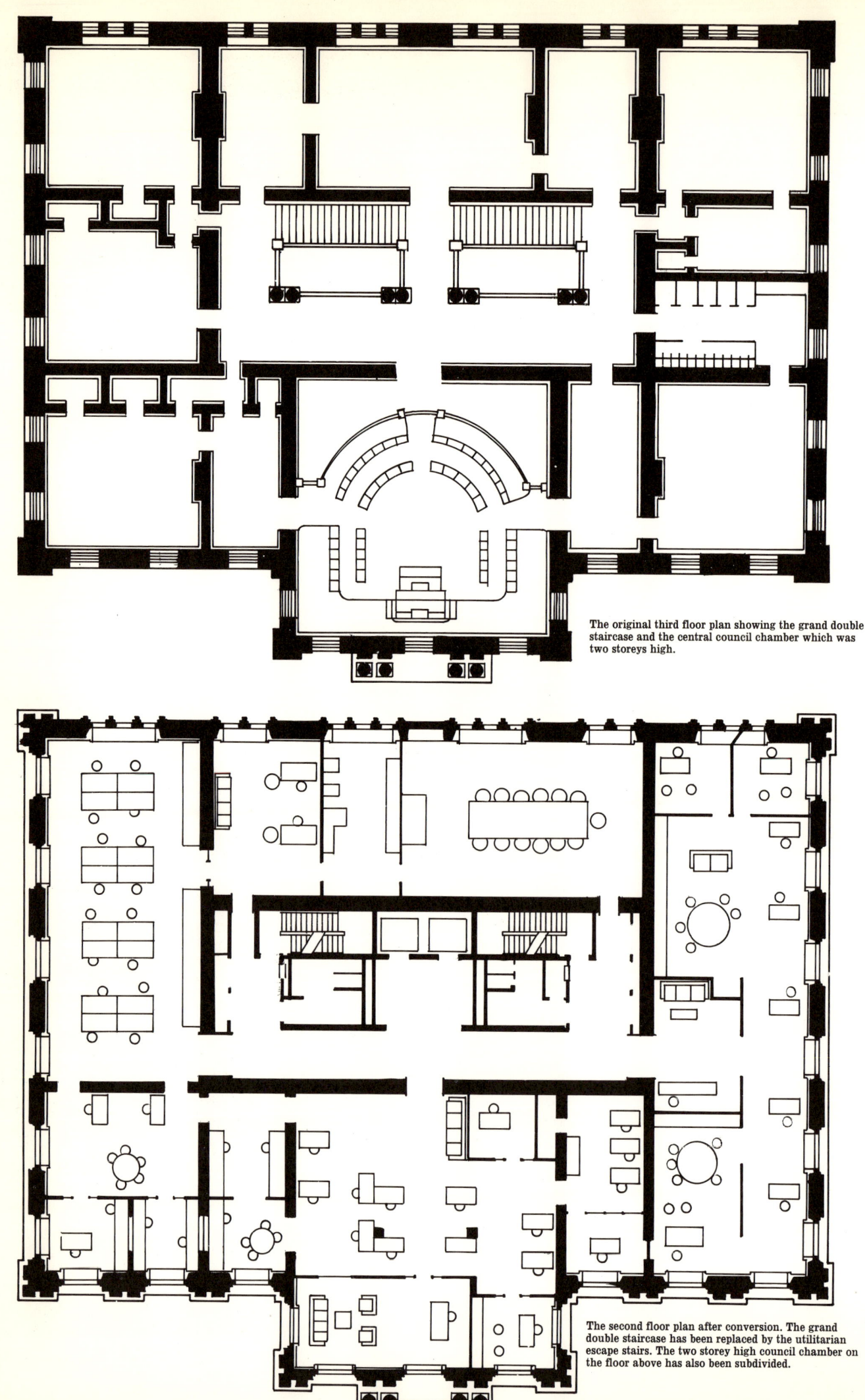

The original third floor plan showing the grand double staircase and the central council chamber which was two storeys high.

The second floor plan after conversion. The grand double staircase has been replaced by the utilitarian escape stairs. The two storey high council chamber on the floor above has also been subdivided.

RAILWAY STATION, BRUNSWICK, GERMAN FEDERAL REPUBLIC

1, Ottmer's original station of 1845 from an engraving by J. M. Kolb after a drawing by L. Rohbock. Behind the main station building can be seen one of the colonnaded wings flanking the vast trainshed.

Architect: Hannes Westermann

Client: Brunswick State Bank, subsequently the Norddeutsche Landesbank

Site: An open site at the south end of the old town. The main north facade faces part of the moat (an artificial arm of the Oker River) which used to encircle the old town. On the axis of this facade and on the opposite side of the moat is the Friedrich Wilhelm Platz. The approach from the north is over two old bridges which have been restored. To the south, where the railway line used to come in, major roadworks are in progress.

History: Designed by Carl Theodor Ottmer (the architect of the first station and later of the Ducal Palace), it was opened in 1845, two years after Ottmer's death. The original building, which was considered to be one of the finest stations in Germany, had a vast train shed (108m. by 21m.), flanked by colonnaded wings, appended to its south side. In 1932–34 the train shed, which had been designed to take two lines, was finally turned into a mere concourse, additional lines having been added over the years outside the shed. Serious bomb damage in the last war left the walls of the main building standing, but the rest of the station virtually destroyed. The main building was patched up and used as a station until 1960 when the State Bank bought it together with some land and promoted a competition for what was intended to be a new building. Instead the prize was awarded to an ingenious design which saved as much as it could of the old building and so enabled the organisation, which had originally helped to finance the railway, restore the station for its own use.

Character: A two-storey neoclassical building with the central part on the north facade in the form of a Roman triumphal arch. This and the end bays project slightly. All the openings on the ground floor are arched; those on the first floor are rectangular except that the windows in the side pavilions have arched hoods with decorated tympana. The roof was originally hipped, giving

2, the main station building in 1890

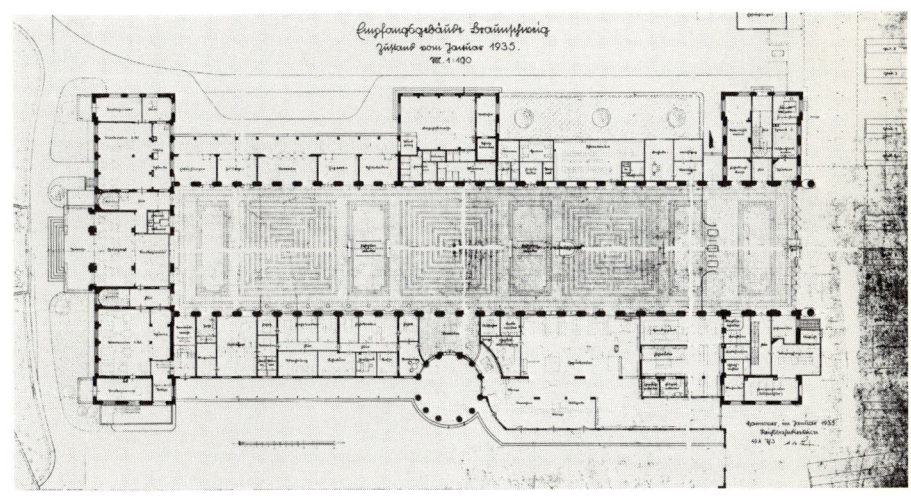

3, plan of the whole station showing the conversion of the train shed into a concourse, completed circa 1935. The surviving block is the main station building at the extreme left end

4, the facade of the main station building and, 5, the interior of the concourse after bomb damage in 1945

255

more emphasis to the parapets over the side pavilions than does the continuous strip of attic windows which now lines up with them. The long wings flanking the train shed were lower, the west wing having a charming rotunda as a side entrance. The train shed was entered through a monumental archway which echoed in a simpler style its counterpart on the north facade.

Internally the main building consisted of a double-height central hall flanked by two storeys of offices. The train shed, covered by a single-span cast-iron roof, was also flanked by two-storey wings which continued the pattern of arched openings on the ground floor and rectangular openings on the first floor.

Work done: The walls of the old building were found to be supported on beech piles and tie beams which had rotted as a result of the lowering of the water table. Before any rebuilding could take place the walls had to be underpinned with concrete, steel piles driven and pile caps laid to support the new columns. The basement had to be properly tanked to keep water out. The north facade and walls of the side wings were faithfully restored except for the fixed plate glass windows without mullions or glazing bars which betray a fully air-conditioned interior. The stucco was painted yellow and the mouldings picked out in white. The south facade, which used to face the train shed, was not restored. Instead an uncompromisingly modern facade of aluminium and glass, echoing the proportions of the north facade, was fixed to the edge of the new reinforced concrete floor structure of the interior. This structure, which is supported on two lines of columns, the north wall and the walls of the end wings, is trimmed to provide a double-height space (recalling the old entrance hall) across the front of the building, and again at second floor level to allow views up the whole height (nearly three storeys) of the great central arch. A new attic floor is set back on the south side to provide a continuous balcony and is lit by both ordinary windows and skylights.

Accommodation: Basement—dining room, kitchen, stores, lavatories, plant
Ground floor—open office space
Mezzanine—gallery, single offices, lavatories
First floor—directors' floor with board room, small dining room and kitchen, large reception area, single offices, lavatories
Attic floor—open office space, lavatories

Date of completion Summer 1966

Cost: 5·98 million DM, including new foundations

Rate: 2063 DM per m²

6, the building's last day as a railway station —1 October 1960

7, the north facade of the main station building after conversion. The old mullioned windows have been replaced by fixed sheets of plate glass

8, the south facade which was masked by the trainshed until its recent demolition. Except for the side pavilions, this side has been restored in an uncompromisingly modern manner

9, view from the south-east showing one of the original side pavilions

10, one of the arched openings in the side pavilions which has been converted into an entrance door with an access balcony of simple and elegant design

257

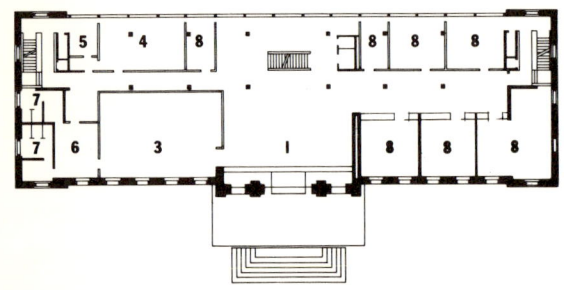

11, the main entrance hall with the new reinforced concrete staircase. The interiors are also uncompromisingly modern

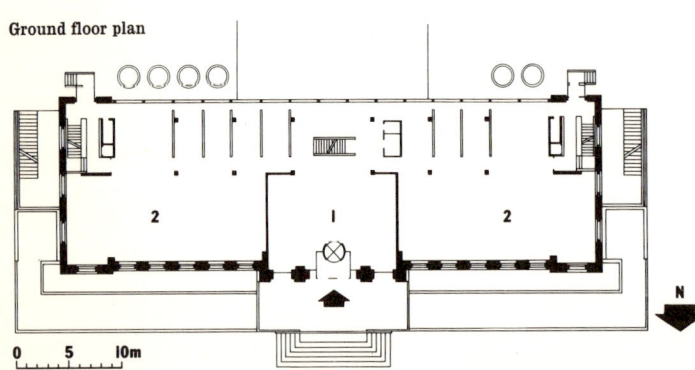

First floor plan

Ground floor plan

key

1, reception
2, open offices
3, conference room
4, dining room
5, kitchen
6, foyer to conference room
7, lavatories
8, office

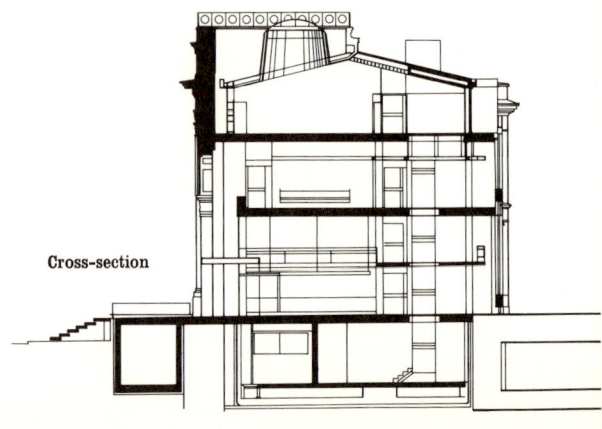

Cross-section

THE ROUND HOUSE, CAMDEN, LONDON

Designer: R. J. Simpson

Client: The Round House Trust Ltd.

Site: The Round House is situated in an urban site in Camden, north London. It fronts on to Chalk Farm Road and backs on to a network of railway lines which form part of the London-to-Glasgow route. It is outside the entertainment centre of London's West End, but easily accessible by underground or car.

History: The Round House was built in 1847 as an engine shed to the design of Robert Stephenson. Such was the rate of progress, however, that within 15 years of its erection, the engines and tenders became too long for the turntable and bays. The building became a goods shed before being leased to W. & A. Gilbey Ltd., who used it as a liquor store.

In 1964 the Round House was acquired (with the help of a gift from Louis Mintz) by Centre 42, a group under the directorship of Arnold Wesker, whose aim was to ensure a greater participation by the Trade Union Movement in all cultural activities. But their schemes for developing the building were too grandiose for the money at their disposal, and after the Round House Trust had been formed and put into commercial use under the directorship of George Hoskins, Arnold Wesker relinquished all claim to it. It is used for various shows—plays, pop concerts, dances, circuses—a variety which is a tribute to its versatility.

Recently, the last of the old debts was paid off by selling a plot of land to a development company, who erected new dressing rooms, a rehearsal theatre, a club cinema and workshops, designed by Richard Seifert, on part of the site, and leased it free to the Round House Trust for ninety years. The money left over after paying off debts was used to buy the Round House freehold. The next plan is to develop the land to the west of the building, bought from British Rail by Camden Council, as a children's playground.

Character: The Round House is circular, 160ft. in diameter, and of a brick, timber and cast-iron construction. The roof is supported on twenty-four cast-iron pillars and radial arches which meet at the apex. The ground floor is supported by forty-eight radial brick walls, arched at the top and bottom. Originally there was a turntable in the centre and ashpits between each pair of columns but these were filled in and the turntable removed when the Round House became a warehouse. In 1920 Gilbeys erected a crudely constructed gallery supported on timbers on the same radii as the columns to create extra storage space.

Work done: When the Round House was first used as a theatre, the barest minimum was done to make it habitable:

1, the Round House seen from an adjoining scrap yard

2, 'interior of the new great circular engine-house, at the Camden Town depot of the North Western Railway.' The roof is supported on 24 cast-iron columns, the building having been designed to hold 23 engines, one between each pair of columns, with one track left free for access. In the centre a turntable served the individual engine bays, each of which was designed for one engine and tender and had below it a long pit for maintenance purposes

3, the gallery was added in 1920 by W. and G. Gilbey who had been using the building for more than 50 years as a liquor store.

lavatories and offices were put in, entrance steps and fire escapes built. Later the building was strengthened by Bickerdike, Allen, Rich and Partners, who were brought in initially as acoustic consultants. They repaired the broken ring beam which had caused a twist in the roof. In 1969 Robbie Simpson was appointed technical manager, and he has undertaken the remaining restoration work, including sandblasting of the brickwork and the installation of a projection room, ventilation system, staircase up to the gallery, foyer and box office. No permanent seating arrangement has been erected; stacking chairs are set out on wooden rostra which are movable by hand and may be rearranged several times a week. A new gallery on brick arches that is being built to replace the old unsafe one will house an exhibition area, a soundproof children's theatre and club rooms as well as more seating space for the theatre. The vaults have been cleared and will be used as a night club and restaurant, and there will also be a new restaurant on the ground floor.

The conversion has been largely determined by financial shortages. This has been fortunate for the Round House, which would not have retained its character with a more lavish conversion. Although the aims of Centre 42 were never achieved, the building in its present form is much nearer to Wesker's original idea than it would have been had his plans been carried out.

Accommodation: Basement—future restaurant and night club
Ground floor—theatre, box office, bar, future restaurant, lavatories, administrative offices
Gallery—(proposed) additional seating for theatre, exhibition area, children's theatre, club rooms

Date of completion: No fixed date. Work will be continued as money becomes available.

4, today the makeshift character of the interior seems to fulfil a specific need in the world of theatre and music

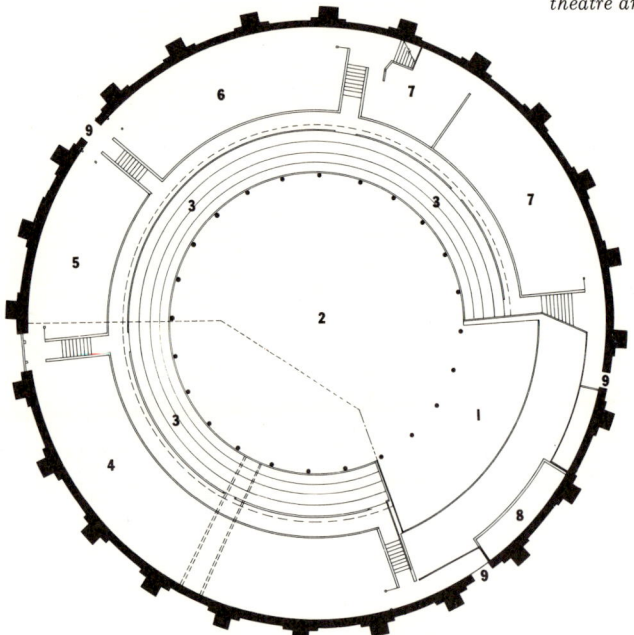

Plan at proposed new gallery level. Scale 1/48in. = 1ft.

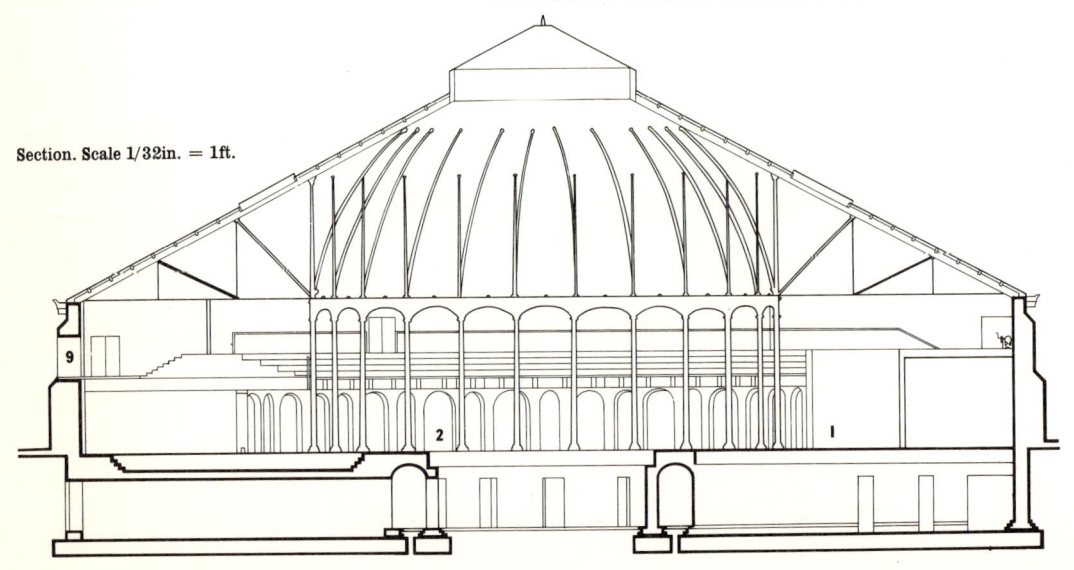

Section. Scale 1/32in. = 1ft.

key
1, acting area below
2, auditorium below
3, new gallery with raked seating
4, exhibition room
5, club room
6, bar and social area
7, children's area
8, winch gear
9, exit

THREE PUMPING STATIONS

introduced by Denis Smith

Steam power was a product of Georgian England and was first used to operate pumps—an application which was to prove a continued incentive to its development. The massive atmospheric beam engine of Thomas Newcomen appeared in the second decade of the eighteenth century and both it and its improved successors were ideally suited for driving reciprocating pumps for mines and land drainage, public water supply and sewage disposal. After many improvements the beam engine and subsequently the direct-acting compound and triple-expansion steam engines were increasingly used in pumping installations up to the early part of this century. These large machines had to be protected from the weather, and the beam engine, in particular, led to the building of the distinctively tall engine house, which often achieved a unique integration of the structure and machinery where the engines were 'house-built' and relied on the walls for support as well as enclosure.

The disused pumping stations of today are largely a legacy of the Victorian period, reflecting urban growth in the nineteenth century and the public health problems which this posed. Rapidly growing populations and disastrous epidemics of cholera and other diseases forced local authorities to face the development of water supply and of the treatment and disposal of sewage. This led to considerable civil engineering work and architectural opportunities, involving the construction of reservoirs, pipe-lines, treatment works and pumping stations. These pumping stations, although functional, purpose-built structures, are often splendid examples of the civic pride which the Victorians lavished on their municipal buildings. Typical buildings make elaborate use of multi-coloured brickwork, carved

1, the Abbey Pumping Station at Leicester which is being converted into a museum of technology for the East Midlands. Four Leicester-built beam engines are preserved in the engine house, 2

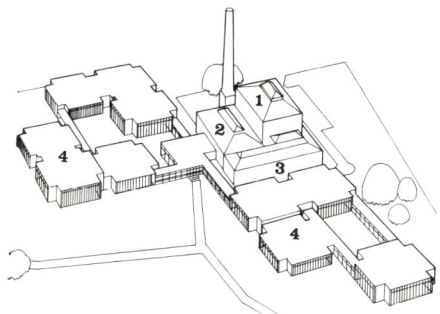

Perspective of Abbey pumping station

key
1, engine house (1891)
2, boiler house (1891)
3, electric pump house (1926)
4, new extensions for three road transport galleries

3, 4, Ryhope pumping station south of Sunderland. It is being converted into a tourist attraction which will include a museum of pumping and water supply

stone, decorative cast and wrought iron, glazed tiling, stained glass, oak handrails and brass door furniture. The beam engines were also architectural in character with the sculptural quality of fluted cast-iron columns, foliate capitals, panelled plinths and entablatures which perfectly matched their setting. In addition the buildings are often placed in well-kept gardens which are a source of continuing pride.

With the growth of electric power distribution in this century many pumping stations had steam plant removed, to be replaced by the ubiquitous vertical-spindle electrically driven pump. Others remain in steam, although many have been closed during the last twenty years. There are two main reasons for this, the first of which is the question of boiler insurance while the second, related to it, is the desire to rationalise the network of small municipal undertakings. Another problem is the labour-intensive nature of steam plant and the increasing difficulty of finding men with the necessary skills and experience for its maintenance. Faced with expenditure on the boilers the authorities often decide to electrify, although there may be years of life left in the engines. At this stage an alternative exists: either to put electric pumps in the existing building and remove the steam engines (for scrap or preservation), or to build a new pumping station on another site. In the first case we are often left with a building of

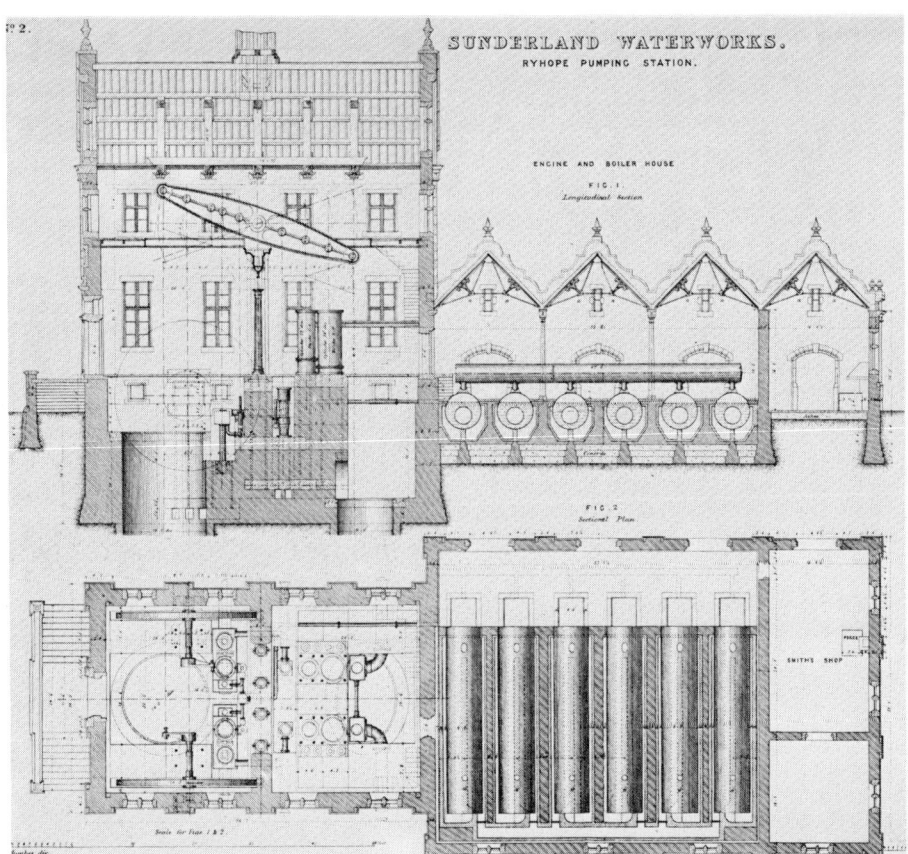

architectural interest continuing as a working station, but with a modern plant: the question of a new use for the building obviously does not arise. In the second case the steam plant is merely shut down, and both the machinery and its building become redundant; if there is no pressure for site redevelopment they could remain in position for many years. Once the steam is shut off, however, the buildings become cold and damp, and machinery, which was lovingly cared for during a lifetime of service, rapidly deteriorates. It is a melancholy experience to revisit a pumping station and find a cold, dark building with broken windows, and the only sound that of disturbed pigeons above the rusting machinery.

What should be done with these buildings? Are they worth preserving? Should the taxpayer's money be spent on them? These and other questions are often asked in connection with disused pumping stations with widely differing answers in particular cases. In recent years there has been a growing interest in industrial archaeology and, in order to find out what does remain in the field, a nation-wide survey was inaugurated with information steadily accumulating in the National Record of Industrial Monuments at Bath University. There is, however, no national preservation policy at the moment, and what is done is largely left to local initiative and enthusiasm. Nevertheless, in 1971, the Standing Commission on Museums and Galleries published its report *The Preservation of Technological Material* (HMSO 1971, 36½p) and among its recommendations it says of the in situ preservation of industrial monuments that 'while continuing to be the responsibility of the Secretary of State for the Environment, it should be the subject of considerably increased expenditure by this Department, both in grants and on staff'. This report led the Government to award an annual grant-in-aid of £150 000 for England and Wales with a further £25 000 for Scotland which should help in the preservation and creative re-use of industrial buildings and machinery. It makes clear, however, the need for local preservation trusts and appeal committees to continue their work in order to match money received from the central grant fund which is administered by the Science Museum.

The Abbey pumping station at Leicester—a sewage lift station—is being converted into a new museum of technology for the East Midlands. Red brick buildings of 1891 on a seven-acre riverside site form the nucleus. Four Leicester-built beam engines are preserved in the engine house, and one of the Lancashire boilers remains in the boiler house which has been converted into a road transport gallery. In the grounds there is a growing collection including a locomotive, stationary steam engines, a railway bridge, and other items awaiting restoration. The phased building programme will extend over a period of fifteen years. The first phase, which will cost £70 000, includes the conversion of the existing buildings,

5, the Markfield sewage works at Haringey converted into a children's playground. The main playground area from the outside, looking like a miniature desert fort

6, the concrete mound incorporating a metal slide behind the central group of buildings

7, the main playground area from inside, with the ski slope in the background (left) and the central group of buildings with the beam engine house (right)

the preservation of the beam engines, the building of an entrance hall, reception areas and three new galleries. The City of Leicester has promised £35 000 providing the rest is raised by donations and grants. The city has indicated that it will underwrite the running costs once the museum has been established. In the meantime it has provided a small qualified staff under curator of technology. This scheme is expected to become a living museum with the beam engines eventually under steam and facilities for for apprentice education and technical research.

The Ryhope pumping station is just south of Sunderland, County Durham, on the east coast. The tall beam engine house contains two engines built in the 1860's which worked until the station closed in July 1967. A great deal of work has been done on the site, which is administered by a trust and run by a keen group of volunteers helped by the Sunderland and South Shields Water Company. The project was one of the first to receive assistance from the English Tourist Board, and facilities at the site include ample car parking, a café, a souvenir shop, lavatories, and a museum showing the history of pumping and water supply.

The local authority in Haringey, London, under Parks Chief Superintendent A. Egan and landscape architect Mary Mitchell, has transformed a six-and-one-half acre sewage works at Haringey into a children's playground. Bold ground modelling and generous planting screen the concrete bays from the adjacent railway lines and industrial estates. The fine beam engine, which belongs to the Lea Valley Regional Park Authority, is being restored to form the nucleus of a future museum. The cost of landscape works and hard surfacing was £26 000, and minor repairs to the building amounted to £1500. The scheme was financed by government loans, part of which will rank for Grant Aid under Section 9 of the Local Government Act of 1966, 'Reclamation of Derelict Land'.

floors is timber on stout joists. The first and second floors are supported by round cast-iron columns and RSJs (introduced into the building around 1947 because of the weight of the grain). The attic/studio floor at the top has a fine sweeping timber raftered roof with a number of valleys. Large beams are tied into it and supported by timber posts. Access to the building was by very steep and small ladder stairs. The whole space, about 1500 sq. ft. on each floor, was unencumbered except for holes for funnels and shafts.

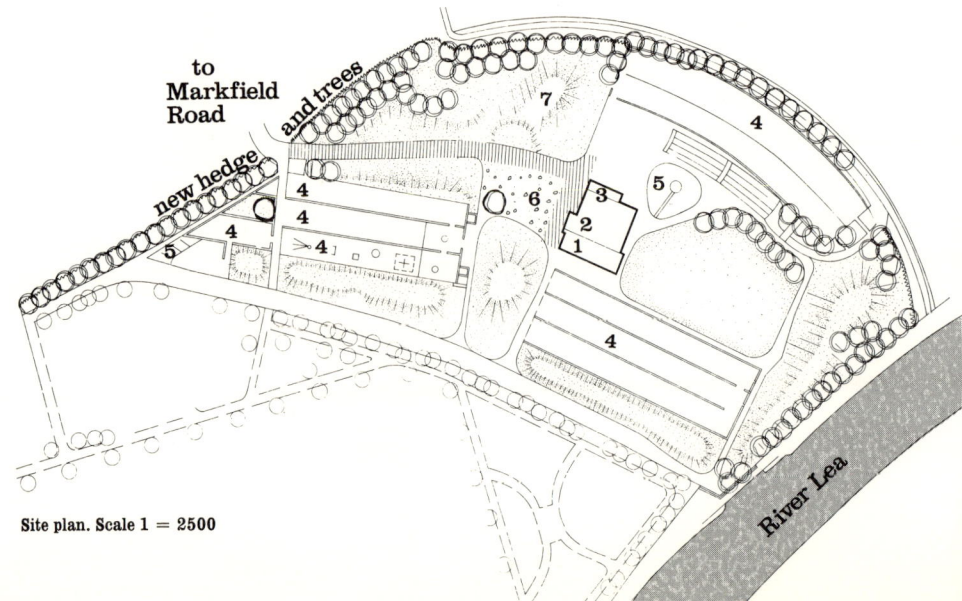

Site plan. Scale 1 = 2500

key
1, beam engine house
2, indoor play
3, play leader
4, playgrounds out of sewage beds
5, slide
6, car park
7, ski slope

Kirtley Library
Columbia College
8th and Rogers
Columbia, MO. 65201